Michael Brawne

The New Museum

Architecture and Display

The Architectural Press, London

4799

C (BRA)

85139   484   1

Published in the U. K. and Commonwealth
(except Canada) by
The Architectural Press, London, 1965
© 1965 by Verlag Gerd Hatje, Stuttgart
Printed in Germany

Translated into German: Wolfgang Pehnt

Michael Brawne   **The New Museum**

Contents

Inhalt

Acknowledgements

Dank des Autors

I am extremely grateful to the architects and directors of many museums who supplied illustrations of their buildings and information about their activities and several of whom devoted a great deal of time showing me around: to Verlag Gerd Hatje and particularly to Gerd Hatje and Antje Pehnt who with great tact and patience extracted material from frequently reluctant sources; to Ivor Haberfeld who with considerable endurance translated drawings into publishable plans, sections and details; to the Editors of the *Architectural Review* who allowed me to use some of the ideas which originally appeared in two of my articles on museums; to my fellow members of the Illuminating Engineering Society Panel on museum lighting who made me aware of many problems in this difficult field; to Francis Haskell, librarian of the Faculty of Fine Arts & Architecture, University of Cambridge, who drew my attention to early outdoor display; to my wife who patiently read and re-read the typescript and proofs.

Mein herzlicher Dank gilt den Architekten und Direktoren zahlreicher Museen, die mir Abbildungs- und Informationsmaterial über die Bauten und die Arbeit ihrer Institutionen zur Verfügung stellten; einige haben auch nicht die Mühe gescheut, mich selbst durch ihre Häuser zu führen. Ich danke weiter dem Verlag Gerd Hatje, vor allem Gerd Hatje und Antje Pehnt, die mit viel Takt und Geduld schwer zugängliches Material beschafften; Ivor Haberfeld, der beträchtliche Mühe darauf verwandte, Zeichnungen in publikationsfähige Grundrisse, Schnitte und Details zu übertragen; den Herausgebern der *Architectural Review* für die Erlaubnis, Gedankengänge auszuwerten, die ich dort in zwei Artikeln über Museumsfragen zuerst veröffentlichte; meinen Kollegen vom Illuminating Engineering Society Panel, die mich auf viele Probleme im schwierigen Bereich der Museumsbeleuchtung aufmerksam machten; dem Bibliothekar der Faculty of Fine Arts and Architecture an der University of Cambridge, Francis Haskell, der mich auf frühe Freilicht-Ausstellungen hinwies; schließlich meiner Frau für das geduldige Lesen von Manuskript und Korrekturen.

At the end of the second floor of the Museo Correr – running parallel with the long south side of the Piazza San Marco – is a small room reserved for eight paintings by the Bellinis (see Figs. page 7 and 8). These, together with a Descent from the Cross by Antonello da Messina and Carpaccio's portrait of two courtesans on a balcony among Venetian pigeons, are the great treasures of the collection. Three of the eight Bellini paintings are on easels, two back to back, the third diagonally opposite the door; five are on walls and of these, two are at a slight angle, hinged as it were on one side.

On entering the room, seven of the paintings can almost be seen at a glance, each clear in its own space. On approach, each picture fills the field of vision, the remainder drop away. And at the end of the sequence, the eighth painting – secular, unrelated in subject to the rest, and most familiar – Gentile Bellini's life size head of the Doge, is suddenly within view on the last easel.

The galleries of the first and second floor which precede this room hold the lanterns of the Doge's ceremonial barges, tapestries, the armour of Venetian noblemen, painting and sculpture from the quattrocento and through the open balcony doors always relate these to the square below. The gallery floors are terazzo or tile, the Bellini room is carpeted; so is the Antonello room and the Carpaccio recess.

Each of these visual and tactile experiences is intended to sharpen the encounter between object and observer, to make possible a communication between artefact and individual.

Since the museum is a medium of communication these are important intentions. It is primarily, but not necessarily exclusively, concerned with the visual communication of objects of cultural and scientific interest, both cultural and scientific used in their widest sense. Unless therefore, the museum is able to fulfil this task it is failing in its purpose. Museum design, both in terms of architecture and display, must thus at least make possible such communication and, preferably, actively contribute to it.

The museum is not, obviously, the only available medium of visual communication; on the contrary, the cinema, television and the printed illustration are much more widely disseminated. The museum is, like the cinema or television, also a mass medium, but unlike them, does not presuppose a simultaneous audience; it is, like the illustrated book or journal, able to communicate to an individual at a time. Yet though it shares characteristics with each of these media, it profoundly differs from them. The printed illustration, the cinema screen and the television set are only able to transmit reproductions of the object, they create a new image; the museum is able to exhibit the object itself. Museum architecture and display must, therefore, exploit this unique sense of immediacy, this direct encounter between viewer and viewed.

Successful communication depends on the clear reception of signals and this clarity is dependent on the absence of interference – of "background noise", that is to say of any intruding element – and the correct adjustment of the receiver. This holds good whether the signals are the Morse Code or art forms. Carlo Scarpa's design of the Bellini Room at the Museo Correr achieves both conditions by means which, though they leave no doubt as to the ends in view, yet do not interfere with the primary communication of the paintings themselves. Their cunning stems from an analysis of the operation of viewing, from their self-confidence and from the realisation that the objects on display are not anonymous but specific.

The definition of the proper function of the museum has, of course, not remained unchanged since Cicero described the Verres collection nor has there necessarily always been a general acceptance of a single definition. That just put forward is, judging at least by so much

Museo Correr, Venice (1953–61). Bellini room. Architect: Carlo Scarpa.

Museo Correr, Venedig (1953–61). Bellini-Raum. Architekt: Carlo Scarpa.

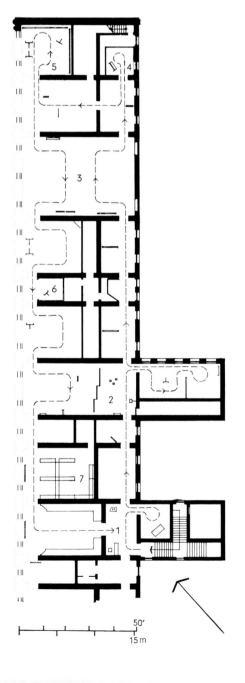

Museo Correr, Venice. Plan of second floor.
Museo Correr, Venedig. Grundriß zweites Geschoß.
1 Entrance from floor below / Aufgang vom Erdgeschoß
2 Sculpture room / Plastik-Raum
3 Room of the Four Doors / Raum der vier Türen
4 Antonello room / Antonello-Raum
5 Bellini room / Bellini-Raum
6 Carpaccio recess / Carpaccio-Nische
7 Majolica ware / Majolika-Sammlung

50'

15 m

museum display, unlikely to find universal acceptance today; the confused legacy of the past is too strong.

Until the 15th century, collections served two disparate purposes: they were the accumulation of objects for either religious ends or personal enjoyment. The treasures of the sanctuaries of Delphi, the Athenian Acropolis or the mediaeval pilgrimage churches served the first aim, the acquisition of the rare, the curious and the beautiful by the princes and popes of the Italian Renaissance the second. The notion of works of art – other than architecture – as public property or at least as public enjoyment is of relatively recent origin. There is previously only a hint of it in the occasional public display of the loot of returning armies. In this sense the Museo Correr is flanked by another: by the Byzantine horses on the West front of St. Mark's taken from Constantinople.

The notion is also largely of Western origin. Despite the very long art history of China the concept of a public museum, as Malraux has remarked, did not arise. To most oriental cultures the appreciation of art, except in its religious sense, presupposes ownership and its contemplation in seclusion – the unfurling of a scroll, the handling of a carving or a bowl. That it is of Western inception is probably due to two causes: a level of physical wealth which allows an abundant production of art and a form of culture in which this art is seen as a kind of surplus not immediately wanted in any everyday secular or religious activity. The idea of a museum does not seem possible as long as the amount of art produced is so small, as in the case of Eskimo carvings, that it is only sufficient for personal and family possession or where, however abundant, as in the case of Byzantine ikons, it is of everyday relevance.

The two prerequisites necessary for a museum occurred during the Hellenistic and Roman period which saw the founding of private collections and a search for antiquities and again during the late Renaissance in Italy. From there the spread of the notion of the museum runs parallel with the spread of the renaissance ideal, an ideal in which at every level the acquisitive instinct played a significant part.

It is thus perhaps not surprising that it was Pope Sixtus IV – known for his acquisition of great funds by simony – who should have been the first to create a museum in the now understood sense by the opening of the Capitoline collection in 1471. This act was followed by others, first in Italy then in the rest of Europe. The Cesarini Museum in Rome opened in 1500, the Farnese in 1546, the Uffizi in 1581 and then, almost a hundred years later, there is the foundation of the Ashmolean at Oxford in 1679, to house a collection first started by John Tradescant, a gardener employed by Queen Henrietta Maria after he had visited Virginia in 1637 and which then consisted of botanical and natural history specimens. In France there is the opening of the Louvre in 1681. In the subsequent century the British Museum started in Old Montague House as a result of Sir Hans Sloane's bequest in 1759 and in Germany William VIII of Hesse established the Kassel Gallery in 1760. In America the first museum was a room set aside at Harvard University in 1750 for a collection of interesting objects – stuffed animals and birds, a model of a ship, tanned human skin, the skull of an Indian warrior – and called the "Repository of Curiosities".

It was, however, the decree of August 30th 1792, passed by the French National Convention, declaring museums the property of the community and the subsequent opening of the Louvre as a Museum of the Republic in 1793, which firmly set in motion the great 19th century period of museum creation.

At the beginning of that century the motive was national and civic pride, towards the end, philanthropy. Thus, on the one hand, it was the public exhibition in Berlin in the autumn of 1815 of the returned art treasures taken during the Napoleonic Wars which eventually led to Schinkel's great Greek revival design for the Altes Museum in 1823 and its completion seven years later. On the other, it was as the result of a gift from Sir Andrew Barclay Walker to the corporation of Liverpool in 1877 that the Walker Art Gallery came into being. Similarly it was Charles Lang Freer of Detroit who deeded to the Smithsonian Institution in 1906 what is now the Freer Gallery of Art in Washington D. C.

The internal arrangements and the display methods were naturally made to further the assumptions from which 19th century museums had originated. In the case of pride in acquisition, the display had inevitably to be ostentatiously rich and complete; as much as possible of the amassed treasure had to be visible. The aim of the communication was in fact not the object on view but the existence of national or local wealth. The museum became the cultural counterpart of that other Victorian innovation, the department store. In the case of philanthropy, the name of the donor having been made obvious and suitably perpetuated, it remained to execute his intentions. These invariably centred about an improvement of the minds of the less fortunate; the museum, like the public library became a tool of Victorian public pedagogy. 19th century education having been essentially literary, it is hardly surprising that a large number of provincial museums became, in the end, a series of well illustrated labels.

The assumptions on which the museums of the 19th century were based have undergone radical transformation during the last forty years. That is not to say that they have entirely disappeared, only that those originally dominant are no longer the determinants. The economic, social and technological changes which have occurred and their effect on education, leisure and mobility have become almost commonplace in their documentation. They do not need further emphasis. Each has had its effect on a wide variety of museum aspects from lighting to the range of the visitors' visual knowledge. In the early part of this century a museum would only have been open during the hours of daylight and its visitors, unless exceptionally well travelled specialists, familiar with only one or two other institutions.

What had been less fully appreciated, however, until André Malraux elaborated the thesis in his *La Psychologie des Arts* was the very considerable impact of photography on the function of the museum. Reproductions, art books and films have made it possible to study both the visual details and the historical association of works of art in seclusion and at any desired time. They have done for the visual arts what the gramophone has done for music. Art books in particular have enabled a whole school of painting or sculpture as well as the complete works of a single artist to be seen synoptically while at the same time concentrating attention on the minutest detail of brush stroke or carved form. They have also enormously widened the range of material immediately available. The frescoes of Serbian churches, the woodcuts of Japan and the portraits of Coptic Egypt are as reachable as Rembrandt, Leonardo or Cézanne.

Neither the gramophone record nor the art book are, however, able to present reality itself; there is an inevitable and proper difference between the high fidelity reproduction and the concert performance, between the Skira print and the painting itself. The two are complementary and a critical assessment of the object may well

The outdoor exhibition, an early form of public display, was at first associated with religious festivals but later in the 18th Century became a less disguised method of showing and selling pictures. Among the well known exhibitions were those in the Piazza San Marco and at San Rocco in Venice and in the colonnade of the Pantheon in Rome. Canaletto's painting shows the square in front of San Rocco as it appeared during the festivities on the Saint's feast day, August 16th. These were attended by the Doge, Senate and the foreign ambassadors. Painters who are known to have exhibited at San Rocco include Tiepolo, S. Ricci, A. Longhi and Canaletto who showed a painting of San Giovanni e Paolo in 1725.

Die Ausstellung im Freien, eine frühe Form der öffentlichen Zurschaustellung, war zunächst mit kirchlichen Festen verbunden, entwickelte sich aber im Laufe des 18. Jahrhunderts immer mehr zu einem Anlaß, Bilder zu zeigen und zu verkaufen. Zu den bekannten Ausstellungen gehörten die auf der Piazza San Marco und vor San Rocco in Venedig und unter den Kolonnaden des Pantheon in Rom. Canalettos Gemälde zeigt den Platz vor der Kirche San Rocco während der Feiern am 16. August, dem Festtag des heiligen Rochus. Der Doge, der Senat und die auswärtigen Gesandtschaften wohnten den Festlichkeiten bei. Maler wie Tiepolo, Ricci, Longhi und Canaletto, der 1725 ein Gemälde von San Giovanni e Paolo zeigte, haben auf dem Campo San Rocco ausgestellt.

require both. The purpose of the museum as the place of display of the object itself thus becomes obvious and the visual exploitation of this special condition a natural consequence.

Moreover, the proliferation of printed matter, part of what Daniel Boorstin has called the "graphic revolution", places an added responsibility on the museum. Professor Boorstin discusses in his book The Image an advertisement which shows a motorist on the edge of the Grand Canyon looking at coloured slides of the Grand Canyon rather than the Canyon itself. It is important that the museum should create an encounter with reality which differs from that with a facsimile; that it should persuade the motorist not only to look at the Canyon, but to get out of his car and appreciate it wholly. It ought to do this if only to encourage a continuous reassessment of the insidiously familiar copy.

This influence of the photograph as a reproduction of the image is quite separate, and should not be confused, with its significance as a form of visual expression to be displayed in its own right within a museum. Both the photograph and the poster have fortunately ceased to be cold shouldered as unworthy of museum space. The Stedelijk has examples of both almost always on view.

Photography has had its most drastic effect on the interior of the museum – on selection and the method of display. The exterior and the location of the building have on the other hand possibly been more strongly influenced by the shift in social outlook. Historically the museum has been a personal, national or civic palace and like any other palace, aloof and superior, harbouring an esoteric existence. This has meant a monumental architecture and a location not in the mainstream of urban life. But the contents of the museum, though still full of wonder, are no longer to most either aloof or esoteric. In any case

even the assumption that these objects are only understood and appreciated by a few has ceased to be acceptable. The posters of the Stedelijk Museum which enliven the lamp posts and tram stops of Amsterdam are a measure of the change; of the museum becoming part of our everyday existence.

Location is, of course, of crucial importance to any museum and its nature may well be determined by it. The Louisiana Museum at Humlebæk, on the coast north of Copenhagen in the centre of a recreational area is a place for a Saturday afternoon visit, for coffee in the sun overlooking the Sound, a concert in the evening indoors or dancing on the lawn. While the Museum of Modern Art in New York is also crowded at the week-end it is, two minutes off Fifth Avenue, sufficient temptation to meet a friend for lunch in the penthouse and see an exhibition afterwards. In both cases the museum is nevertheless still a closed, rather special place. It is possible, however, to imagine a situation in which the space of the museum and that of say a shopping arcade mingled without more definition than that of a threshold, where art was on view as publicly as in the Loggia dei Lanzi facing the Piazza della Signoria in Florence. It would not, for example, require a great deal of architectural ingenuity to coax the first floor of the Museo Correr down its great staircase into the arcades surrounding the Piazza San Marco. Some commercial art galleries, of course, almost achieve such a link. Such an imperceptible transition may make the apparently separate realities of outside and inside less divergent; may also make possible a cross-reference between painting and street so that the first may become more real, the second less squalid.

Some display can, in fact, be taken completely out of the context of the museum and put on view in places not normally associated with it. The London County Council attempted this when it organised sculpture exhibitions in

its public parks or when in 1962 the Italian Ministry of Fine Arts staged a display of sculpture among the mediaeval buildings and Roman ruins of Spoleto in the Umbrian hills. This sort of open air viewing need not, however, be confined to such durable objects as stone or metal sculpture. The Swedish Society of Industrial Art has, for instance, selected examples of industrial design and put these on view within a public park in Stockholm and every year there are a number of shows in London in which painters display their work on screens put up along a public pavement. In Boston, Mass. the same thing is done within tents on the Common in the centre of the town.

The public library whose function in terms of communication has after all considerable similarities to that of the museum has become increasingly open and inviting and its location more firmly rooted to the everyday paths of its users. This often means building on land of high commercial value. Libraries and museums are both uses which require both capital and considerable recurring annual expenditure. Unless therefore these buildings are used, the money spent on them is not invested as soundly as it might be. A building site within a shopping precinct may thus, in the long run, despite its high initial cost, be the most economically justified choice. The local savings bank of Lund may have been aware of the strength of this argument when it built the new Art Gallery on the edge of the market place in the old part of the town and presented it to the citizens in 1957 (see Fig. page 11). Klas Anshelm's design achieves there a dramatic and direct transition from cobbled market place to gallery interior. Museums need not, and probably should not, be sterilised in cultural centres isolated in cultural parks. This does not mean that they themselves should not be centres of cultural interest in the widest possible sense; a position in the main stream of community activity

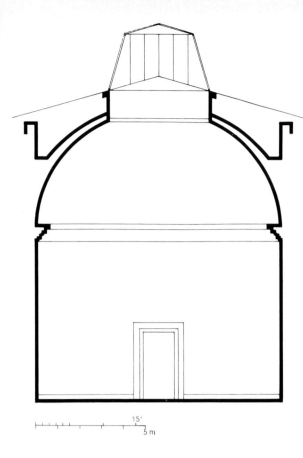

Alte Pinakothek, Munich (1836). Section. Architect: Leo von Klenze.

Alte Pinakothek, München (1836). Schnitt. Architekt: Leo von Klenze.

should in fact encourage this more general function. Such a wider view of the museum is, moreover, entirely in accord with the original definition of the museum as a medium of communication of objects of cultural and scientific interest. Although the method of communication is mainly visual and of a particular kind – a moving observer looking at stationary objects – it need not be exclusively so. It may, for example, be as effective to communicate certain aspects of art through an actual attempt at its performance as through its observation. The art classes of the São Paulo Museum of Art or the children's painting room at the entrance to Louisiana are thus complimentary to the display. Similarly films may be essential for an understanding of an ethnographic exhibition or early 20th century art. They are regularly shown, for example, at the Museum of Geography and Ethnography in Rotterdam and the Museum of Modern Art in New York. Visual communication will, what is more, be sharpened by intellectual understanding so that lectures and discussions are yet another aspect of museum activity. Most museums hold regular lectures both for school children and adults and have conducted tours of the galleries.

Every museum label should, of course, provide some of this information unobtrusively yet legibly at a range not too dissimilar from that at which the object is normally seen. Although the 19th century may have gone too far in asserting itself through excessive length and a passion for detailed references, the current tendency towards the sparsest possible label may be equally mistaken. What is probably wanted is a simple identification near the object itself coupled with a more descriptive label acting as an introduction to a section or group of exhibits. It is a method which takes into account the sequence of museum viewing and is one frequently used by the Museum of Modern Art in New York.

Systems of transmitting verbal information to individual viewers through small radio receivers – hired by them at the entrance desk – are now also widely available so that visual communication can be simultaneously reinforced by the spoken word. Unlike the crowded guided tour or the elaborate notes of a catalogue, such systems do not seem to destroy the immediacy which would appear to be essential to museum viewing. The museum as an institution is in its fullest and most useful sense thus more than a series of rooms in which objects happen to be put on display.

It is the total method of communication which will in the end determine the architectural organisation of the museum. The anatomy of the building will be shaped by the social role envisaged and the emphasis to be given to different aspects of that communication. Inevitably foremost among these must be the encounter between individual and object; this is after all the essence of the museum, it is what distinguishes it from other building types. And this uniqueness, this difference from other buildings, may well also be the clue to its design.

The last premise rests, of course, on certain architectural assumptions which are open to question. It can no doubt be argued that the museum is no more than a well lit warehouse, an anonymous volume in which certain criteria of illumination are satisfied and which happens to contain pictures, porcelain or push-button models of coal mines. The argument is based on criteria of flexibility and an insistence that all possible and even unforeseen conditions must be capable of being met. The more undefined the spaces, the more unlimited the choices, the better is the answer considered to be. Several museums have aimed at this goal – Cullinan Hall, the Kunsthaus in Zürich, São Paulo's Museum of Art, the Helena Rubinstein Pavilion in Tel Aviv – though none perhaps has yet achieved this ideal.

It may be that further design will get closer to limitless flexibility and undifferentiated space. Whether the pursuit of this goal is in fact worthwhile is, however, another matter since it rests on two profound misconceptions of art and architecture. The first assumes that there is a kind of competition between art and environment and that unless this environment is completely negated the work on display will be crushed; the second, which is a corollary to the first, suggests that each work has such a degree of independence that it can be shown anywhere, that it is entirely free of its background. Both assumptions are abstract notions unrelated to the actual process of viewing and the total experience of visiting a museum. Neither art nor architecture is anonymous. One of the acknowledged distinguishing characteristics of art is a sense of uniqueness – not necessarily of individuality linked to a particular person, but of form, colour, emotion; inherent thus not only in Picasso but equally in Balinese textiles. Similarly architecture is the enclosure of space for human use, or to paraphrase Kahn's definition, 'the thoughtful enclosure of space for human use', and neither the use nor the thought can be anonymous. Both are geared to a purpose.

Art in a museum is like the performance of a symphony in a concert hall: it exists as part of its environment. The auditorium impinges on the music through its acoustics and the performance as heard is the interaction of the two. In the same way the museum impinges on the display through its appearance because what is seen and appreciated at any one moment is conditioned by the images seen previously and those even peripheral in the field of vision. It is, therefore, not a matter of competition between art and its environment, between picture and architecture, in which one or other aspect has to be negated but of arriving at a working relationship between the two. That this is in fact possible has been shown in Italy during the last ten years.

A concert performance, apart from the music, is also in any case more than a matter of adjusted acoustics. It is the visual excitement of the orchestra, the crowd movement in the foyer, the awareness of joint participation within the auditorium, the sense of occasion which together make up the appreciation of the event. Similarly museum display, apart from the quality of the objects on view, is more than a case of the correct background or balanced illumination. It is again the totality of the experience which becomes an event in its own right and within this totality, architecture, as space manipulation, must of necessity assume a positive function. To aim at an environment of nothingness is to abrogate architectural responsibility.

Both in biology and architecture there is a complex and important interaction between function and anatomy. Each influences and modifies the other. The architectural anatomy of a museum will be strongly influenced by two aspects of function: the general role assigned to that particular museum and the crucial relation within it of object and spectator. The first will affect the relative disposition of spaces, the second their nature.

The second aspect is also, of course, the characteristic which is likely to influence the most important spaces, those in fact unique to the museum, and it becomes thus the cell structure, as it were, from which the anatomy is later to be built up.

A good deal of architectural interest has been devoted to this problem, most of it pursuing the theme of an ideal section relating observer, object and light source. It is the basis of Cockerell's design for the completion of the Fitzwilliam Museum in Cambridge from 1845 onwards, for his project for the National Gallery in London and for Van der Steur's Boymans in Rotterdam as much as for Frank Lloyd Wright's solution at the Guggenheim, Bassi and Boschetti's attempt at Turin or the work of the Building Research Station at Birmingham (see Figs. page 12.) Most of these designs, particularly the more recent, assume that once this theoretical ideal is established it can be multiplied without limit. But the ideal is not a static repetitive solution and the architectural section of a museum cannot be extruded like aluminium. The ideal, in so far as it exists, is a situation varied in terms of space and light. Ignazio Gardella's design for the Pavilion of Contemporary Art at the Gallery of Modern Art in Milan is based on a complete awareness of this necessity. The pavilion is about 120 ft. long and 90 ft. at its greatest width (see pages 36–37). Within the two storey height there are five different kinds of space. A two-storey high narrow side-lit entrance hall; up half a flight, a one and a half-storey high gallery area top-lit and divided by screens into five bays each a different length; on one side and down several steps this opens on to a gallery the full length of the main exhibition space completely glazed with a view of trees and shrubs; a whole flight of steps up from the main gallery floor there is a balcony again top-lit and beyond it a long narrow enclosed room with artificial lighting. These differences correspond to differences in use. The side-lit space is intended for sculpture, seen there so that its three dimensional qualities are enhanced and its silhouette is against foliage; the large area with its controllable toplighting and variable screens is for paintings; the two smaller upper level spaces are for drawings and small objects and the enclosed room is especially for prints.

Similar changes in space and light can be seen at Louisiana, at the Art Gallery in Lund, at Scarpa's Venezuelan Pavilion in the Biennale Garden in Venice and, in a greatly simplified form, at Rietveld's Zonnehof in Amersfoort. These examples, like the Milan pavilion, are small buildings which have benefited from thorough study and the absence of any necessity to make a monumental gesture. There is, however, an equal need and an even greater validity for the same approach when designing larger museums.

The need stems from a double functional necessity for not only do the objects on view benefit from conditions sympathetic to their particular nature but the observer's perception demands such changes in order to remain alert. It is known that in terms of bodily comfort, for example, the continually and slightly fluctuating conditions of a spring day are those which are at the same time the most stimulating and comfortable. Much the same appears true of vision. Physiological research on the detailed mechanics and chemistry of the eye has shown that there is a continuous photochemical reaction going on in the receptor rods of the retina and that the retina itself is in constant vibration shifting the image across the receptors. The eye relies, in fact, for effective sight on alternate moments of action and inaction, the most apparent symptom of which is blinking. It is in this instant of darkness that the photochemical process is reversed and regenerated. It would seem from experience that very similar conditions are needed on the larger scale of vision as well, that action and inaction and regeneration are equally vital and that change with its demand for new adaptation provides the necessary stimuli.

It may well be that in many cases museum fatigue is thus not only due to the inevitable mental and emotional concentration combined with the physical effort of standing and walking, but also, perhaps, to the tiring effects of excessively static illumination. The museum visitor may often, though probably less consciously, be as eye tired as foot sore, particularly since seeing is such a dominant part of the whole activity. Visual alertness and the capacity to appreciate will both diminish with tiredness; communication will become inefficient.

The attempt to define an ideal has also led to a considerable development of artificial illumination. That such lighting is in fact required can no longer be in dispute for the new social role of the museum demands quite clearly that it should be open in the late afternoon and evening. The late opening of many European and American museums which now occurs on one or more days of the week and, particularly in America, on Sunday, has proved a great success. But the principle of change applies equally to artificial as to natural lighting and the single ideal is again an illusory concept.

Fluorescent tubes, for example, are available in three categories of colour temperature corresponding roughly to daylight from a north sky, afternoon sunlight and the light of tungsten lamps. The position and extent of such fluorescent tubes or of tungsten lighting is also highly variable. It can, to take only three examples, be a general luminous light source in the plane of the ceiling or wall, it can be a highly localized beam from a projector with a lens system and a masking screen cut to light only the object itself or it can be a shaped and shielded cold cathode tube within a display cabinet. The details of such systems and their possible applications are discussed later in relation to particular display methods. What is important to establish at the moment, is the inappropriateness of completely uniform conditions where the communication of highly individual objects is concerned and where uniformity impairs the receptiveness of the observer.

Uniformity is in any case undesirable on purely functional grounds. Different objects demand different qualities of light in order to become "visible". The sculpture in the diffusely lit sculpture room of the Boymans, off-white objects against off-white walls, loses many of its sculptural qualities; it fails to communicate. The choice of lighting will depend on the nature of the object – the reflectivity of its surface, its roundness or flatness, its degree of opacity, its colour. Thus the glow and glitter of jewellery which is brought out by display methods is the result of quite different conditions of illumination from those that define the form of Rococco furniture or bring out the colour of stained glass (see Fig. page 17). Light is variable in direction and intensity, it can come straight from a source or be reflected, it can be concentrated or diffused – there is nothing in the nature of light to suggest a single or a static solution.

While this is common knowledge in the theatre it is not so in the museum. That even there lighting need not be static was demonstrated some time ago by the Louvre where in the Oriental Antiquities section a room containing sculpture taken from the 8th century palace at Khorsabad had its light change from spot lighting to diffuse illumination, first revealing the low relief as ghost-like apparitions from the past, then showing it so that all its detail may be carefully viewed. Such devices need careful consideration so that they do not become obtrusive and do not interpose themselves between the exhibit and the visitor.

Museum lighting is, in general, halfway between that for the theatre aiming at predetermined dramatic effects and that for a laboratory or classroom in which various objects are to be examined in visual comfort. The great difference, however, between stage lighting and museum lighting is that in the theatre the viewer is static and normally outside the area in which the lighting is taking place. In the museum, on the other hand, he is within this illuminated zone, casting shadows, obscuring the light source, continually in danger of being dazzled. The difference between classroom and museum illumination is that in a teaching space the examination of an object may be prolonged and is usually performed by a stationary observer, in the museum the examination is relatively short since each object is only part of a series and the observer is moving so that change is expected and natural.

Uniformity is also undesirable as far as the conservation of the museum collection is concerned. There is some anxiety among those responsible for conservation that the high levels of illumination which are becoming increasingly frequent in museums will damage many of the objects on display. Most of the damage occurs from ultraviolet radiation. This can be filtered and rooms exhibiting tapestries, textiles, paintings and any other light-sensitive materials in daylight or under fluorescent lighting should include such filters. All light is, however, to some extent damaging and Gary Thomson, Conservator of the National Gallery, London, has therefore suggested maximum levels to safeguard the material on display which may vary from 300 lux for metal or stone to 50 lux for watercolours or tapestries. These levels and the use of ultraviolet filters are discussed later.

The light levels of both natural and artificial lighting which are currently in use have to some extent been taken over from lighting research related to industrial or commercial uses. As Thomson has, however, pointed out these standards apply to various tasks performed as part of regular work and are therefore not applicable to museum viewing, though they may be correct for the critical tasks of a picture restorer in his workshop. The level of lighting has also been rising because the use of fluorescent tubes and the emphasis on the exclusion of sunlight has increased the proportion of light in the blue end of the spectrum. The eye, however, is on the contrary conditioned to accepting progressively lower levels of illumination as the light shifts towards the red end of the spectrum – towards low sunlight, the light from a tungsten filament, an oil lamp, a candle. Rooms lit by fluorescent tubes of the daylight type need therefore to be brighter to appear as well lit as the same room in incadescent light. This has forced levels well above the 150 lux which, it has been suggested, might be considered safe as a general rule.

The acceptance of lower levels of lighting has two important architectural implications. In the first instance it reduces the preoccupation – so often questionable – with a search for an ideal lighting solution and the consequent manipulation of the roof section at the expense of other considerations. In the second instance it demands more gradual transitions from the brightness of the open air so that the eye may accommodate to these lower levels. The approaches to the collection may have to be considered as zones of transition in which the lighting is so manip-

Art Gallery, Lund, Sweden (1956–57). Exterior view. Architect: Klas Anshelm.

Kunstgalerie, Lund, Schweden (1956–57). Außenansicht. Architekt: Klas Anshelm.

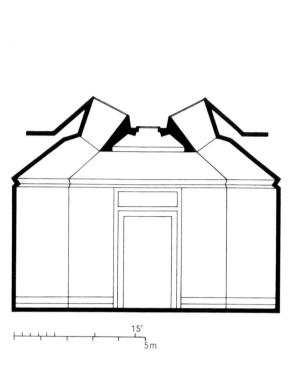

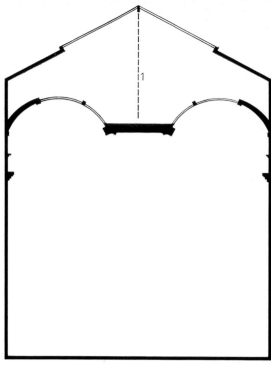

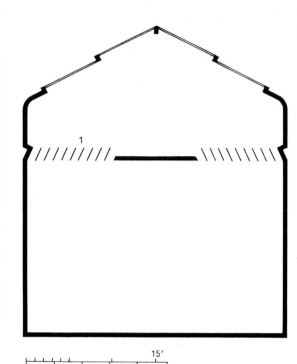

Fitzwilliam Museum, Cambridge, England (after 1845).
Section through typical gallery. Architect: C. R. Cockerell.
Fitzwilliam Museum, Cambridge, England (nach 1845).
Schnitt durch einen Ausstellungsraum. Architekt: C. R. Cockerell.

National Gallery, London. Section. Proposal by C. R. Cockerell, 1850.
National Gallery, London. Schnitt. Projekt von C. R. Cockerell, 1850.
1 Sunblind / Sonnenblende

Boymans-van Beuningen Museum, Rotterdam (1931–35).
Section. Architect: A. van der Steur.
Museum Boymans-van Beuningen, Rotterdam (1931–35).
Schnitt. Architekt: A. van der Steur.
1 Louvres / Lamellen

New Galleries, Birmingham City Museum and Art Gallery (1957). Section. Architects: City Architect, A.G. Sheppard Fidler with John Bickerdike of the Building Research Station.
Neugestaltung des Städtischen Museums und der Kunstgalerie, Birmingham (1957). Schnitt. Architekt: Stadtbauamt, A.G. Sheppard Fidler mit John Bickerdike von der Building Research Station.
1 Existing roof light / Vorhandenes Oberlicht
2 Metal vane / Metall-Diopter
3 Aluminium eggcrate velarium / Untergehängte Rasterplatte aus Aluminium

The Solomon R. Guggenheim Museum, New York, N.Y. (1956–59). Section. Architect: Frank Lloyd Wright.
The Solomon R. Guggenheim Museum, New York, N.Y. (1956–59). Schnitt. Architekt: Frank Lloyd Wright.
1 Glass dome / Gläserne Kuppel

Gallery of Modern Art, Turin (1954–59). Cross section.
Architects: Carlo Bassi and Goffredo Boschetti.
Galleria d'Arte Moderna, Turin (1954–59). Querschnitt.
Architekten: Carlo Bassi und Goffredo Boschetti.
1 Wired glass / Drahtglas
2 Acrylic diffuser / Plexiglasplatten

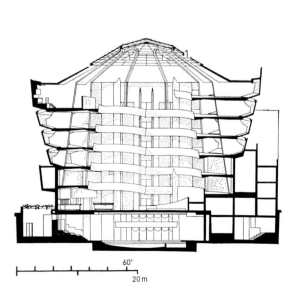

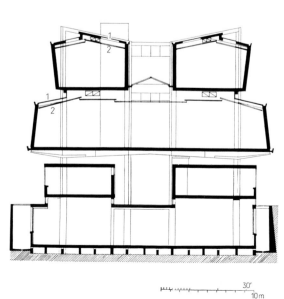

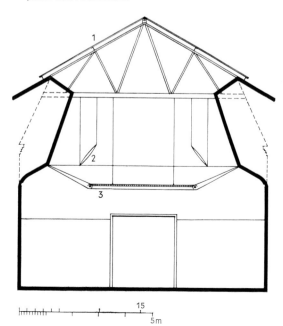

ulated – usually by being greatly subdued – that low levels of illumination inside the building appear bright by contrast. Similarly views of the outside, and particularly of the sky, from the exhibition areas must be restricted and controlled.

These are some of the considerations which influence the process of looking at objects and which can at once be related to some aspect of environmental control. The perception of the object is also, however, a matter of history. Both those who make the object, whether it be painting, sculpture, illustration or utensil, and those who look at it are, as Professor E. H. Gombrich has demonstrated in his *Art and Illusion*, conditioned by certain previous experiences which create a "schema" into which they attempt to fit the object. This "mental set" is certainly at work in all museum viewing. Prof. Gombrich discusses, for example, two illustrations of French Cathedrals, one drawn in 1635, the other in 1836 and compares both with photographs. The 17th century topographical artist has made the side of Notre Dame more symmetrical than it is and rounded the pointed Gothic windows, he has made it conform more closely to Renaissance concepts; the 19th century illustrator, on the other hand, drawing the west facade of Chartres has elongated and pointed the rounded Romanesque windows to fit his "schema" of a cathedral as a Gothic building.

Somewhat the same sort of fitting into predetermined stylistic notions inevitably occurs when looking at painting or sculpture in a museum. This has, of course, certain advantages for it enables amongst other things a rapid change of critical standpoint. The expectation on seeing a Uccello is not the same as before a Corot. Fitting into categories – the habit of looking at the label before the picture – has equally very great dangers for the "mental set" may already be so rigidly fixed that the object will fail to communicate. When, therefore, Studio BBPR surround Michelangelo's unfinished *Pietà Rondanini* at the Castello Sforzesco with a stone embrasure and reveal it suddenly after a sharp turn at the foot of a flight of steps, they do not only intend the sculpture to be seen undisturbed by other objects in the room but also, through a measure of surprise, to destroy the preconceived responses which any work by Michelangelo is so likely to arouse.

The visual surprise of this design depends, as all museum arrangement, on a relation between a stationary exhibit and a moving observer. This is spatially the reverse of the cinema. But, like the cinema, the experience of a museum consists of a series of images seen in sequence (see Fig. page 15). This series can be organised and the juxtaposition of events within the sequence deliberately manipulated. The organisation of the Bellini Room at the Museo Correr, for example, depends on such sequential viewing and the position of the almost bare "Room of the Four Doors" on the same floor of the Correr acts twice as a pause within the sequence of the floor as a whole.

At the most obvious level sequence is made to parallel chronology so that objects are seen in historical order. Many museums have, of course, adopted this course. It is wholly appropriate where the evolution of an idea or a process is to be demonstrated. The development of the Paisley shawl, for instance, from patterns brought from India and its relation to the Jacquard loom is probably best shown in such chronological order and the local museum arranges its collection in this way.

Sequence need not, however, always have this one directional sense. In the late summer of 1961 the Stedelijk Museum in Amsterdam had an exhibition showing the two parallel streams of Apollonian and Dionysian tendencies in art. The gallery in the new wing of the museum is side-lit from windows down both long sides and screens were arranged at right angles to these with a gangway down the middle. On one side there was sculpture and painting representing the Dionysian stream, on the other the Apollonian. Within each half the examples were arranged chronologically. It was thus possible by going down the length of the room to examine each stream in historical sequence or by going from side to side across its width to see the two streams as they existed at any one period. Walking down the centre gangway and looking left and right it was also possible to get a quick impression of the apparent opposition between the two tendencies.

Similar opportunities of cross-reference within the sequence of serial viewing become possible when the spatial organisation of the building is sufficiently open to allow a simultaneous view of several areas which at other times are seen only at close range. James Johnson Sweeney, the first curator of the Guggenheim Museum, has described the effects inherent in the openness of Wright's great spiralling space:

"This possibility of seeing three levels of exhibit at once across the empty centre of the building makes the composition of the wall, from the point of view of critical or historical apposition of exhibits, in a way no conventional gallery affords. For example, side by side within a single bay, paintings or sculptures may be grouped for comparison or contrasts at close range. The contents of the bays on each side may be related to this – again at close range – for serial viewing by the visitor as he proceeds up or down the ramp. In addition to these critical or historical single level associations, the bays immediately above and below may be arranged likewise in critical or historical relationship to be seen from a distance – from across the empty central well.... To enjoy to full advantage the opportunities the building offers, each level, each bay, must therefore be related to one another up and down, from level to level and across the empty centre, as well as backwards and forwards along the ramp, if the spectator is to be led without effort on his part from critical point to critical point in the essay which the exhibition installation should provide."

It is thus not surprising that the importance of certain visual juxtapositions can often be shown much more clearly in an exhibition than through any other medium since, as in the two examples just described, it is possible to exploit a considerable variety of spatial arrangements. It obviously becomes possible to provide greater differences of viewing than in a book held at a roughly constant distance and having a limited size. The sort of visual relationships which were exploited in Gyorgy Kepes's exhibition "The New Landscape" at the Massachusetts Institute of Technology in 1951 or Paul Rudolph's arrangement of "The Family of Man" photographic exhibition shown in New York in 1955 and subsequently elsewhere, could not be repeated in Kepes's later book of the same title or in the volume which reproduced the photographs originally assembled by Edward Steichen for the Museum of Modern Art. The dance of the recurring "Family of Man" theme photograph of the smiling boy and his magic flute or the contraction of space in the section on death before the unfolding of Cartier-Bresson's great panorama of Indian women seen against the mountains of Kashmir was possible in a museum but not in a book.

The choice of sequence and the ability to make quick general appraisals before or after detailed examination which was characteristic of the Stedelijk exhibition is impossible with any of the systems so far proposed which reverse the accepted method of museum viewing and place moving objects before a fixed observer. These depend on some method of mechanically handling exhibits – most suggestions only apply to pictures – by attaching them to revolving drums or some form of conveyor. Lina Bo Bardi has suggested a number of revolving drums placed on a revolving stage and Cicero Diaf has put forward a design for a museum consisting of a number of enclosed drums housing pictures on turnstiles from which two or three can be selected at a time to appear mechanically on a wall at the side of this drum (see Fig. page 18). Luc Benoist and Charles Friese have also discussed the possible mechanisation of the museum and put forward projects in which the building consisted of vertically superimposed viewing platforms facing a kind of paternoster carrying pictures.

The nearest working example of such a mechanised display occurred at the "International Labour Exhibition" in Turin in 1961 where Albini and Bonfante hung display panels from an overhead conveyor in the section devoted to "Increase in Production". The panels of photographs and captions moved vertically and horizontally along the periphery, the noise and appearance of the conveyor deliberately suggesting the inside of a factory, while the spectators stood or sat in the middle of the room. The display showed both the strengths and weaknesses of the method. While it was possible to rest or at least stand still, the information had to be absorbed at a predetermined pace and in a set sequence. In terms of museum communication both these latter restrictions may well be serious. The sort of viewing which was possible in the "Dionysian-Apollonian" Exhibition, for example, would be extraordinarily difficult to achieve in any mechanised display. And to some extent this going backwards and forwards and making a quick survey goes on almost every time one enters a gallery. But what is perhaps even more important is that any form of mechanical conveyance of objects tends to destroy that sense of immediacy which is at the core of all museum communication; it interposes itself between viewer and viewed.

Museum planning is to a great extent influenced and often even defined by the assumption that there will be a viewing sequence. Le Corbusier's studies, for instance, have always assumed this and made growth an extension of the established sequence (see Fig. page 20). The design of the Guggenheim is wholly and rigidly determined by it. It is almost the starting point for the plan. This is equally true of Franco Minissi's ingenious conversion of the Villa Giulia where the insertion of a mezzanine level within the existing structure aimed primarily to create an unbroken succession of exhibition rooms. Sequence considered as linear continuity stems of course from much earlier museum planning which was itself an adaptation of the Renaissance palace in which all the principal rooms formed a connected series of spaces opening off each other. Von Klenze's plan for the Alte Pinakothek in Munich is thus, except for its brilliant staircase slot, essentially the modification of a palace floor plan (see Fig. page 21).

There is a certain dogmatism about any plan which defines circulation as a closed circuit; a presumption that once safely on the cultural conveyor belt it would be a mistake to step off. This may not matter much in a small museum such as Louisiana where different pavilions link to form a continuous route but can become extraordinarily irritating in a large building such as the main part of the Rijksmuseum in Amsterdam. There may after all be considerable sections which one does not want to see on a particular visit or which are so obviously second-rate that they tend to devalue the remainder.

The closed circuit is also, to a large extent, an attempt to enforce a certain clarity and sense of order on the plan. As long as linear progression can be maintained the circulation is clear and determined even if visually that clarity cannot be grasped. But a large museum is not unlike an interior city and its galleries may be as disconcerting as a labyrinth of undifferentiated streets. This situation can occur even before the amorphous vastness of the Louvre, needing a copy of a floor plan continually before one, is reached.

Some of the elements which impose visual order and which, as a result, become important in direction finding and orientation have been analysed by Kevin Lynch in *The Image of the City*. He has listed those which are important within an urban framework as paths, edges, districts, nodes and landmarks. Each has a recognisable architectural equivalent relevant to orientation within a museum and to its total image.

Paths are, of course, the routes of movement and in a museum usually the spaces left between the exhibits. These can be controlled and channeled by screens or rigidly defined as in the suspended galleries of the Villa Giulia. In any serial viewing the relationship between the path and object will also largely determine the sequence in which things will be seen. Thus when that control is absolute, as around the *Pietà Rondanini* the sequence is equally predetermined. Occasionally the expression of the route becomes the dominant architectural theme; this is the case at the Guggenheim and, to a lesser degree, at Louisiana. In many older museums the main paths were delineated and thus made obvious by axial vistas of the framed openings between enfiladed rooms.

Edges are linear elements which are not paths but boundaries between parts. In the city they are, for example, shore lines or railway embankments. Gardella's Pavilion in Milan has three clearly defined edges parallel to each other; the long glass wall between the sculpture gallery and the park, the change in level between sculpture gallery and the main area for paintings and the balcony line above this space. Each edge defines, separates, yet helps to make the whole coherent.

Districts are sections which can be grasped mentally and which one recognises as having entered. Studio BBPR acknowledged the value of such separateness when they put the link between the ground and first floors of the first section of the Castello Sforzesco out-doors. Although the route is covered it makes a distinct break between the two districts by first passing over a bridge looking down into a courtyard moist and green from a fountain and then ascending a staircase which terminates in an open loggia with a view of the space between the two wings of the museum and the entrance tower. Scarpa has used similar devices with equal success at the Castelvecchio in Verona. Such separateness not only provides a pause between sections of a museum, but makes each a more recognisable and visually graspable unit. It becomes, as a result, a more easily memorable division.

Nodes are focal points from which and to which one moves because paths converge there or because there is at those points a concentration of activity. Le Corbusier's central three-storey space lit by a pyramidal sklylight and containing the main element of vertical movement is obviously the node of the National Museum of Western Art in Tokyo about which its organisation is structured. The great top-lit court of the Munson-Williams-Proctor Institute acts in much the same way. Nodes need not, of course, be central nor need a museum have only one. Each district can have its own node and even in a museum in which the route is strictly circumscribed there could be two nodes, each node, for example, formed by a dominant space containing a staircase. One district could be seen as one ascends the building, the other as one descends. It is probably also possible to create nodes by having dominant enclosed volumes – service elements or storage – as visually fixed points within open or only partially screened areas, particularly if these volumes are linked to stairs or bridges leading to new groups of spaces. Landmarks are points of reference which remain external and which, unlike nodes, are not entered. They may equally be distant objects or quite small signs which give a clue to position. Courtyards about which one pivots but which one does not enter or views of the outside such as those of the Piazza San Marco from the Museo Correr or of the sea at the Musée Maison de la Culture in Le Havre can act as landmarks. At a shorter range, the narrow slots intended for the passage of large pictures which can be seen at the Palazzo Abbatellis or in some of the newly arranged rooms of the Uffizi and which just reveal something of the next room make out of the disclosed object a landmark, a distant goal to be reached (see Fig. page 22). These elements of space manipulation are, of course, only some of the tools which enable the functional organisation of the building to be made comprehensible. They impose an order and a clarity related to use which is an aid to the understanding of the spaces of the building. Such an understanding is able to reinforce the communication which the museum is attempting to convey. It is, moreover, an order which is not in conflict with the exhibition but in fact arises out of it.

These considerations, though relevant throughout the museum building, are of particular importance in its public spaces. A museum has, in terms of Kahn's definition, a very clear organisation of served and servant spaces. The primary areas are those directly devoted to communication – display galleries, lecture rooms, class rooms, libraries, book and post card counters – and these are served by spaces – work-shops, laboratories, storage rooms, offices, mechanical plant rooms – which make the functioning of the primary spaces possible. The first group is the zone to which the public has immediate access, the second is a private zone of internal housekeeping. The relative size of the two zones will vary with the nature of the museum but in general the amount of servant space required has often been severely underestimated. Both are vital to the proper functioning of the museum and neither can be neglected in any architectural planning. There is a third zone of ancillary spaces – restaurants, washrooms, coat rooms, club rooms – which are of social or personal importance. The floor area of this group will depend on the number of visitors expected during peak hours.

James Johnson Sweeney has suggested that only about one-seventh of a museum's area be used for displaying pictures. This seems a small proportion and may have been influenced by the fact that the Guggenheim of which he was director had such meagre storage that part of the top of the display ramp had to be allocated to picture racks. It is however reasonable when it is realised that only 10% of the Guggenheim collection is on view at time and 90% is in storage and on loan.

Other collections have a greater proportion of their exhibits on view: the Yale Art Gallery shows about 60%, the Palazzo Abbatellis in Palermo 50%, the Shimane Prefectural Museum in Matsue 25%. In terms of floor area Philip Johnson has advocated a proportion of one-third for exhibits to two-thirds backstage. The backstage area does, of course, include the whole range of ancillary spaces and part of it may house the study collections which are open to students.

In view of the considerable proportion of the total building which must be given over to storage and other ancillary elements, it is surprising that this has been exploited so little in terms of architectural form. Libraries, for example, often turn the existence of a large book stack to advantage by making it a core element ringed by reading areas needing light. Only Ahrbom and Zimdal's Municipal Museum at Linköping completed in 1939 uses narrow storage rooms as dividing spaces under a directional toplighting arrangement (see Figs. page 23). There has been no development of this notion of using servant spaces to fill the less usable zones of the primary volumes and to organise with them certain spatial subdivisions; the unseen portions of the museum iceberg have remained submerged. Perhaps the demarcation between the primary exhibits on the one hand and the study collections and the workshops on the other, has been overly rigid. It ought to be possible for a visitor to make a transition from the first zone to at least parts of the second two with ease. This is not to suggest that all parts of the collection ought to be equally on view; only that since it would seem that if exhibits are to make their proper impact the number which can be shown in an area at one time is limited, access to the remainder ought to be simple and direct. The less frequently exhibits are seen and the less casually they are normally viewed, the denser can their arrangement be organised. Study collections can, like footnotes, be packed tighter than the main statement. Such accessible study collections must, however, be housed so that their organisation is obvious and they can be used without close supervision. A number of museums have paid as much attention to the display of these collections as to the main exhibition areas. The enterprising Ethnographical Museum at Neuchâtel, for instance, keeps the pottery of its reference collection in cabinets and display cases which have the ordered and workmanlike character appropriate to such a section and which have evidently been as carefully considered as the showcases and lighting of the main gallery (see Fig. page 24). The method of viewing differs considerably, however, in these two spaces. In the main gallery it is always a sequence of objects seen by a moving observer; in the study collections on the other hand the objects are selected and closely examined for a considerable time so that the person is normally standing or sitting. There is thus a need for both storage and study space. Such areas are in their function in fact very like the reading rooms of a library adjacent to open access book stacks.

The transition to the workshop area needs greater control if these are to perform their tasks efficiently. It would seem, nevertheless, possible to have at least certain aspects of conservation on view, perhaps through glass panels or during guided tours. The Brooklyn Museum is considering this possibility. The techniques used are certainly sufficiently fascinating to arouse interest; to see a pot assembled, a textile repaired, an animal preserved or a picture cleaned satisfies not only proper curiosity but emphasises the complexity of preservation and the painstaking efforts which are necessary to maintain things intact for the future. Museum communication can be seen to be dependent on conservation.

The amount and frequency of maintenance is very much related to the nature of the environment. The more it can be controlled and, especially, kept constant the less is there likely to be a need for drastic repairs. It is for this reason, of course, that full air conditioning giving control over temperature, humidity and air pollution including dust is advisable. It is particularly necessary in rooms housing organic materials – wood, textiles, paintings, paper, fur, bones, leather – and in highly variable climates especially if there are wide fluctuations in relative humidity. Certain relevant design factors for such environmental control are tabulated on page 179.

Some form of mechanical ventilation becomes necessary as soon as totally enclosed, artificially illuminated spaces are created. That is to say, air has to be introduced into these zones mechanically even if that air is not heated, cooled or cleaned. It will in most climates, however, have to be heated at some time of the year and at other times it may well be essential to cool it, particularly as the heat given off by artificial lighting is considerable. The design of the air-handling system must pay special regard to the amount of lighting there is likely to be and should assume that at some time or other the maximum may be reached in every gallery. It is an extremely worthwhile investment in future flexibility.

The great additional virtue of air conditioning, of cleaned air, is that a number of protective enclosures which interpose themselves between object and the observer can be removed. Paintings need no longer hide behind glass reflecting the gallery and its spectators and many other vulnerable objects can dispense with their dust-protecting cases. The removal of such cases may create problems of security but these can often be overcome by other methods such as the ingenious linking of the Swedish copper-plate money on show in the Royal Coin Cabinet in Stockholm to an electric burglar alarm. Air-conditioning can be seen – and justified – as an aid to direct communication. Museum buildings should thus make provision for air-handling ducts and plant rooms even if the equipment cannot be installed at first. Adequate horizontal and vertical voids ought to form part of the original design and be distributed throughout the building so that eventually every part of it may be air conditioned.

Restaurants and club rooms, part of the third zone of ancillary spaces, are a relatively new addition to the museum plan. The Victorians would have considered them frivolous and, therefore, harmful in what was intended as a pedagogic warehouse. They are now on the contrary welcomed as adding to the extrovert nature of the museum.

The best museum restaurants are civilised spaces designed for their purpose and not left over corners in the basement. They usually exploit some particular situation: the Museum of Modern Art in New York has its penthouse and roof terrace as a members' restaurant and the long ground floor room facing a terrace in front of its sculpture garden as a public cafeteria (see Fig. page 25); the Stedelijk in Amsterdam puts its restaurant next to the library as two linked communal rooms and extends it on to a paved terrace looking out over a pool and sculpture with a children's play space beyond; Louisiana, eighteen miles north of Copenhagen, terminates its last pavilion with a restaurant and shaded out-door eating space overlooking the Sound.

Club rooms and meeting rooms, provided they are not taken over by a pseudo-artistic coterie, can serve an equally valuable function. Although objects within a museum can only communicate to individuals, that communication can, as a result, frequently become more intelligible. Such rooms might well, of course, be multi-purpose spaces so that they can be used for lectures, film shows or painting classes. Only in this way are they likely to justify themselves economically.

Such spaces and their varied uses will, like the inclusion of a library, make it more likely that the museum becomes

a community building and that appreciation and understanding become many sided. The museum library, for instance, deserves to be considered as a primary space as much connected to the main zone of public circulation as an exhibition gallery. The reading room at the Stedelijk in Amsterdam, sited in a pivotal position between the old building and the new wing, encourages reference to historical material or a glance at an art magazine which may put the current exhibition in its proper setting. Once provided such facilities are certainly used; the library of the Museum of Modern Art in New York containing 15,000 items consisting of books, periodicals and catalogues is open to all museum visitors and is consulted by about 5000 readers each year. Such information ought thus not only be available to the research staff or on sale at the postcard counter, as is so often the case, but accessible to the public in surroundings as congenial as the reading area around a fireplace at Louisiana. And the fact that museums may occasionally be visited by large numbers should not deter one from attempting to create such intimate places.

Reading rooms, restaurants, storage, galleries, lighting are only some of the elements which together form a museum building and however excellent any one of these may be, it cannot itself create a satisfactory museum. What matters is the total experience, the architecture of the whole.

It is the ordering of these elements, varied and occasionally conflicting, so that they may together cause what Le Corbusier has called the "correct, wise and magnificent play of forms under light" which will create an architecture. There is an infinite possibility to this play of forms; in the last resort it will have as many variants as there are architects. Yet certain trends, certain historically changing intellectual assumptions can be found even if not always defined.

When Mercier writing in 1770 foresaw an utopian museum for the year 2000 he placed on its facade the words "An Abridgement of the Universe". Though his vision may yet come true, it would seem, at the moment at any rate, unlikely. The supposedly rational assumption that a museum can be a kind of concrete encyclopaedia, complete and all informative, has long been disproved. Not only has the amount of information increased to an extent where this is no longer possible, but the attempt to acquire such universal knowledge through a single medium has been abandoned. We are content with perhaps lesser but more realisable aims. We accept the museum as one of several media of communication and at the same time recognise that its strength lies in the performance of a specific and specialised function, the presentation of the object itself.

The manner of this presentation will be considered in greater detail in the later section on display. The approach to the design of such display, however, as well as to that of its architectural setting will be strongly influenced by the architectural and social outlook which the architect and his client accept. It is thus not fortuitous that the Amon Carter Museum in Fort Worth is a glazed adaptation of a classical portico and the new wing of the Stedelijk in Amsterdam a kind of glazed warehouse. The first was designed by Philip Johnson for one of the most affluent towns of America highly and self-consciously intent on making its mark as a centre of culture, the second in the office of the Amsterdam City Architect in collaboration with W. Sandberg, then curator of the Stedelijk and one of the men most responsible in Europe for destroying the image of the museum as an esoteric cultural palace.

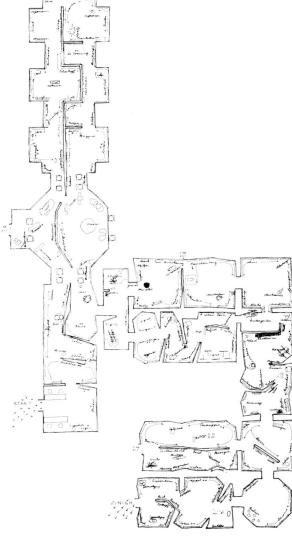

Alison and Peter Smithson's design for a temporary exhibition at the Tate Gallery, London, in 1964 fully recognised the idea of sequence as being vital to museum viewing. The painting and sculpture of the decade 1954–1964 in the Gulbenkian Collection was shown so that only a few related exhibits were seen at a time and arranged in such a way that important groups of sculpture, less brightly lit than the pictures, formed punctuation marks in the sequence of connected spaces.

Alison und Peter Smithson gingen bei der Gestaltung einer Sonderausstellung in der Tate Gallery (London, 1964) davon aus, daß die Abfolge der Kunstwerke für den Museumsbesucher von entscheidender Bedeutung ist. Die Bilder und Skulpturen der Jahre 1954 bis 1964 aus der Sammlung Gulbenkian waren so angeordnet, daß der Besucher jeweils nur einige aufeinander bezogene Objekte mit einem Blick erfassen konnte; Gruppen wichtiger Plastiken, die weniger hell erleuchtet waren als die Bilder, setzten in der Abfolge miteinander verbundener Räume die Akzente.

The acceptance of some limitations on the role of the museum carries with it also certain architectural implications. The museum is no longer a palace, royal and dominant. Its architecture need not thus have the rather obvious – possibly even now banal – quality of dominance through size and material ostentation which may at one time have been thought appropriate. Sheer size has in any case proved functionally unsound since it merely induces visual and mental numbness. However generous future museum finance may be – in most countries a laughably unlikely assumption – it seems extremely improbable that one would ever create a museum on the scale of the Louvre or the Smithsonian Institution with its 55,000,000 catalogued objects.

This reluctance towards the elephantine is, quite apart from the malaise of museum fatigue, strengthened by two further considerations. In the first place museum attendance has considerably increased in recent years. A good deal of this increase is not only due to the museum attracting a wider audience but to the fact that the same people may go several times each year. The large attendance figures of London's Tate Gallery or New York's Museum of Modern Art, for instance, are to a great extent made up from recurring visits. The museum is thus able to display very much less for a limited time so that all display can in a sense be considered as a series of temporary exhibitions. Such arrangements also attract publicity and are much more likely to make the museum and its activities interesting and relevant to the public. Certain Japanese firms are exploiting this publicity by arranging special exhibitions of art treasures – often of quite exceptional pieces on loan from temples – in the Tokyo department stores. These like the "Rinascente" design exhibitions organised as part of the display of their Milan shop serve to reduce the overly rigid barriers which have accumulated around anything which is ever labelled "art". The same result tends to be achieved by the reverse situation, the display within museums of objects normally on sale in shops. Exhibitions of household articles and other items of industrial design occur regularly at the Museum of Modern Art in New York and elsewhere. On at least two occasions the New York exhibitions have included motor cars positioned on the terraces of the sculpture garden.

Secondly, we no longer take as self-evident that the museum must be the final resting place of any worthwhile work of art or scientifically interesting object. A sense of this was very strong in the 19th century. The British Museum was, for instance, until 1963 not permitted under the ordinances governing its collections to dispose of any item on its premises or even to lend an object abroad without a special Act of Parliament. We now accept that the museum will select, sift and discard. Under its statutes the Louisiana Foundation, for example, may sell or – in collaboration with the artist – exchange pictures. Within the museum world it may also be advantageous to move objects from one collection to another. In New York the Museum of Modern Art has such an arrangement with the Metropolitan Museum and in London, the Tate Gallery with the National Gallery. Other media may keep more comprehensive records and should in fact do so since they are able to abstract and condense information. The museum dealing with the object itself has to accept a more limited but equally effective task. And in order to fulfil this efficiently it has to guard against becoming simply a depository of the currently unwanted.

Museum architecture does not, of course, exist in isolation as some special branch of design but is inevitably and properly part of the general trend of architectural thought. If it is of sufficient calibre it will itself in turn exert an influence on this trend. This is certainly true at present in Italy and was probably equally true and with wider significance as a result of the design of the Barcelona Pavilion in 1929, in effect a museum building. Mies van der Rohe's later unbuilt project of a "Museum for a Small City" in 1942 (see Figs. page 26, 27) may have been less influential in terms of architecture as a whole but certainly created an image of flexible museum space which no reality, including Mies's own, has so far matched. Le Corbusier's image of the expanding museum has been equally powerful and remains equally unrealised.

This discrepancy between idea and reality may, like the inevitable doubts about the Guggenheim Museum, be due to the fact that the designs of these buildings have taken very general concepts – universal space, growth, organic form – as their starting point and really only used the museum as a demonstration. They have only marginally concerned themselves with the primary purposes of the building. The interest of the current Italian contribution lies in the opposite direction: that new solutions have been achieved from a detailed consideration of particular situations involving the museum's main function – the confrontation of object and observer.

Such a notion may have validity outside the immediate area of museum design or the scale of museum display and is, in fact, in evidence in a great deal of recent architectural thinking. It has so far had its most publicised realisation in Kahn's laboratory building at the University of Pennsylvania. This is not to claim that the Richards Medical Research Building was influenced by the work of Albini or Scarpa, but only to suggest that a number of Italian museums are early and relevant examples of a design approach which is probably of considerable general significance. It is an approach rooted in our increasing affluence which makes specialised uses of spaces economically possible and thus a design attitude which starts from a specific situation architecturally viable. The trend towards the specialised and the specific in architecture is one that runs parallel to a very similar trend in the design and use of tools and other implements of environmental control. The degree of such specialisation is to a large extent the measure of technological advance – of the gap between a universal implement like the neolithic flint and a specialised cutting edge on an automatic lathe programmed for a specific task. The museum being a building type essentially dependent on a high level of affluence, it is perhaps not surprising that it should also, in certain cases at any rate, have been among the early instances of the realisation of this design approach.

The general rise in the level of wealth and thus also of leisure in Western society and soon, one hopes, in the remainder of the world, is thus most likely to accentuate this trend and to create conditions in which there will be a demand for a large number and variety of museums. The demand is certainly already evident in the United States. It is much more likely to lead to the growth of small and medium sized museums – institutions of the size of the Kalamazoo Institute of Arts, the Museum of Art, Science and Industry in Fairfield County, Conn., or the Munson-Williams-Proctor Institute at Utica – that is to say to the creation of local centres of activity borrowing travelling collections, arranging lectures and classes, lending exhibits and books, working closely with schools, rather than towards a further increase in the number of great national or metropolitan institutions. The large established museums have a considerable programme of renovation and remodelling as well as of a certain amount of expansion ahead of them so that their enormous collections may be arranged in a way which will again allow each particular item to communicate its message. Both programmes will need a great deal of architectural ingenuity and study before workable and humane places are achieved. In the case of museum design a focussing of attention on the particular has brought with it a further and important contribution; the ability to come to terms with some of the greatest examples of the past without in any way compromising the present. A small number of recent museums have done this with very considerable success. Architecturally this may be their most important pointer to the future.

Im Museo Correr in Venedig ist am Ende des zweiten Stockwerks, das parallel zu der langen Südseite der Piazza San Marco läuft, ein kleiner Raum für acht Gemälde der Bellinis vorbehalten (Abb. S. 7, 8). Diese Bilder gehören zu den größten Schätzen der Sammlung – zusammen mit Antonello da Messinas Kreuzabnahme und Carpaccios Porträt zweier Kurtisanen, die umgeben von venezianischen Tauben auf einem Balkon sitzen. Drei der acht Bellinis stehen auf Staffeleien, zwei Rücken an Rücken, der dritte schräg gegenüber der Tür; fünf hängen an den Wänden. Von diesen fünf sind zwei leicht abgewinkelt, sozusagen nach einer Seite hin gedreht.

Wenn man den Raum betritt, lassen sich sieben Bilder fast mit einem Blick erfassen, die jeweils von dem nötigen Freiraum umgeben sind. Beim Nähertreten füllt jedes einzelne Bild das Blickfeld aus, die übrigen bleiben beiseite. Am Ende dieser Sequenz fällt plötzlich das Auge auf die letzte Staffelei, auf ein wohlvertrautes, profanes Bild, dessen Gegenstand nichts mit denen der anderen Werke zu tun hat: Gentile Bellinis lebensgroßer Dogenkopf.

Im ersten und zweiten Geschoß zeigen die Räume, die dem Bellini-Kabinett vorausgehen, Laternen von den repräsentativen Gondeln der Dogen, Tapisserien, Waffen venezianischer Adliger, Gemälde und Skulpturen aus dem Quattrocento. Durch die offenen Balkontüren sind alle diese Kunstwerke auf den Markusplatz unten bezogen. Die Böden sind aus Terrazzo oder Kacheln, der Bellini-Raum ist mit Teppichen ausgelegt, ebenso der Antonello-Raum und die Carpaccio-Nische.

Jede dieser visuellen und haptischen Erfahrungen dient dazu, die Begegnung zwischen Gegenstand und Betrachter zu vertiefen, eine Beziehung zwischen Artefakt und Individualität herzustellen.

Da das Museum ein Mittel der Kommunikation ist, sind diese Intentionen wesentlich. Das Museum befaßt sich, wenn auch nicht ausschließlich, mit der visuellen Kommunikation von Gegenständen kulturellen und wissenschaftlichen Interesses, wobei »kulturell« und »wissenschaftlich« im weitesten Sinne verstanden sind. Wenn das Museum diese Aufgabe nicht erfüllt, verfehlt es seine Bestimmung. Die Gestaltung von Museen, die Architektur wie die Darstellung der Objekte, muß daher zumindest eine solche Kommunikation möglich machen, am besten aber aktiv dazu beitragen.

Es liegt auf der Hand, daß das Museum nicht das einzige Kommunikationsmittel ist; im Gegenteil, Kino, Fernsehen und gedruckte Illustration sind viel weiter verbreitet. Wie Kino und Fernsehen ist auch das Museum ein Massenmedium, aber im Unterschied zu ihnen setzt es nicht die gleichzeitige Teilnahme vieler voraus; darin gleicht es dem illustrierten Buch oder der Zeitschrift, die sich dem einzelnen zu einer von ihm gewählten Zeit mitteilen. Trotz aller Gemeinsamkeiten unterscheidet sich das Museum radikal von allen diesen Medien. Illustriertes Buch, Leinwand und Bildschirm vermitteln Reproduktionen von Gegenständen, sie schaffen ein neues Bild; das Museum kann den Gegenstand selber zeigen. Museumsarchitektur und -einrichtung muß daher diese einmalige Chance der unmittelbaren Gegenwärtigkeit, diese direkte Begegnung zwischen Betrachter und Betrachtetem ausnutzen. Erfolgreiche Kommunikation hängt von der eindeutigen Wahrnehmung von Signalen ab. Diese Eindeutigkeit beruht ihrerseits auf der Abschirmung aller störenden Elemente, aller »Geräusche im Hintergrund« sowie auf der richtigen Einstellung des Empfängers. Dabei spielt es keine Rolle, ob die Signale in Morsezeichen oder Kunstformen bestehen. Carlo Scarpas Gestaltung des Bellini-Raums im Museo Correr erfüllt diese Bedingungen, weil sie keinen Zweifel über ihre eigentlichen Absichten läßt, aber dennoch die spontane Aussagekraft der Bilder selber nicht in Frage stellt. Der wohlberechnete Erfolg erklärt sich aus einer Analyse des Sehvorganges, aus dem Vertrauen auf die Wirkung der verwendeten Mittel und aus der Einsicht, daß die dargestellten Gegenstände nicht anonym sind, sondern spezifische Eigenschaften besitzen.

Seitdem Cicero die Sammlung des Gaius Verres beschrieb, ist die eigentliche Aufgabe des Museums immer wieder anders definiert worden. Auch haben sich die verschiedenen Zeitalter wohl nur selten auf eine einzige jeweils gültige Definition einigen können. So ist es unwahrscheinlich, daß heute eine solche Formel allgemeine Zustimmung finden wird – zumindest lassen die vorliegenden praktischen Lösungen diesen Schluß nicht zu. Das verworrene Erbe der Vergangenheit ist dafür zu groß. Bis zum 15. Jahrhundert dienten die Sammlungen zwei ganz verschiedenen Zwecken: Die Objekte wurden entweder aus religiösen Gründen zusammengetragen oder um des persönlichen Vergnügens willen. Die Schätze der Heiligtümer von Delphi, der Akropolis in Athen oder der mittelalterlichen Pilgerkirchen fielen in die erste Kategorie, in die zweite Rubrik gehört die Sammeltätigkeit italienischer Renaissance-Fürsten und -Päpste, die alles erwarben, was selten, merkwürdig und schön war. Die Auffassung vom Kunstwerk als öffentlichem Eigentum oder doch wenigstens als Gegenstand öffentlichen Interesses ist – die Architektur ausgenommen – verhältnismäßig neueren Ursprungs. Allenfalls die öffentliche Schaustellung des Beuteguts zurückkehrender Armeen deutete bereits in diese Richtung. So gesehen findet sich in der nächsten Nachbarschaft des Museo Correr ein anderes »Museum«: die Westfassade von San Marco mit den byzantinischen Pferden, die aus Konstantinopel stammen.

Diese Konzeption hat sich weitgehend im Abendland entwickelt. Trotz der sehr langen Geschichte der chinesischen Kunst trat in China, wie Malraux bemerkt hat, der Begriff eines öffentlichen Museums nicht auf. Für die meisten orientalischen Kulturen setzt der Umgang mit Kunst, sofern er nicht religiös bestimmt ist, ein Eigentumsverhältnis voraus. Kunst wird in der Zurückgezogenheit aufgenommen: das Entfalten einer Rolle, die Benutzung eines geschnitzten Geräts oder einer Schale. Die abendländische Herkunft des Museumsgedankens läßt sich wahrscheinlich auf zwei Ursachen zurückführen, auf einen allgemeinen materiellen Wohlstand, der eine reiche Kunstproduktion erlaubt, und auf eine Form der Kultur, bei der Kunst als eine Art Überschuß betrachtet wird, für den im profanen oder religiösen Bereich des Alltags kein unmittelbarer Bedarf besteht. Die Idee eines Museums kommt so lange nicht auf, wie Kunstgegenstände – zum Beispiel die Schnitzereien der Eskimos – nur in geringen Mengen hergestellt werden und für den Bedarf des einzelnen oder der Familie gerade eben ausreichen. Dasselbe ist dort der Fall, wo die Kunst, auch wenn sie reichlich produziert wird, einen Platz im Alltagsleben einnimmt, wie etwa die byzantinischen Ikonen. Die beiden Voraussetzungen des Museumsgedankens wurden im hellenistischen und im römischen Zeitalter und dann wieder in der italienischen Spätrenaissance erfüllt. Privatsammlungen entstanden, die Nachfrage nach antiken Kunstschätzen stieg. Der Begriff des Museums entwickelte sich von da an parallel zur Ausbreitung der Renaissance-Ideale, Ideale, bei denen der Erwerbstrieb in vielfacher Hinsicht eine Rolle spielte. Daher ist es kaum verwunderlich, daß gerade Papst Sixtus IV., der beträchtliche Gelder durch Simonie zusam-

International Exhibition of Modern Jewellery 1890–1961, London, 1961. Architect: Alan Irvine.

Internationale Ausstellung modernen Schmucks 1890 bis 1961, London, 1961. Architekt: Alan Irvine.

menbrachte, als erster ein Museum im heutigen Sinne schuf, indem er 1471 die kapitolinischen Sammlungen öffnete. Sein Beispiel fand erst in Italien, dann im übrigen Europa Nachfolge. Das Museum Cesarini in Rom wurde 1500 der Öffentlichkeit zugänglich gemacht, das Museum Farnese 1546, die Uffizien 1581. Fast hundert Jahre später, 1679, wurde das Ashmolean Museum in Oxford gegründet. Es nahm eine botanische und naturhistorische Sammlung auf, die John Tradescant, ein Gärtner der Königin Henrietta Maria, nach seiner Virginia-Reise 1637 begonnen hatte. Der Louvre wurde 1681 geöffnet. In das folgende Jahrhundert fallen die Anfänge des British Museum im Old Montague House (1759), das auf ein Vermächtnis von Sir Hans Sloane zurückgeht. In Deutschland gründete Landgraf Wilhelm VIII. von Hessen die Kasseler Galerie (1760). Das erste Museum in Amerika war ein Raum in der Harvard University, der 1750 mit einer Sammlung interessanter Gegenstände wie ausgestopften Tieren und Vögeln, einem Schiffsmodell, einer gegerbten Menschenhaut, dem Schädel eines indianischen Kriegers eingerichtet und »Repository of Curiosities« (Aufbewahrungsort für Kuriositäten) genannt wurde.

Aber erst das Dekret der Französischen Nationalversammlung vom 30. August 1792, das die Museen zum Gemeinbesitz erklärte, und die 1793 folgende Umwandlung des Louvre in ein Museum der Republik waren der Auftakt für die vielen Museumsgründungen im 19. Jahrhundert.

Das Motiv dieser Bewegung zu Anfang des Jahrhunderts bildete der Stolz der Nationen und der Bürger, am Ende des Jahrhunderts die Philanthropie. So war die öffentliche Ausstellung in Berlin im Herbst 1815, bei der die während der Napoleonischen Kriege geraubten und nun zurückgekehrten Kunstschätze gezeigt wurden, der Anlaß zu Schinkels großem antikisierenden Entwurf für das Alte Museum (1823, fertiggestellt sieben Jahre später). Aber in der zweiten Hälfte des 19. Jahrhunderts ging etwa die Walker Art Gallery von 1877 auf eine Stiftung von Sir Andrew Barclay Walker an die Gemeinde Liverpool zurück. Ebenso vermachte Charles Lang Freer aus Detroit der Smithsonian Institution 1906 die heutige Freer Gallery of Art in Washington.

Die Inneneinrichtung und die Ausstellungsmethoden entsprachen selbstverständlich den Intentionen, die den Museen des 19. Jahrhunderts zugrunde lagen. Der Besitzerstolz führte unweigerlich zu einer betont reichhaltigen und umfassenden Darbietung; die gehäuften Schätze sollten so vollständig wie möglich gezeigt werden. Der Zweck dieser »Kommunikation« war denn auch nicht das einzelne sichtbare Objekt, sondern der nationale oder lokale Reichtum, den es repräsentierte. Das Museum wurde zum kulturellen Gegenstück des Kaufhauses, jener anderen viktorianischen Neuerung. Im Falle der philanthropischen Stiftungen kam es darauf an, daß der Name des Spenders deutlich sichtbar gemacht und überliefert wurde. Die Absichten der Stifter zielten bei diesem Museumstyp auf Weiterbildung der wenig Begüterten: Museum und öffentliche Bibliothek waren Werkzeuge viktorianischer Volkspädagogik. Da die Erziehung im 19. Jahrhundert hauptsächlich literarisch orientiert war, nimmt es nicht wunder, daß eine große Zahl von Provinzmuseen letzten Endes zu einer Serie gut illustrierter Bildunterschriften wurde.

Während der letzten vierzig Jahre haben sich die Voraussetzungen, auf denen noch die Museen des 19. Jahrhunderts basierten, von Grund auf geändert. Sie sind nicht völlig weggefallen, aber doch in den Hintergrund getreten. Die wirtschaftlichen, sozialen und technischen Veränderungen und ihre Auswirkungen auf Erziehung, Muße und geistige Beweglichkeit müssen nicht näher ausgeführt werden. Jede von ihnen hat das Museum in seinen heutigen Aspekten beeinflußt, von der Beleuchtungstechnik bis zu dem Ausmaß an Kenntnissen und visuellen Erfahrungen, die der Besucher mit ins Museum bringt. Noch zu Beginn dieses Jahrhunderts war ein Museum gewöhnlich nur so lange geöffnet, wie das Tageslicht ausreichte, und seine Besucher kannten allenfalls eine oder zwei ähnliche Institutionen, sofern es sich nicht um vielgereiste Spezialisten handelte.

Erst André Malraux rückte mit seiner *Psychologie der Kunst* ein anderes Problem ins allgemeine Bewußtsein, nämlich den beträchtlichen Einfluß, den die Fotografie auf die Funktion des Museums genommen hat. Reproduktionen, Kunstbücher und Filme ermöglichen es, die Details und den historischen Zusammenhang eines Kunstwerks jederzeit in Ruhe zu studieren. Für die visuellen Künste haben sie das geleistet, was das Grammophon für die Musik bedeutet. Vor allem das Kunstbuch kann eine ganze Schule von Malern und Bildhauern oder das Gesamtwerk eines Künstlers vorführen und zugleich die Aufmerksamkeit auf kleinste Details wie Pinselführung oder Materialbehandlung lenken. Die Skala der verfügbaren Objekte hat sich unendlich erweitert. Die Fres-

ken serbischer Kirchen, japanische Holzschnitte und die Portraits des koptischen Ägyptens sind ebenso erreichbar wie Rembrandt, Leonardo oder Cézanne.

Aber weder die Schallplatte noch das Kunstbuch geben die Wirklichkeit selber. Zwischen der High-Fidelity-Aufnahme und der Konzertaufführung, zwischen einem Skira-Druck und dem Bild selbst liegt ein unüberbrückbarer qualitativer Unterschied. Das eine ergänzt das andere, und ein kritisches Verständnis des Objektes kann sich beider bedienen. Sinn des Museums ist daher, den Gegenstand selbst auszustellen, und es ist nur natürlich, daß das Museum aus dieser nur ihm eigenen Bestimmung Konsequenzen in der visuellen Darstellung zieht.

Überdies hat das Übermaß an Druckerzeugnissen, die »graphische Revolution«, wie Daniel Boorstin es genannt hat, dem Museum eine zusätzliche Verpflichtung auferlegt. Professor Boorstin erörtert in seinem Buch *The Image* eine Reklame, die einen Autofahrer am Rande des Grand Canyon zeigt, wie er Farbdias betrachtet, statt des Canyons selbst. Es kommt darauf an, daß das Museum eine Begegnung mit der Realität schafft, die sich von der mit einem Faksimile unterscheidet; es muß den Autofahrer überreden, nicht nur einen Blick auf den Canyon zu werfen, sondern aus seinem Wagen auszusteigen und die Landschaft ganz in sich aufzunehmen. Und wäre es auch nur, damit der so gefährlich vertrauten Kopie Gerechtigkeit widerfährt!

Der Einfluß der Fotografie als einer Reproduktion des Bildes sollte nicht verwechselt werden mit der ganz anders gearteten Bedeutung, die sie als visuelle Ausdrucksform hat. In dieser Eigenschaft, als selbständiges Ausdrucksmittel, kann sie selber einen Platz im Museum beanspruchen. Fotografie und Plakat werden – glücklicherweise – nicht länger mehr über die Achsel angesehen. Das Stedelijk Museum in Amsterdam zeigt fast immer Beispiele von beiden in seinen Räumen.

Die Fotografie hat außerordentlich drastische Wirkungen auf das Innere des Museums gehabt, auf die Auswahl und die Art der Aufstellung. Das Äußere und der Standort des Bauwerks sind dagegen wohl mehr von einem Wechsel der soziologischen Perspektive beeinflußt worden. In der Geschichte war das Museum ein privater, städtischer oder nationaler Palast und zog sich wie jeder andere Palast erhaben und hochmütig in ein esoterisches Dasein zurück. Seine Architektur war monumental, sein Platz abseits des betriebsamen Lebens der Stadt. Aber für die meisten ist heute der Inhalt eines Museums, so viele Wunder er auch verheißen mag, weder erhaben noch esoterisch. Auf jeden Fall verfängt die Annahme nicht mehr, daß diese Objekte nur von wenigen verstanden und gewürdigt werden können. Die Plakate des Stedelijk Museums, die Laternenpfähle und Straßenbahnhaltestellen beleben, sind ein Beweis für diesen Wandel; das Museum wird ein Teil unseres Alltagslebens.

Von Bedeutung ist natürlich die Lage, die für den Charakter eines Museums entscheidend sein kann. Das Louisiana Museum in Humlebæk an der Küste nördlich von Kopenhagen liegt inmitten eines Erholungsgebietes, ein Ausflugsziel für den Samstagnachmittag, für Kaffeetrinken in der Sonne mit dem Blick auf den Sund, für Abendkonzerte und Tanz im Garten. Das New Yorker Museum of Modern Art, das am Wochenende ebenfalls überfüllt ist, bietet dagegen – zwei Minuten von der Fifth Avenue entfernt – einen günstigen Treffpunkt für den Lunch auf dem Dachgarten und einen anschließenden Ausstellungsbesuch. Trotz aller Unterschiede sind beide Museen Orte, die von ihrer Umgebung abstechen. Es ließe sich jedoch auch denken, daß ein Museum und

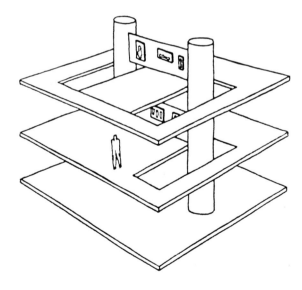

In Cicero Diaf's proposal for a picture gallery the paintings are housed on turnstiles within large drums and mechanically selected to appear on a wall before the visitor.

Bei Cicero Diafs Entwurf für eine Kunstgalerie sind die Bilder an Drehkreuzen innerhalb großer Trommeln befestigt und erscheinen mechanisch auf einer Wand vor dem Besucher, der sie ausgewählt hat.

Page / Seite 19:

Exhibition of the work of Carlo Crivelli and his followers, Palazzo Ducale, Venice, 1961. Architect: Egle Trincanato. The route defined by the openings of enfiladed rooms.

Ausstellung »Carlo Crivelli und sein Kreis«, Palazzo Ducale, Venedig, 1961. Architekt: Egle Trincanato. Die Wegführung wird durch die Öffnungen der hintereinanderliegenden Räume bestimmt.

etwa eine Ladenpassage eng miteinander verbunden werden und nicht mehr als eine Türschwelle sie voneinander trennt; daß Kunst so öffentlich sichtbar wird wie in der Loggia dei Lanzi an der Piazza della Signoria in Florenz. Beispielsweise braucht es nicht viel architektonische Phantasie, sich die erste Etage des Museo Correr das große Treppenhaus hinunter bis zu den Arkaden fortgesetzt zu denken, die die Piazza San Marco umgeben. Einige private Kunstgalerien haben eine solche Verbindung fast erreicht. Ein unmerklicher Übergang könnte die unterschiedlichen Wirklichkeitsbereiche von innen und außen einander annähern, könnte Kunst und Straße so aufeinander beziehen, daß die eine realer und die andere weniger armselig würde.

Manche Ausstellungsgegenstände können ja tatsächlich aus dem Zusammenhang des Museums genommen und an Orten aufgestellt werden, wo man sie normalerweise nicht erwartet. Der London County Council unternahm mit seinen Plastikausstellungen in öffentlichen Anlagen Versuche in dieser Richtung, und 1962 stellte das italienische Ministerium für die Schönen Künste Skulpturen zwischen den mittelalterlichen Bauwerken und römischen Ruinen von Spoleto in Umbrien auf. Solche Freilichtausstellungen müssen nicht auf wetterfeste Objekte wie Stein- oder Metallskulpturen beschränkt bleiben. Die schwedische Gesellschaft für Industrial Design präsentierte zum Beispiel ausgesuchte Produkte industrieller Formgebung in einem Stockholmer Park, und in London finden jedes Jahr einige Ausstellungen statt, bei denen Maler ihre Arbeiten an Wänden zeigen, die öffentlich im Freien aufgestellt werden. Boston, Massachusetts, veranstaltet ähnliche Ausstellungen, für die Zelte in einem Park mitten im Stadtzentrum aufgeschlagen werden.

Öffentliche Bibliotheken, deren Funktion als Kommunikationsmittel sie den Museen vergleichbar macht, haben immer mehr diesen offenen und einladenden Charakter angenommen und sind von ihrem Standort her dem Alltagsleben ihrer Benutzer nähergerückt. Das bedeutet häufig Bauplätze mit hohen Grundstückspreisen. Bibliotheken wie Museen sind Institutionen, die beträchtliches Kapital und große jährliche Zuschüsse verlangen. Die investierten Beträge zahlen sich erst dann aus, wenn diese Einrichtungen auch wirklich benutzt werden. Ein Bauplatz in einem Einkaufsviertel kann daher, auf die Dauer gesehen, trotz der hohen Anfangskosten die wirtschaftlichste Lösung sein. Für die Stadtsparkasse von Lund dürfte dieses Argument entscheidend gewesen sein, als sie die neue Kunstgalerie im alten Teil der Stadt am Marktplatz errichtete und 1957 den Bürgern übergab (Abb. S. 11). Klas Anshelm erreicht in seinem Entwurf einen dramatischen und direkten Übergang vom Marktplatz mit seinem Granitpflaster zum Inneren der Galerie. Museen müssen nicht – und dürfen vielleicht nicht einmal – in sterilen Kulturzentren isoliert werden.

Das heißt nicht, daß die Museen selbst nicht Zentren kulturellen Interesses im weitesten Sinne bilden sollten; ihre Position im Gemeindeleben sollte diese allgemeinere Aufgabe erleichtern. Eine solche großzügige Auffassung des Museums stimmt völlig mit seiner Definition überein, Vermittler von Objekten kultureller oder wissenschaftlicher Bedeutung zu sein. Obwohl seine Darstellungsmethoden vor allem auf dem Optischen in einer bestimmten Ausprägung beruhen – ein Betrachter in Bewegung, der ruhende Gegenstände in sich aufnimmt –, muß sich die Aufgabe des Museums nicht notwendig darauf beschränken. So können gewisse Aspekte der Kunst ebenso wirkungsvoll durch einen Versuch zur eigenen Ausübung verdeutlicht werden wie durch Anschauung. Die Kunstklassen des Kunstmuseums in São Paulo oder das Malzimmer für Kinder am Eingang des Louisiana

Museums ergänzen die Ausstellungen. Ebenso können Filme wesentlich zum Verständnis einer völkerkundlichen Sammlung oder der Kunst des Jahrhundertbeginns beitragen. Das Museum für Geographie und Völkerkunde in Rotterdam und das Museum of Modern Art in New York zeigen regelmäßig solche Filme. Schließlich kann die Anschauung durch das intellektuelle Verständnis vertieft werden, so daß Vorträge und Diskussionen ein weiterer Aspekt der Museumsarbeit sind. Die meisten Museen veranstalten Vorträge für Schulkinder wie für Erwachsene und Führungen durch die Galerien.

Einen Teil der nötigen Information vermittelt die Bildbeschriftung. Sie soll unaufdringlich angebracht, aber aus einer Entfernung lesbar sein, die von der normalen Distanz des Betrachters vom Gegenstand nicht allzu sehr differiert. Das 19. Jahrhundert mag in seiner Leidenschaft für das Detail und in der übertriebenen Länge der Texte zu weit gegangen sein, aber die heutige Tendenz zur sparsamsten Formulierung hat auch ihre Nachteile. Wünschenswert wäre wohl eine ganz knappe Bezeichnung am Objekt selbst, verbunden mit einem ausführ-

licheren Text, der als Einführung zu einer Gruppe von Gegenständen dient. Diese Methode, die das Museum of Modern Art in New York benutzt, stellt die zeitliche Abfolge bei einem Museumsbesuch mit in Rechnung.

Auch die Möglichkeit, erklärende Informationen über kleine Radioempfänger zu vermitteln, die der einzelne Besucher am Eingang ausleihen kann, ist heute weithin gegeben, so daß der visuelle Eindruck gleichzeitig durch das gesprochene Wort ergänzt wird. Im Gegensatz zu den überfüllten Führungen oder den detaillierten Angaben eines Kataloges wird bei einem solchen Verfahren nicht die Unmittelbarkeit der Anschauung gestört, die für den Museumsbesuch so wichtig ist. Die Institution des Museums in ihrem umfassenden Sinn schließt also mehr ein als nur eine Raumfolge, in der Objekte mehr oder weniger zufällig zur Schau gestellt sind.

Kommunikation, die eigentliche Aufgabe des Museums, entscheidet letzten Endes über die architektonische Organisation. Die Anatomie des Bauwerks wird bestimmt durch die Rolle, die das Museum in der Gesellschaft

spielen soll, und durch die Akzente, die auf die verschiedenen Aspekte der Kommunikation gesetzt werden. Im Vordergrund muß zwangsläufig die Begegnung zwischen dem Einzelnen und dem Objekt stehen, denn hier liegt das Wesen des Museums begründet – das, was es von anderen Bauaufgaben unterscheidet. Diese Eigenart, dieser Unterschied zu anderen Bauten bietet auch den Schlüssel zum Entwurf des Museums.

Eine solche Behauptung setzt bestimmte architektonische Thesen voraus, über die sich streiten läßt. Natürlich kann man der Meinung sein, ein Museum sei nichts anderes als ein gut ausgeleuchtetes Warenhaus, ein anonymes Raumvolumen, in dem bestimmte lichttechnische Ansprüche erfüllt sein müssen und das im übrigen nur durch Zufall Bilder, Porzellan oder Miniaturmodelle von Kohlenbergwerken enthält. Diese Ansicht kann sich auf das Argument der Flexibilität berufen: Alle denkbaren und auch die unvorhergesehenen Konstellationen sollen von vornherein berücksichtigt werden. Je weniger die Räume definiert sind, je weniger die Möglichkeiten begrenzt sind, desto besser die Lösung. Eine Reihe von Museumsbauten haben dieses Ziel angestrebt, wenn auch wohl keiner bisher dieses Ideal erfüllt: das Cullinan Hall, das Kunsthaus in Zürich, das Kunstmuseum in São Paolo, der Helena-Rubinstein-Pavillon in Tel Aviv.

Es mag sein, daß die künftige Entwicklung noch näher an die unbegrenzte Flexibilität und den undifferenzierten Raum heranführt. Ob aber dieses Ziel den Einsatz lohnt, ist eine andere Frage. Zwei Mißverständnisse, der Kunst wie der Architektur, liegen ihm zugrunde. Da ist einmal die Annahme, daß zwischen der Kunst und ihrer Umgebung eine Art Konkurrenz herrscht und daß das ausgestellte Werk erdrückt wird, sofern die Umgebung nicht völlig neutral gehalten wird. Die zweite These, die mit der ersten zusammenhängt, ist die, daß jedes Produkt in sich so unabhängig von der Umwelt, so frei von jedem background ist, daß es überall gezeigt werden kann.

Beide Vermutungen sind abstrakte Vorstellungen, die nichts mit dem tatsächlichen Vorgang des Sehens und dem Gesamterlebnis Museum zu tun haben.

Weder Kunst noch Architektur sind anonym. Einer der allgemein anerkannten, konstitutiven Faktoren der Kunst ist ihre Einmaligkeit. Darunter ist nicht unbedingt eine Individualität zu verstehen, die mit einer bestimmten Person verbunden wäre, sondern eine Individualität der Form, der Farbe, des Empfindens. Sie gehört zu einem Picasso ebenso wie zu balinesischen Textilien. Entsprechend ist Architektur, um Kahns Definition zu variieren, »durchdachte Raumumschließung für einen menschlichen Zweck« – und weder der Zweck noch das Denken kann anonym sein. Beide sind auf ein Ziel bezogen.

Kunst im Museum ist wie die Aufführung einer Sinfonie im Konzertsaal: Sie existiert als Teil ihrer Umgebung. Der Raum wirkt dank seiner Akustik auf die Musik ein, und die Aufführung in der Form, wie sie ans Ohr dringt, entsteht aus der Wechselwirkung beider. Ebenso beeinflußt das Museum durch seine äußere Erscheinung die Gegenstände, die es zeigt. Denn alles, was in einem bestimmten Augenblick aufgefaßt wird, hängt ab von den vorhergehenden Wahrnehmungen – Wahrnehmungen auch von Bildern, die nicht zentral im Blickfeld lagen. Deshalb kann nicht von einer Konkurrenz zwischen Kunst und ihrer Umgebung, zwischen Bild und Architektur, die Rede sein. Zwischen beiden »Parteien« muß nicht der eine oder andere Aspekt unterschlagen werden, sondern beide müssen in eine fruchtbare Verbindung gebracht werden. Daß ein solches Ziel möglich ist, hat Italien in den letzten zehn Jahren bewiesen.

Eine Konzertaufführung ist, auch abgesehen von der Musik, in jedem Fall mehr als nur eine Frage der richtigen Akustik. Die sichtbare Bewegung im Orchester, die Menschenmenge im Foyer, die spürbare Anteilnahme der Zuhörer, das Gefühl für den bedeutenden Augenblick, das alles gehört zu dem Erlebnis eines solchen Ereignisses dazu. So hängt auch die Einrichtung eines Museums nicht nur von der Qualität der ausgestellten Objekte, der richtigen Wahl des Hintergrundes und einer ausgewogenen Beleuchtung ab. Auch hier geht es um die Einheit des Erlebens, und die Architektur, die den Raum schafft und ordnet, muß innerhalb dieser Einheit notwendig eine positive Rolle spielen. Nur ein neutrales Gehäuse zu errichten, hieße die Verantwortlichkeit der Architektur leugnen.

In der Biologie wie in der Architektur bestehen vielfältige und bedeutungsvolle Wechselbeziehungen zwischen Funktion und Anatomie. Eines beeinflußt und verändert das andere. Die architektonische Anatomie eines Museums wird von zwei wichtigen funktionellen Gesichtspunkten bestimmt: der allgemeinen Rolle, die das betreffende Museum spielt, und der entscheidenden Relation zwischen Objekt und Betrachter. Vom ersten Punkt hängt die Aufgliederung der zur Verfügung stehenden Räume ab, vom zweiten Charakter und Auffassung des Raumes schlechthin. Dieser zweite Aspekt bildet überdies das Charakteristikum, das die wichtigsten – und nur dem Museum eigenen – Teile des Gebäudes bestimmt. Von hier aus ergibt sich sozusagen die Zellstruktur, aus der sich die Anatomie aufbaut.

Diesem Problem war ein guter Teil des architektonischen Interesses gewidmet. Zumeist verfolgen die Architekten das Ziel, eine ideale Konstellation von Betrachter, Objekt und Lichtquelle zu erreichen: So bei den Entwürfen für den Weiterbau des Fitzwilliam Museums in Cambridge (nach 1845) und für die National Gallery in London, beide von Cockerell, bei van der Steurs Museum Boymans in Rotterdam, bei Frank Lloyd Wrights Guggenheim Museum, bei dem Experiment von Bassi und Boschetti in Turin oder der Arbeit der Building Research Station in Birmingham (Abb. S. 12). Die meisten dieser Entwürfe, vor allem die neueren, setzen voraus, daß das einmal gefundene theoretische Ideal beliebig vervielfältigt werden könne. Aber eine reproduzierbare statische Lösung ist kein Ideal, und der Querschnitt eines Museums kann nicht gestreckt werden wie Aluminium. Das Ideal, sofern es überhaupt eines gibt, ist deshalb eine in Raumgestaltung und Lichtführung variierte architektonische Situation.

Ignazio Gardellas Pavillon zeitgenössischer Kunst für die Galleria d'Arte Moderna in Mailand beruht auf der klaren Einsicht in diese Notwendigkeit. Der Bau ist rund 40 Meter lang, bis zu 30 Meter tief und hat eine Höhe von zwei Geschossen (Seite 36-37). Fünf verschiedenartige Raumtypen entstanden: eine enge, zwei Stockwerk hohe Eingangshalle mit Seitenlicht; einige Stufen führen zu einer Ausstellungsfläche hinauf, die anderthalb Geschosse hoch ist, Oberlicht besitzt und von Scherwänden in fünf verschieden tiefe Nischen geteilt wird; von dort gehen ein paar Stufen nach unten zu einer Galerie, die sich in der vollen Länge des Hauptraums erstreckt, an der einen Seite vollverglast ist und einen Blick auf Bäume und Büsche bietet; schließlich führt, ebenfalls von der Hauptausstellungsfläche aus, eine Treppe zu einem Balkon mit Oberlicht und dahinter einem langen, schmalen, abgeschlossenen Raum mit Kunstlicht. Diese Unterschiede entsprechen unterschiedlichen Raumfunktionen. Die Galerie mit Seitenlicht ist für Skulpturen vorgesehen, so daß die dreidimensionale Wirkung der Plastiken unterstrichen wird und ihre Silhouetten gegen Laubwerk gesetzt sind. Die große Fläche mit ihrem kontrollierbaren Oberlicht und den variablen Stellwänden ist für Bilder gedacht. Die beiden schmalen oberen Räume nehmen Zeichnungen und kleinere Objekte auf, wobei der umschlossene, von Kunstlicht beleuchtete Raum speziell für Druckgraphik bestimmt ist.

Einen ähnlichen Wechsel in Raum und Licht zeigen Louisiana, die Kunstgalerie in Lund, Scarpas Venezolanischer Pavillon auf der Biennale in Venedig und, in einer sehr vereinfachten Form, Rietvelds Zonnehof in Amersfoort. Diese Beispiele sind ebenso wie Gardellas Mailänder Museum kleine Bauten, die von einer gründlichen Planung und dem Verzicht auf monumentale Geste profitiert haben. Aber bei größeren Museen sind diese Prinzipien ebenso sehr, wenn nicht noch mehr am Platze.

Das Bedürfnis nach einem solchen Wechsel läßt sich zweifach begründen: Einmal gewinnen die ausgestellten Gegenstände durch Bedingungen, die ihrem jeweiligen Charakter entsprechen, zum anderen verlangt die Aufnahmefähigkeit des Betrachters Veränderungen, um wach und gespannt zu bleiben. Es ist bekannt, daß zum Beispiel die wechselnden meteorologischen Verhältnisse eines Frühlingstages für das körperliche Wohlbefinden am günstigsten sind. Für die optische Wahrnehmung gilt weitgehend dasselbe. Die Physiologie der mechanischen und chemischen Vorgänge im Auge hat ermittelt, daß in den Rezeptoren der Netzhaut eine ständige photochemische Reaktion vor sich geht und daß die Netzhaut selber sich ununterbrochen in Bewegung befindet, wobei die Lichtreize in Nervenerregungen umgesetzt werden. Das Auge ist, um sehen zu können, auf alternierende Ruhe und Bewegung angewiesen; einleuchtendstes Symptom ist das Blinzeln der Augenlider. Im Moment der Dunkelheit kehrt sich der photochemische Prozeß um und erneuert sich. Die Erfahrung zeigt, daß im großen Maßstab – bei der Wahrnehmung und Betrachtung von Gegenständen – Bewegung, Ruhe und Regeneration ebenso wichtig sind und daß der Wechsel mit seiner Forderung nach neuer Anpassung einen notwendigen Stimulus bedeutet.

Museumsmüdigkeit ist sehr wahrscheinlich nicht nur eine Folge der unvermeidlichen geistigen und emotionalen Konzentration, zu der noch die physische Anstrengung des Stehens und Gehens kommt, sondern erklärt sich auch aus der ermüdenden Wirkung einer zu statischen Beleuchtung. Wenn es ihm auch weniger bewußt wird, so dürfte der Museumsbesucher ebensooft augenwie fußmüde sein; schließlich spielt das Sehen eine wichtige Rolle in der gesamten Aktivität des Menschen. Die visuelle und intellektuelle Aufnahmefähigkeit nimmt mit wachsender Müdigkeit ab; die Kommunikation wird unzureichend.

Der Versuch, das ideale Museum zu definieren, hat zur Weiterentwicklung der künstlichen Beleuchtung geführt. Kunstlicht ist unbestreitbar durch die neue Rolle des Museums im sozialen Leben notwendig geworden; Museen sollten heute auch am späten Nachmittag oder Abend geöffnet sein. Viele europäische und amerikanische Museen sind an einem oder mehreren Tagen der Woche oder – vor allem in Amerika – auch am Sonntag noch spät offen, und diese Maßnahmen haben sich als großer Erfolg herausgestellt. Aber die Forderung nach Abwechslung gilt ebenfalls für künstliches und natürliches Licht; Einseitigkeit ist auch hier von Übel.

Leuchtstoffröhren zum Beispiel sind in drei verschieden temperierten Farbwerten erhältlich, die ungefähr dem Tageslicht von Norden, dem Sonnenlicht am Nachmittag und dem Licht von Wolframbirnen entsprechen. Die Anbringung und Anwendung von Leuchtstoffröhren oder Wolframlampen ist ebenfalls außerordentlich variabel. Um nur drei Möglichkeiten anzuführen: Es wären denkbar etwa eine gleichmäßig ausleuchtende Lichtquelle in der Ebene der Decke oder der Wand; ein örtlich streng begrenzter Lichtstrahl aus einem Scheinwerfer mit Linsensystem und Abblendschirm, der nur das Objekt selber punktförmig erhellt; oder das kalte Licht einer abgeschirmten Kathodenröhre in einer Vitrine oder einem Raum mit ausgestellten Gegenständen. Solche Systeme und ihre Anwendungsmöglichkeiten werden später zusammen mit den verschiedenen Ausstellungsmethoden erörtert. Wichtig bleibt festzuhalten, daß gleichförmige Lichtverhältnisse ungeeignet sind, wo es sich um individuelle Gegenstände handelt und wo die Aufnahmebereitschaft des Betrachters unterstützt werden soll.

Unterschiedliche Objekte verlangen qualitativ verschiedenes Licht, wenn sie »sichtbar« werden sollen. Unter dem diffusen Licht des Plastiksaals im Museum Boymans verlieren die weißen Skulpturen vor den weißen Wänden viele ihrer plastischen Qualitäten: Sie teilen sich dem Besucher nicht mit. Die Wahl des Lichtes muß von den Eigenschaften der Objekte abhängen, von der Reflexwirkung ihrer Oberflächen, ihrer plastischen Rundung oder flächigen Auffassung, ihrer materiellen Dichte, ihrer Farbe. So ergeben sich Glut und Glanz des Schmuckes, die von der Ausstellungstechnik unterstrichen werden, aus Lichtverhältnissen, die wieder völlig ungeeignet wären, um die Form eines Rokokomöbels oder die Farbe von Glasbildern herauszuarbeiten (Abb. S. 17). Licht läßt sich nach Richtung und Intensität verändern, es kann direkt von der Lichtquelle ausgehen oder reflektiert werden, es kann gebündelt oder gestreut werden – es gibt kein einziges Charakteristikum in der Beschaffenheit des Lichtes, das für eine bestimmte oder auch nur eine statische Lösung spräche.

Das sind Binsenweisheiten im Bereich des Theaters, aber nicht in dem des Museums. Daß aber sogar im Museum dynamische Lichtverhältnisse möglich sind, demonstrierte der Louvre vor einiger Zeit. In der Orientalischen Abteilung wechselte in einem Raum, der Skulp-

turen des Palastes in Khorsabad aus dem 8. Jahrhundert enthielt, das Licht von punktförmiger Beleuchtung bis zum gleichmäßigen Streulicht. Dabei wirkten die flachen Reliefs zunächst wie Geistererscheinungen aus einer fernen Vergangenheit, dann wurden sie in allen ihren Details deutlich und konnten eingehend betrachtet werden. Solche Einrichtungen müssen natürlich genau überlegt werden, damit sie nicht aufdringlich wirken und sich nicht zwischen Gegenstand und Besucher stellen.

Die Lichtführung im Museum liegt im großen und ganzen zwischen der im Theater, wo es auf vorherbestimmte dramatische Wirkungen ankommt, und der Beleuchtung eines Laboratoriums oder Hörsaals, wo Objekte unter günstigen visuellen Bedingungen untersucht werden müssen. Der große Unterschied zwischen Bühnen- und Museumsbeleuchtung liegt jedoch darin, daß der Zuschauer sich im Theater statisch verhält und sich normalerweise außerhalb der beleuchteten Fläche befindet. Im Museum bewegt er sich dagegen in der erhellten Zone, wirft Schatten, verdunkelt die Lichtquelle und kann jeden Augenblick geblendet werden. Zum Hörsaal oder Klassenzimmer besteht der Unterschied darin, daß die Untersuchung eines Objekts sich dort länger hinauszögern kann und gewöhnlich von einem sitzenden oder stehenden Beobachter vorgenommen wird. Im Museum dauert die Betrachtung verhältnismäßig kurze Zeit, da jedes Objekt Teil einer ganzen Reihe von Gegenständen ist und der Besucher sich bewegt, so daß ein Wechsel erwartet und natürlich ist.

Uniformität ist aber auch mit Rücksicht auf den Erhaltungszustand der Sammlungen nicht wünschenswert. Die verantwortlichen Museumsbeamten kennen die Sorge, daß die sehr intensive Beleuchtung, die in Museen immer mehr üblich wird, den ausgestellten Gegenständen schadet. Solche Schäden sind meistens auf ultraviolette Strahlen zurückzuführen. Räume, in denen Tapeten, Textilien, Gemälde und andere lichtempfindliche Materialien bei natürlichem oder Fluoreszenz-Licht gezeigt werden, sollten deshalb mit Filtern gegen ultraviolette Strahlen versehen sein. In gewissem Ausmaß zerstört jedes Licht. Gary Thomson, Konservator der National Gallery in London, hat deshalb angeregt, Höchstwerte festzusetzen, um die ausgestellten Materialien zu schützen. Die Skala reicht dabei von 300 lx für Metall und Stein bis zu 50 lx für Aquarelle oder Tapisserien. Diese Lichtstärken und die Verwendung ultravioletter Filter werden später besprochen.

Die heute üblichen Lichtstärken bei natürlichem und künstlichem Licht sind bis zu einem gewissen Grade von Untersuchungen für industrielle oder kommerzielle Zwecke übernommen worden. Thomson hat aber darauf hingewiesen, daß diese Maße sich auf den Bereich der normalen Arbeit beziehen und deshalb nicht auf den Museumsbesuch angewendet werden können; für die exakte Arbeit eines Bilderrestaurators in seiner Werkstatt mögen sie zutreffen. Auch aus einem anderen Grund haben die Lichtmeßwerte zugenommen: Die Verwendung von Fluoreszenzröhren und die Verbannung des Sonnenlichtes aus dem Museum führten dazu, daß der Anteil des Lichtes von der blauen Seite des Spektrums zugenommen hat. Das Auge ist aber gewöhnt, im gleichen Maße niedrigere Lichtstärken zu akzeptieren, wie das Licht sich zum roten Ende des Spektrums hin bewegt: Licht bei tiefstehender Sonne, Licht von Wolframfäden, Öllampen, Kerzen. Ein Raum, der von Fluoreszenzröhren mit Tageslicht-Qualität erhellt wird, wirkt nur bei höheren Lichtstärken ebenso gut ausgeleuchtet wie derselbe Raum bei objektiv dunklerem Glühbirnenlicht. Die Meßwerte sind infolgedessen beträchtlich über die 150 lx hinausgegangen, die noch als sicher gelten dürfen.

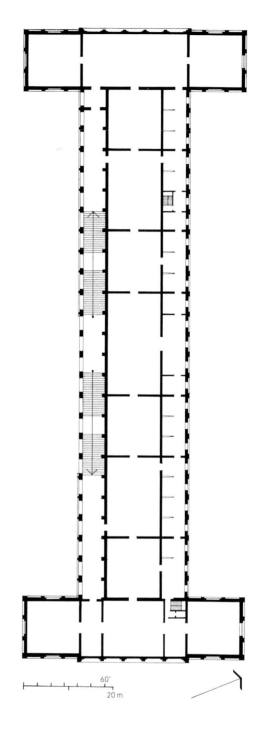

60'
20 m

Alte Pinakothek, Munich. Original design by Leo von Klenze completed in 1836; the plan shows the museum in its reconstructed form after damage in 1943 and 1944. Plan of first floor, 1957.

Alte Pinakothek, München. Der ursprüngliche Entwurf von Leo von Klenze wurde 1836 fertiggestellt; der Grundriß zeigt das Museum in seiner wiederhergestellten Form, nachdem es im Krieg 1943 und 1944 schwer beschädigt wurde. Grundriß Erdgeschoß, 1957.

Page / Seite 20:

Museum of Unlimited Expansion (Project, 1939). Architect: Le Corbusier.

Museum mit der Möglichkeit unbeschränkten Wachstums (Projekt, 1939). Architekt: Le Corbusier.

21

New arrangement, Uffizi Gallery, Florence (1956). Architects: Ignazio Gardella, Giovanni Michelucci, Carlo Scarpa, Guido Morozzi. Interior view; the narrow slot allows for the movement of large pictures from room to room.

Neugestaltung der Uffizien, Florenz (1956). Architekten: Ignazio Gardella, Giovanni Michelucci, Carlo Scarpa, Guido Morozzi. Innenansicht; durch den schmalen Wandschlitz können Bilder von einem Raum in den anderen transportiert werden.

Die Wahl niedrigerer Lichtstärken hat für die Architektur zwei wichtige Konsequenzen. Erstens wird dadurch die oft so fragwürdige Bedeutung reduziert, die die Beleuchtungsfrage und infolgedessen auch die Behandlung der Dachzone auf Kosten anderer Erwägungen beanspruchen. Zweitens müssen allmähliche Übergänge von der Helligkeit draußen zu den niedrigeren Lichtstärken innen geschaffen werden, damit das Auge sich umstellen kann. Der Weg zu den Schauräumen hin muß in der Lichtführung so behandelt werden, daß – vor allem durch Dämpfung des Lichtes – die geringeren Lichtwerte im Inneren vergleichsweise wieder hell erscheinen. Ausblicke von Museumsräumen ins Freie, vor allem auf den Himmel, müssen entsprechend eingeschränkt und unter Kontrolle gehalten werden.

Das sind einige der Überlegungen, die einen Einfluß auf die Begegnung zwischen Betrachter und Objekt haben und zugleich in das Kapitel »Gestaltung der Umgebung« gehören. Die Wahrnehmung von Gegenständen hat zugleich aber auch einen historischen Aspekt. Sowohl derjenige, der das Objekt herstellt, ob es sich nun um Bilder, Skulpturen, Illustrationen oder Geräte handelt, wie auch derjenige, der es betrachtet, sind durch gewisse vorausgehende Erfahrungen bestimmt. Solche Bedingungen führen, wie Ernst Hans Gombrich in *Art and Illusion* dargelegt hat, zu einem »Schema«, in das der Gegenstand so weit wie möglich eingeordnet wird. Diese »geistige Fixierung« spielt bei jedem Museumsbesuch mit. Professor Gombrich bespricht zum Beispiel zwei Darstellungen französischer Kathedralen, die eine 1635 gezeichnet, die andere 1836, und vergleicht sie mit Fotografien. Der Topograph des 17. Jahrhunderts faßte die Seitenansicht von Notre Dame symmetrischer auf als sie tatsächlich ist und rundete die gotischen Spitzbogenfenster ab, so daß der Bau den Vorstellungen der Renaissance näherkommt. Der Illustrator des 19. Jahrhunderts dagegen verlängerte in seiner Zeichnung der Chartreser Westfassade

die romanischen Rundbogenfenster und spitzte sie zu, damit sie in sein »Schema« der Kathedrale als eines gotischen Bauwerks paßte.

Ein ähnlicher Vorgang, in dem das wahrgenommene Bild einem vorgegebenen Stilbegriff angepaßt wird, findet auch im Museum statt. Das hat natürlich bestimmte Vorteile, es erlaubt zum Beispiel einen schnellen Wechsel des kritischen Standpunkts. Einem Uccello tritt man mit anderen Erwartungen als einem Corot gegenüber. Das Einpassen in Kategorien, die Gewohnheit, erst auf das Schild, dann auf das Bild zu blicken, hat aber ebenso große Gefahren. Die »geistige Fixierung« kann bereits so starr sein, daß das Objekt selber sich nicht mehr mitteilt. Im Mailänder Castello Sforzesco umgaben die Architekten, das Studio BBPR, Michelangelos unvollendete *Pietà Rondanini* mit einer Steinwand, die sich erst öffnet, wenn der Besucher einige Stufen hinuntergeht und eine scharfe Wendung vollzieht. Die Architekten wollten nicht nur ermöglichen, daß die Skulptur ungestört von den anderen, im selben Raum ausgestellten Dingen betrachtet werden kann, sondern sie wollten auch durch einen Überraschungseffekt die von vorneherein festliegende Reaktion vermeiden, die ein Werk Michelangelos auszulösen pflegt.

Die Überraschung, die von dieser Lösung visuell ausgeht, hängt wie jedes Museumsarrangement von der Beziehung zwischen unbeweglichem Objekt und sich bewegendem Betrachter ab. Räumlich gesehen, handelt es sich hier um das Gegenteil des Kinos. Aber wie im Kino besteht auch das Museumserlebnis in einer Reihe von Wahrnehmungen in zeitlicher Abfolge (Abb. S. 15). Diese Abfolge läßt sich organisieren und durch Zwischenschaltung bestimmter Erlebnisse behutsam manipulieren. So rechnet die Einrichtung des Bellini-Raums im Museo Correr mit einem solchen zeitlichen Ablauf des Sehvorgangs, und der fast kahle »Raum der vier Türen«, ebenfalls im zweiten Stockwerk des Museo Correr, wirkt

zweimal als Pause in der Raumfolge der gesamten Etage. Die Anordnung eines Museums folgt üblicherweise der Chronologie, so daß die Objekte in der historischen Reihenfolge gezeigt werden. Dieses System haben natürlich viele Museen übernommen. Es ist überall dort angemessen, wo die Entfaltung einer Idee oder überhaupt ein geschichtlicher Vorgang illustriert werden sollen. Die Entwicklung des Schals von Paisley, einer schottischen Textilstadt, aus indischen Mustervorlagen und die Beziehung zum Jacquard-Webstuhl werden sicherlich am besten in der chronologischen Anordnung deutlich, und entsprechend organisiert denn auch das lokale Museum seine Sammlung.

Die Aufstellung muß jedoch nicht notwendig nur in eine einzige Richtung orientiert sein. Im Spätsommer 1961 veranstaltete das Stedelijk Museum in Amsterdam eine Ausstellung über das Apollinische und das Dionysische in der Kunst. Die Galerie im neuen Flügel des Museums hat Fenster an beiden Langseiten; die Scherwände wurden rechtwinklig zu den beiden Fensterwänden errichtet und ließen in der Mitte einen Gang frei. Auf der einen Seite wurden Plastik und Malerei der dionysischen Richtung, auf der anderen Seite die der apollinischen gezeigt. Innerhalb jeder Hälfte waren die Werke chronologisch geordnet. Man konnte deshalb den Raum entlanggehen und jede der beiden Strömungen in ihrem historischen Ablauf verfolgen oder aber von einer Seite zur anderen wechseln und die beiden Ausdrucksmöglichkeiten vergleichen, wie sie gleichzeitig in den betreffenden Epochen nebeneinander existiert haben. Und natürlich war es auch möglich, sich einen raschen Eindruck von der Gegensätzlichkeit der beiden Tendenzen zu verschaffen, wenn man den Mittelgang abschritt und nach links oder rechts blickte.

Solche Möglichkeiten, trotz konsequenter Abfolge Querverbindungen herzustellen, sind dann gegeben, wenn die architektonische Organisation des Gebäudes den Blick in andere Räume erlaubt, die sonst nur von nahem besichtigt werden können. James Johnson Sweeney, der erste Direktor des Guggenheim Museums in New York, hat die Wirkungen beschrieben, die von Wrights großem offenen Spiralraum ausgehen:

»Die Tatsache, daß über den leeren Kern der Spirale hinweg gleichzeitig drei verschiedene Niveaus der Ausstellungsfläche einzusehen sind, ermöglicht eine völlig unkonventionelle Hängung an den Wänden und dadurch eine kritische Auseinandersetzung mit dem Gegenstand, wie sie keine normale Galerie zuläßt. So können zum Beispiel innerhalb einer Koje Bilder oder Plastiken zum Vergleich oder im Kontrast zusammengestellt werden. Der Inhalt der Kojen zu beiden Seiten läßt sich darauf abstimmen, so daß sich für die Betrachtung aus der Nähe ein geschlossener Ablauf ergibt, wenn der Besucher die Rampe hinauf- oder hinuntergeht. Zu dieser von kritischen oder historischen Gesichtspunkten bestimmten Anordnung auf einem einzigen Rampenniveau treten die kritischen oder historischen Beziehungen, die für die Betrachtung aus der Distanz, über den leeren Lichtschacht hinweg, zu den darüber- oder darunterliegenden Kojen geschaffen werden können ... Wenn die Möglichkeiten, die das Gebäude bietet, voll ausgenutzt werden sollen, so muß jedes Rampenniveau, jede Koje nach oben wie unten in Beziehung gesetzt werden, von Geschoß zu Geschoß, quer über die leere Mitte hinweg und entlang der Rampe nach vorn und hinten. Nur so wird der Betrachter ohne Anstrengung seinerseits in dem Essay, den die Ausstellung darstellen soll, von einem Argument zum anderen geführt.«

Es überrascht daher nicht, daß eine Ausstellung visuelle Beziehungen klarer machen kann als irgendein anderes Medium. Beide Beispiele, die Ausstellung des Stedelijk Museums und das Guggenheim Museum, gestatten eine beträchtliche Zahl räumlicher Querbeziehungen. Im Gegensatz zum Buch mit seinem beschränkten Format und dem relativ gleichbleibenden Abstand zwischen Auge und Buchseite ermöglicht das Museum ein weitaus differenzierteres Sehen. Die optische Aussage von Gyorgy Kepes' Ausstellung »The New Landscape« im Massachusetts Institute of Technology (1951) oder von Paul Rudolphs Gestaltung der Fotoschau »The Family of Man« in New York (1955, später an vielen anderen Orten) wurde von keiner der nachfolgenden Publikationen erreicht: weder von Kepes' Buch mit demselben Titel noch von dem Band, der die (ursprünglich von Edward Steichen für das Museum of Modern Art ausgewählten) Fotos reproduzierte. In einem Museum, aber nicht in einem Buch sind solche Eindrücke möglich wie der Tanz des leitmotivisch verwendeten »Family of Man«-Fotos mit dem lächelnden Jungen und seiner Zauberflöte oder die Verengung des Raumes in dem Teil der Ausstellung, der dem Tod gewidmet war, kurz bevor sich Cartier-Bressons großes Panorama mit den indischen Frauen vor den Bergen von Kaschmir entfaltete.

Die Stedelijk-Ausstellung ließ dem Besucher die Wahl offen, in welcher Reihenfolge er die Werke betrachten wollte, und erlaubte ihm vor dem detaillierten Studium einen raschen Überblick über das Ganze. Das ist nicht möglich bei den bisher bekanntgewordenen Systemen, die das traditionelle Verhältnis umkehren und den ruhenden Betrachter mit sich bewegenden Objekten konfrontieren wollen. Dabei spielen stets in irgendeiner Form mechanische Vorrichtungen eine Rolle. Die meisten dieser Anregungen lassen sich nur auf Bilder anwenden, die auf drehbaren Trommeln oder laufenden Bändern befestigt werden sollen. Lina Bo Bardi hat rotierende Zylinder vorgeschlagen, die auf einer Drehbühne angebracht sind. Cicero Diaf entwickelte ein Museumsprojekt mit einem System umschlossener Trommeln, die Bilder an Drehkreuzen enthalten; zwei oder drei können jeweils ausgewählt werden und erscheinen dann mechanisch auf einer Wand an der Seite einer solchen Trommel (Abb. S. 18). Auch von Luc Benoist und Charles Friese existieren Entwürfe für die Mechanisierung des Museums, und zwar sind dabei übereinanderliegende Beobachtungsplattformen und ein Paternoster vorgesehen, der die Bilder transportiert.

Ein ausgeführtes Beispiel für mechanisierte Ausstellungstechnik, das diesen Vorstellungen am nächsten kommt, bot die »Internationale Arbeitsausstellung« in Turin (1961). In dem Sektor, der sich mit »Organisation, Produktivität, Markt« beschäftigte, hatten die Architekten Albini und Bonfante Förderbänder installiert, von denen Tafeln mit Fotos und Texten herabhingen. Die Hängetafeln bewegten sich horizontal und vertikal entlang der Raumbegrenzung, während die Zuschauer in

der Mitte des Raumes standen oder saßen. Der Lärm und das technische Erscheinungsbild der Laufbänder suggerierte dabei absichtlich das Innere einer Fabrik. Diese Anordnung zeigte Vorzüge und Nachteile der Methode. Während der Besucher sich ausruhen oder wenigstens stillstehen konnte, mußte er die Informationen, die ihm mitgeteilt wurden, in vorbestimmten Zeitabständen und in festgelegter Reihenfolge verarbeiten. Für die Wirksamkeit des Museums können sich diese Einschränkungen als schädlich erweisen. Die Bewegungsfreiheit, die beispielsweise in der Stedelijk-Ausstellung apollinischer und dionysischer Kunstwerke gegeben war, läßt sich bei jeder mechanisierten Ausstellungsform nur außerordentlich schwer erreichen. Und in einem gewissen Maß nutzt jeder Besucher einer Galerie die Möglichkeit aus, vor- und rückwärts zu gehen oder sich schnell einen Überblick zu verschaffen. Aber was noch wichtiger ist: Jede mechanische Vermittlung von Objekten neigt dazu, sich zwischen Betrachter und Betrachtetem zu drängen und die Unmittelbarkeit der Begegnung zu zerstören, die zum Wesen des Museums gehört.

Die Planung von Museen wird weitgehend, oft sogar vollständig von der Annahme bestimmt, daß ein bestimmter Ablauf der Betrachtung geschaffen werden müsse. Le Corbusiers Entwürfe zum Beispiel gehen davon aus; wenn er Erweiterungen vorsah, so dachte er an Verlängerung und Ausweitung bestehender Abfolgen (Abb. S. 20). Das Konzept des Guggenheim Museums wird ganz von dieser Forderung bestimmt, die geradezu den Ausgangspunkt der Planung bildete. Dasselbe gilt für Franco Minissis intelligenten Umbau der Villa Giulia. In den bestehenden Bau wurde ein Zwischengeschoß eingezogen, das vor allem einen ununterbrochenen Ablauf der Raumfolge ermöglichen sollte. Dieser Grundsatz – Ablauf als lineare Aufeinanderfolge – kommt natürlich von einer viel älteren Auffassung des Museums her. In letzter Instanz geht er auf den Palazzo der Renaissance zurück, in dem alle wichtigen Räume en filade angeordnet waren, das heißt eine Folge von untereinander verbundenen Räumen bildeten. Der Grundriß von Klenzes Alter Pinakothek in München war, abgesehen von dem großartigen Treppenhausschacht, in erster Linie die Variation eines Palazzo-Grundrisses (Abb. S. 21).
Jedem Grundriß, der die Wegführung als geschlossenen Zirkel organisiert, haftet dabei eine gewisse Dogmatik an. Stillschweigend wird dabei vorausgesetzt, daß jeder Schritt zur Seite einen Fehler bedeutet, wenn das Fließband der Kultur einmal in Gang gesetzt ist. Das ist weiter kein Nachteil bei kleinen Museen wie Louisiana, wo verschiedene Pavillons so miteinander verbunden sind, daß sich ein kontinuierlicher Weg ergibt. Aber bei großen Institutionen wie dem Hauptgebäude des Amsterdamer Rijksmuseums irritiert diese Anordnung sehr. Immerhin möchte man nicht bei jedem Besuch jede Abteilung sehen, und in manchen Fällen sind einzelne Räume so offenkundig zweitrangig, daß sie den Gesamteindruck beeinträchtigen.
Die ringförmige Wegführung versucht, dem Grundriß eine gewisse Klarheit und Ordnung aufzuzwingen. So lange lineare Fortbewegung möglich ist, spielt sich der innere Verkehr im Museum konsequent ab, auch wenn diese Konsequenz visuell nicht deutlich wird. Aber ein großes Museum läßt sich einem Stadtkern vergleichen. Seine Galerien können so verwirrend wirken wie ein Labyrinth von Straßen, die sich zum Verwechseln ähnlich sehen. Diese Situation stellt sich nicht erst bei Museen von der amorphen Ausdehnung des Louvre ein, wo man ständig seinen Grundriß vor Augen haben müßte. Einige Elemente, die zu optischer Gliederung verhelfen

Municipal Museum, Linköping, Sweden (1938–39). View from gallery to storage room and cross section. Architects: Nils Ahrbom and Helge Zimdal.

Städtisches Museum, Linköping, Schweden (1938–39). Blick vom Ausstellungsraum in ein Magazin und Querschnitt. Architekten: Nils Ahrbom und Helge Zimdal.

1 Roof light / Oberlicht
2 Louvres / Lamellen
3 Storage / Magazin

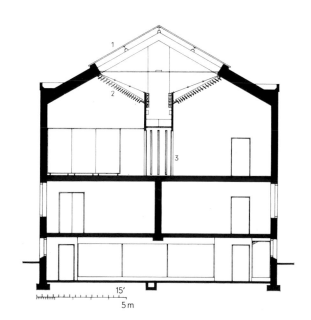

und daher die Orientierung erleichtern, sind vor kurzem in dem Buch *Das Bild der Stadt* von Kevin Lynch analysiert worden. Er bezeichnete diese Bestandteile städtischer Ordnung als Weg, Begrenzung, Bezirk, Knotenpunkt und Wegmarke. Jedes dieser Elemente hat eine Parallele für die Orientierung im Museum und für das Gesamterlebnis des Museums.

Unter »Weg« ist natürlich die Bewegungsspur der Besucher zu verstehen, im allgemeinen also der Raum, der zwischen den ausgestellten Gegenständen frei bleibt. Der Weg läßt sich durch Stellwände kontrollieren und kanalisieren; oder er kann so genau vorgeschrieben werden wie bei den nachträglich eingezogenen Galerien der Villa Giulia. Die Beziehung zwischen Weg und Objekt bestimmt zum großen Teil die Reihenfolge, in der die Dinge wahrgenommen werden. Wenn diese Kontrolle vollständig ist – zum Beispiel bei der *Pietà Rondanini* – so ist auch die Abfolge festgelegt. Manchmal wird der Ausdruck des Weges zum beherrschenden architektonischen Thema; das ist der Fall beim Guggenheim Museum und in geringerem Maße im Louisiana. In vielen älteren Museen sind die Hauptwege durch die Achsen festgelegt, die sich aus dem Blick durch die Türrahmen der Raumfluchten ergeben.

»Begrenzungen« sind lineare Elemente – nicht Wege, sondern Trennlinien zwischen verschiedenen Teilen. In der Stadt sind es zum Beispiel Flußufer oder Eisenbahndämme. Gardellas Pavillon in Mailand besitzt drei klar definierte Begrenzungen, die parallel zueinander laufen: die lange Glaswand zwischen Skulpturengalerie und Park, der Wechsel im Bodenniveau zwischen der Skulpturengalerie und der Hauptausstellungsfläche für Gemälde, schließlich die Balkonlinie oberhalb dieses Raumes. Jede Begrenzung trennt und definiert, hilft aber

gerade damit, den Zusammenhang des Ganzen herzustellen.

»Bezirke« sind Abschnitte, die als deutlich wahrnehmbare Teileinheiten erkannt werden können. Das Studio BBPR erfaßte den Wert solcher Gliederungen, als es in der ersten Abteilung des Castello Sforzesco das Verbindungsglied zwischen dem Erdgeschoß und dem ersten Stockwerk nach außen verlegte. Obwohl die Strecke überdeckt ist, markiert sie einen Einschnitt zwischen den beiden Bezirken. Zunächst geht der Weg über eine Brücke, von der der Blick auf einen feuchten und bemoosten Brunnenhof fällt. Dann führt eine Treppe empor zu einer offenen Loggia; von hier aus wird der Hof zwischen den Flügeln des Museums und dem Eingangsturm sichtbar. Scarpa benutzte mit demselben Erfolg ähnliche Mittel im Castelvecchio in Verona. Solche Unterteilungen schaffen eine Zäsur zwischen den verschiedenen Bereichen eines Museums und lassen seine Teile als visuell erfaßbare Einheiten wirken. Die Gliederung des Museums prägt sich infolgedessen leichter ins Gedächtnis ein.

Mit »Knotenpunkten« sind Stellen gemeint, von denen her oder auf die hin der Besucher sich bewegt, sei es, weil sich hier Wege kreuzen oder weil sich an solchen Punkten Aktivität konzentriert. In Le Corbusiers Nationalmuseum für abendländische Kunst in Tokio ist der große, drei Geschosse hohe Zentralraum ein solcher Kern, um den sich das Gebäude organisiert. Er wird von einem pyramidenförmigen Oberlicht beleuchtet und enthält das wichtigste vertikale Verkehrselement. Ähnlich liegt der Fall bei dem großen Lichthof des Munson-Williams-Proctor Institute in Utica. Knotenpunkte müssen natürlich nicht zentral angelegt werden, ebenso wie sie in einem Bau auch mehrfach auftreten können. Jeder Bezirk kann einen Knotenpunkt aufweisen, und auch Museen, in denen der Ablauf streng vorgezeichnet ist, können mehrere dieser Zentren besitzen – beispielsweise in Gestalt dominierender Räume mit Treppenhäusern. Ein Bezirk wird dann beim Hinaufgehen sichtbar, der andere beim Herabsteigen. Denkbar wären auch Knotenpunkte als akzentuierende, geschlossene Volumen (Festpunkte oder Abstellräume), die auf offenen oder nur teilweise abgeschirmten Flächen als optische Markierungen wirken, vor allem dann, wenn sie mit Treppen oder Brücken verbunden sind, die zu neuen Raumgruppen führen.

Als »Wegmarken« lassen sich Bezugspunkte definieren, die – im Gegensatz zu Knotenpunkten – nicht betreten werden können. Es kann sich dabei um weit entfernte Objekte handeln, aber auch um kleinere Hinweiszeichen, die der Orientierung dienen. Ein Hof, den man umkreist, aber nicht betritt, ein Blick nach draußen auf die Piazza San Marco vom Museo Correr oder auf das Meer vom Musée Maison de la Culture in Le Havre aus, wirken als Wegmarken. In geringerer Entfernung erlauben die engen Wandschlitze, die für den Transport großer Bilder gedacht sind, im Palazzo Abbatellis oder in einigen neu eingerichteten Räumen der Uffizien, einen Einblick in den Nachbarraum (Abb. S. 22). Das Objekt, das auf diese Weise sichtbar gemacht ist, wird zu einer Wegmarke, zu einem erreichbaren Ziel.

Diese räumlichen Gestaltungselemente sind natürlich nur einige Mittel, mit denen die funktionelle Organisation des Bauwerks veranschaulicht werden kann. Die Ordnung und die Klarheit, die dadurch zustande kommen, sind eng auf den Zweck des Museums bezogen und helfen seine Raumgliederung klären. Sie tragen zu der Kommunikation bei, die das Museum herzustellen sucht.

Diese Überlegungen gelten zwar für das ganze Museumsgebäude, haben aber besondere Bedeutung für seine öffentlich zugänglichen Teile. Ein Museum ist, um mit

Kahn zu sprechen, durch eine sehr klare Gliederung in »dienende« und »bediente« Räume charakterisiert. Primärräume sind solche, die unmittelbar für die Kommunikation bestimmt sind – Ausstellungssäle, Vortrags- und Klassenräume, Bibliotheken, Verkaufsstände für Bücher und Postkarten. Sie werden bedient durch Sekundärräume: Werkstätten, Laboratorien, Magazine, Verwaltungsräume mit technischen Installationen, die alle erst das Funktionieren der Primärräume ermöglichen. Die erste Gruppe bildet die Zone, die jedermann betreten darf, die zweite den privaten Bereich, der dem inneren Betrieb des Hauses vorbehalten ist. Das Größenverhältnis beider Zonen zueinander ändert sich mit der Art des Museums, aber im allgemeinen wird der Anteil der nötigen Sekundärräume unterschätzt. Beide sind unentbehrlich, wenn das Museum seiner Aufgabe nachkommen will, und keine von beiden darf bei der architektonischen Planung vernachlässigt werden. Schließlich gibt es eine dritte Zone mit Nebenräumen wie Restaurants, Waschräume, Garderoben, Klubzimmer, die der Bequemlichkeit des einzelnen dienen oder von sozialer Bedeutung sind. Die Fläche, die von dieser Gruppe beansprucht wird, hängt von der Zahl der Gäste in den Hauptbesuchszeiten ab.

James Johnson Sweeney hat vorgeschlagen, daß nur ein Siebtel der Gesamtfläche für Ausstellungszwecke benutzt werden sollte. Diese Zahl scheint allerdings viel zu gering und mag sich aus der Tatsache erklären, daß das Guggenheim Museum, dessen erster Direktor er war, so wenig Depotfläche hatte, daß ein Teil der oberen – für die Ausstellung vorgesehenen – Rampe zum Bilderlager gemacht werden mußte. Die Proportion erscheint dagegen weniger unvernünftig, wenn man sich vor Augen hält, daß nur etwa 10 Prozent der Sammlung Guggenheim zu gleicher Zeit gezeigt wird und daß 90 Prozent magaziniert oder ausgeliehen sind.

Andere Kollektionen zeigen einen größeren Teil ihrer Bestände: die Yale Art Gallery etwa 60 Prozent, der Palazzo Abbatellis in Palermo 50 Prozent, das Shimane Prefectural Museum in Matsue 25 Prozent. Philip Johnson befürwortet ein Verhältnis von einem Drittel Ausstellungsfläche zu zwei Dritteln sonstiger Nutzfläche. In diesen zwei Dritteln sind natürlich sämtliche Nebenräume eingerechnet, ebenso die Studiensammlungen, die Wissenschaftlern und Studenten zugänglich sind.

Angesichts des beträchtlichen Anteils, den Magazine und andere Nebenräume im Museum beanspruchen, ist es überraschend, daß die architektonische Seite des Problems so wenig untersucht worden ist. Bei Bibliotheksbauten zum Beispiel wird häufig aus der Notwendigkeit eines großen Bücherdepots ein Kernelement entwickelt, das von Lesesälen, die Tageslicht benötigen, umgeben ist. Nur im Städtischen Museum von Linköping (Architekten Ahrbom und Zimdal, fertiggestellt 1939) sind enge Magazine als trennende Elemente unter einer Oberlichtkonstruktion mit gelenktem Lichteinfall verwendet (Abb. S. 23). Dieser Gedanke, die weniger günstigen Zonen der primären Raumvolumen durch Sekundärräume auszunutzen und dadurch bestimmte räumliche Unterteilungen zu erreichen, hat keine Schule gemacht. Die unsichtbaren Teile des Eisbergs Museum sind unter der Wasseroberfläche geblieben. Wahrscheinlich ist die Trennungslinie zwischen der eigentlichen Ausstellung auf der einen Seite und den Studiensammlungen und Werkstätten auf der anderen zu streng gezogen worden. Übergänge von der einen Zone wenigstens zu Teilbereichen der zweiten sollten erleichtert werden. Das heißt nicht, daß alle Bestände der jeweiligen Sammlung gezeigt werden müßten. Aber da die Zahl der ausgestellten Gegenstände begrenzt ist, wenn sie ihre Wirkung tun sollen, so müßte der Zugang zu dem übrigen Material einfach und direkt sein. Je seltener und je intensiver Objekte besichtigt werden, desto gedrängter können sie aufbewahrt werden. Studiensammlungen lassen sich wie Fußnoten enger darbieten als der Haupttext, die Schausammlung.

Zugängliche Studiensammlungen müssen jedoch übersichtlich gegliedert sein und ohne strenge Aufsicht benutzt werden können. Eine Reihe von Museen haben der Anordnung dieser Sammlungen ebensoviel Aufmerksamkeit gewidmet wie der Hauptausstellungsfläche. Das unternehmungslustige Museum für Völkerkunde in Neuchâtel verwahrt beispielsweise die Töpferwaren seiner Arbeilssammlung in Räumen und Vitrinen, die in ihrer Anordnung und ihrem Werkstattcharakter ihrer Bestimmung angemessen sind und offensichtlich genauso sorgfältig wie die Vitrinen und die Beleuchtung der Hauptgalerie geplant wurden (Abb. S. 24).

Unterschiedlich ist dagegen die Art und Weise, wie der Betrachter sich in den beiden Abteilungen des Museums zum Gegenstand verhält. In der Schausammlung handelt es sich immer um eine Folge von Objekten, die von einem in Bewegung befindlichen Betrachter wahrgenommen wird; in der Studiensammlung werden dagegen die Objekte ausgewählt und längere Zeit untersucht, so daß der Betrachter normalerweise steht oder sitzt. Es muß also sowohl für Depotfläche wie für Arbeitsplätze gesorgt werden. In der Funktion sind diese Bereiche des Museums den Lesesälen einer Bibliothek mit frei zugänglichen Bücherregalen verwandt.

Die Verbindung zu den Werkstätten muß stärker kontrolliert werden, wenn der Arbeitsbetrieb nicht behindert werden soll. Immerhin sollte es möglich sein, bestimmte Aspekte der Restaurationsarbeiten sichtbar zu machen, etwa durch Glasflächen hindurch oder an Hand von Führungen. Das Brooklyn Museum erwägt diese Möglichkeit. Die Restaurationstechniken sind faszinierend genug, um allgemeines Interesse zu erwecken. Zu sehen, wie ein Topf zusammengesetzt, eine Textilarbeit restauriert, ein Tier präpariert oder ein Bild gereinigt wird, befriedigt nicht nur die – hier wohlangebrachte – Neugierde, sondern zeigt, wieviel Gewissenhaftigkeit und Mühe notwendig sind, um solche Dinge heil der Zukunft zu überliefern. Die Mittlertätigkeit des Museums wäre ohne Pflege und Erhaltung des Überlieferten nicht möglich.

Wie oft und in welchem Umfang Restaurationsarbeiten durchgeführt werden müssen, hängt weitgehend von den Bedingungen der Umgebung ab. Je mehr diese Bedingungen kontrolliert und vor allem konstant gehalten werden können, desto entbehrlicher werden drastische Eingriffe. Wünschenswert ist deshalb die Kontrolle über Temperatur, Feuchtigkeitsgehalt und Luftverschmutzung durch Vollklimatisierung. Sie ist besonders dort notwendig, wo organische Materialien wie Holz, Textilien, Bilder, Papier, Felle, Knochen, Leder aufbewahrt werden, und in Zonen mit sehr unterschiedlichem Klima, vor allem mit großen Schwankungen der Luftfeuchtigkeit. Eine Reihe von Angaben, die in dieser Hinsicht für den architektonischen Entwurf aufschlußreich sind, finden sich auf Seite 179.

Mechanische Belüftung in irgendeiner Form ist bei allen völlig abgeschlossenen, künstlich beleuchteten Räumen notwendig. Das heißt, Luft muß auf mechanischem Wege zugeführt werden, auch wenn sie nicht erwärmt, gekühlt oder gereinigt wird. Unter den meisten klimatischen Bedingungen muß sie jedoch zu bestimmten Jahreszeiten erwärmt oder gekühlt werden, letzteres schon deshalb, weil von der künstlichen Beleuchtung beträchtliche Wärmemengen abgegeben werden. Die

Klimaanlage muß infolgedessen die Lichtwerte berücksichtigen, die in den Sälen jetzt oder später einmal auftreten, so daß die erforderliche Leistung jederzeit in jedem Raum erreicht werden kann. Diese Überlegung macht sich bei der Flexibilität eines Museums bezahlt.

Ein weiterer großer Vorteil der Klimatisierung, die Reinigung der Luft, hat zur Folge, daß eine Reihe trennender Vorrichtungen zwischen Objekt und Betrachter wegfallen können. Bilder müssen nicht mehr mit Glas geschützt werden, das den Saal und seine Besucher reflektiert, und viele andere empfindliche Gegenstände können ohne staubschützende Gehäuse auskommen. Es mögen dadurch Sicherheitsprobleme entstehen, die sich aber durch andere Vorkehrungen lösen lassen – wie zum Beispiel im Falle des Königlichen Münzkabinettes in Stockholm, wo die ausgestellten schwedischen Kupfermünzen mit einem elektrischen Warnsystem verbunden sind. Zu Recht darf Klimatisierung also auch als ein Mittel gelten, das die Unmittelbarkeit der Kommunikation fördert. Bei Neubauten von Museen müßten deshalb die Kanäle und die nötigen Räumlichkeiten für Klimazentralen von vornherein mit eingeplant werden, auch wenn solche Anlagen erst später installiert werden können. Entsprechende horizontale und vertikale Hohlräume sollten schon im Entwurf berücksichtigt sein, so daß sich jeder Teil des Gebäudes klimatisieren läßt.

Restaurants und Klubräume, die zur dritten Sparte, den Nebenräumen, gehören, haben erst seit relativ kurzer Zeit einen Platz im Museum erhalten. In der viktorianisch-wilhelminischen Epoche wäre das als frivol angesehen worden, ja geradezu als schädlich für die Ziele des Museums, des pädagogischen Warenhauses. Heute sind diese Ergänzungen willkommene Erweiterungen, die den extrovertierten Charakter des Museums unterstreichen. Die besten Museumsrestaurants sind eigens für ihren Zweck entworfen und nicht irgendwo in einen Winkel des untersten Stockwerks verwiesen. Meistens ziehen sie Nutzen aus einer besonderen Situation: Das Museum of Modern Art in New York hat Dachgeschoß und Dachterrasse als Restaurant für seine Mitglieder und den langen Raum im Erdgeschoß vor einer Terrasse des Skulpturengartens als öffentliche Cafeteria eingerichtet (Abb. S. 25). Das Stedelijk Museum in Amsterdam installierte sein Restaurant in der Nachbarschaft der Bibliothek – beides öffentlich zugängliche miteinander verbundene Räume; das Restaurant dehnt sich nach außen auf eine gepflasterte Terrasse aus, von der der Blick über einen Teich, über Plastiken und dahinter einen Kinderspielplatz geht. In Louisiana, dreißig Kilometer nördlich von Kopenhagen, ist der letzte Pavillon einem Restaurant und schattigen Freiplätzen mit Blick über den Sund vorbehalten.

Klubzimmer und Versammlungsräume können eine ähnlich nützliche Funktion ausüben, sofern sie nicht von einer pseudo-interessierten Clique mit Beschlag belegt werden. Museumsobjekte teilen sich zwar nur dem einzelnen mit, aber diese »Mitteilung« kann diskutiert und verglichen werden und wird dadurch oft verständlicher. Solche Räume können natürlich für verschiedene Zwecke dienen, etwa für Vorträge, Filmvorführungen, Malkurse; auf diese Weise lassen sie sich auch ökonomisch rechtfertigen.

Mehrzweckräume dieser Art führen – ebenso wie die Einrichtung von Bibliotheken – dazu, daß das Museum einen festen Platz im Leben der betreffenden Gemeinde einnimmt und vielseitige Auseinandersetzungen ermöglicht. So sollte beispielsweise die Museumsbibliothek

Museum for a Small City (Project, 1942). Plan and perspective. Architect: Ludwig Mies van der Rohe.

"Two openings in the roof plate (3 and 7) admit light into an inner court (7) and into an open passage (3) through one end of the building. Outer walls (4) and those of the inner court are of glass. On the exterior, free-standing walls of stone would define outer courts (1) and terraces (10). Offices (2) and wardrobes would be free-standing. A shallow recessed area (5) is provided, around the edge of which small groups could sit for informal discussions. The auditorium (8) is defined by free-standing walls providing facilities for lectures, concerts and intimate formal discussions. The form of these walls and the shell hung above the stage would be dictated by the acoustics. The floor of the auditorium is recessed in steps of seat height, using each step as a continuous bench. Number (6) is the print department. Above it is a space for special exhibits. Number (9) is a pool." (Mies van der Rohe.)

durchaus als Primärraum betrachtet und wie die Ausstellungssäle mit der allgemein zugänglichen Verkehrsfläche verbunden werden. Im Amsterdamer Stedelijk Museum ist der Lesesaal zwischen dem alten Bau und dem neuen Flügel eingerichtet, so daß der Besucher ermutigt wird, sich der Nachschlagewerke zu bedienen oder einen Blick in die Kunstzeitschriften zu werfen – Informationen, die unter Umständen die jeweils gezeigten Ausstellungen in ein anderes Licht rücken. Wenn solche Einrichtungen einmal geschaffen sind, werden sie auch benutzt. Die Bibliothek des Museum of Modern Art in New York, die rund 15000 Bücher, Zeitschriften und Kataloge umfaßt, steht allen Besuchern des Museums offen und wird von etwa 5000 Lesern im Jahr aufgesucht. Informierende Werke sollten nicht nur für die Mitarbeiter des Museums verfügbar sein oder an den Postkartenständen verkauft werden, sondern der Allgemeinheit in einer Umgebung zugänglich gemacht werden, die dem genius loci so entspricht wie es etwa in Louisiana der Lesebereich am Kamin tut. Die Tatsache, daß Museen zeitweise große Besucherzahlen aufzuweisen haben, spricht nicht dagegen, solche intimen Zonen zu schaffen.

Lesezimmer, Restaurants, Magazine, Säle, Lichtführung sind nur Elemente, die zusammen das Museum bilden. Wie brillant jedes für sich gelöst sein mag, allein kann es kein zufriedenstellendes Ganzes ausmachen. Was zählt, ist das Gesamterlebnis, die Architektur als untrennbare Einheit.
Erst die Ordnung aller Elemente, ihre Abwandlung und gelegentlich auch der Konflikt, in den sie zueinander treten, schafft Architektur; erst ihr Zusammenwirken führt zu dem »genauen und wunderbaren Spiel der Formen im Licht«, wie Le Corbusier es genannt hat. Es gibt unendlich viele Möglichkeiten für dieses Spiel der Formen – ebenso viele wie Architekten. Trotzdem lassen sich bestimmte Tendenzen, bestimmte historisch bedingte Auffassungen nachweisen, auch wenn sie nicht immer definiert worden sind.
Als Mercier 1770 ein Museum für das Jahr 2000 entwarf, setzte er auf die Fassade die Worte »Ein Abriß des Uni-

versums«. Im Augenblick jedenfalls ist es nicht wahrscheinlich, daß seine Utopie sich realisiert. Die rationale Voraussetzung, daß ein Museum so etwas wie eine konkrete, umfassende und belehrende Enzyklopädie sein könne, hat sich seit langem als Trugschluß erwiesen. Nicht nur der Wissensstoff hat sich in ungeahntem Maße vermehrt, sondern auch der Versuch, universale Kenntnisse durch ein einziges Medium zu erwerben, ist fehlgeschlagen. Wir begnügen uns mit vielleicht weniger hochgesteckten, dafür aber erreichbaren Zielen. Wir akzeptieren das Museum als eines von mehreren Kommunikationsmitteln, dessen Stärke in einer bestimmten und spezialisierten Aufgabe liegt, der Darbietung des Objekts selbst.
Wie das Objekt präsentiert wird und wie die Architektur dabei mitwirkt, hängt in starkem Maße von den architektonischen und sozialen Vorstellungen des Architekten und seines Auftraggebers ab. Nicht zufällig wirken das Amon Carter Museum in Fort Worth wie eine gläserne Variante des klassischen Portikus und der Anbau des Amsterdamer Stedelijk Museums wie eine Art verglasten Warenhauses. Das Amon Carter Museum wurde von Philip Johnson in einer der wohlhabendsten Städte Amerikas errichtet und gibt sich selbstbewußt als ein Zentrum der Kultur zu erkennen. Das Stedelijk Museum wurde vom Amsterdamer städtischen Baubüro in Zusammenarbeit mit W. Sandberg entworfen, dem damaligen Direktor des Stedelijk, der mehr als irgend jemand in Europa dazu getan hat, die Vorstellung vom Museum als einem esoterischen Ort der Kultur zu zerstören.
Daß die Rolle des Museums in gewissem Grade eingeschränkt worden ist, hat Konsequenzen für die architektonische Lösung gehabt. Das Museum ist kein mächtiger und dominierender Palast mehr. Die Architektur muß deshalb nicht mehr durch Größe und Baumaterial beeindrucken, was einst als angemessen und heute doch wohl eher als banal empfunden wird. Die bloße Größe hat sich sowieso als funktionell unbrauchbar erwiesen, da sie visuell und geistig nur zur Abstumpfung führt. Wie günstig die finanzielle Lage des Museums in Zukunft auch sein mag – in den meisten Ländern eine verwegene Hy-

pothese –, zu Museen von der Größenordnung des Louvre oder der Smithsonian Institution mit ihren 55 Millionen katalogisierten Objekten dürfte es kaum kommen.
Abgesehen von der drohenden Museumsmüdigkeit sprechen zwei Überlegungen gegen die Aufblähung des Museums. Zunächst einmal hat der Museumsbesuch in den letzten Jahren beträchtlich zugenommen. Zum guten Teil ist diese Zunahme nicht nur darauf zurückzuführen, daß das Museum weitere Kreise anzieht, sondern daß dieselben Leute mehrere Male im Jahr kommen. Die großen Besucherzahlen beispielsweise für die Londoner Tate Gallery oder das New Yorker Museum of Modern Art sind weitgehend mit solchen wiederholten Besuchen zu erklären. Deshalb braucht das Museum in einer bestimmten Zeitspanne viel weniger auf einmal zu präsentieren, so daß alles, was es zeigt, gewissermaßen als eine Folge wechselnder Ausstellungen aufgefaßt werden kann. Auf diese Art werden das Museum und seine Tätigkeit für die Öffentlichkeit interessant und wichtig. Einige japanische Firmen profitieren von dieser Publizität, indem sie in Kaufhäusern in Tokio Sonderausstellungen von Kunstschätzen veranstalten; oft handelt es sich dabei um ganz ungewöhnliche Stücke, die aus Tempeln entliehen sind. Auch die Ausstellungen, die der Rinascente-Konzern in seiner Mailänder Filiale mit Beispielen der Formgebung durchführt, helfen die respektvolle Distanz zu allem verringern, was das Schild »Kunst« trägt. Der umgekehrte Fall hat die gleiche Wirkung, nämlich die Präsentation von Gegenständen im Museum, die normalerweise in Geschäften verkauft werden. So sind Haushaltsartikel und andere Beispiele industrieller Formgebung regelmäßig im Museum of Modern Art in New York, aber auch anderswo ausgestellt. Bei wenigstens zwei Gelegenheiten wurden dabei in New York sogar Automobile auf den Terrassen des Skulpturengartens gezeigt.
Weiterhin gilt es heute nicht mehr als selbstverständlich, daß das Museum der Aufbewahrungsort für jedes wertvollere Kunstwerk oder wissenschaftlich interessante Objekt zu sein hat. Im 19. Jahrhundert war diese Meinung weit verbreitet. Das British Museum zum Beispiel durfte

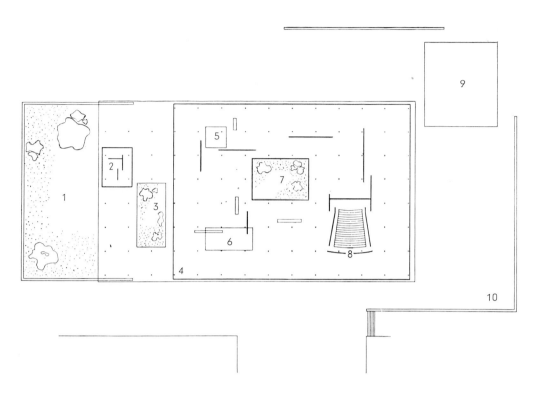

Museum für eine kleine Stadt (Projekt, 1942). Grundriß und Perspektive. Architekt: Ludwig Mies van der Rohe.

»Zwei Öffnungen in der Dachplatte (3 und 7) lassen Tageslicht in einen Innenhof (7) und in einen offenen Gang (3) am einen Ende des Gebäudes eintreten. Die Außenwände (4) und die Wände des Innenhofes sind aus Glas. Außerhalb des Gebäudes bilden freistehende Steinwände äußere Höfe (1) und Terrassen (10). Büroräume (2) und Garderoben stehen frei. Eine flache Nische (5) bietet Sitzplatz für kleine private Diskussionsgruppen. Das Auditorium (8), durch freistehende Wände begrenzt, ist für Vorträge, Konzerte und kleinere öffentliche Diskussionen vorgesehen. Die Form dieser Wände und der über der Bühne eingehängten Deckenschale wird von der Akustik bestimmt. Der Boden des Hörsaals steigt stufenförmig an, wobei jede Stufe als durchlaufende Sitzbank ausgebildet ist. Der Bauteil (6) ist das Graphikkabinett, darüber ist Raum für Sonderschauen. (9) ist ein Wasserbassin.« (Mies van der Rohe.)

noch 1963 nach den geltenden Vorschriften kein Objekt seiner Bestände veräußern oder auch nur ins Ausland verleihen, es sei denn, es wurde durch ein besonderes Gesetz des Parlamentes dazu ermächtigt. Wir heute sind der Meinung, daß das Museum auswählen, sieben und aussondern darf. Die Statuten der Louisiana-Stiftung erlauben beispielsweise, daß Bilder verkauft oder – in Zusammenarbeit mit dem Künstler – ausgewechselt werden. Oft erweist es sich auch als nützlich, daß Objekte innerhalb der Museumswelt von der einen in die andere Sammlung wandern. In New York hat das Museum of Modern Art eine solche Abmachung mit dem Metropolitan Museum, in London die Tate Gallery mit der National Gallery. Bei anderen Medien können und sollen weitergehendere Vereinbarungen getroffen werden, da sie sich mit Information befassen, die nicht an reale Gegenstände gebunden ist und kondensiert werden kann. Das Museum, das sich mit dem Objekt selber beschäftigt, begnügt sich mit einer begrenzteren, aber in gleichem Maße wirkungsvollen Aufgabe. Um sie so gut wie möglich zu lösen, muß es sich davor hüten, zu einem Depot aller derzeit nicht erwünschten Dinge zu werden.

Es versteht sich von selber, daß Museumsarchitektur nicht einen isolierten Spezialsektor darstellt, sondern daß sie an der allgemeinen Entwicklung des architektonischen Denkens teilhat. Wenn sie genügend Durchschlagskraft aufbringt, wird sie ihrerseits diese Entwicklung beeinflussen. Das gilt gegenwärtig vor allem für Italien, und es galt mit noch mehr Recht für den Barcelona-Pavillon (1929), der ja ein Museumsbau war. Sein Architekt, Mies van der Rohe, entwarf später ein nicht ausgeführtes »Museum für eine kleine Stadt« (1942), das auf die Architektur als ganzes wohl weniger Einfluß ausgeübt hat (Abb. S. 26, 27). Aber damit war das Vorbild eines flexiblen Museumsraumes geschaffen, das bislang von der gebauten Wirklichkeit einschließlich dem Werk Mies van der Rohes nicht erreicht worden ist. Le Corbusiers Gedanke eines erweiterungsfähigen Museums war ebenfalls eindrucksvoll und blieb ebenfalls unverwirklicht. Diese Diskrepanz zwischen Idee und Wirklichkeit, zu der

auch die unvermeidliche Skepsis über das Guggenheim Museum gehört, erklärt sich dadurch, daß diese Entwürfe von einem allgemeinen Konzept ausgehen. Am Anfang stehen Vorstellungen wie universaler Raum, Erweiterungsfähigkeit, organische Form, und das Museum wird nur als Demonstrationsmöglichkeit benutzt. Die Hauptprobleme des Museumsbaus sind dabei nur am Rande berührt worden. Dagegen liegt die Bedeutung des gegenwärtigen italienischen Beitrags in der entgegengesetzten Richtung: Neue Lösungen entstanden aus der detaillierten Beschäftigung mit konkreten Situationen, und es ging dabei jedesmal um die wichtigste Funktion des Museums, die Gegenüberstellung von Objekt und Betrachter.

Ein solches Verfahren läßt sich nicht nur für den Bereich des Museumsbaus oder der Ausstellungstechnik feststellen, sondern stimmt mit einem weiten Bereich des heutigen architektonischen Denkens überein. Meist publiziertes Beispiel ist Kahns Laboratoriumsgebäude der University of Pennsylvania. Das soll nicht heißen, daß das Richards Medical Research Building von Albini oder Scarpa beeinflußt ist; aber zweifellos sind eine Reihe italienischer Museumsbauten frühe und aufschlußreiche Belege für eine neue, allgemein bedeutungsvolle Einstellung zum architektonischen Entwurf. Ermöglicht wird die neue Haltung durch den zunehmenden Wohlstand Jetzt ist der spezialisierte Verwendungszweck bestimmter Räume wirtschaftlich zu vertreten und damit eine Architekturkonzeption, die von einer spezifischen, architektonisch auswertbaren Situation ausgeht. Die Tendenz zur Spezialisierung hat Parallelen im Design von Geräten und anderen Werkzeugen zur Bewältigung der Umwelt. Dabei ist das Ausmaß der Spezialisierung weitgehend ein Gradmesser des technischen Fortschritts – von dem steinzeitlichen Feuerstein, der für alle möglichen Zwecke gedient hat, bis zu dem hochspezialisierten Drehstahl einer automatischen Drehbank, der für eine spezifische Aufgabe konstruiert ist. Da das Museum als Bautyp von einem hohen allgemeinen Lebensniveau abhängt, verwundert es nicht, wenn zumindest in einigen Fällen diese Entwurfsmethoden angewendet worden sind.

Die Verbesserung des Lebensstandards und damit auch die vermehrte Mußezeit in der westlichen Gesellschaft (und hoffentlich auch bald in der übrigen Welt) dürfte diese Tendenz verstärken. Damit wächst der Bedarf für Museen der verschiedensten Art. In den USA ist diese Entwicklung bereits deutlich. Sie wird kaum zu neuen nationalen oder weltstädtischen Institutionen führen, statt dessen aber zu Neugründungen kleiner oder mittelgroßer Museen von der Größe des Kalamazoo Institute of Arts, des Museum of Art, Science and Industry in Fairfield County (Connecticut) oder des Munson-Williams-Proctor Institute in Utica. Das heißt: Die meisten Chancen haben lokale Zentren der Aktivität, die Wanderausstellungen zeigen, Vorträge und Kurse veranstalten, Ausstellungsobjekte und Bücher verleihen und eng mit den Schulen zusammenarbeiten. Erweiterungen in gewissem Umfang und ein großes Programm von Neuordnungen und Renovierungen erwarten die größeren traditionellen Museen; ihre riesigen Bestände müssen so organisiert werden, daß jedes einzelne Objekt seine Botschaft mitteilen kann. Alle diese Aufgaben werden den Architekten ihren ganzen Einfallsreichtum und ihre ganze Bereitschaft zur Auseinandersetzung abverlangen, damit brauchbare und menschliche Stätten entstehen. Im Museumsbau hat die Konzentration auf das Einzelne und Besondere zu einer bedeutenden Leistung geführt: die Vergangenheit in einigen ihrer größten Beispiele zu bewältigen, ohne darüber die Gegenwart zu verraten. Eine kleine Zahl neuerer Museen hat gültige architektonische Lösungen dieser Aufgabe gefunden; darin besteht ihr wichtigster Beitrag für die Zukunft.

Museums have been grouped in the following pages by countries or regions and arranged within each group in chronological order. The development of techniques within a country can thus be followed. Suprisingly enough despite the publication of display in UNESCO's *Museum*, a quarterly with an international circulation, and frequent conferences arranged by ICOM, ideas do not seem to cross frontiers easily. A very considerable timelag is involved.

Within each museum the photographs are, wherever possible, placed in the sequence in which these views would be seen by a museum visitor. The illustrations thus try to preserve the characteristic sequential nature of museum viewing.

Die Museen auf den folgenden Seiten sind nach Ländern angeordnet; innerhalb der Ländergruppen erscheinen sie in chronologischer Reihenfolge, so daß sich die Entwicklungstendenzen der einzelnen Länder verfolgen lassen. Obwohl die UNESCO eine vierteljährlich erscheinende internationale Zeitschrift über Ausstellungsgestaltung mit dem Titel *Museum* herausgibt und obwohl der ICOM (International Council of Museums) häufig Tagungen veranstaltet, vermögen neue Konzeptionen nicht ohne weiteres und nur mit erheblichen Verzögerungen die Grenzen zwischen den Ländern zu überwinden.

Bei den einzelnen Museen sind die Abbildungen – soweit möglich – in der Reihenfolge angeordnet, in der ein Museumsbesucher die Eindrücke aufnimmt. Die Abbildungsreihen suchen also die für das Museum typische Sehfolge zu erhalten.

Both as regards quantity and quality the post-war Italian contribution to museum design has been astonishing. Museums throughout the country have participated in a resurgence which has been notable not only for the attention lavished on the execution of the display but for the intentions underlying its design. This is as true of large as of small or isolated institutions; of the Castello Sforzesco in Milan, the National Gallery and Capodimonte in Naples, the museums in Pisa, Bergamo, Perugia, Verona, Venice and Palermo as of the small extension to the Canova Gallery of casts at Possagno near Cesena.

Part of the success is undoubtedly due to the work done in the first instance by a small number of architects – Albini, Gardella, Scarpa, Studio BBPR – who saw themselves not as rebels against history but as part of a continuous tradition the most marked aspect of which is a simultaneous belief in the present and an acceptance of the past. What is obvious from a design such as Carlo Scarpa's restoration and rearrangement of the Castelvecchio in Verona is that it was based both on thought and emotion.

With this understanding came the realization that objects had to be shown so that they could be seen; that it was not only a matter of warehousing but of communication; of a communication which is, what is more, individual and specific. As Bruno Zevi, the editor of *L'Architettura* said in 1958:

"We had been accustomed to museums conceived architecturally on a monumental scale, a shell into which the works of art were inserted at a later stage. But now this concept is being reversed: the works of art themselves create the architecture, dictating the spaces and prescribing the proportions of the walls. Each picture and statue is studied for the best possible view: it is then set in the necessary spatial quantity."

Exhibition design at the Milan Triennale, at the Turin "Italia '61" celebration, at the many temporary exhibitions such as that of Crivelli and his followers in the Doge's Palace in 1961 and the Italian contributions at the Venice Biennale, particularly Scarpa's Venezuelan Pavilion, are all part of the same movement.

Although these ideas have been current in Italy since at least 1950, they are only now finding acceptance elsewhere. When they eventually make their way into the general stream of museum design and are perhaps combined with certain other notions of the museum as a community building which are now being developed in the United States and Scandinavia, our whole concept of the museum as an institution and as a place may be radically altered.

Nach Quantität und Qualität ist der Beitrag, den Italien nach dem letzten Krieg zum Museumswesen geleistet hat, erstaunlich. Überall im Lande sind Museen erneuert oder neu errichtet worden, wobei nicht nur die Auseinandersetzung mit den ausstellungstechnischen Detailproblemen bemerkenswert ist, sondern auch die grundsätzlichen Erwägungen, die für die Gestaltung maßgebend waren. Das gilt für große wie für kleine oder isoliert liegende Institutionen, für das Castello Sforzesco in Mailand, das Museo Nazionale und das Museo di Capodimonte in Neapel, die Museen in Pisa, Bergamo, Perugia, Verona, Venedig und Palermo oder für den kleinen Erweiterungsbau des Museo Canoviano in Possagno bei Cesena.

Zum Teil ist dieser Erfolg zweifellos der Arbeit einer kleinen Gruppe von Architekten zuzuschreiben. Albini, Gardella, Scarpa oder das Architektenteam BBPR betrachteten sich nicht als Rebellen gegen die Historie, sondern fühlten sich einer ununterbrochenen Tradition verpflichtet; sie glaubten an die Gegenwart und akzeptierten zugleich die Vergangenheit. Eine Lösung wie die Restaurierung und Neugestaltung des Castelvecchio in Verona von Carlo Scarpa zeigt, wie sehr hier der Intellekt und die emotionale Seite beteiligt waren.

Damit zusammen ging die Einsicht, daß Objekte gezeigt werden müssen, damit sie gesehen werden können; daß Kommunikation – und zwar eine auf das Individuelle, Spezifische ausgehende Kommunikation – an die Stelle des Warenhaus-Denkens treten muß. Bruno Zevi, der Herausgeber der Zeitschrift *L'architettura*, sagte 1958:

»Wir waren an Museen gewöhnt, deren Architektur monumental konzipiert war, Gehäuse, in denen die Kunstwerke nachträglich, nach der Planung des Bauwerks, untergebracht wurden. Diese Vorstellung ist heute umgekehrt worden: Die Kunstwerke schaffen ihrerseits die Architektur, bestimmen die Räume und schreiben die Abmessungen der Wände vor. Jedes Bild und jede Skulptur werden darauf überprüft, wie sie sich am besten darbieten: Erst dann erhalten sie den Raum, den sie benötigen.«

Zeitlich begrenzte Ausstellungen wie die Mailänder Triennale, die »Internationale Arbeitsausstellung 1961« in Turin, Veranstaltungen wie die Crivelli-Ausstellung im Dogenpalast 1961 und die italienischen Beiträge zur Biennale in Venedig, vor allem der Venezolanische Pavillon von Scarpa, sie alle haben Teil an dieser Bewegung.

Obwohl diese Gedankengänge in Italien zumindest seit 1950 aktuell sind, werden sie erst jetzt auch anderswo allmählich akzeptiert. Wenn sie einmal allgemein die Begriffe von Museumsgestaltung bestimmt haben und mit anderen Ideen kombiniert werden – etwa der Auffassung des Museums als Gemeinschaftszentrum, wie sie gegenwärtig in den USA und in Skandinavien entwickelt wird –, dürfte sich unsere ganze gegenwärtige Vorstellung vom Museum, von der Institution und vom Bauwerk, radikal ändern.

1

1–3. The Villa Giulia in Rome was converted and enlarged by Franco Minissi between 1955 and 1960 through the introduction of an intermediate floor within the existing two-storey volume. The new floor becomes a bridge between supports and its balustrade holds showcases as well as narrow spotlights.

1–3. Das Museo Nazionale di Villa Giulia in Rom wurde zwischen 1955 und 1960 von Franco Minissi umgebaut und erweitert. Minissi zog in das zwei Geschosse hohe Raumvolumen ein Zwischengeschoß ein. Das neue Geschoß bildet eine Brücke zwischen Stützen. Auf der Balustrade sind Vitrinen angebracht; schmale Spotlights beleuchten die unterhalb der Balustrade aufgestellten Werke.

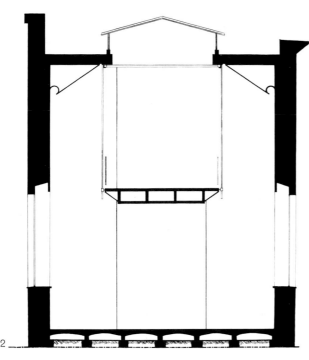

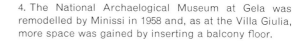

4. The National Archaelogical Museum at Gela was remodelled by Minissi in 1958 and, as at the Villa Giulia, more space was gained by inserting a balcony floor.

4. Das Museo Nazionale Archeologico in Gela baute Minissi 1958 um. Wie bei der Villa Giulia gewann der Architekt auch hier durch Einziehen eines Zwischengeschosses mehr Platz.

3

4

Palazzo Bianco Museum, Genoa (1950–51)

Architect: Franco Albini

This museum reconstruction was the first to question the accepted methods of display and to provide solutions which were to prove enormously influential later. Nowhere is this more obvious than in the mounting of the fragment from the tomb of Margaret of Brabant. The Palazzo was heavily damaged during a bombing raid in 1942 but enough survived to make possible a reconstruction by the Department of Civil Engineering in 1945. Franco Albini's arrangements were designed within this setting.

Caterina Marcenaro, Director of Fine Arts of the City of Genoa, who collaborated with Albini, has described some of the aspects which were considered important.

"The present solution is based on considerations of quality. Some of the former exhibits have been withdrawn, on the ground that they were not of the finest quality, were negligible from the standpoint of visual education, and liable to confuse the mind of the uninformed visitor. They have been replaced by others which are, qualitatively and technically, of greater interest. . . .

In the interests of education, the palace concept was abandoned and the museum criterion strictly adhered to. In other words, the works of art were treated not as the decorative part of a given setting, but as a world in themselves, sufficient to absorb the visitor's full attention. To avoid distracting that attention, care was taken when arranging the rooms so far as possible to dispense with all embellishments either in material, form or colour – the intention being to provide the tranquil visual background that is desirable, if not essential, for the contemplation of a work of representational art. . . . Certain paintings stand mounted on iron supports fixed into capitals or bases of Roman or Gothic pillars. This solution has given rise to some criticism on the ground of what is held to be too close an association of the new with the old. In my opinion, however, this view is unfounded; every cultural problem – and it cannot be denied that museums are part of culture – must be solved in terms, not of what is old and what is new, but of what is true and what is false. It is the business of culture to search for truth, no matter whether the truth will in fact be discovered. . . .

Special methods were adopted for the display of certain particularly distinctive and important items. For instance, the fragment from the tomb of Margaret of Brabant, by Giovanni Pisano, has been mounted on a cylindrical steel support which can be raised and swivelled as desired. This solution has been much discussed, not always with approval. Apart from the fact that there were no original designs or later documentary evidence to show how the work had been set up in the first place, it consists simply of a fragment, and considerable freedom is thus permissible in its display. Moreover it is, though a fragment, of such quality that it was essential for it to be easily viewable; it had, therefore, to be mobile and to be set in a place apart. The fact that mobility was obtained by the use of a revolving, electrically – operated steel cylinder is due, not to lack of respect for Giovanni, but to simplicity and humility of approach in respect of a great work of art. To have placed the fragment on a pedestal or in the shadow of a marble or other niche would have been, not only to resort to arbitrary treatment and revive the thorny question of the genuine versus the spurious, but to bring undue influence to bear on the work, especially as regards proportion, thus confusing the general public and disturbing the atmosphere of purity and tranquillity which I consider essential when a visitor – particularly an uninformed visitor – approaches a real masterpiece."
(*Museum*, Volume VII, Number 4, 1954.)

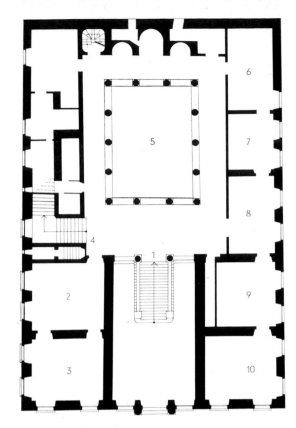

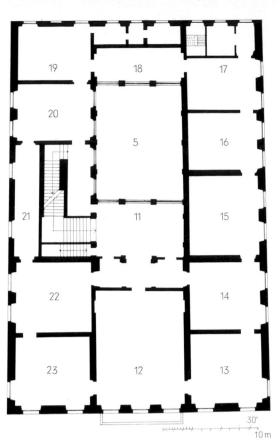

1

2

Plans, first and second floor / Grundrisse erstes und zweites Geschoß.

1 Stairs from ground floor entrance hall / Treppe von der Eingangshalle des Erdgeschosses
2 Room I / Raum I
3 Room II / Raum II
4 Stairs to second floor / Treppe ins zweite Geschoß
5 Courtyard / Innenhof
6 Temporary teaching exhibitions / Wechselnde Lehrausstellungen
7 Room XIX / Raum XIX
8 Room XVI / Raum XVI
9 Room XVII / Raum XVII
10 Room XVIII / Raum XVIII
11 South loggia, room III / Loggia nach Süden, Raum III
12 Room IV / Raum IV
13 Room V / Raum V
14 Room VI / Raum VI
15 Room VII / Raum VII
16 Room VIII / Raum VIII
17 Room IX / Raum IX
18 North loggia, room X / Loggia nach Norden, Raum X
19 Room XI / Raum XI
20 Room XII / Raum XII
21 Room XIII / Raum XIII
22 Room XIV / Raum XIV
23 Room XV / Raum XV

1. The Palazzo Bianco as arranged in 1893.
2. The staircase leading up to the first floor with the courtyard beyond, the first exhibition room is to the left of the top of the stairs.

1. Der Palazzo Bianco im Jahre 1893.
2. Vom Erdgeschoß führt eine Treppe ins erste Geschoß; dahinter der Innenhof. Oberhalb der Treppe liegt links der erste Ausstellungsraum.

3

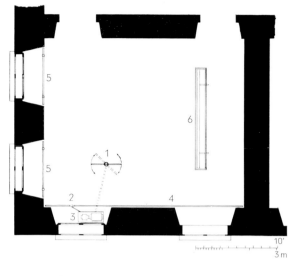

Plan of room II / Grundriß von Raum II.
1 Hydraulic lifting and rotating device / Hydraulische Dreh- und Hebevorrichtung
2 Control switch / Kontrollschalter
3 Motor and pump / Motor und Pumpe
4 New slate wall / Neue Schieferverkleidung
5 Venetian blinds / Lamellen
6 Byzantine pallium in a glass case / Byzantinisches Pallium in einer Glasvitrine

10'
3 m

3. Room I with a crucifix by Caravana, the case containing the Byzantine pallium can be seen through the opening. The natural light falling into the room is regulated by venetian blinds.

3. Raum I mit einem Kruzifix von Caravana. Die Vitrine im angrenzenden Raum enthält ein byzantinisches Pallium. Der Lichteinfall wird durch Lamellenstores geregelt.

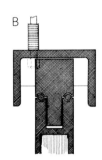

A. Hydraulic lifting device / Hydraulische Hebevorrichtung.
B. Rotating head on roller bearing / Rotationskopf auf Kugellager.

4"
0,10 m

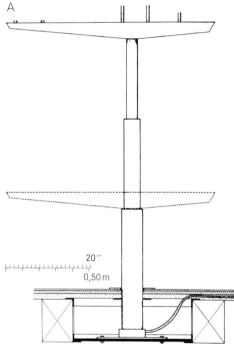

A

4–6. The fragment from the tomb of Margaret of Brabant by Giovanni Pisano and the 13th century Byzantine pallium in Room II. The marble fragment is mounted on an adaptation of a hydraulic car hoist; the Byzantine fabric in a double-sided glass case illuminated by a fluorescent tube so that both sides of the material can be seen. Spotlights provide additional lighting. The motor and pump needed for the rotating lifting device are in a recess behind the slate wall. While the floors of the other rooms are of marble, Room II is carpeted.

4–6. Raum II zeigt das Fragment von Giovanni Pisanos Grabmal der Margarete von Brabant und das byzantinische Pallium aus dem 13. Jahrhundert. Das Marmorfragment ist auf einen Träger montiert, der ähnlich wie ein hydraulischer Autoheber funktioniert. Motor und Pumpe für die Dreh- und Hebevorrichtung sind hinter der Schieferverkleidung in die Wand eingelassen. Spotlights geben zusätzliches Licht. Das byzantinische Gewebe kann in der verglasten, durch eine Leuchtstoffröhre erhellten Vitrine von beiden Seiten betrachtet werden. Im Gegensatz zu den Marmorböden der übrigen Säle ist dieser Raum mit Teppichen ausgelegt.

20"
0,50 m

4

5

6

Museo di Palazzo Bianco, Genua (1950–51)

Architekt: Franco Albini

Bei der Neugestaltung dieses Museums wurden zum erstenmal die traditionellen Ausstellungsmethoden in Frage gestellt; Albinis Lösungen erwiesen sich später als außerordentlich einflußreich. Nirgendwo wird das deutlicher als bei der Aufstellung des Fragments vom Grabmal der Margarete von Brabant. Der Palazzo wurde 1942 durch einen Luftangriff schwer beschädigt, doch blieb noch soviel von dem Gebäude übrig, daß das Hochbauamt 1945 mit dem Wiederaufbau beginnen konnte. Franco Albinis Konzeptionen sind auf diesen Rahmen zugeschnitten.

Caterina Marcenaro, Direktorin der Städtischen Kunstsammlungen in Genua, die mit Albini zusammenarbeitete, hat in *Museum* VII, Heft 4, 1954, die wichtigsten Aspekte der Neugestaltung beschrieben:

»Die gegenwärtige Lösung beruht auf der Forderung nach Qualität. Einige früher ausgestellte Werke werden nicht mehr gezeigt, da sie nicht höchsten Ansprüchen gerecht wurden, von der visuellen Kommunikation her bedeutungslos erschienen und den uninformierten Besucher nur verwirrt hätten. Sie wurden durch andere ersetzt, die in Qualität und Technik interessanter sind ... Aus kunstpädagogischen Erwägungen heraus wurde der Palazzo Bianco von einem Palast zu einem Museum umgewandelt; dieser Gesichtspunkt wurde streng eingehalten. Die Kunstwerke sollten also nicht die Dekoration gegebener Räumlichkeiten, sondern eine Welt für sich darstellen und die ungeteilte Aufmerksamkeit des Besuchers beanspruchen. Um jede Ablenkung zu vermeiden, wurden Materialien, Formen und Farben so zurückhaltend wie möglich gewählt. Es sollte ein optisch ruhiger Hintergrund geschaffen werden, der für die Betrachtung eines Kunstwerks wünschenswert, wenn nicht sogar notwendig ist ... Einige Gemälde wurden an Eisenstangen befestigt, die in römische oder griechische Säulenkapitelle oder -basen eingelassen sind. Diese Lösung hat mehrfach Kritik hervorgerufen, da das Alte angeblich zu eng mit dem Neuen verbunden ist. Meiner Meinung nach entbehrt eine solche Ansicht jedoch der Grundlage; bei jedem kulturellen Problem – und eine kulturelle Institution ist das Museum ohne Zweifel – sind nicht alt oder neu, sondern wahr oder falsch die Kriterien der Lösung. Es gehört zu unseren Aufgaben, nach der Wahrheit zu forschen, ohne Rücksicht darauf, ob wir sie auch tatsächlich finden ...

Für das Arrangement bestimmter besonders wichtiger Kunstwerke wurden spezielle Aufstellungsmethoden angewandt. So wurde zum Beispiel das Fragment von Giovanni Pisanos Grabmal der Margarete von Brabant auf einem zylindrischen Stahlträger montiert, der drehbar und in der Höhe variabel ist. Auch diese Lösung wurde viel diskutiert und fand nicht immer Zustimmung. Abgesehen davon, daß keine Originalzeichnungen oder späteren Dokumente vorliegen, die zeigen könnten, wie das Werk ursprünglich angebracht war, handelt es sich nur um ein Fragment; bei der Ausstellung eines solchen Kunstgegenstandes ist deshalb die größte Freiheit gegeben. Darüber hinaus besitzt das Fragment eine solche künstlerische Qualität, daß es von allen Seiten gut sichtbar sein muß. Aus diesem Grunde wurde es beweglich montiert und an einem besonderen Platz aufgestellt. Daß für die Beweglichkeit ein drehbarer, elektrisch betriebener Stahlzylinder sorgt, zeugt nicht von mangelndem Respekt vor Giovanni Pisano, sondern von einer schlichten und demütigen Haltung gegenüber einem großen Kunstwerk. Wenn man das Fragment auf einen Sockel oder in den Schatten einer Marmornische gestellt hätte, so wäre durch eine solche willkürliche Plazierung wieder die schwierige Frage von echt und unecht aufgetaucht. Außerdem wäre das Werk – vor allem durch das Problem der Proportionen – ungünstigen Einflüssen ausgesetzt gewesen. Das hätte wiederum das Publikum verwirrt und die Atmosphäre der Ruhe und Klarheit gestört, die ich für außerordentlich wichtig halte, wenn ein Besucher – und insbesondere ein unvoreingenommener Besucher – sich mit einem wirklichen Meisterwerk vertraut macht.«

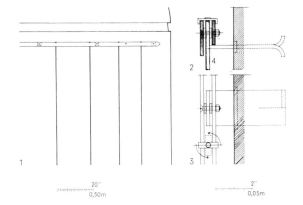

Detail.
1 Elevation of picture suspension rods / Ansicht der Aufhängevorrichtung
2 Section of top bars bracketed out from wall / Vertikalschnitt der in der Wand verdübelten Schienen
3 View from above / Ansicht von oben
4 ¼" bar / 6 mm dicker Stab

7, 8. Paintings by 15th and 16th century Flemish, French-Flemish and Dutch masters are hung in Room IV. These are attached to long iron rods suspended from iron bars at the top of the wall. The rods can be moved so that there is cosidenrable flexibility and the walls remain undamaged. Only pictures in the corners of the room are fixed to the wall and turned to face the visitor. Lighting is by cold cathode tubes running parallel with the walls.

7, 8. In Raum IV hängen Gemälde flämischer, französisch-flämischer und holländischer Maler aus dem 15. und 16. Jahrhundert. Die Bilder wurden an Eisenstäben angebracht, die entweder in Kapitellen und Basen eingelassen oder unterhalb der Decke an eisernen Schienen befestigt sind. Die Stäbe können verschoben werden, so daß die Aufhängung der Bilder flexibel ist und die Wände keinen Schaden erleiden. Nur die Gemälde in den Ecken des Raumes sind auf Schwenkarmen an der Wand montiert und wenden sich dem Besucher zu. Die Beleuchtung erfolgt durch Leuchtstoffröhren mit kaltem Licht, die parallel zu den Wänden verlaufen.

7

8

9. Room V contains Italian paintings of the 15th and 16th centuries and, beyond it, the openings leading into the remaining rooms on the east side of the second floor.
10. The north loggia acts as the connecting space between the east and west sides of the Palazzo. Pictures are frequently fixed to iron rods held in Roman or Gothic column bases or capitals.

9. Raum V zeigt italienische Malerei aus dem 15. und 16. Jahrhundert. Die Türen im Hintergrund führen zu den weiteren Räumen auf der Ostseite des zweiten Obergeschosses.
10. Der im Norden gelegene Raum verbindet die Ost- und Westseite des Palazzo. Die meisten Bilder hängen an Eisenstäben, die in romanischen oder gotischen Säulenbasen und -kapitellen befestigt sind.

9

10

11. Tapestries, such as this 16th century Flemish work in Room XVIII, are hung from iron rails at the top of the wall by means of rods holding a horizontal round bar passing through straps sewn to the tapestry. It was thought important to have movable seating so that the position from which exhibits were to be looked at could be chosen by the visitor. The seats are of natural leather and black pearwood and are the only definite colours which were introduced; the remaining colours are shades of black and grey.

11. An die Tapisserien wurden – wie bei diesem flämischen Werk aus dem 16. Jahrhundert in Raum XVIII – Schlingen genäht, durch die eine runde horizontale Eisenstange führt. Die Stange wird von dünneren Stäben gehalten, die ihrerseits unterhalb der Decke an einer Eisenschiene befestigt sind. Die Sitzgelegenheiten sind beweglich, damit der Besucher sich selbst den richtigen Blickwinkel auswählen kann. Die Stühle sind aus Naturleder und schwarz gestrichenem Birnbaumholz – die einzigen Farben, die zugelassen wurden; sonst finden sich in dem Museum nur Schwarz- und Grauschattierungen.

11

Gallery of Modern Art, Milan (1954)

Architect: Ignazio Gardella

Galleria d'Arte Moderna, Mailand (1954)

Architekt: Ignazio Gardella

This is a new pavilion added to the existing gallery buildings. Within a single volume it provides three distinct types of space each intended for a particular function and each having a character of its own. Yet the spaces are only separated by changes of level. The design shows that flexibility in arrangement can be achieved without creating wholly anonymous volumes; such anonymous voids may in fact produce serious limitations since they make impossible a specific relation of object to environment.

The structure consists of steel columns and roof trusses. The pitched roofs are covered with wired glass.

Der neue Pavillon zeitgenössischer Kunst schließt sich an die bestehenden Museumsgebäude an. Er enthält innerhalb eines einzigen Bauvolumens drei verschiedene Raumtypen, die jeweils einer bestimmten Funktion dienen. Jeder Bereich besitzt einen spezifischen Charakter, obwohl die Räume nur durch verschiedene Niveauhöhen gegeneinander abgesetzt sind. Der Pavillon beweist, daß eine Flexibilität der Anordnung auch dann erreicht werden kann, wenn die Räume nicht völlig anonym gehalten werden. Ein anonymer Hohlraum kann sogar im Gegenteil Beschränkungen auferlegen, da er es unmöglich macht, das Ausstellungsobjekt in eine Beziehung zu seiner Umgebung zu setzen.

Die Gebäudekonstruktion besteht aus Stahlstützen und Dachträgern. Die Satteldächer sind mit Drahtglas bedeckt.

1. The three levels within the single volume are seen from the half-landing of the stairs to the gallery. The lowest level overlooking the park is intended for sculpture, the middle level for pictures, the top balcony and a room immediately behind it for drawings, prints and small objects.

1. Die drei Niveaus des Pavillons, gesehen von der Treppe zur Galerie. Das niedrigste Niveau zum Park hin ist für Plastik bestimmt, das mittlere für Bilder und der obere Balkon sowie ein Raum unmittelbar dahinter für Zeichnungen, Druckgraphik und kleinere Gegenstände.

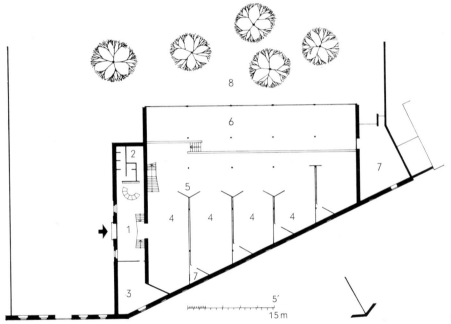

Plan, ground floor / Grundriß, Erdgeschoß

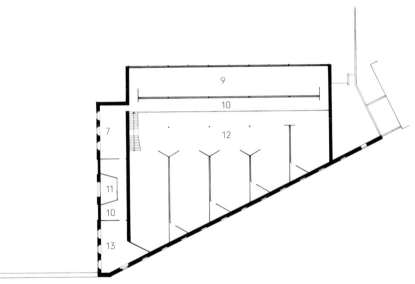

Plan, first floor / Grundriß erstes Geschoß

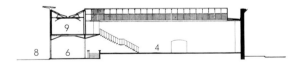

Transverse section / Querschnitt

1 Entrance / Eingang
2 Cloakroom / Garderobe
3 Boiler room / Zentralheizung
4 Picture gallery / Ausstellungsraum für Gemälde
5 Movable partitions / Bewegliche Trennwände
6 Sculpture gallery / Ausstellungsraum für Plastik
7 Storage / Magazin
8 Garden / Garten
9 Prints and drawings gallery / Ausstellungsraum für Zeichnungen und Druckgraphik
10 Balcony / Balkon
11 Upper part of entrance hall / Luftraum Eingangshalle
12 Upper part of main gallery / Luftraum Hauptausstellungssaal
13 Workshop and storage / Werkstatt und Magazin

1

2, 3. The lowest of the three levels facing the park, although here used for pictures, is meant for sculpture so that the exhibits may be seen silhouetted against foliage and their three dimensional quality brought out by directional lighting.

4, 5. The middle level, one and a half storeys high, seen from the balcony, is top lit through a double layer of adjustable aluminium slats painted white. It is subdivided into five separate bays by movable partitions to allow certain groupings and to provide greater wall space for pictures.

2, 3. Der untere Raum mit Blick auf den Park nimmt hier zwar Bilder auf, ist aber an sich für Skulpturen gedacht, die sich gegen die Bäume abheben sollen. Die dreidimensionalen Eigenschaften der Plastiken werden durch das einfallende Seitenlicht hervorgehoben.

4, 5. Das mittlere Niveau, das anderthalb Geschosse einnimmt, vom Balkon aus gesehen. Das Oberlicht wird durch eine Doppellage weißgestrichener, verstellbarer Aluminiumlamellen reguliert. Der Raum ist durch bewegliche Trennwände in fünf Bereiche unterteilt. Dadurch lassen sich die Bilder in bestimmten Gruppierungen anordnen, und es wird zusätzliche Wandfläche für die Aufhängung der Gemälde geschaffen.

2

3

4

5

6

6. Both the lower and upper levels and the park outside are visible from the main space.

7. The south side facing the garden with the long glass wall of the lowest level. Counterweighted grilles can be lowered over this glass area to provide security.

6. Vom Hauptraum aus sind das untere und obere Niveau wie auch der Park zu sehen.

7. Die Südseite mit der langen Glaswand des unteren Ausstellungsniveaus zum Garten hin. Zur Sicherung können vor die Glaswand Gitter herabgelassen werden, die in Schienen laufen und an Gegengewichten aufgehängt sind.

7

Palazzo Abbatellis, National Gallery of Sicily,
Palermo (1954)

Architect: Carlo Scarpa

This 15th century palace had been a convent for four centuries and was damaged during the war. The National Gallery of Sicily which was formed from the State collection of medieval and modern art in Palermo previously in the National Museum is now housed here. The palace is a square two-storey building around a central courtyard with a porch and an open gallery on one side. The courtyard, the windows screened with Gothic tracery, the bare stone walls and the vaulted ceilings are all part of the museum display and all add to the creation of a specific and memorable environment. Scarpa's design is in entire sympathy with a statement made by the Director of the Gallery, Giorgio Vigni, that, "works of art are individuals requiring to live in their own special environment, and as such are endowed with a personality which gives form and rhythm to their allotted space."

The ground floor is given over to sculpture except for a large 15th century fresco, *The Triumph of Death*, which takes up the whole end wall of the apse of the church which had been attached to the convent. The second floor is devoted to paintings and small frescoes.

Palazzo Abbatellis, Galleria Nazionale della Sicilia,
Palermo (1954)

Architekt: Carlo Scarpa

Der Palazzo Abbatellis stammt aus dem 15. Jahrhundert und beherbergte vierhundert Jahre lang ein Nonnenkloster. Während des zweiten Weltkrieges wurde er schwer beschädigt. Heute ist in dem Palazzo die Nationalgalerie von Sizilien untergebracht; sie besteht aus der staatlichen Sammlung mittelalterlicher und moderner Kunst, die früher zum Nationalmuseum von Palermo gehörte. Das quadratische, zweigeschossige Gebäude ist um einen Innenhof angeordnet, der an einer Seite von einer zweigeschossigen offenen Galerie begrenzt wird. Der Innenhof, die Fenster mit dem gotischen Maßwerk, die nackten Steinwände und die gewölbten Decken sind in die Museumsgestaltung einbezogen und helfen eine charakteristische Umgebung zu schaffen. Scarpas Entwurf entspricht völlig einer Erklärung des Galeriedirektors Giorgio Vigni, daß nämlich »Kunstwerke Individuen sind, die eine eigene Umgebung brauchen; sie besitzen eine Persönlichkeit, die dem umgebenden Raum Form und Rhythmus verleiht«.

Das Erdgeschoß nimmt nur Plastik auf, mit Ausnahme des großen Freskos *Der Triumph des Todes* aus dem 15. Jahrhundert. Das Fresko erstreckt sich über die gesamte Stirnwand in der Apsis der Kirche, die an das Kloster angebaut ist. Das zweite Geschoß enthält Gemälde und kleine Fresken.

1. The new staircase, part of Scarpa's internal rearrangement, joins the existing stair going from the courtyard to the loggia on the first floor.

1. Die Treppe im größten der drei Plastiksäle, die Scarpa neu einzog, stößt auf die alte Treppe vom Innenhof zu der Loggia im ersten Geschoß.

2, 3. Plans, ground and first floor. These rough plans show better than any accurate drawing of the completed installation the sort of considerations which guided Scarpa in the design. His placing of arrows indicating either movement or sequence of views controls the positioning of objects.

2, 3. Grundrisse Erdgeschoß und erstes Geschoß. Diese Skizzen zeigen besser als jede exakte Zeichnung, welche Vorstellungen Scarpa bei dem Umbau des Palazzo leiteten. Die Pfeile geben Bewegung oder Blickfolge an und bestimmen die Aufstellung der Kunstwerke.

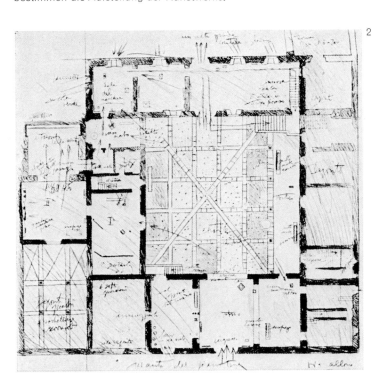

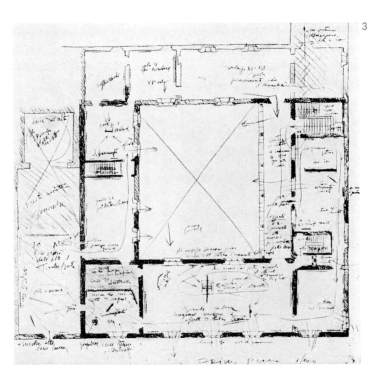

4, 5. A sequence of three sculpture rooms terminating with Laurana's bust of Eleanor of Aragon.

6. Francesco Laurana's bust at the end of this vista is raised slightly above its support so that none of its lines should be visually interrupted. The background of green painted panels emphasizes the outline of the marble and at the same time provides an environment in scale with the size of the sculpture and the delicacy of its carving.

7, 8. The *Head of a Page*, also by Francesco Laurana, stands in front of a window in the central of the three rooms and is lit from behind so as to bring out the carving of the hair. A dark wood panel on the wall emphasizes the profile and helps, on approach, to isolate the small piece from the large grey wall behind it.

9. A 13th century crucifix from Pisa stands turned towards the light isolated in its rectangular metal frame in the first room opening off the loggia.

4, 5. Drei aufeinanderfolgende Plastiksäle; im Hintergrund Lauranas Büste der Eleonore von Aragon.

6. Die Büste von Francesco Laurana ist durch zwei Stifte vom Exponatträger abgehoben, damit die Linienführung nicht optisch unterbrochen wird. Die grüngestrichenen Platten im Hintergrund und an der Seite betonen die Um-

risse der Marmorbüste; sie schaffen gleichzeitig eine Umgebung, die den Proportionen der Plastik und der Feinheit der plastischen Behandlung entspricht.

7, 8. Der *Pagenkopf* von Laurana steht vor einem Fenster im mittleren Raum und wird von hinten beleuchtet, so daß die Linien des Haares hervortreten. Die dunkle Holztafel an der Wand bildet einen Hintergrund für das Profil und isoliert die kleine Plastik von der großen, grauen Wand.

9. Das Kruzifix aus Pisa (13. Jh.) ist dem Fenster zugekehrt. Es steht in dem ersten Raum, der sich von der Loggia des Obergeschosses aus öffnet, und ist durch den rechteckigen Metallrahmen von der Umgebung isoliert.

10

10. One of the two crucifixes in the main hall on the first floor; both are painted on two sides and therefore stand free in the room. The two long walls of the hall are unplastered and are the background to frescoes by Tommaso de Vigilia; the two end walls, on the other hand, are plastered and painted to provide a surface more in scale with the triptychs painted on gold ground.

11. Immediately to one side of the main hall there is a small room, partly screened by wood panelling, with paintings by Antonello da Messina. The three saints on the left are set into fabric covered panels hinged to brass rods so that they may be turned to face the light.

12. Antonello's famous Annunziata stands in the middle of the room. The wooden screen is hollow and can be opened on one side. The painting is protected by glass within a red velvet covered recess.

13. The Mabuse Triptych in the Flemish collection is mounted within an opening in the movable screen so that both sides can be seen.

11

12   13

10. Eines der beiden Kruzifixe im Hauptsaal des Obergeschosses; die Kruzifixe sind auf beiden Seiten bemalt und stehen deshalb frei im Raum. Die Längswände des Saales sind roh belassen; sie bilden den Hintergrund für Fresken von Tommaso de Vigilia. Die beiden Stirnwände sind dagegen verputzt und gestrichen, damit sie besser mit den auf Goldgrund gemalten Triptychen zusammengehen.

11. An eine Seite des Hauptsaales schließt sich ein kleiner Raum an, der teilweise mit Holz verkleidet ist und Gemälde von Antonello da Messina enthält. Die drei Heiligenbilder links sind in stoffverkleidete Platten eingesetzt. Die Platten wurden mit Scharnieren an Messingstangen befestigt und können zum Licht hin ausgeschwenkt werden.

12. Antonellos berühmte *Annunziata* steht in der Mitte des Raumes. Das Bild ist in einer mit rotem Samt verkleideten Vertiefung angebracht und wird durch eine Glasscheibe geschützt. Der Holzrahmen ist innen hohl und läßt sich auf einer Seite öffnen.

13. Das Triptychon von Mabuse in der flämischen Sammlung ist in die Öffnung einer beweglichen Stellwand eingelassen, so daß beide Seiten des Bildes betrachtet werden können.

Castello Sforzesco Museum, Milan (1954–64)

Architects: Studio Architetti BBPR (Lodovico B. Belgiojoso, Enrico Peressutti, and Ernesto N. Rogers)

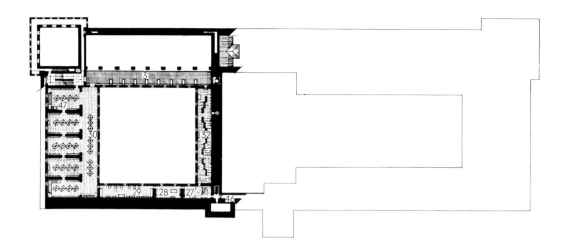

The issue of *Casabella* which first illustrated this museum also carried a leading article on "Modern Architecture since the Generation of the Masters" by Ernesto Rogers, its editor and one of the architects concerned with this reconstruction. It was headed by a quotation from William James, "Real culture lives with sympathies and admiration not by dislikes and disdains." The effect of such an attitude and particularly of its relevance to the relation of past to present is obvious in every detail of the Castello.

It is an attitude which in its application requires considerable effort; there are no ready made answers and no universal solutions. The design of the museum assumes for instance different degrees of flexibility for different groups of objects: in the Scarlioni Room (see Figs. 15, 16, 17), Michelangelo's sculpture is within a relatively fixed enclosure, Bishop Battista Bagaroto's funeral monument stands on the floor at the head of the room – movable but obviously part of the composition of the space – while on the walls held by iron supports are smaller pieces of sculpture with room for further such items clearly indicated by the unused bronze wall pegs. Every object is considered individually and its mounting or support related both to itself and the objects around it. 600 drawings apart from sketches and perspectives and models of the main exhibits were needed for the rearrangement of the two floors of the first part of the Castello.

The design also relates the exhibition to the historical building which houses it and which, as in the case of Leonardo's fresco, itself often becomes the exhibit. The museum experience is thus dependent on the total environment – on exhibits, their sequence, the building. This was a significant innovation which has now considerably influenced subsequent museum design.

The building was heavily damaged during air raids in August 1943 and it was therefore necessary to undertake this extensive reconstruction of what is now the Municipal Museum of Milan. The first section, designed in 1952 and built between 1954 and 1956, consists of two floors, the lower being devoted to sculpture, armour, a few tapestries and the Leonardo fresco, the upper floor to paintings, furniture and tapestry. The second section was finished seven years later and is on the upper floors around the courtyard immediately to the other side of the entrance tower. It exhibits mainly ceramics, bronzes, jewellery, tapestries and a large collection of musical instruments.

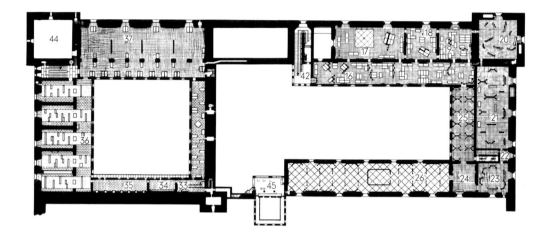

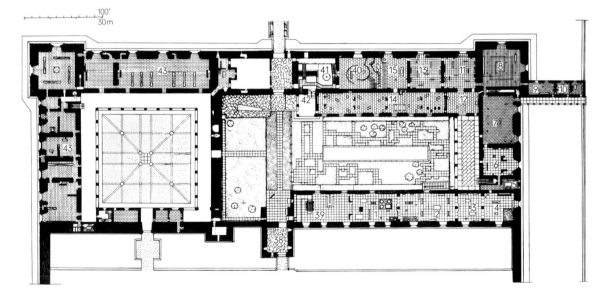

Plan, second floor / Grundriß zweites Geschoß.
Plan, first floor / Grundriß erstes Geschoß.
Plan, ground floor / Grundriß Erdgeschoß.

1–6 Rooms 1–6, sculpture / Räume 1–6, Skulpturen
7 Room 7, tapestry / Raum 7, Gobelins
8 Room 8, Sala delle Asse with frescoe by Leonardo/ Raum 8, Sala delle Asse mit Fresko von Leonardo
9–11 Rooms 9–11, sculpture / Räume 9–11, Skulpturen
12 Room 12 / Raum 12, Capella Ducale
13 Room 13, sculpture / Raum 13, Skulpturen
14 Room 14, armour / Raum 14, Waffen und Rüstungen
15 Room 15 / Raum 15, Sala degli Scarlioni
16–19 Rooms 16–19, furniture / Räume 16–19, Möbel
20 Room 20, paintings / Raum 20, Gemälde
21 Room 21, main picture gallery / Raum 21, Hauptausstellungsraum für Gemälde
22–25 Rooms 22–25, paintings / Räume 22–25, Gemälde
26 Room 26, paintings (previously tapestries) / Raum 26, Gemälde (ursprünglich Gobelins)

27 Room 27, ante-room / Raum 27, Vorraum
28 Room 28, metal work / Raum 28, Metallarbeiten
29–30 Rooms 29–30, ceramics / Räume 29–30, Keramik
31 Room 31, porcelain on gallery overlooking room 37/ Raum 31, Galerie über Raum 37 mit Porzellangegenständen
32 Upper level gallery to room 30 / Auf höherem Niveau gelegener Ausstellungsraum zu Raum 30
33 Room 33, ante-room / Raum 33, Vorraum
34 Room 34, textiles / Raum 34, Textilien
35 Room 35, textiles and costumes / Raum 35, Textilien und Kleidung
36 Room 36, musical instruments / Raum 36, Musikinstrumente
37 Room 37, tapestries and musical instruments / Raum 37, Gobelins und Musikinstrumente

38 Tower / Turm
39 Entrance / Eingang
40 Pietà Rondanini
41 Courtyard with fountain / Brunnenhof
42 Stairs from ground floor to first floor / Treppen vom Erdgeschoß zum ersten Geschoß
43 Parts not completed summer 1964 / Im Sommer 1964 noch nicht fertiggestellte Teile
44 Hall to be used for musical performances / Für musikalische Darbietungen vorgesehene Halle
45 Stairs to second floor of second section / Treppen zum zweiten Geschoß des zweiten Abschnitts
46 Entrance from first floor of first section / Eingang vom ersten Geschoß des ersten Abschnitts
47 Stairs to upper level gallery / Treppe zur höher gelegenen Galerie

Museo del Castello Sforzesco, Mailand (1954–64)

Architekten: Studio Architetti BBPR (Lodovico B. Belgiojoso, Enrico Peressutti und Ernesto N. Rogers)

Die Ausgabe von *Casabella*, die sich zum erstenmal mit dem Castello Sforzesco befaßte, enthielt auch einen Artikel über die »Moderne Architektur seit der Generation der Meister « von Ernesto Rogers, dem Herausgeber der Zeitschrift und Mitarbeiter an der Neugestaltung des Museums. Ein Zitat von William James leitete den Aufsatz ein: »Wirkliche Kultur lebt durch Sympathien und Bewunderung, nicht durch Antipathien und Verachtung. « Diese Einstellung wird in jedem Detail des Castello deutlich und äußert sich vor allem in der Verbindung von Altem und Neuem. Für eine solche Haltung gibt es keine Vorbilder und keine Patentlösungen. Beim Castello Sforzesco wurde zum Beispiel Flexibilität für die einzelnen Kategorien von Objekten in verschiedenen Graden vorgesehen: In dem Scarlioni-Raum (vgl. Abbildungen 15, 16, 17) ist zum Beispiel Michelangelos Skulptur innerhalb einer relativ festen Umgrenzung aufgestellt. Das Grabmal des Bischofs Battista Bagaroto steht auf dem Fußboden am Ende des Raumes; es ist zwar beweglich, bildet aber einen Bestandteil der Gesamtkomposition. An den Wänden sind kleinere Plastiken an Eisenträgern befestigt; daß hier weitere Ausstellungsgegenstände Platz finden sollen, machen die unbenutzten bronzenen Wanddübel deutlich. Bei diesem Museum wird also jedes Objekt individuell behandelt, und seine Anbringung oder Aufstellung hängt von ihm selbst und von den umgebenden Gegenständen ab. Für die Neuordnung der zwei Geschosse im ersten Teil des Castello waren 600 Zeichnungen sowie Skizzen, Perspektiven und Modelle der wichtigsten Ausstellungsstücke nötig.

Der Entwurf des Architekten setzt den Ausstellungsbereich in eine Beziehung zu dem historischen Gebäude, das bisweilen – wie bei Leonardos Fresken – selbst zum Ausstellungsobjekt wird. Zum Erlebnis des Museumsbesuches trägt also die gesamte Umgebung bei – die Kunstwerke, ihre Abfolge, das Gebäude. Diese Konzeption trat beim Castello Sforzesco zum erstenmal auf und hat einen starken Einfluß auf die Museumsgestaltung ausgeübt.

Das Bauwerk wurde im August 1943 durch Luftangriffe schwer beschädigt, so daß umfangreiche Wiederaufbauarbeiten notwendig waren, bis das Städtische Museum von Mailand seinen Einzug halten konnte. Der erste Abschnitt (entworfen 1952, gebaut 1954–56) umfaßt zwei Geschosse. Das untere enthält Plastik, Rüstungen, einige Tapisserien und das Leonardo-Fresko, das obere Gemälde, Möbel und Tapisserien. Der zweite Abschnitt wurde sieben Jahre später fertiggestellt; er umfaßt die Teile der oberen Stockwerke, die den Hof auf der anderen Seite des Eingangsturmes umgeben. Ausgestellt sind vor allem Keramik, Bronzen, Schmuck, Tapisserien und eine große Sammlung von Musikinstrumenten.

1

2

3

4

5

6

7

1. The entrance doors and the staircase which link this part of the museum to the second section. The approach to the entrance is through a portal at the foot of one of the castle towers.
2. The entrance space has a photographic exhibition on the history of the building. Postcards are on sale at the counter on the left.
3. The 14th century *Portale della Pusterla dei Fabbri* which closes the entrance space and acts as a sort of triumphal arch to the beginning of the ground floor exhibition area.
4. Room 7 which used to be the reception hall of the Milan Municipality now contains a group of 17th century Brussels tapestries.
5. Room 2, the central part of the long sculpture gallery which can be seen from the stone archway.
6. The end room of the sculpture gallery. The exhibits are held by brackets which fit on to bronze pegs let into the wall; rest on shelves fixed to such brackets; are attached to low sloping partitions or rest on the floor. In each case there is some separation between the exhibit and its immediate surroundings.
7. An iron frame straddles the end of Room 5 to support a 13th century wooden figure of Christ. This small room acts as a pause between the preceeding sculpture gallery and the series of large rooms to come.

1. Die Eingangstüren und die Treppe, die den ersten Teil des Museums mit der zweiten Abteilung verbindet. Als provisorischer Eingang dient ein Portal neben einem der Schloßtürme.
2. Im Eingangsbereich erläutern Fotografien die Geschichte des Bauwerks. Am Tisch links werden Postkarten verkauft.
3. Das *Portale della Pusterla dei Fabbri* aus dem 14. Jahrhundert schließt den Eingangsbereich ab und markiert als eine Art Triumphbogen den Beginn der Ausstellungsräume im Erdgeschoß.
4. Raum 7 wurde früher als Empfangssaal der Stadt Mailand benutzt; er enthält Brüsseler Gobelins aus dem 17. Jahrhundert.

5. Raum 2, der zentrale Bereich der langen Skulpturengalerie, die durch den steinernen Torbogen zu sehen ist.
6. Der letzte Raum der Plastikgalerie. Die Skulpturen werden von Wandarmen gehalten, die ihrerseits von bronzenen, in die Wand eingelassenen Dübeln aufgenommen werden; sie stehen auf Brettern, die auf diesen Wandarmen ruhen, sind an niedrigen, schrägen Stellflächen angebracht oder auf dem Boden aufgestellt. In jedem Falle distanziert sich das Ausstellungsobjekt in gewissem Maße von seiner unmittelbaren Umgebung.
7. Ein Eisengerüst im Hintergrund von Raum 5 trägt eine hölzerne Christusfigur aus dem 13. Jahrhundert. Dieser kleine Raum bildet ein Intervall zwischen den vorhergehenden Sälen und den folgenden großen Räumen.

8, 9. The tapestries are suspended from cast bronze brackets which also hold the light fittings in two brass channels, one pointing upwards at the painted ceiling, the other downwards at the tapestries, and these are held taut at the bottom by being fastened back to pegs in a wooden board.

8, 9. Die Gobelins hängen an Armen aus Gußbronze und sind am Boden straff mit Schlingen und Stiften an einem Holzsteg befestigt. Die Bronzearme tragen außerdem zwei Messingleisten mit Leuchtröhren; die oberen sind auf die bemalte Decke, die unteren auf die Teppiche gerichtet.

8

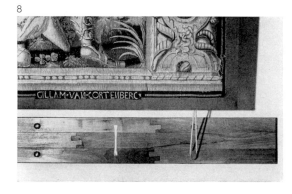

9

43

10

10. Skulpturen und Fragmente wie die beiden Engel, die ursprünglich zu einem Hochrelief gehörten, sind in den Räumen 11 und 13 ausgestellt. Als Träger dienen starke Bretter aus Walnußholz auf Bronzestützen mit kreuzförmigem Durchschnitt.

11. Detail von Raum 14. Die Wände sind in hellem Smaragdgrün gestrichen, die Büsten und Puppen, die Helme oder Rüstungen tragen, sind rotlackiert.

12. Die eisernen Lampenträger und die gezackte Wandtäfelung in Raum 8 betonen den Freiluftcharakter von Leonardos Weinspalier-Fresko, das auf die Decke und den oberen Teil der Wände gemalt ist. Die Tafeln aus massivem Walnußholz in der Mitte des Raumes bilden ein Labyrinth; sie sind auf der Innenseite mit blauem Filz bespannt und können für Wechselausstellungen benutzt werden.

13. Zwischen restaurierten Fresken aus dem 15. Jahrhundert ist an der Wand eine Madonna mit Kind angebracht, die sich von einem topasfarbenen Samtvorhang abhebt. Gegenüber steht auf einem Sockel aus rotem Porphyrmarmor die *Anbetende Madonna*, die Pietro Solari zugeschrieben wird.

14. Drei Renaissance-Portale unterteilen Raum 14 und bilden einen Hintergrund für die Waffen und Rüstungen aus dem 15. bis 17. Jahrhundert.

11

10. Sculpture, mostly in the form of fragments like the two angels which were part of a high relief, is displayed in Room 11 and 13. The stands consist of walnut boards on cruciform bronze uprights.

11. A detail of Room 14. The walls are painted a light emerald green, the dummies supporting the armour are lacquer red.

12. The iron lamp posts and the tooth edged wall panelling are intended to emphasize the outdoor character of Leonardo's fresco of a vine trellis painted on the ceiling and the upper part of the walls in Room 8. The wooden panels in the centre of the room form a maze and are solid walnut on the outside but lined with blue felt on the inner face so that they may be used for temporary displays.

13. On the wall between restored 15th century frescoes is a Madonna and Child against a dark background of topaz coloured velvet; facing her on a red porphyry marble pedestal, the *Worshipping Madonna* attributed to Pietro Solari.

14. Three Renaissance portals which punctuate Room 14 and provide a background for 15th–17th century armour.

12

13

14

44

15

16

17

15. The Scarlioni Room with the steps going down towards Michelangelo's *Descent from the Cross* placed behind the stone embrasure on the right and the olive wood screen which turns the visitor towards it. No part of the unfinished sculpture is visible until one has turned at that screen.

16. After leaving the Pietà there is again a view of the whole room, this time looking up towards the funeral monument at the top and the zig-zag wall pattern which was found during the restoration. The suspended ceiling is made of walnut boards and the light fittings suspended from it are brass cylinders.

17. The *Pietà Rondanini* in its niche made of interlocking stone slabs.

18, 19. The fountain court beyond the Scarlioni Room ends the sequence of ground floor spaces. After crossing the balcony there is staircase to the upper floor. This

outdoor room acts as a punctuation mark and divides the two parts of the first section of the museum into distinct districts.

20. Before entering the rooms on the second floor there is an oblique view of the courtyard between the two wings of the museum seen here head on from above.

15. Im Scarlioni-Raum führen Stufen hinunter zu Michelangelos *Kreuzabnahme,* die hinter der polygonalen Steinmauer rechts aufgestellt ist; eine Stellwand aus Olivenholz leitet den Besucher in die Nische. Die Skulptur wird erst sichtbar, wenn der Besucher dieser »Aufforderung« gefolgt ist.

16. Wenn der Besucher die Nische verläßt, kann er wiederum den ganzen Raum 17 überblicken. Im Hintergrund

das Grabmal des Bischofs Battista Bagaroto, an der Wand das Zickzackmuster, das bei der Restaurierung aufgedeckt wurde. Die eingehängte Decke besteht aus Walnußbrettern; für die künstliche Beleuchtung sorgen zylindrische Hängelampen aus Messing.

17. Michelangelos unvollendete *Pietà Rondanini* in ihrer Nische, die sich aus ineinander verzahnten Steinplatten zusammensetzt.

18, 19. Der Brunnenhof hinter dem Scarlioni-Raum liegt am Ende der Raumfolge im Erdgeschoß. Wenn man den Balkon überquert, gelangt man über eine Treppe ins obere Geschoß. Der Innenhof bildet einen Orientierungspunkt und trennt die beiden Teile im ersten Abschnitt des Museums in deutlich geschiedene Bereiche.

20. Bevor der Besucher die Räume des zweiten Geschosses betritt, kann er von oben her den Hof zwischen den Flügeln des Museums überblicken.

18

19

20

21

22

23

24

25

26

21, 22. Platforms and movable screens define groups of furniture, tapestries and paintings in Rooms 16 to 19. Platforms are at three different levels and covered with various materials: wood; felt; blue, yellow-green and purple ceramic tiles.

23. The main picture gallery, Room 21, is top lit by a continuous skylight in which the light is filtered by movable wooden louvres seen in detail on page 174. Fabric covered screens with metal uprights and bronze bases subdivide the space.

24. Brickwork panels are angled towards the light which comes from two windows in Room 20. The tallest screen carries Andrea Mantegna's *Madonna with Angels*. This corner room with its isolated pictures seen against a solid background of unfinished plaster comes as a pause after the crowded spaces of the furniture galleries and is an introduction to the long top lit gallery which follows it.

25. The whole of one wing of the second floor was given over to twelve tapestries from the workshop of Vigevano. Each represents a month of the year and is based on drawings by Bramantino. They are displayed as if in a triumphal parade, hanging from wooden crossbeams supported by bright brass poles springing from shaped marble blocks in the floor. The tapestries have now been re-hung in Room 37, which is the main space of the part completed in 1963, and are shown in their new setting on Fig. 28.

26. Room 31 is a long gallery inserted into the double height of the largest volume of the second section, Room 37. The metal cases containing porcelain are cantilevered from the wall and have their own lighting.

27. The low part of Room 37 with windows facing the courtyard on the right lighting a display of musical instruments. The structure of the gallery overhead consists of steel beams painted a rust brown with exposed terracotta pots spanning between these.

28. Large hanging tapestries divide the two storey high space of Room 37. These formerly formed the triumphal parade in Room 24. The facetted ceiling of timber boards recalls the ceiling of the Scarlioni Room, the most important space in the first section of the museum.

29, 30. The bridge and staircase which link the second section back to the first and which, like the fountain court after the Scarlioni Room, provide the clear division between the various parts.

27

21, 22. Plattformen und bewegliche Stellwände akzentu-
ieren die Gruppen von Möbeln, Tapisserien und Gemälden in den Räumen 16 bis 19. Die Plattformen haben drei
verschiedene Höhen und sind mit unterschiedlichen
Materialien ausgelegt: Holz, Filz, blaue, gelbgrüne und
rote Keramikkacheln.

23. Die Gemäldegalerie in Raum 21 erhält Deckenbeleuchtung; das Licht wird durch verstellbare Holzlamellen gefiltert, die im Detail auf Seite 174 gezeigt sind. Stoffbespannte Stellwände mit Bronzefüßen und Metallstüt-
zen, die außerdem durch Drahtseile an der Decke befestigt sind, unterteilen den Raum.

24. In Raum 20 sind die Trennwände aus verputztem
Backstein so angeordnet, daß sie das von den beiden
Fenstern einfallende Licht auffangen. Die größte Wand
trägt Andrea Mantegnas *Madonna mit Engeln*. Dieser
Eckraum mit seinen isolierten Bildern, die sich von dem
ungestrichenen Putz der Zwischenwände abheben, bildet nach den vollgestellten Möbelsälen ein Intervall und
leitet zu einem langgestreckten Oberlichtsaal über.

25. Im zweiten Geschoß war ein ganzer Flügel zwölf Gobelins aus der Werkstatt von Vigevano gewidmet. Die Tapisserien beruhen auf Zeichnungen von Bramantino und
stellen die zwölf Monate des Jahres dar. Sie sind an Holzträgern aufgehängt, die auf gekreuzten Messingstangen
ruhen. Die Stangen sind am Boden in plastisch geformte
Marmorblocks eingesetzt. Diese Gobelins wurden nun in
Raum 37, der den Hauptraum des 1963 fertiggestellten
Teils darstellt, neu aufgehängt. Die jetzige Anordnung
der Gobelins zeigt Abb. 28.

26. Raum 31 ist eine lange Galerie, die in Raum 37, den
zwei Geschosse hohen und damit größten Ausstellungsbereich des zweiten Abschnitts, eingezogen wurde. Die
Metallvitrinen, in denen Porzellan gezeigt wird, kragen
aus der Wand aus und sind mit eigenen Lichtquellen versehen.

27. Der untere Teil von Raum 37; die Fenster zum Hof auf
der rechten Seite sorgen für die Beleuchtung der Sammlung von Musikinstrumenten. Die Konstruktion der eingezogenen Galerie besteht aus rostbraun gestrichenen
Stahlträgern mit dazwischengespannten unverputzten
Terrakotta-Platten.

28. Große Gobelins unterteilen die zwei Geschosse hohen
Raum 37. Sie bildeten früher den »Triumphzug« in
Raum 24. Die Holzriemendecke erinnert an die Decke
des Scarlioni-Raumes, des wichtigsten Saales im ersten
Teil des Museums.

29, 30. Die Brücke und die Treppe, die den zweiten Abschnitt wieder mit dem ersten verbinden. Wie der Brunnenhof hinter dem Scarlioni-Raum sorgen diese Elemente für eine klare Trennung zwischen den verschiedenen
Teilen des Museums.

28

29

30

Museum of the Treasury, San Lorenzo Cathedral, Genoa (1956)

Architect: Franco Albini

Schatzkammer der Kathedrale San Lorenzo, Genua (1956)

Architekt: Franco Albini

The Treasury is partly a museum, partly a depository of religious objects still used in the ceremonies of the cathedral. One of the design problems was thus to relate the exhibition space as closely as possible to the cathedral. This was achieved by sinking the museum 10 feet below the ground level in the courtyard adjoining the apse. A ramp connects it to the sacristy; the public entrance is by a flight of steps. The Treasury is also a permanent collection of a limited number of objects which is very unlikely to be altered. It was thus possible and desirable to design a series of spaces specifically related to these objects and to exploit the sense of permanence and of the special and sacred nature of many of the relics.

The ceiling is flat in the circulation areas, conical inside the tholos and is composed of concrete ribs balanced on the enclosing walls. The paving of the courtyard above repeats the pattern of these ribs. All spaces are air conditioned giving humidity control, essential in this underground situation.

Die Schatzkammer dient teils als Museum, teils als Verwahrungsort für religiöse Gegenstände, die noch bei liturgischen Handlungen in der Kathedrale verwendet werden. Es war also wichtig, den Ausstellungsraum so eng wie möglich mit der Kirche zu verbinden. Das Museum wurde deshalb im Hof an der Apsis 3 m unter Bodenniveau gelegt. Es ist durch eine Rampe mit der Sakristei verbunden; für das Publikum führt der Zugang über eine Treppe hinunter. Die Schatzkammer enthält unter anderem eine ständige Ausstellung von nicht sehr zahlreichen Kunstgegenständen, die wahrscheinlich nicht mehr erweitert oder verändert wird. Es war deshalb möglich und wünschenswert, eine Reihe von Räumen zu schaffen, die speziell auf die Objekte bezogen sind und dem sakralen Charakter der Kunstgegenstände Rechnung tragen.

Die Decke ist in den Bereichen, die der Zirkulation dienen, flach und innerhalb der Rundräume konisch. Sie besteht aus Betonrippen, die auf den umschließenden Wänden aufliegen. Der gepflasterte Hof darüber folgt dem Muster dieser Rippen. Alle Räume sind mit Klimaanlagen versehen, die die Luftfeuchtigkeit regulieren – hier ein besonders wichtiger Faktor, da das Museum unter der Erde liegt.

1. The steps down to the museum as seen from the public entrance; the door to the sacristy is on the left and some of the doors to the storage cupboards are open.
2. View from the entrance corridor past a statue of St. Lawrence to the first tholos containing the Holy Grail.
3. The Holy Grail, a first century A. D. Roman glass vessel, held on a three pronged support within a circular glass case.
4, 5. The main circulation area. Lighting, which is entirely artificial, is by spotlights fixed to conduit running in a groove between ceiling and wall, or by lights within the showcases, or immediately above them.
6. The vestments are displayed in glass cases lit by fluorescent lamps within a metal enclosure separated from the cases. The top layer of diffusing glass acts as a partial filter of the ultraviolet light emitted by the lamps which is liable to cause damage to the fabric.

1. Die Treppe, die hinunter zum Museum führt, vom öffentlichen Eingang aus gesehen; links die Tür zur Sakristei. Die Türen zu den Aufbewahrungsschränken sind hier geöffnet.
2. Blick vom Eingangskorridor zu einer Statue des heiligen Laurentius. Im Hintergrund der erste Rundraum mit dem Heiligen Gral.
3. Der Heilige Gral, ein römisches Glasgefäß aus dem ersten Jahrhundert nach Christus, wird durch einen dreigabeligen Ständer gehalten und von einem runden Glaskasten umschlossen.
4, 5. Die Zirkulationsfläche zwischen den Rundräumen. Für die – ausschließlich künstliche – Beleuchtung sorgen Spotlights, die an die in einer Rinne zwischen Decke und Wand verlaufende Leitung angeschlossen sind. Außerdem sind in den Vitrinen oder unmittelbar darüber Leuchtkörper installiert.
6. Die Meßgewänder sind in Glasvitrinen ausgestellt. Sie werden durch Leuchtstoffröhren erleuchtet, die in Metallrahmen über den Vitrinen angebracht sind. Das diffuse Glas, das die Vitrinen nach oben hin abschließt, wirkt als Filter und wehrt die ultravioletten Strahlen der Leuchtkörper zum Teil ab, da ultraviolettes Licht den Geweben schaden könnte.

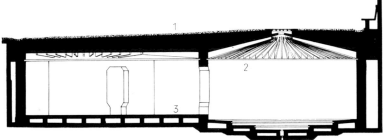

Plan / Grundriß.
1 Public entrance / Eingang für das Publikum
2 Entrance from the sacristy / Eingang von der Sakristei
3 Storage / Magazin
4 Air conditioning / Klimaanlage
5 Statue of San Lorenzo / Statue des heiligen Laurentius
6 Holy Grail / Heiliger Gral
7 Golden casket for the Holy Ashes / Goldener Schrein
8 Altar front / Altarantependium
9 Statue of the Virgin / Marienstatue
10 Vestments / Meßgewänder
11 Byzantine cross / Byzantinisches Zacharias-Kreuz
12 Relics / Reliquien
13 Shrine of the Ashes of St. John / Schrein für die Asche des Evangelisten Johannes
14 Altar fronts / Altarantependien

Transverse section / Querschnitt.
1 Cobble stone paving / Kopfsteinpflaster
2 Reinforced concrete beams / Betonrippen
3 Stone flooring / Steinfußboden

1

2

3

4

5

6

7

8

7, 8. The polygonal showcases in the two larger rooms follow the line of the top step; the main exhibit, in one case a pair of altar fronts, in the other a shrine for the ashes of St. John the Evangelist, are set within the circle formed by the lowest step.

7, 8. Die polygonalen Vitrinen in den beiden größeren Räumen folgen in der Linienführung der oberen Stufe; die wichtigsten Objekte, in dem einen Falle zwei Altarantependien, in dem anderen ein Schrein für die Asche des Evangelisten Johannes, sind in der kreisförmigen Vertiefung aufgestellt, die durch die untere Stufe entsteht.

9

9. Looking into the second tholos with the Byzantine Zachariah cross seen just beyond the entrance. This is on a hammered iron support with a flat glass front and a curved glass back.

9. Blick in den zweiten Rundraum mit dem byzantinischen Zacharias-Kreuz. Das Kreuz ist auf einem schmiedeeisernen Träger angebracht und wird von vorn durch eine flache, von hinten durch eine gekrümmte Glasplatte geschützt.

Gallery of Modern Art, Turin (1954–59)

Architects: Carlo Bassi and Goffredo Boschetti

Galleria d'Arte Moderna, Turin (1954–59)

Architekten: Carlo Bassi und Goffredo Boschetti

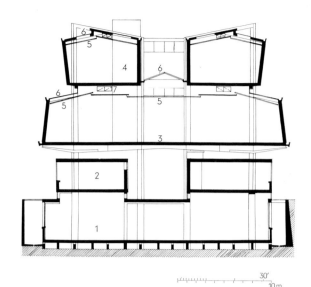

The Gallery, at the edge of the centre of the town, consists of three zones: a central main exhibition area, a smaller wing for temporary exhibitions and a subsidiary wing containing a library and a large lecture room. The design was considerably influenced by an attempt to devise an ideal lighting solution within a multistorey building and the section is undoubtedly the building's most interesting feature. Due to the cantilevered first floor, the splay of the exterior walls and the light-well in the centre it was possible to give sufficient toplight to both floors of the main exhibition building. Whether the devices necessary to produce this solution are in the end worthwhile in terms of the gallery as a whole is, however, very much open to question.

The lower floors facing the garden are entirely side lit, the upper ones mainly top lit except at the north end and in the centre of the main exhibition wing where there are glass doors opening on to balconies. The top lighting, both natural and artificial from fluorescent tubes, is diffused by corrugated acrylic sheet.

Das Museum, das am Rande des Stadtzentrums liegt, umfaßt drei Flügel: einen zentralen Ausstellungsbereich, einen kleineren Bau für Wechselausstellungen und einen weiteren Trakt mit Bibliothek und Vortragssaal. Es ging den Architekten vor allem darum, in dem mehrgeschossigen Hauptgebäude ideale Lichtverhältnisse zu schaffen. Diese Konzeption hatte starken Einfluß auf die Gesamtplanung, und der Schnitt ist wohl das interessanteste Merkmal des Gebäudes. Durch das Auskragen des ersten Obergeschosses, durch die unterschiedlichen Neigungswinkel der Außenwände und den Lichtschacht in der Mitte war es möglich, beide Hauptgeschosse des zentralen Ausstellungsbaus mit ausreichendem Oberlicht zu versehen. Fraglich erscheint, ob der Aufwand, den die Lösung des Beleuchtungsproblems erforderte, auch für die Gesamtwirkung des Museums günstig ist.

Die unteren Geschosse haben ausschließlich Seitenlicht, die oberen hauptsächlich Deckenlicht. Nur vor den Ruheräumen in der Mitte des Hauptflügels und an der Nordseite öffnen sich Glastüren auf Balkons. Das Deckenlicht (Tageslicht und Leuchtstoffröhren) wird durch gewellte Plexiglasplatten gefiltert.

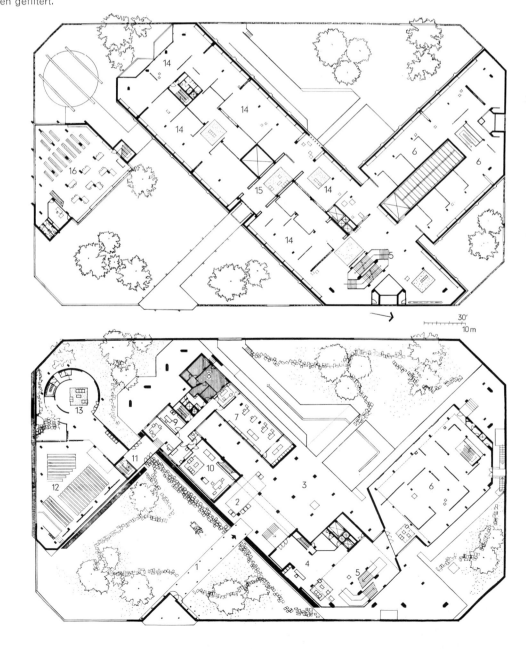

Transverse section / Querschnitt.
1 Storage / Magazin
2 Offices / Büros
3 First floor gallery / Ausstellungsräume im ersten Geschoß
4 Second floor galleries / Ausstellungsräume im zweiten Geschoß
5 Acrylic diffuser / Plexiglasplatten
6 Wired glass / Drahtglas
7 Air conditioning ducts / Klimaanlage

Plan, first floor / Grundriß erstes Geschoß.
Plan, ground floor / Grundriß Erdgeschoß.
 1 Covered way / Überdeckter Weg
 2 Fountain and pool / Wasserbecken mit Springbrunnen
 3 Porch / Vorhalle
 4 Entrance hall / Eingangshalle
 5 Main double stair / Doppelläufige Haupttreppe
 6 Temporary exhibition gallery / Raum für Wechselausstellungen
 7 Secretary's offices / Büros
 8 Flat / Wohnung
 9 Curator / Kurator
10 Director / Direktor
11 Stair to library / Treppe zur Bibliothek
12 Lecture hall seating 350 / Vortragssaal mit 350 Plätzen
13 Foyer to lecture hall / Foyer des Vortragssaales
14 Exhibition gallery / Ausstellungsräume
15 Rest area / Ruheraum
16 Library / Bibliothek

1. The central exhibition building with the covered way leading to the entrance.
2. Pictures are hung on free standing screens or on wires stretched over frames which stand clear of the sloping outside walls on the upper two floors.
3. The covered entrance space with a pool and fountain on the left, the steps to the main entrance on the right. Such covered transitional zones can help to adapt the eye to the difference in light levels between outside and inside.
4. The main staircase consists of two interlocking stairs, one to be used ascending, the other descending.
5. In the basement, paintings are stored on wire mesh screens supported on aluminium tubing.

1. Das Hauptausstellungsgebäude mit dem überdeckten Weg zum Eingang.
2. Die Bilder hängen an frei stehenden Stellwänden oder an Drähten, die an Holzleisten befestigt sind. Die Leisten wurden frei vor den geneigten Außenwänden der beiden oberen Geschosse angebracht.
3. Der überdeckte Eingangsbereich; links ein Wasserbecken mit Springbrunnen, rechts die Treppe zum Haupteingang. Solche Übergangszonen tragen dazu bei, das Auge an die Lichtunterschiede zwischen Außen und Innen zu gewöhnen.
4. Die Haupttreppe zum ersten Geschoß setzt sich aus zwei Treppenläufen zusammen, von denen der eine zum Hinaufgehen, der andere zum Hinuntergehen benutzt wird.
5. Im Untergeschoß, das das Magazin enthält, hängen die Bilder an Maschendrahtelementen, die an Gestellen aus Aluminiumröhren befestigt sind.

6

7

6. One of the galleries on the top floor.
7. The balcony on the north end of the first floor interrupting the sequence of top lit spaces and giving a glimpse of the garden.
8, 9. Two of the subsidiary spaces in the east wing: a lecture hall seating 350 on the ground floor and a library for 20,000 volumes on the first floor.

6. Einer der Säle im zweiten Geschoß.
7. Der Balkon an der Nordseite des ersten Geschosses gibt Seitenlicht und erlaubt einen Blick in den Garten. Die angrenzenden Räume erhalten Deckenlicht.
8, 9. Der Ostflügel des Museums enthält im Erdgeschoß einen Vortragssaal mit 350 Plätzen und im ersten Geschoß eine Bibliothek für 20000 Bände.

8

9

Municipal Museum of Castelvecchio, Verona (1958–61)

Architect: Carlo Scarpa

Museo Civico di Castelvecchio, Verona (1958–61)

Architekt: Carlo Scarpa

Scarpa's reconstruction of the museum in the Castelvecchio is based on very much the same principles as his work at Palermo and achieves here with an extraordinary economy of means a unique museum and an unambiguous restoration of a 14th century building. The economy is deliberate and stems from the most careful and thorough consideration of every object and every detail. As a result there is also no doubt that there is a reciprocal action between object and enclosure, that the museum gains enormously by being within a worthy architectural setting and that the building in turn benefits by housing a museum.

The Castelvecchio was considerably restored between 1923 and 1926. Certain of these restorations were kept when further rebuilding became necessary after the damage caused in 1945 when the bridges across the Adige were blown-up. Superficial restorations were however removed and the original fabric revealed. Additions to the building – stairs, gates, linking bridges – bear no stylistic resemblance to their surroundings but are complementary to them. They carry the unmistakable imprint of the work of Scarpa.

Scarpas Neugestaltung des Museums im Castelvecchio beruht weitgehend auf den Prinzipien, die er in Palermo angewandt hatte. Mit außerordentlich sparsamen Mitteln schuf er ein eindrucksvolles Museum in einem vorzüglich restaurierten Gebäude aus dem 14. Jahrhundert. Diese Ökonomie der Mittel wurde ermöglicht durch die Sorgfalt, mit der Scarpa jeden Gegenstand und jedes Detail berücksichtigte. Dadurch entstand ein Wechselspiel zwischen Objekt und Umgebung; wie das Museum durch den würdigen architektonischen Rahmen gewinnt, so gewinnt umgekehrt das Gebäude dadurch, daß es ein Museum aufnimmt.

Das Castelvecchio ist zwischen 1923 und 1926 stark restauriert worden. Als nach den Zerstörungen des zweiten Weltkrieges – verursacht durch die Sprengung der Etsch-Brücken – der Wiederaufbau begann, wurden einige Ergebnisse dieser Restaurierungen beibehalten. Veränderungen der Wandflächen wurden jedoch entfernt, damit die ursprüngliche Struktur wieder zum Vorschein kommen konnte. Die Elemente, die Scarpa hinzufügte – Treppen, Tore, Verbindungsbrücken –, haben keine stilistische Verwandtschaft mit dem eigentlichen Gebäude, sondern sind als Ergänzungen kenntlich gemacht. Sie tragen den charakteristischen Stempel des Architekten.

1–3. The ground floor sequence of rooms contains sculpture of the 13th and 14th century from Verona. It is always arranged to form groups which can be seen as a whole and which are related to an observer moving from room to room but which can nevertheless be studied individually.
4. The reveals of the windows are splayed so as to grade the light coming in.
5, 6. Small pieces of sculpture are bracketed out from the wall or set within a recess which has been coloured so as to establish a distinction between wall and display.
7. Large pieces of sculpture rest on simple pedestals of precast concrete; the slot down the centre and the boardmarks on the concrete do something to preserve a sense of scale between the 14th century sculpture and its support.

1–3. Die Raumflucht im Erdgeschoß zeigt Veroneser Plastik aus dem 13. und 14. Jahrhundert. Die Skulpturen sind so angeordnet, daß ein von Raum zu Raum schreitender Besucher sie als Gruppen, aber natürlich auch als einzelne Kunstwerke betrachten kann.
4. Die Fensterlaibungen wurden abgeschrägt, um das einfallende Licht besser zu differenzieren.
5, 6. Kleinere Plastiken sind auf Wandkonsolen befestigt oder in Wandvertiefungen eingesetzt, die farbig gestrichen wurden, damit sich der Ausstellungsgegenstand von der Mauer abhebt.
7. Große Skulpturen sind auf einfachen Sockeln aus Beton-Fertigelementen aufgestellt. Der Schlitz in der Mitte und die Schalungsstreifen des Betons tragen dazu bei, die Proportionen zwischen der Plastik des 14. Jahrhunderts und dem Sockel in Übereinstimmung zu bringen.

1 Courtyard / Hof
2 Entrance hall / Eingangshalle
3 Galleries, ground floor / Ausstellungsräume, Erdgeschoß
4 Morbio Gate / Porta del Morbio
5 Tower / Turm
6 Library / Bibliothek
7 Offices / Büros
8 Parts of the Castle not belonging to the museum / Gebäudeteile, die nicht zum Museum gehören
9 Bridge / Verbindungsbrücke
10 Staircase from ground to second floor / Treppe vom Erdgeschoß ins zweite Geschoß
11 Large hall / Große Ausstellungshalle
12 Galleries, first floor / Ausstellungsräume, 1. Geschoß
13 Galleries (these are seen after those on second floor reached from Room 11) / Ausstellungsräume (der Besucher gelangt in diese Räume, nachdem er von Raum 11 aus die Säle im 2. Geschoß besichtigt hat)
14 Concert hall / Konzertsaal
15 Galleries, 2nd floor / Ausstellungsräume, 2. Geschoß
16 Stairs down to galleries on the first floor / Treppe zu den Ausstellungsräumen im ersten Geschoß

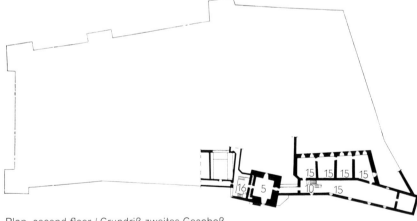

Plan, second floor / Grundriß zweites Geschoß.

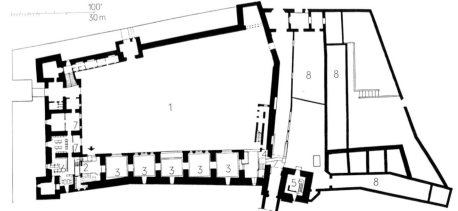

Plan, ground floor / Grundriß Erdgeschoß.

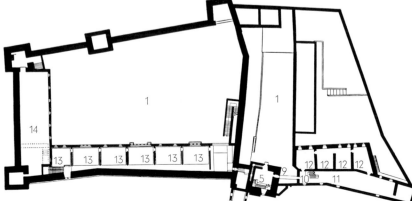

Plan, first floor / Grundriß erstes Geschoß.

1

2

3

4

5

6

7

8. The new sliding folding metal screen is the entrance to the 12th century *Morbio Gate*, part of a castle tower which acts as the pivotal point within the museum layout.

9. The new staircase within the tower.

10. The tower is linked to the picture gallery on the first floor by a new bridge from which there is a view of a courtyard and foliage.

11. To the side of the large hall there are four smaller interconnecting rooms; pictures are held clear of the wall so as to be more sharply defined and to let the air circulate on both sides.

8. Durch die eiserne Schiebe- und Falttür gelangt man zur neuerdings freigelegten *Porta del Morbio* aus dem 12. Jahrhundert. Sie ist Teil eines Burgturms, der innerhalb der Museumsneugestaltung eine Art Scharnier bildet.

9. Die neue Treppe im Turm.

10. Der Turm ist mit der Bildergalerie im ersten Geschoß durch eine neue Verbindungsbrücke verbunden, die einen Blick auf den Hof freigibt.

11. Neben der großen Halle liegen vier miteinander verbundene kleinere Räume. Die Bilder sind frei vor der Wand angebracht, so daß sie sich deutlicher abheben und die Luft auf beiden Seiten zirkulieren kann.

11

12

13

14

12, 15. The end room of the second floor with Stefano da Zevio's *Madonna in the Rose Garden* between two iron rods and the remaining pictures on easles, on the wall or, like pages of a book, turned to face the light.

13, 14, 16. Part of the large hall immediately beyond the bridge is at first screened by a new staircase to the second floor and its angular shape is not fully revealed until one has walked past the crucifix. Objects are placed within the room so that they relate to the light coming in and at the same time punctuate the long space; a gold altar piece glows in the furthest corner.

12, 15. Der hinterste Raum des zweiten Geschosses mit Stefano da Zevios Gemälde *Madonna im Rosengarten*, das zwischen zwei Eisenstäben befestigt ist. Die übrigen Bilder stehen auf Staffeleien, hängen an den Wänden oder sind wie die Seiten eines Buches auf Schwenkarmen dem Licht zugekehrt.

13, 14, 16. Von der großen Halle hinter der Brücke führt eine neue Treppe in das zweite Geschoß. Die winklig gebrochene Form der Halle wird erst dann ganz deutlich, wenn der Besucher an dem Kruzifix vorbeigegangen ist. Die Kunstwerke sind so angeordnet, daß sie das einfallende Licht auffangen und gleichzeitig den langen Raum artikulieren. Im Hintergrund der Halle ein goldener Altaraufsatz.

15

16

Museo Correr, Venice (1953–61)

Architect: Carlo Scarpa

Museo Correr, Venedig (1953–61)

Architekt: Carlo Scarpa

The Museo Correr in the Procuratie Nuove facing the Piazza San Marco in Venice contains paintings and sculpture acquired by Teodoro Correr, the 19th century founder of the museum. Its fame rests on its collection of early Venetian paintings and on works by Antonello, the Bellinis and Carpaccio. The historical section of the museum occupies the first floor of the building and was arranged by Carlo Scarpa in 1953. The picture gallery on the second floor was opened in 1961 and it is this part which is illustrated in the pages which follow.
Like the Palazzo Abbatellis in Palermo and the Castelvecchio in Verona, the Correr shows Scarpa's great awareness of the museum as an experience dependent on viewing objects in sequence, a sequence which, like a piece of literature, requires punctuation and a choice of language related to content.

Das Museo Correr in den Neuen Prokurazien an der Piazza San Marco in Venedig enthält Malerei und Plastik aus dem Besitz von Teodoro Correr, der im 19. Jahrhundert das Museum gründete. Der Ruhm des Museums beruht vor allem auf seiner Sammlung früher venezianischer Gemälde und auf den Werken von Antonello, den Bellinis und Carpaccio. Die historische Abteilung des Museums nimmt das erste Geschoß des Gebäudes ein und wurde 1953 von Carlo Scarpa gestaltet. Im zweiten Geschoß befindet sich die Bildergalerie (eröffnet 1961), von der hier die Rede ist.
Wie der Palazzo Abbatellis in Palermo und das Castelvecchio in Verona zeigt auch das Museo Correr, daß Scarpa den Museumsbesuch als ein Erlebnis auffaßt, das weitgehend von der optischen Aufeinanderfolge der Ausstellungsgegenstände abhängt. Für eine solche Abfolge ist – wie bei einem literarischen Werk – eine Sprache notwendig, die dem Inhalt angemessen ist und Akzente setzt.

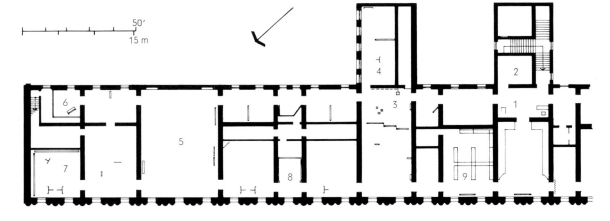

Plan, second floor / Grundriß zweites Geschoß.
1 Entrance and stair from floor below / Eingang und Treppe vom ersten Geschoß
2 Gallery containing the first Venetian painting on wood / Ausstellungsraum mit der ersten venezianischen Holzmalerei
3 Sculpture room / Plastik-Raum
4 Venetian Gothic paintings / Gemälde der venezianischen Gotik
5 Room of the Four Doors / Raum der vier Türen
6 Antonello room / Antonello-Raum
7 Bellini room / Bellini-Raum
8 Carpaccio recess / Carpaccio-Nische
9 Majolica ware / Majolika-Sammlung

1. A room in the Correr with 16th century paintings and a coin collection as it appeared when arranged in 1939.
2. The mahogany wall which screens the entrance from the first room.

1. Ein Ausstellungsraum des Museums mit einer Münzsammlung und Gemälden aus dem 16. Jahrhundert, wie er im Jahre 1939 aussah.
2. Eine Holzwand aus Mahagoni schirmt den Eingang gegen den ersten Ausstellungsraum ab.

3

4

3, 4. The kneeling figure of a Venetian Doge – a statue of Tommaso Mosenigo by Jacobello delle Mesegne – is first seen in profile from an adjoining room and only later head-on against a blank wall behind it and subsequently again in a three quarter view against the screen in the corner. The statue stands on a stone pedestal shaped somewhat like a capital and slotted over an iron support which thrusts it forward as if offered, suggesting its possible original position on a monument or altar.

3, 4. Die kniende Gestalt des venezianischen Dogen Tommaso Mosenigo von Jacobello delle Mesegne wird zunächst von einem benachbarten Raum aus im Profil sichtbar, danach en face vor der weißen Wand, dann in Dreiviertelansicht vor dem Schirm in der Ecke. Die Statue ruht auf einem geschlitzten Steinsockel, dessen Form an ein Kapitell erinnert. Der Sockel ist auf einen nach vorn ausgewinkelten Eisenträger gestülpt und bietet sozusagen die Gestalt dar; die ursprüngliche Aufstellung auf einem Grabmal oder Altar wird auf diese Weise angedeutet.

5

6

7

5–7. The figure of the Doge faces a room which goes across the width of the building and which is crossed twice during the circuit of the museum. The two paths are separated by a translucent glass screen and by fragments of a stone balustrade set in a metal frame which corresponds in length to the original length of the complete balustrade. The head-on view of the Doge from the far side of the room acts as a reminder of one's first encounter and provides a clue to one's position in the sequence of rooms.

5–7. Die Dogenstatue blickt auf einen Raum, der sich über die ganze Breite des Museums erstreckt und vom Besucher bei einem Rundgang zweimal durchschritten wird. Die beiden Zirkulationswege sind durch eine transparente Glaswand und durch Fragmente einer Steinbalustrade getrennt, die in Metallrahmen eingefaßt sind. Die Rahmen bezeichnen die ursprüngliche Länge der Balustrade. Die Frontalansicht des Dogen vom anderen Ende des Raumes erinnert an den ersten Anblick der Statue und dient so als Orientierung innerhalb der Raumfolge.

8

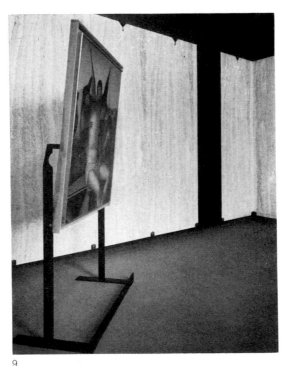

9

8. The painted crucifix in the room devoted to 14th century Venetian painting is able to pivot so that it can be turned towards the window during the day, towards the artificial light at night.

9. Antonello da Messina's *Pietà* is in a small room at the end of the second floor. Two of the walls are partially obscured by a travertine screen and to signal the special quality of this room the floor is carpeted. The plaster wall behind the travertine is painted brown so that all the attention is focussed on the lower half of the space and particularly the painting tilted slightly towards the visitor.

8. Das bemalte Kruzifix in dem Raum, der venezianische Malerei aus dem 14. Jahrhundert zeigt, kann tagsüber zum Fenster hin gedreht werden und abends entsprechend der künstlichen Beleuchtung durch die Deckenleuchten.

9. Die *Pietà* von Antonello da Messina ist in einem kleinen Raum am Ende des zweiten Geschosses untergebracht. Zwei Wände des Raumes sind bis zu halber Höhe mit Travertinplatten verkleidet. Um den besonderen Charakter dieses Raumes hervorzuheben, wurde der Boden mit Teppichen ausgelegt. Die verputzte Wand hinter den Travertinplatten ist braun gestrichen, so daß die Aufmerksamkeit sich auf die untere Hälfte des Raumes und vor allem auf das Bild konzentriert, das sich dem Besucher leicht entgegenneigt.

10

11

12

10. Many of the pictures, particularly those near windows, are shown on specially designed metal easels with movable ledges.

11. The support of a bust which stands in front of the translucent glass screen.

12. Two related paintings inclined towards each other.

10. Eine große Zahl von Bildern wird – vor allem in der Nähe von Fenstern – auf speziell entworfenen, verstellbaren Staffeleien gezeigt.

11. Der eiserne Träger einer Büste, die vor der transparenten Glaswand steht.

12. Zwei zusammengehörige Bilder sind mit Hilfe einer zweiteiligen Rahmenkonstruktion eng aufeinander bezogen.

13

14

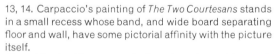

13, 14. Carpaccio's painting of *The Two Courtesans* stands in a small recess whose band, and wide board separating floor and wall, have some pictorial affinity with the picture itself.

15, 16. The last two rooms before the exit contain a collection of majolica ware in black steel framed cases. These are lit from above through a diffusing screen made of linen stretched across the top sheet of glass.

13, 14. Carpaccios Gemälde *Die zwei Kurtisanen* ist in einer kleinen Nische untergebracht. Der Wandstreifen und die breiten Leisten zwischen Fußboden und Wand sind auf bildnerische Elemente des Gemäldes bezogen.

15, 16. Die beiden letzten Räume vor dem Ausgang zeigen eine Majolika-Sammlung in Vitrinen mit schwarzlackierten Stahlrahmen. Die oberen Glasplatten der Vitrinen sind mit Leinen bespannt, so daß das von oben einfallende Licht der Scheinwerfer gestreut wird.

15

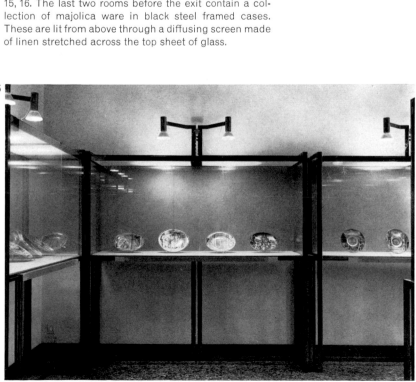

16

1

Palazzo Rosso, Genoa (1953–61)

Architect: Franco Albini

The Palazzo Rosso is the third in the series of Genoese museums for which Albini has been responsible. The fourth, a restoration of the church of Sant'Agostino in which sculpture and architectural fragments will be exhibited in the cloisters and in a new addition, is under consideration. The three completed works all exemplify Albini's great concern for the museum as a working combination of space and exhibit and for the subtle relationship between old and new.

The palazzo dates from 1671–1677 and was built for two brothers, Rodolfo and Giò Francesco Brignole-Sale, by Matteo Lagomaggiore. Each brother had his own piano nobile so that the building now has the curious section of two principal floors each with its own mezzanine. The building is one of the best surviving examples of baroque in Genoa and the new arrangement by Albini, done like the Palazzo Bianco in collaboration with Caterina Marcenaro, is deliberately intended to make the architecture the main object of display. The studiedly detailed glass screens emphasise and exploit the transparency and continuity of internal spaces and allow the frescoes of the upper piano nobile to play their full part.

Certain of the details are very similar to those at the Palazzo Bianco. This applies particularly to the flexible system of supporting pictures on rods suspended from a continuous metal bar at cornice level. Lights also come down from this bar and consist of metal cones around Zeiss projectors with corrugated mirrors.

Key to plans / Legende zu den Plänen:
1 Entrance / Eingang
2 Temporary exhibitions / Wechselausstellungen
3 Lavatories / Toiletten
4 Control room / Kontrolle
5 Courtyard / Hof
6 Photographic exhibitions / Fotoausstellungen
7 Staff room / Raum für Museumsangestellte
8 Garden / Garten
9 North Loggia / Nordloggia
10 Exhibition galleries / Ausstellungsräume
11 South Loggia / Südloggia
12 Textile storage / Magazin für Textilien
13 Staircase / Treppe
14 Exhibition galleries in subsidiary wing / Ausstellungsräume im Nebenflügel
15 Ceramics storage / Magazin für Keramik
16 Storage / Magazin
17 Terrace / Terrasse

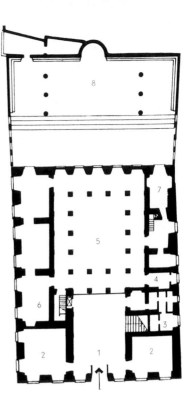

Plan, ground floor / Grundriß Erdgeschoß.

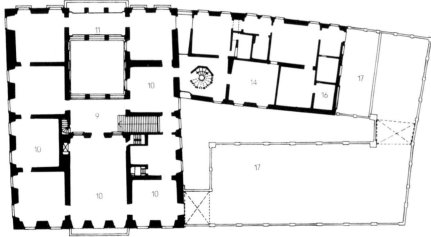

Plan, first piano nobile / Grundriß erster piano nobile.

Plan, second piano nobile / Grundriß zweiter piano nobile.

1

2

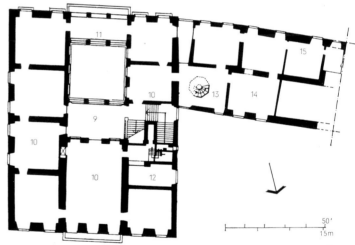

6

Palazzo Rosso, Genua (1953–61)

Architekt: Franco Albini

Der Palazzo Rosso ist das dritte Museum in Genua, für das Franco Albini verantwortlich zeichnet. Das vierte, das aus der restaurierten Kirche Sant'Agostino mit ihren Kreuzgängen sowie einem neuen Anbau bestehen und Plastik und Architekturfragmente ausstellen soll, wird zur Zeit geplant. Die drei fertiggestellten Museen veranschaulichen, wie sehr Albini das Museum als eine Einheit von Raum und Ausstellungsgegenstand auffaßt und sich für eine harmonische Verbindung von alt und neu einsetzt. Der Palazzo wurde 1671–77 von Matteo Lagomaggiore für die Brüder Rodolfo und Giò Francesco Brignole-Sale errichtet. Jeder Bruder hatte seinen eigenen piano nobile, so daß das Gebäude kurioserweise in zwei Hauptgeschosse mit je einem Zwischengeschoß eingeteilt ist. Der Palazzo ist eines der besten noch erhaltenen Beispiele für Barockarchitektur in Genua, und die Neugestaltung Albinis (wie beim Palazzo Bianco in Zusammenarbeit mit Caterina Marcenaro) sucht bewußt die Architektur zum wichtigsten Ausstellungsgegenstand zu machen. Die geschickt angebrachten Glaswände betonen die Transparenz und die Kontinuität der Raumfolgen und bringen die Fresken im oberen piano nobile zu voller Geltung.
Einige Details sind denen im Palazzo Bianco sehr ähnlich. Das trifft besonders auf das flexible System zu, bei dem die Bilder an Stäben hängen, die an einer in Gesimshöhe

3

4

umlaufenden Metallschiene befestigt sind. Auch die Beleuchtung, die aus konischen Metallschirmen um Zeiss-Projektoren mit gewellten Spiegeln besteht, ist an dieser Schiene angebracht.

5

1. The entrance hall at ground level with a view through the glass screen to the central courtyard. The main staircase to the upper floors is on the right. The screen has opening sections between columns, fixed glazing in front of them. The glass is held by dark bronze members. The space under the arch is filled by glass set into the plaster. A horizontal sheet of glass joins the screen to these inset pieces to give continuous enclosure.
2. The doorway at the end of the vista seen at night.
3. The two superimposed southern loggias face the central courtyard and their sparse glass screens allow this inner space to go through to the outside.
4. There is a small walled garden on the south side of the building. The three new lower doors allow a view through from the entrance hall and the courtyard to a baroque doorway in the garden wall. The restored ground floor wall is grey mauve, the original cornices are red, the shutters white on their inner faces, green on their outer.
5. The central room on the first piano nobile. The floor is white marble, the walls grey plaster. The paintings by Bordone on either side of the door are on swivelling supports.

1. Die Eingangshalle im Erdgeschoß mit Blick durch die Glaswand auf den Hof. Rechts die Haupttreppe zu den oberen Geschossen. Zwischen den Stützen sind Glasflächen an dunklen bronzenen Halterungen befestigt. Die Verglasung der Bögen ist in den Putz eingelassen. Ein horizontales Glasband verbindet die in verschiedenen Ebenen angeordneten vertikalen Glasflächen.
2. Das Tor am Ende der Eingangsachse bei Nacht.
3. Die beiden übereinanderliegenden Südloggien öffnen sich zum zentralen Hof hin; dank der Glaswände scheint sich der Innenraum nach außen fortzusetzen.
4. An der Südseite des Gebäudes liegt ein von einer Mauer umgebener kleiner Garten. Die drei neuen niedrigeren Türen erlauben einen Blick von der Eingangshalle über den Hof zu einem barocken Tor in der Gartenmauer. Die restaurierte Wand des Erdgeschosses ist von einem hellen Grauviolett, die alten Gesimse sind rot, die Fensterläden innen weiß und außen grün.
5. Der Hauptraum auf dem ersten piano nobile. Der Boden ist weißer Marmor, die Wände sind grau getüncht. Die Bilder von Bordone zu beiden Seiten der Tür sind auf schwenkbaren Stützen angebracht.

6

6. Certain of the pictures can be turned towards the light; these are mounted on swivelling arms cantilevered from a steel pipe fixed to the wall.

7. The steel arm consists of a sleeve within which a further arm with a vertical cross piece is able to slide. This is fixed to the back of the picture and can be adjusted to fit its size. The back of the paintings has been covered with red fabric. The holes are for ventilation.

6. Einige Bilder können zum Licht gedreht werden. Sie sind auf Schwenkarmen montiert, die von einem an der Wand befestigten Stahlrohr auskragen.

7. Der Stahlarm besteht aus einem Führungselement und einem ausziehbaren Arm mit einem vertikalen Kreuzungsstück, das an der Rückseite des Bildes befestigt und dem Format entsprechend variiert werden kann. Die Rückseiten der Bilder sind mit rotem Stoff verkleidet; die Löcher dienen der Ventilation.

7

8

9

10

11

13

12

8. A painting by Giò Antonio Galli turned away from the wall on its swivelling bracket.

9. The Southern Loggia on the second piano nobile contains a ceiling frescoe by Paolo Gerolamo Piola and a *trompe l'oeil* painting of a crumbling brick arch on the end wall by Niccolò Viviano. Both gain greatly by the complete transparency of the two glass screens.

10. At the nodal point between the palace and the service wing a new octagonal staircase goes through four floors. This is held by eight outer rods hanging from each floor slab and eight inner rods suspended from the top floor ceiling. The continuous timber handrail is covered in leather, the treads with red carpet.

11. The service wing houses the less important exhibits. Most of these are in glass cabinets cross-shaped on plan, the arms having unequal lengths. The structure is made up of steel angles. Lights are contained within the cabinet at the outer recessed edge of the upper shelf: one fluorescent light shining downwards, the other upwards.

12. Small cabinets are suspended from the high level steel bars rather like the pictures on the main floors of the palace. The vulnerable corners of openings between rooms are protected by round grey marble edges.

13. The passage between the palace and its service wing above the first floor with a new staircase connection in white marble. A cabinet containing weights is suspended on rods on the far wall.

14. The top floors of the building contain museum offices, the library and the offices of the Municipal Fine Art Commission.

15. Part of the library under the steeply sloping roof forms the gallery to the room seen in Fig. 14. The floor is made up in the traditional lozenge-shaped pattern of marble and slate.

8. Ein Gemälde von Giò Antonio Galli, das auf seinem Schwenkarm von der Wand weggedreht ist.

9. Die Südloggia im zweiten piano nobile enthält ein Dekkenfresko von Paolo Gerolamo Piola und an der Stirnseite ein Wandfresko von Niccolò Viviano, das eine zerbrökkelnde Säulenarchitektur darstellt. Beide Kunstwerke profitieren von der völligen Transparenz der zwei Glaswände.

10. An dem Verbindungspunkt zwischen dem Palazzo und dem Nebenflügel führt eine neue oktagonale Treppe durch vier Geschosse. Sie wird außen von acht Stahlstangen gehalten, die jeweils an den Geschoßflächen abgehängt sind, und innen von acht weiteren Stahlstangen, die an der Decke des obersten Geschosses hängen. Der durchgehende Handlauf aus Holz ist mit Leder verkleidet; die Stufen sind mit rotem Teppich ausgelegt.

11. Der Nebenflügel nimmt die weniger wichtigen Ausstellungsgegenstände auf. Sie sind meist in Glasschränken von kreuzförmigem Grundriß bei ungleichmäßiger Länge der Kreuzarme untergebracht. Die Konstruktion besteht aus Stahlwinkelprofilen. In den Schränken ist am zurückgesetzten äußeren Rand des oberen Fachbodens die Beleuchtung angebracht: eine Leuchtstoffröhre gibt Licht nach unten ab, die andere nach oben.

12. An den in Gesimshöhe befestigten Stahlstäben hängen Vitrinen, ähnlich wie die Bilder in den Hauptgeschossen des Palazzo. Die empfindlichen Kanten der Öffnungen zwischen den Räumen werden durch runde Profile aus grauem Marmor geschützt.

13. Die Verbindung zwischen dem Palazzo und dem Nebenflügel oberhalb des ersten Geschosses mit der neuen Treppe aus weißem Marmor. An der Wand im Hintergrund hängt an Stäben eine Vitrine mit Gewichten.

14. In den oberen Geschossen des Gebäudes sind Verwaltung, Bibliothek und die Büros der Städtischen Kunstkommission untergebracht.

15. Ein Teil der Bibliothek unter dem Steildach bildet die Galerie, die in dem Raum auf Abb. 14 eingezogen ist. Der Boden ist mit Marmor und Schiefer im herkömmlichen Rautenmuster belegt.

14

15

Van der Steur's design interest while working on the Boymans in Rotterdam which opened in 1935 obviously centred on the means of controlling daylight. The Boymans is one of the earliest examples of a serious study of throwing light on the wall surface apart from certain experiments in the 19th century.

The same interest is evident in Henry van de Velde's design for the Kröller-Müller in Otterlo which though in the middle of a National Park of unspoilt forest and heath is a series of enclosed and entirely top lit rooms. Only the sculpture gallery at the far end of the building in any way reveals the scenery outside. The intention seems perverse and the bleaching effect of the unrelieved skylight does nothing in fact to enhance the great collection of Van Goghs.

Sandberg's emphasis on side lighting in the addition to the Stedelijk in Amsterdam, built while he was its director, and, equally, on the creation of a total museum environment is thus all the more significant. It was part of a move to make museum going a more everyday activity. The move has proved enormously successful and its most recent architectural manifestation is Rietveld's small gallery, the Zonnehof, at the edge of the town centre of Amersfoort. It is a single two-storey rectangular room, partly side-lit, partly top-lit, with a gallery on three sides. It is even more straightforward than his pavilion at the Biennale or the brick sculpture pavilion he designed for a temporary exhibition at Arnhem. This feeling of simplicity is now a recurring theme in Dutch exhibition design and can be found, for instance, in a little exhibition space which the printers de Jong added to their works in Hilversum and which though it doubles as a works' canteen is nevertheless a greatly sought after gallery.

Bei seinem Entwurf für das Museum Boymans in Rotterdam, das 1935 eröffnet wurde, befaßte sich A. van der Steur besonders eingehend mit der Regulierung des einfallenden Tageslichts: Er lenkte das Licht durch Lamellen von der Decke her auf die Wandflächen der Ausstellungsräume. In der Tat gehört das Museum Boymans – abgesehen von einigen Experimenten des 19. Jahrhunderts – zu den ersten Museumsbauten, bei denen das Problem der Lichtführung sorgfältig untersucht wurde.

Die Räume in Henry van de Veldes Museum Kröller-Müller in Otterlo sind ausschließlich durch Oberlichter erhellt. Obwohl das Bauwerk im Nationalpark Hoge Veluwe liegt und von Wald und Heide umgeben ist, kann der Besucher nur von dem Plastiksaal im neuen Flügel des Museums einen Blick auf die Landschaft werfen. Die Konzeption des Architekten entspricht also nicht den Gegebenheiten, und die bleichende Wirkung des ungemilderten Tageslichts ist für die umfangreiche Van-Gogh-Sammlung nicht gerade günstig.

Um so bedeutsamer erscheint es daher, daß Sandberg bei dem Anbau des Stedelijk Museums in Amsterdam für Seitenbeleuchtung plädierte und einen umfassenden Museumsbereich schuf. Er wollte den Museumsbesuch in den Alltag einbeziehen – eine Ansicht, die sich in der Folge immer mehr durchsetzte. Das jüngste Beispiel für diese Tendenz ist Rietvelds kleines Museum Zonnehof am Rande des Stadtzentrums von Amersfoort, ein rechteckiger Ausstellungssaal mit Seiten- und Oberlichtbeleuchtung, der zwei Geschosse hoch und an drei Seiten von Galerien umgeben ist. Das Bauwerk wirkt noch schlichter als Rietvelds Holländischer Pavillon für die Biennale in Venedig (1954) oder als sein Backstein-Pavillon für eine Plastikausstellung in Arnhem. Die Vorliebe für einfache Formen ist überhaupt ein Charakteristikum der neueren Ausstellungsbauten in den Niederlanden. Sie findet sich zum Beispiel auch in dem Ausstellungsraum der Druckerei de Jong in Hilversum, einer vielbesuchten Galerie, die gleichzeitig als Werkskantine benutzt wird.

1, 2. Boymans-van Beuningen Museum, Rotterdam (1931 to 1935). Architect: A. van der Steur. Various louvre arrangements were used in the ceiling to direct the light from the overhead skylights onto the wall surface or sculpture. The artificial lighting is in the space between the louvres and the skylight.

1, 2. Museum Boymans-van Beuningen, Rotterdam (1931 bis 1935). Architekt: A. van der Steur. Metall-Lamellen an der Decke lenken das Tageslicht von den Oberlichtern auf Wände oder Skulpturen. Die künstliche Beleuchtung ist zwischen den Lamellen und dem Oberlicht installiert.

1

2

Stedelijk Museum, Amsterdam (1954)

Architect: Architectural Dept. Municipality of Amsterdam;
Interior F. A. Eschauzier, Collaborator Bart van Kasteel

Stedelijk Museum, Amsterdam (1954)

Architekt: Stadtbauamt Amsterdam; Innenausstattung
F. A. Eschauzier, Mitarbeiter Bart van Kasteel

The Stedelijk stands at the edge of a large square in Amsterdam which is closed at one end by the vast brick complex of the Rijksmuseum and at the other by the Concertgebouw building. One might therefore suppose it to be part of a self-contained monumental cultural centre, remote and forbidding. Yet nothing could be further from the truth. W. Sandberg who was its director for sixteen years until his retirement at the end of 1962 has, on the contrary, made it one of the most simple and lively museums in Europe. It is one of the few in which children seem – and are – as naturally part of the place as in a school. The main building was completely renovated internally in 1945 and a new wing meant for temporary exhibitions was added at right angles to the existing building in 1954. This is a two-storey building entirely side-lit down its two long walls.

Das Stedelijk Museum liegt an einem großen Amsterdamer Platz, der an der einen Seite von dem riesigen Backsteinkomplex des Rijksmuseums, an der anderen vom Concertgebouw begrenzt wird. Man könnte das Museum deshalb für den Bestandteil eines autonomen, monumentalen Kulturzentrums halten, für eine Institution, die sich souverän und abweisend gebärdet. Nichts wäre weiter von der Wirklichkeit entfernt. W. Sandberg, der das Stedelijk sechzehn Jahre lang bis zu seiner Pensionierung Ende 1962 leitete, hat daraus eines der einfachsten und lebendigsten Museen Europas gemacht. Es zählt zu den wenigen, in denen Kinder genauso selbstverständlich am Platze scheinen – und sind – wie in der Schule. Das Innere des Hauptgebäudes wurde 1945 vollständig renoviert; 1954 wurde im rechten Winkel zum alten Bau ein neuer Flügel für Wechselausstellungen errichtet. Der Anbau, eine Stahlbetonkonstruktion, hat zwei Geschosse, die durch das an den Längsseiten einfallende Tageslicht beleuchtet werden.

1

Plan, ground floor / Grundriß Erdgeschoß.
1 Main entrance in existing building / Haupteingang im alten Gebäude
2 Restaurant
3 Library / Bibliothek
4 Terrace / Terrasse
5 Pool / Wasserbecken
6 Lavatories / Toiletten
7 Connecting corridor / Verbindungsgang
8 New gallery for temporary exhibitions / Neuer Ausstellungsbereich für Wechselausstellungen
9 Covered entrance / Überdeckter Eingang
10 Stair to first floor gallery / Treppe zu den Ausstellungsräumen im ersten Geschoß

1. Posters announcing the current exhibitions can be seen throughout Amsterdam.
2. A park and a children's playground form part of the large square towards which the back of the museum faces. The new wing is on the left.

1. An vielen Stellen Amsterdams machen Plakate auf die jeweiligen Ausstellungen aufmerksam.
2. Auf der Rückseite des Museums liegt ein großer Platz mit Park und Kinderspielplatz. Links der neue Flügel.

2

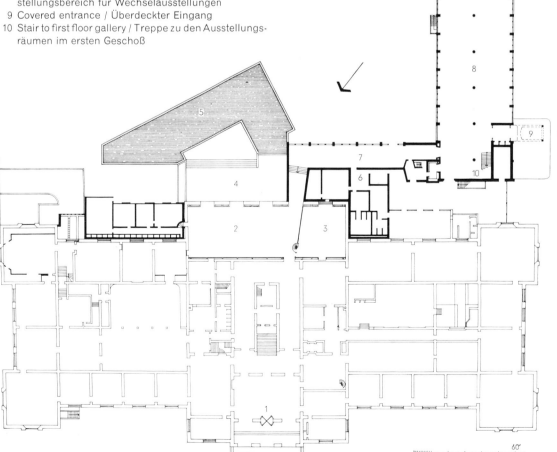

60'
20 m

3

4

3. The main entrance space has a sign post indicating the various sections. Coats can be deposited in the room on the left.

4. The print room is artificially lit by spotlights and fluorescent tubes which are installed behind blinds. It is reached from the half-landing of the main stair. This is a low U-shaped space with its walls lined in wood. The reflection from these helps to "warm" the light from the fluorescent tubes (colour temperature 4,200°K).

5. Quite a large room on the first floor opposite the principal stair is given over to selling postcards, catalogues and reproductions; this is recognised as an important activity.

6. A mobile by Calder hangs above the main staircase to the first floor of the old building.

7. One of the rooms on the first floor of the old building with subsidiary display shown horizontally. A taut fabric canopy acts as a light diffuser.

3. Am Haupteingang weisen Schilder den Weg zu den verschiedenen Abteilungen. Links im Hintergrund die Garderobe.

4. Das Kabinett für Druckgraphik, das auf halber Höhe der Haupttreppe liegt, ist künstlich durch Punktleuchten und Leuchtstoffröhren hinter Blenden beleuchtet. Die Wände des niedrigen, U-förmigen Raumes sind mit Holz verkleidet. Die Reflexion der Holzwände »wärmt« das Licht der Leuchtstoffröhren (Farbtemperatur 4200° K).

5. In einem relativ großen Raum im ersten Geschoß gegenüber der Haupttreppe werden Postkarten, Kataloge und Reproduktionen verkauft; im Stedelijk Museum wird diese Nebentätigkeit ernst genommen.

6. Ein Mobile von Calder hängt über der Haupttreppe zum ersten Geschoß des alten Baus.

7. Raum im ersten Geschoß des alten Gebäudes. Zusätzliche Ausstellungsstücke sind horizontal auf Kästen angeordnet. Ein eingespannter Stoffhimmel sorgt für diffuses Licht.

5

6

7

68

8. Part of the library extends into the two-storey restaurant as a narrow balcony. The link to the new wing is through the opening next to the library.

9. The restaurant opens out onto a terrace facing a pool and a park with a children's sand pit.

8. Ein schmaler Balkon, der noch zur Bibliothek gehört, erstreckt sich in das zwei Geschosse hohe Restaurant. Durch die Öffnung neben der Bibliothek gelangt der Besucher in den Verbindungsgang zum neuen Flügel.

9. Von der Terrasse des Restaurants blickt man auf ein Wasserbecken und die Parkanlage mit einem Sandkasten für Kinder.

10

11

10, 11. The ground floor room of the new wing arranged for two different exhibitions, seen in one case during the day (11), in the other at night (10). Floodlights are mounted on the columns; their light is reflected by the white ceiling.

10, 11. Zwei verschiedene Ausstellungen im Erdgeschoß des neuen Flügels, bei Tag (11) und abends (10). An den Stützen sind Scheinwerfer montiert, deren Licht von der weißen Decke reflektiert wird.

12

12. An international poster exhibition on the first floor of the new wing; aluminium venetian blinds screen the windows on both sides. Parallel to the windows, there is a louvered recess in the ceiling for fluorescent lighting.
13. The library is open to the public and is clearly one of the important spaces of the museum.

12. Internationale Plakatausstellung im ersten Geschoß des neuen Flügels; Lamellenstores aus Aluminium mildern auf beiden Seiten das Tageslicht. Parallel zu den Fensterfronten sind über einem Lamellensystem Leuchtstoffröhren in die Decke eingezogen.
13. Die Bibliothek ist dem Publikum zugänglich und gehört zu den wichtigsten Einrichtungen des Museums.

13

Let us try to create surroundings
where the vanguard feels at home
wide
clear
on human scale
no large halls, pompous stairways, ceiling lights
doors like gates, uniformed officials
but a place where people dare talk, laugh
and be themselves
a real centre for present life
generous
elastic
music's home, home also for photography
painting and sculpture, for dance and movies
for experiment
and for everything that will brighten the features of the
face of our time for every contribution to the form
of the present.

(W. Sandberg. in: *NU – in the Middle of the 20th century, art and its function in life*, 1959.)

14

15

16

17

14, 15. Exhibits are whenever possible left unprotected and are, in this case, touched and thus understood by the blind.
16, 17. Children learn about painting through listening as well as doing.
18, 19. The roof of the original building houses both offices and workshops.

14, 15. Die Ausstellungsgegenstände werden nach Möglichkeit nicht abgeschirmt. Hier können Blinde den Gegenstand betasten und dadurch verstehen.
16, 17. Kinder lernen etwas über Malerei, indem sie zuhören – und es selber versuchen.
18, 19. Das Dachgeschoß des alten Gebäudes nimmt Büros und Werkstätten auf.

Laßt uns versuchen, eine Umgebung zu schaffen
in der die Avantgarde zu Hause ist
weit
klar
in menschlichem Maßstab
keine riesigen Hallen, keine pompösen Treppen und Deckenleuchter, keine Türen, die Portale sind,
keine uniformierten Wärter sondern einen Ort, an dem die Menschen es wagen, zu lachen und zu reden
und sich natürlich zu bewegen
ein wahres Zentrum des heutigen Lebens
großzügig
anpassungsfähig
eine Heimstätte der Musik und auch der Fotografie
der Malerei und der Plastik, des Balletts und des Films und der Experimente
eine Stätte für alles, was unsere Zeit heller macht
für jeden Beitrag zu der Formensprache der Gegenwart.

(W. Sandberg, in: *NU – In der Mitte des 20. Jahrhunderts, Kunst und ihre Funktion im Leben*, 1959.)

18

19

Gallo-Roman Lapidary Museum, Buzenol-Montauban, Belgium (1960)

Architect: Constantin L.-Brodzki

Musée lapidaire gallo-romain, Buzenol-Montauban, Belgien (1960)

Architekt: Constantin L.-Brodzki

This building is an extension of the Musée Gaumais at Virton and was designed to display the collection of funerary monuments being excavated on this site. It was built on a portion of the ground which had already been cleared by the archaeologists.

Great care was taken in the design to produce a building which could survive unattended and unheated but which could nevertheless be unobtrusively sunk into the ground. As a result the actual museum is an inner shell set clear of an outer retaining wall and roof with a large fully ventilated space between the two. Unlike the sunk Treasury at San Lorenzo in Genoa, this building does not rely on air-conditioning. The division of the museum into bays makes certain groupings of objects possible. Although the extent of the building is revealed from the entrance, not all its spaces are made immediately visible. There is thus always an element of suprise even in this very small interior. On the outside, on the other hand, the serrated bays reduce the apparent impact of the building on the landscape.

Das Gebäude gehört zu dem Musée Gaumais in Virton und enthält eine Sammlung von Grabmonumenten, die unmittelbar in der Nähe ausgegraben wurden. Der Baugrund selbst ist von den Archäologen bereits durchforscht.

Für den Entwurf war bestimmend, daß das Museum keine Heizung und keinen sonstigen Unterhaltungsaufwand erfordern sollte, aber trotzdem in den Boden eingelassen werden konnte. Das Gebäude besteht aus einem inneren Kern, der von den äußeren Stützwänden und dem Dach abgesetzt ist; dazwischen liegt ein voll ventilierter Bereich. Im Gegensatz zu der unterirdischen Schatzkammer von San Lorenzo in Genua ist das Museum nicht mit Klimaanlagen ausgestattet. Die Aufteilung in einzelne Zellen ermöglicht es, die Gegenstände in Gruppen anzuordnen. Obwohl vom Eingang aus der Raum in seiner ganzen Tiefe sichtbar wird, können die verschiedenen Bereiche nicht auf den ersten Blick hin eingesehen werden. Selbst bei dieser relativ kleinen Ausstellungsfläche ist also ein Überraschungsmoment gegeben. In der Außenansicht bewirkt die Staffelung der Zellen eine unauffälligere Einfügung des Bauwerks in die Landschaft.

1, 2. The museum is entered from the uphill side; all that is visible is a stair leading down between two stone retaining walls.

1, 2. Das Museum wird von oben, von der Bergseite her betreten; der Besucher erblickt zunächst nur eine Treppe, die zwischen steinernen Stützmauern nach unten führt.

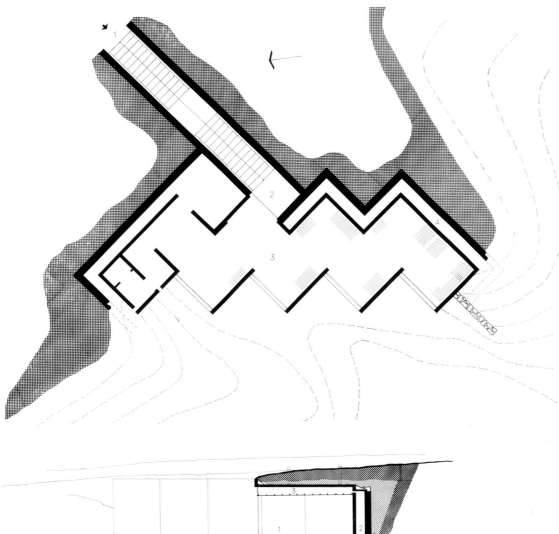

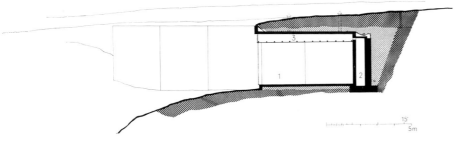

Plan / Grundriß.
1 Steps down to the museum from ground level / Treppe an der Bergseite, die hinunter zum Museum führt
2 Entrance / Eingang
3 Exhibition area / Ausstellungsräume
4 Hollow space between retaining wall and inner wall of exhibition area / Hohlraum zwischen äußeren Stützwänden und Innenwänden des Ausstellungsbereichs

Section / Schnitt.
1 Exhibition area (side lit) / Ausstellungsbereich (Seitenlicht)
2 Hollow space between retaining wall and inner wall / Hohlraum zwischen äußerer Stützwand und Innenwand
3 Hollow space between ceiling and structural slab. These voids are ventilated through fixed louvres above the windows. Extracts above ground ventilate the hardcore on top of the roof slab / Hohlraum zwischen Dach und eingezogener Decke. Die Hohlräume werden durch feststehende Lamellen über den Fenstern belüftet. Ventilationsschlote über dem Bodenniveau sorgen für die Belüftung der Schüttpacklage auf dem Flachdach des Gebäudes

15'
5m

3. On the downhill side the museum reveals five serrated bays, four of them fully glazed overlooking a steep wooded valley. The louvres above the glass ventilate the airspace between the roof and ceiling.

4. The four exhibition bays seen diagonally from the entrance. The stone retaining wall on the left is at the foot of the stairs.

5. The roman funerary fragments are shown on metal stands or suspended from the wall. The large sheets of glass are fixed except in the end bay, seen on the left, where there is a centrally pivotted door.

3. Ansicht von Nordwesten. Auf der Hangseite hat das Museum fünf gegeneinander versetzte Zellen, von denen vier verglast sind. Der Blick geht in ein steil abfallendes, bewaldetes Tal. Die Lamellen über den Glasfronten ventilieren den Luftraum zwischen Decke und Dach.

4. Die vier Ausstellungsbereiche, diagonal vom Eingang her gesehen. Die steinerne Stützmauer links befindet sich am Fuß der Treppe.

5. Die römischen Grabsteinfragmente sind auf Ständern oder Wandkonsolen aus Stahl befestigt. Die großen Fenster sind fest verglast, mit Ausnahme der letzten Nische links, wo die Glastür sich um die Mittelachse drehen läßt.

Scandinavian museum design, unlike that in Italy perhaps, has been interested rather more in the achievment of a complete environment, rather less in the technique of display. It has tried to emphasise the museum as a natural part of civilised life, a place of enjoyment to be visited regularly for a number of activities. As often as not the building is related to a particular landscape setting – the Maihaugen set against a pine clad ridge is part of the outdoor folk museum established there, the floating Wasa Dockyard Museum is part of the water landscape of Stockholm, Louisiana part of the recreational area bordering the sea north of Copenhagen – and the museum derives some of its interest from its setting. The landscape fulfills much the same role as the urban palace or castle does in the case of the Italian museum conversions: it provides an element which is unique and memorable over and above the display. Interestingly enough Sverre Fehn's Scandinavian Pavilion at the Biennale, see page 198, manages to establish a similar relationship with its corner of a Venetian park.

The example set by these museums has not yet been followed elsewhere; like the Italian attitude to display it has yet to be absorbed into current thinking.

Die skandinavische Museumsarchitektur interessiert sich – anders als die italienische – weniger für die Ausstellungstechnik als für die Planung eines umfassenden Museumsbereichs. Die skandinavischen Architekten haben sich bemüht, das Museum in das tägliche Leben einzubeziehen und es zu einem Zentrum der Aktivität zu machen. Im allgemeinen sind die Museumsbauten in eine Beziehung zur umgebenden Landschaft gesetzt: Das Maihaugen Museum, das zusammen mit rekonstruierten historischen Wohnbauten im Freien eine große Volkskunst-Ausstellung bildet, ist an einen Hang gebaut und von Wald umgeben; das schwimmende Wasa-Schiffswerft-Museum von Howander und Åkerblad ist Teil des Hafenbildes von Stockholm; das Louisiana Museum gehört zu dem Erholungsgebiet, das nördlich von Kopenhagen ans Meer grenzt – und es zieht aus dieser Lage manchen Nutzen. Die Landschaft spielt hier die gleiche Rolle wie etwa der Stadtpalast oder das Schloß bei den italienischen Museumsbauten: Sie schafft einen unverwechselbaren Hintergrund, der noch eindrucksvoller ist als die Ausstellungstechnik. Interessanterweise brachte es Sverre Fehn sogar bei seinem Skandinavischen Pavillon auf der Biennale (vgl. Seite 198) fertig, auf dem kleinen Grundstück im Biennale-Park eine ähnliche Verbindung zur Natur herzustellen.

Dem Vorbild Skandinaviens sind andere Länder bisher noch nicht gefolgt; wie die italienische Ausstellungstechnik muß auch die skandinavische Museumsarchitektur erst noch vom architektonischen Denken unserer Zeit verarbeitet werden.

1. Sverre Fehn and Geir Grung's Maihaugen museum built in 1955–59 is part of a large exhibition of folk art at Lillehammer in Norway which includes reconstructions of old settlements placed among the fir trees.
2. This exhibition building by Bengt Gate (1956) stands near the Orrefors glass factory and consists of two rooms, an open fully glazed one for the present production of the factory and, beyond it, an enclosed historic room with showcases bracketed out from the wall.

1. Das Maihaugen Museum von Sverre Fehn und Geir Grung (erbaut 1955–59) ist ein Teil der großen Volkskunst-Ausstellung in Lillehammer (Norwegen), zu der Rekonstruktionen alter Siedlungsformen gehören.
2. Dieser Ausstellungspavillon von Bengt Gate (1956) steht in der Nähe der Glasfabrik von Orrefors und besteht aus zwei Räumen. Der eine Raum ist voll verglast und enthält die heutigen Produkte der Firma; dahinter liegt der nach außen abgeschlossene historische Raum mit auskragenden Wandvitrinen.

1

2

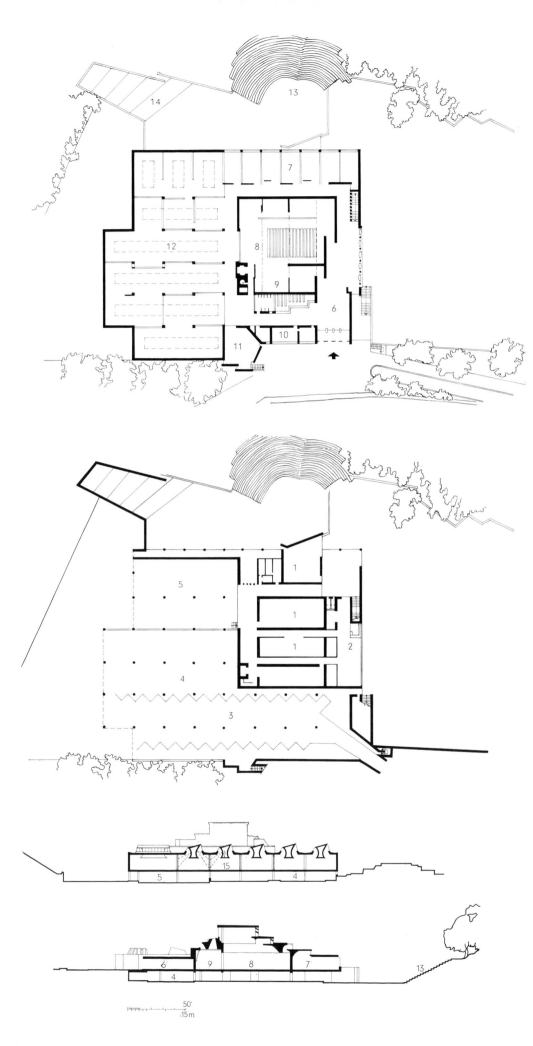

3. The competition design for a museum at Aalborg in Denmark by Elissa and Alvar Aalto and Jean-Jacques Baruël adopts something of Le Corbusier's lighting methods used at Tokyo but does not direct daylight through two layers of glass. Like most other Scandinavian museums it respects and uses the site, in this instance by taking cars to a lower level and parking them under the building and by cutting sculpture terraces and an amphitheatre into the hillside.

3. In dem Wettbewerbsentwurf für ein Museum in Aalborg (Dänemark) von Elissa und Alvar Aalto und Jean-Jacques Baruël sind einige Beleuchtungsprinzipien verwertet, die Le Corbusier in Tokio anwandte; das Tageslicht wird jedoch nicht durch zwei Glasschichten geleitet. Wie bei den meisten skandinavischen Museen wird das Gelände respektiert und einbezogen. Die Autozufahrt ist auf ein niedrigeres Niveau verlegt, und der Parkplatz befindet sich unter dem Gebäude. Außerdem sind Terrassen für Plastikausstellungen und ein Amphitheater in den Hang eingeschnitten.

Plan, upper ground floor / Grundriß Obergeschoß.
Plan, lower ground floor / Grundriß Untergeschoß.
Section through main exhibition gallery / Schnitt durch den Hauptausstellungsbereich.
Section through entrance hall and sculpture gallery / Schnitt durch Eingangshalle und Ausstellungsraum für Plastik.

1 Storage / Magazin
2 Workshop / Werkstatt
3 Car parking / Parkgarage
4 Bicycles / Fahrradraum
5 Service area / Service
6 Entrance hall / Eingangshalle
7 Picture galleries / Ausstellungsräume für Gemälde
8 Lecture hall seating 200 / Vortragssaal mit 200 Plätzen
9 Sculpture gallery / Ausstellungsraum für Plastik
10 Offices / Büros
11 Music room / Musikraum
12 Modern art galleries / Ausstellungsräume für moderne Kunst
13 Amphitheatre / Amphitheater
14 Sculpture terraces / Terrassen für Plastikausstellungen
15 Top-lit main gallery / Hauptausstellungsraum mit Oberlicht

Art Gallery, Lund, Sweden (1956–57)

Architect: Klas Anshelm

The Art Gallery at Lund makes it possible to step straight from the granite paving of the market place into a world of pictures and sculpture without intervention of ticket booths, turnstiles, postcard counters or guards. The gallery, a series of interconnected spaces, some top lit, some side lit and of varying height and outlook, is planned around four sides of an open courtyard. There is no single and dogmatic solution – the steeply sloping skylights, for instance, face in four different directions – and the building gains greatly as a result.

Kunstgalerie, Lund, Schweden (1956–57)

Architekt: Klas Anshelm

Der Besucher der Kunstgalerie in Lund gelangt vom Granitpflaster des Marktplatzes direkt in eine Welt der Bilder und Skulpturen: Keine Kartenschalter, Drehkreuze, Postkartenstände oder Wärter stellen sich ihm in den Weg. Die untereinander verbundenen Räume der Galerie sind um einen quadratischen Innenhof angeordnet; sie werden teils durch Seitenlicht, teils durch Oberlicht erhellt. Die unterschiedlichen Raumhöhen und die individuelle Gestaltung der einzelnen Ausstellungssäle (die schräg gestellten Oberlichter sind zum Beispiel nach vier verschiedenen Richtungen orientiert) lassen das Museum lebendig und undogmatisch erscheinen. Der Bau ist als Stahlbetonkonstruktion errichtet und nach außen mit Backsteinen, zum Hof hin mit Steinplatten verkleidet.

1

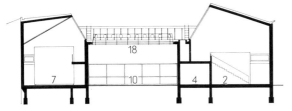

North-south section / Schnitt in Nord-Süd-Richtung.

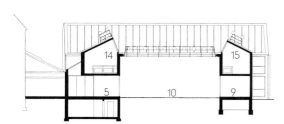

Transverse section / Querschnitt.

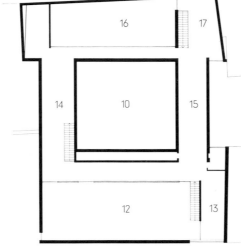

Plan, first floor / Grundriß erstes Geschoß.

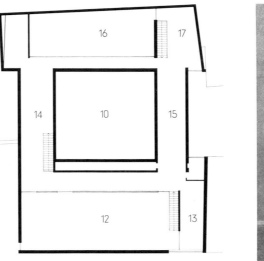

2

1. The red brick building faces the market place in the old part of town and adjoins existing buildings on two sides. Its interior is revealed just sufficiently to arouse curiosity. A further view of the outside is on page 11.
2. A pair of double doors separates the square from the first gallery.

1. Das rote Backsteingebäude liegt am Marktplatz im älteren Teil der Stadt und wird an zwei Seiten von bereits vorhandenen Bauten flankiert. Vom Inneren ist gerade so viel zu erkennen, daß die Neugierde geweckt wird. (Eine weitere Außenaufnahme vgl. Seite 11).
2. Der erste Ausstellungsraum ist nur durch Doppeltüren vom Marktplatz getrennt.

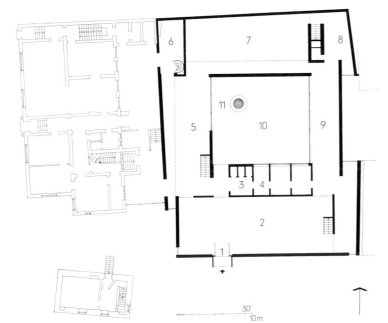

Plan, ground floor / Grundriß Erdgeschoß.

1 Entrance / Eingang
2 Gallery I / Raum I
3 Cloakroom / Garderobe
4 Offices / Büros
5 Gallery II / Raum II
6 Storage / Magazin
7 Gallery III / Raum III
8 Gallery IV / Raum IV
9 Gallery V / Raum V

10 Courtyard / Innenhof
11 Fountain / Brunnen
12 Upper part Gallery I / Luftraum Saal I
13 Cafeteria / Erfrischungsraum
14 Gallery VI / Raum VI
15 Gallery VII / Raum VII
16 Upper part Gallery III / Luftraum Saal III
17 Gallery VIII / Raum VIII
18 Exterior lighting / Äußere Beleuchtungsanlage

3

4

5

6

3, 4. Like the first room, Gallery III is a two-storey space with a balcony, only in this case lit by a skylight facing south. The room is sometimes used in the evening for musical performances.

5. The first room is a double height volume lit from a high window facing north with a slot window at the far end letting in south light.

6. Gallery II has its long wall top lit by a skylight set between the wall and the ceiling. Beyond the stairs there is a window looking out onto the courtyard.

3, 4. Wie der erste Raum ist auch der dritte Ausstellungssaal zwei Geschosse hoch und hat einen Balkon, nur ist das Oberlicht hier nach Süden orientiert. Der Raum wird abends bisweilen für Musikveranstaltungen benutzt.

5. Der zwei Geschosse hohe erste Ausstellungsraum erhält Licht von Norden durch das hohe Oberlicht; vertikale und horizontale Fensterbänder an der Eingangsseite lassen Südlicht ein.

6. Die Längswand des zweiten Ausstellungsraumes wird durch ein Oberlicht erhellt, das zwischen Wand und Decke eingelassen ist. Ein Fenster hinter der Treppe blickt auf den Innenhof.

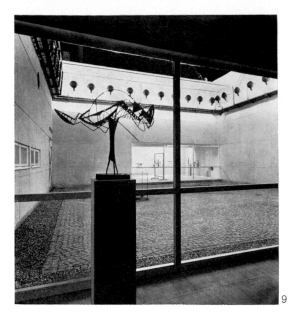

7. The courtyard has a fountain and sculpture and is, like the market square outside, paved with granite blocks set in the same fan-shaped pattern.

8, 9. A narrow room with a view of the courtyard leads back to Gallery I. The rooms are artificially lit by floodlights placed outside the roof glazing on rails running round four sides of the courtyard and by small movable fittings clamped to a channel in the ceiling.

10, 11. Stairs from Gallery I lead to the various balconies and rooms on the first floor.

12. The balcony to the left of the top of the stairs seen in the distance overlooks Gallery I and has a view of the square outside; it is adjacent to a pantry serving refreshments.

7. Im Innenhof sieht der Besucher einen kleinen Brunnen und mehrere Plastiken. Das fächerförmige Pflastermuster entspricht dem des Marktplatzes vor dem Museum.

8, 9. Ein schmaler Raum mit Blick auf den Innenhof führt zurück zum ersten Saal. Für die künstliche Beleuchtung der Ausstellungsräume sorgen Scheinwerfer, die an der Außenseite der Oberlichter installiert sind und auf Schienen um die vier Seiten des Innenhofs laufen. Zusätzliches Licht geben verstellbare Punktleuchten im Inneren, die an einer Deckenrinne befestigt sind.

10, 11. Die Treppe im ersten Ausstellungsraum führt zu den Balkons und Galerien des Obergeschosses.

12. Vom Balkon im Hintergrund, links oberhalb der Treppe, blickt der Besucher auf den ersten Ausstellungssaal und – durch das Horizontalfenster – auf den Marktplatz. An den Balkon schließt sich ein Büfett für Erfrischungen an.

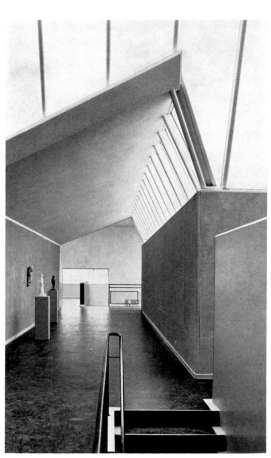

Louisiana Museum, Humlebæk near Copenhagen (1958)

Architects: Jørgen Bo and Vilhelm Wohlert

Founded by Knud W. Jensen, now chairman of the Louisiana Foundation, this private institution is within an important recreation area 30 kilometres north of Copenhagen near the Sound which separates Denmark from the southern tip of Sweden. The new building adjoins a country house built over a hundred years ago and its name does not refer to the State in the U.S.A. but to the fact that its original owner married three times, in each case a woman named Louise. The museum has adopted this name out of respect for such exceptional fidelity. Louisiana is the most important museum to have been built in Scandinavia since the war. Its importance rests not on the merit of its collection but on the total environment which has been created there in terms of architecture, landscape, exhibits and a wide variety of related activities. Jørgen Bo and Vilhelm Wohlert have described their design and some of the notions on which it was based:

"We spent two wonderful weeks in the autumn of 1956, when staying in Louisiana's old house and working in close co-operation with the owner we made the sketches of the new building. Every day we had the ground, the trees, and the Sound in view, and we were surrounded by the works of art, for which we were to create the frame. There were two essential problems to deal with, how to combine the old house naturally with a new building, and how to place the new building in such a way that the exceptional qualities of the park were utilized, but in no way disfigured. We chose to use the old house as an entrance pavilion, thereby giving it a natural function. The new building is situated on the part of the site where the landscape is most varied, the part which during the war with England formed a bastion towards the Sound. And then the problem how to combine these two buildings placed rather far from each other, arose. During the work, however, we found out that the glass corridor which became the connecting link, in itself gave the park a new quality, making the walk through the grounds a new delight to the visitor. When designing the building we wanted partly to subordinate ourselves to nature and partly to emphasize and stress its values. The homely atmosphere conveyed by the old house has in the new wing been kept and developed in harmony with modern thought, by such simple arrangements as working with low levels and much use of side light, which makes it as easy to feel at home in the surroundings as it would be in ordinary living rooms.

As the collection should be considered as a living whole, the building has generally speaking been arranged with a view to making it possible for every room to display all types of art (painting, sculpture and applied art) and also to form the frame around works of art from different periods. Great importance was attached to creating rooms of various character. One walks through a row of alternately open and closed forms. There was an endeavour to avoid the stamp of the institutional, of museology and dogmatism. There are essentially three types of rooms, rooms with side light and removable screens for smaller works of art, some a little higher and lantern-lit, and finally a high side-lit room that can hold works of art which because of their size and their whole character must have plenty of space; there is a room fitted with artificial lighting for water-colours. Direct light from above is only used when a special effect is aimed at. With regard to lighting, an attempt has been made to convey the impression that the works of art are displayed as in an ordinary home. Any museum-like artificial device is avoided, and glimpses of the sun shining on the pictures can be caught here and there, even if direct sunshine is kept out everywhere by curtains. Lantern

light is in itself advantageous, compared with ordinary light from above, because the light is thrown on the walls so that they become the dominating surfaces of the room, an effect that is emphasized by the dark floor and ceiling. This way of lighting is also favourable for sculpture and applied art, because it sets off the shape and textural effect of the exhibited object. The low windows between the main beams are placed there in order to give light on the ceiling, so that dark corners are avoided and a lighter interior obtained.

The buildings had to be white: inside the house because of the works of art, and outside in order to contrast with

1, 2. The new building of whitewashed brick and wood is set among mature trees planted by the first owner of the house.

the green park and link the new and old together. The natural textural effects in brickwork and wood are neutral, and yet they increase the effects of the exhibits.

In the way the materials and the construction appear direct and clear, the architecture of the building represents a Danish tradition, brought about by local conditions with regard to climate and materials. In proportioning the building as a whole and in detail we have attempted to perpetuate primary shapes and proportions in our work. The background of this architectonic asceticism is to be found in the rich contents and the prolific surroundings." (*Mobilia* 38/1958.)

1, 2. Das neue Gebäude aus weiß geschlämmtem Backstein und Holz liegt inmitten von Bäumen, die bereits der erste Besitzer des alten Landhauses gepflanzt hat.

Louisiana Kunstmuseum, Humlebæk bei Kopenhagen (1958)

Architekten: Jørgen Bo und Vilhelm Wohlert

Das Louisiana Museum ist eine private Institution, die von Knud W. Jensen (dem jetzigen Vorsitzenden der Louisiana-Stiftung) ins Leben gerufen wurde. Das Gebäude liegt inmitten eines beliebten Erholungsgebietes 30 km nördlich von Kopenhagen, nahe am Sund, der Dänemark von der Südspitze Schwedens trennt. Das über hundert Jahre alte Landhaus, das sich auf dem Grundstück befand, bauten die Architekten zu einem Eingangspavillon um; dieser Pavillon ist durch einen verglasten Gang mit dem neuen Gebäudekomplex verbunden. Seinen Namen verdankt das Museum nicht etwa dem Staat Louisiana in den USA, sondern der Tatsache, daß der ursprüngliche Eigentümer dreimal heiratete – jedesmal eine Frau namens Louise. Das Louisiana ist das wichtigste Museum, das nach dem Krieg in Skandinavien gebaut wurde. Es ist den Architekten hier gelungen, einen umfassenden Museumsbereich zu schaffen, in dem Architektur, Landschaft und Ausstellungsgegenstände ein harmonisches Ganzes bilden und der eine Vielzahl von Möglichkeiten in der Benutzung bietet. Jørgen Bo und Vilhelm Wohlert haben in der Zeitschrift *mobilia* 38/1958 beschrieben, auf welchen Voraussetzungen ihr Entwurf basierte:

»Im Herbst 1956 verbrachten wir vierzehn herrliche Tage im alten Louisiana-Haus; in enger Zusammenarbeit mit dem Besitzer fertigten wir Entwürfe für das neue Gebäude an. Täglich hatten wir die Landschaft, die Bäume und den Sund vor Augen, und wir waren von den Kunstwerken umgeben, für die wir einen Rahmen schaffen sollten.

Wir mußten beim Entwurf zwei Gesichtspunkte berücksichtigen: Das alte Haus sollte sich harmonisch an das neue Gebäude anschließen, und der Neubau sollte so gelegen sein, daß er die Schönheit des Parks ausnutzte, aber nicht zerstörte. Wir machten aus dem alten Haus einen Eingangspavillon und verliehen ihm dadurch eine natürliche Funktion. Das neue Gebäude erhebt sich auf dem Teil des Grundstücks, der die abwechslungsreichste Landschaft bietet – dem Teil, der während des Krieges gegen England eine Bastion zum Sund hin gebildet hatte. Dann ergab sich das Problem, die beiden relativ weit voneinander weg liegenden Bauten zu verbinden. Im Laufe der Arbeit fanden wir heraus, daß der verglaste Korridor, den wir als Bindeglied wählten, dem Museumsbesucher das zusätzliche Erlebnis eines Parkspaziergangs vermittelte. Wir suchten uns bei unserem Entwurf der Natur zu unterwerfen und gleichzeitig ihre Reize zu entdecken und zu unterstreichen. Die behagliche Atmosphäre des alten Hauses wurde mit modernen Mitteln auch auf den neuen Flügel übertragen. Relativ niedrige Raumhöhen und weitgehende Verwendung von Seitenlicht tragen dazu bei, daß sich der Besucher im Museum so wohl fühlt wie in einem normalen Wohnzimmer.

Da eine Kunstsammlung als lebendes Ganzes aufgefaßt werden sollte, suchten wir die Räume so flexibel zu gestalten, daß sie Malerei ebenso wie Plastik oder Kunstgewerbe aufnehmen und gleichzeitig auch den Rahmen für Werke aus verschiedenen Epochen bilden können. Wir legten außerdem großen Wert darauf, Räume mit individuellen Merkmalen zu schaffen, um jeden Anklang an offizielle, dogmatische Museumsarchitektur zu vermeiden. Offene und geschlossene Raumvolumen wechseln sich ab. Im wesentlichen wurden drei Raumtypen vorgesehen: Räume mit Seitenlicht und beweglichen Stellwänden für kleinere Ausstellungsgegenstände, höhere Räume mit Oberlicht und ein hoher Saal mit Seitenlicht für Kunstwerke, die ihrem Format und ihrem Charakter nach viel Platz beanspruchen; ein Kabinett mit

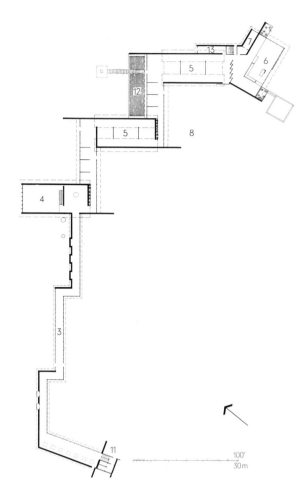

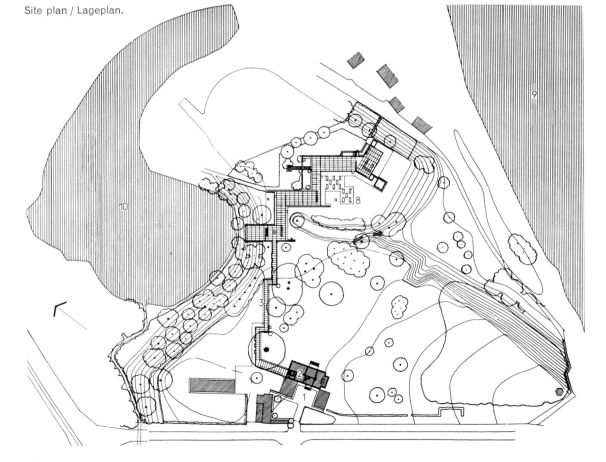

Site plan / Lageplan.

Plan, ground floor / Grundriß Erdgeschoß.
1 Main entrance / Haupteingang
2 Existing house / Vorhandenes Gebäude
3 Connecting corridors (side-lit) / Verbindungskorridor (Seitenlicht)
4 Two storey high gallery / Zwei Geschosse hoher Ausstellungsraum
5 Lantern-lit galleries / Ausstellungsräume mit Oberlicht
6 Library / Bibliothek
7 Kitchen / Küche
8 Cafeteria terrace / Caféterrasse
9 Øresund
10 Lake Humlebæk / Humlebæk-See
11 Entrance from existing house / Eingang durch das vorhandene alte Gebäude
12 Pool / Wasserbecken
13 Storage / Magazin
A large top-lit room for temporary exhibitions is to be added east of the connecting corridor / Ein großer Raum mit Oberlicht für Wechselausstellungen wird östlich des Verbindungskorridors entstehen.

Section (page 81) / Schnitt (Seite 81).
1 Brick paving / Backsteinfliesen
2 Brick walls / Backsteinwände
3 6″ × 18″ laminated wood beams / Träger aus Schichtholz (Querschnitt 15 × 45 cm)
4 Double glazing / Doppelte Verglasung
5 ¾″ boarded ceiling / Mit Holzriemen von 1,75 cm Stärke verkleidete Decke
6 Teak fascias / Teakholzverblendung

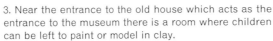

künstlicher Beleuchtung nimmt Aquarelle auf. Direktes Deckenlicht ist nur da angewandt, wo eine besondere Wirkung erzielt werden sollte. Bei der Beleuchtung vermieden wir überhaupt eine künstliche Atmosphäre, wie sie häufig in Museen anzutreffen ist, damit die Kunstwerke wie in einer gewöhnlichen Wohnung zur Geltung kommen. Hier und da fällt ein Sonnenstrahl auf die Bilder, wobei freilich das direkte Sonnenlicht durch Vorhänge ferngehalten wird. Laternen-Oberlichter haben manchen Vorteil gegenüber direktem Deckenlicht: Das einfallende Licht wird auf die Wände geworfen, die dadurch den Raum beherrschen – eine Wirkung, die durch dunkle Böden und Decken noch betont wird. Eine solche Beleuchtungsmethode ist auch für Plastik und Kunstgewerbe günstig, da sie die Formen und Strukturen der Ausstellungsgegenstände hervorhebt. Die niedrigen Fenster zwischen den Holzträgern beleuchten die Decke, so daß keine dunklen Ecken entstehen und das Innere im ganzen heller wirkt.

Die Gebäude mußten innen und außen weiß gestrichen werden. Im Inneren bilden die weißen Flächen den Hintergrund für die Kunstwerke, außen kontrastieren sie mit dem grünen Park und stellen eine Verbindung zwischen dem alten und dem neuen Bauwerk her. Die natürlichen Strukturen von Backstein und Holz sind neutral und steigern gerade dadurch die Wirkung der Kunstwerke. In der Anwendung der Materialien und in seiner klaren Konstruktion vertritt das neue Gebäude eine dänische Tradition, die aus den besonderen Gegebenheiten des Landes entstanden ist. Bei der Gestaltung des Bauwerks haben wir im ganzen wie auch im Detail Grundformen und einfache Proportionen anzuwenden gesucht. Der Grund für diese architektonische Askese liegt in dem reichen Inhalt des Gebäudes und in seiner eindrucksvollen Umgebung. «

3. Near the entrance to the old house which acts as the entrance to the museum there is a room where children can be left to paint or model in clay.
4. A long staggered corridor, glazed on one side, joins the original house to the new museum.
5, 6. The only two-storey high room in the museum overlooks a woodland lake first seen from the top of a stair on entering; views of the sky are obscured by foliage.
7. The small artificially lit room used for the display of watercolours occurs under the balcony of the two-storey high space.
8. Pictures are displayed on white brick walls or on movable screens covered in grass cloth. The floors are covered with red clay tiles.

3. Nahe beim Eingang zum alten Haus, das heute den Zugang zum Museum bildet, ist ein Mal- und Modellierraum für Kinder.
4. Ein langer, winklig gebrochener Korridor, auf einer Seite verglast, verbindet das alte mit dem neuen Gebäude.
5, 6. Der einzige zwei Geschosse hohe Raum des Museums öffnet sich auf einen Waldsee, auf den der Blick zum erstenmal fällt, wenn man den Raum über eine Treppe von oben her betritt. Der Himmel ist durch Laubwerk abgeschirmt.
7. Der kleine Ausstellungsraum für Aquarelle ist künstlich beleuchtet und liegt unter dem Balkon des zweigeschossigen Raumes.
8. Die Bilder hängen auf den weißgetünchten Backsteinwänden oder beweglichen Tafeln mit grob strukturierter Stoffbespannung. Sämtliche Böden sind mit Backsteinfliesen abgedeckt.

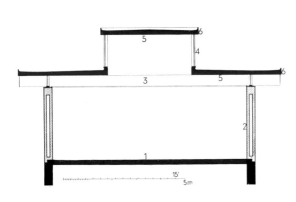

9

10

9, 10. Two of the exhibition rooms are lit by monitor roof lights and a line of clerestory glazing which occurs within the depth of the laminated wood beams. The ends of these are covered with gold-leaf. Curtains can be drawn across the roof lights and Japanese matting over the clerestory windows.

9, 10. Zwei Ausstellungsräume sind durch Laternen-Oberlichter sowie durch ein seitliches Fensterband beleuchtet, das sich über den Längswänden entlangzieht und die Höhe der laminierten Holzträger hat. Die Balkenköpfe sind mit Goldblatt belegt. Die Laternenfenster können mit Vorhängen, die Fensterbänder mit japanischen Matten abgeschirmt werden.

11

12

11, 12. The last but one room is flanked by a pool with a figure by Astrid Noack at the end of the stepping stones.

11, 12. Neben dem vorletzten Raum liegt ein rechteckiges Wasserbecken; am Ende der Trittsteine eine Skulptur von Astrid Noack.

13

13. Concert performances are given in the evening indoors and out and there are also lectures, films, dramatic performances, jazz and poetry recitals. An art course is arranged every year in conjunction with a neighbouring Folk High School.

13. Konzertveranstaltungen finden im Inneren des Museums und im Freien statt. Zum Programm des Museums gehören außerdem Vorträge, Film- und Theatervorführungen, Jazzkonzerte und Rezitationsabende. Einmal jährlich wird in Verbindung mit einer nahe liegenden Volkshochschule ein Kursus für bildende Kunst abgehalten.

14

14. The last gallery of the museum arranged here with a painting by Richard Mortensen and sculpture by Søren Georg Jensen. Artificial lighting is from suspended copper bowls with concentric plastic diffusers.
15. The combined indoor cafeteria and library beyond the last gallery. An L-shaped slightly sunk seating area faces an open fireplace.
16. The outdoor self-service cafeteria under a slatted pergola faces the Sound and the island of Hven.

14. Der am weitesten nach Nordosten gelegene Ausstellungsraum des Museums mit einem Gemälde von Richard Mortensen und einer Plastik von Søren Georg Jensen. Für die künstliche Beleuchtung sorgen Pendelleuchten aus Kupferschalen mit konzentrischem Stufenringraster aus Kunststoff.
15. Der Ruheraum, der gleichzeitig die Bibliothek aufnimmt, liegt hinter dem letzten Ausstellungsraum. Der L-förmige Sitzbereich ist um einen offenen Kamin an-

geordnet und liegt etwas tiefer als der übrige Teil des Raumes.
16. Die Selbstbedienungs-Cafeteria im Freien unter einer Lattenpergola gewährt einen Ausblick auf den Sund und die Insel Hven.

15

16

Forestry Museum, Gävle, Sweden (1960–61)

Architects: Sven H. Wranér, Erik Herløw, and Tormod Olesen

The museum was financed by asking forest owners to contribute the value of two full length logs for each 125 acres of forest in their posession. This ingenious attitude of involving those interested is in evidence throughout the museum: the public, for instance, are encouraged to touch exhibits and to identify woods by smelling samples. Similarly the exhibits deal not only with the nature of timber and the techniques of forestry but equally with the social problems of the forester.
The design of the museum is due to a team consisting of a Danish professor of architecture, the local town architect and a Danish exhibition designer. The construction is, suprisingly, a steel frame enclosed in glass and shingles. It thus clearly demarcates the exhibition from the enclosure.

Museum für das Forstwesen, Gävle, Schweden (1960–61)

Architekten: Sven H. Wranér, Erik Herløw und Tormod Olesen

Die Finanzierung des Museums wurde dadurch ermöglicht, daß zahlreiche Forstbesitzer von je 50 ha ihres Waldes zwei Baumstämme zur Verfügung stellten. Dieser kluge Einfall, die Interessenten einzubeziehen, hat sich auch im Museum selbst geäußert: Die Besucher werden zum Beispiel dazu aufgefordert, die Ausstellungsgegenstände zu berühren und die Holzarten nach dem Geruch zu identifizieren. Die Ausstellung bezieht sich im übrigen nicht nur auf Holzarten und -eigenschaften oder Forstwirtschaft, sondern auch auf die sozialen Probleme der Waldarbeiter.
Der Museumsentwurf entstand in einer Arbeitsgemeinschaft, der ein dänischer Architekturprofessor, ein Architekt des Stadtbauamts und ein Ausstellungsarchitekt angehörten. Die Konstruktion besteht überraschenderweise aus einem Stahlrahmen, der mit Glas und Schindeln verkleidet ist. Dadurch wird eine klare Trennung zwischen Ausstellung und Architektur erreicht.

Plan, ground floor / Grundriß Erdgeschoß.
1 Office building / Bürogebäude
2 Parking / Parkplatz
3 Entrance / Eingang
4 Pool / Wasserbecken
5 Exhibition area / Ausstellungsbereich
6 Lecture hall / Vortragssaal
7 Restaurant
8 Courtyard / Innenhof

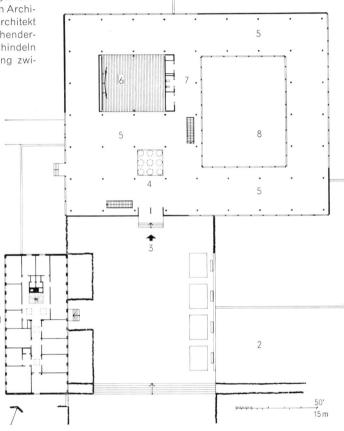

1. The south side of the museum and the main entrance facing a terrace paved with wooden blocks. The natural lighting of the interior is controlled by canvas blinds on the outside and by aluminium venetian blinds on the inside.
2. The entrance hall contains a top-lit pool as its focal point. The introductory part of the exhibition starts on the left of this view; the pivotting screens on the right lead to the lecture hall.

1. Die Südseite des Museums mit dem Haupteingang; der Vorplatz hat Holzpflaster. Das in den Innenraum einfallende Tageslicht wird von außen durch Segeltuchmarkisen und von innen durch Lamellenstores aus Aluminium gedämpft.
2. Den Mittelpunkt der Eingangshalle bildet ein von oben her beleuchtetes Wasserbecken. Die schwenkbaren Wandelemente rechts gehören zum Vortragssaal. Links beginnt die Ausstellung mit einer einführenden Abteilung.

1

2

3

3, 4. The design of the exhibition exploits all the available planes – it is a skilful realisation of Herbert Bayer's concept shown on page 181 – and uses photographs, diagrams and the actual objects themselves to make its point.
5. The introductory part of the exhibition. Exhibits are lit by directional fittings attached to the supporting framework. The uprights fit into sockets in the floor and ceiling spaced on a 4 ft. × 4 ft. grid. A detail of these is shown on page 190.

3, 4. Bei der Ausstellungsgestaltung wurden alle verfügbaren Flächen ausgenutzt – eine gelungene Realisierung von Herbert Bayers Konzeption (vgl. Seite 181), die mit Fotografien, Diagrammen und den Objekten selbst arbeitet.
5. Der einführende Teil der Ausstellung in der Vorhalle. Für die Beleuchtung der Ausstellungsgegenstände sorgen bewegliche Scheinwerfer, die an den Rahmen der Stellwände angebracht sind. Die Stützen sind am Boden und an der Decke in Buchsen befestigt, die einen Raster von 120 × 120 cm bilden (Detail auf Seite 190).

4

5

6

7

6. The lecture hall used for talks, concerts and film shows is an internal space lit from high level. To one side of it there is a small restaurant looking out on an enclosed court.

7. Part of the exhibition showing the growth and structure of trees. The forty year old pine root suspended from the ceiling was taken out of the ground by having the fire department sluice away the earth. Only in this way could the bulk of the fine fibrils be preserved.

8. The courtyard seen from the entrance hall. The stairs lead down to the outside and to the path to the arboretum.

9. The suspended pine tree root seen from below.

10. A range of wooden chairs used as a commentary on how different techniques (and tastes) produce different forms.

11, 12. Visitors are encouraged not only to look but to use their other senses as well, to recognise a timber by its smell or to feel its smoothness.

13. A display panel showing the effect of the tool on the texture of the cut surface. Words are made redundant by representing the tool pictorially.

14. The versatility of timber displayed by playful forms and photographs of it in use; these overhead exhibits annotate those below.

6. In dem Vortragssaal, der bei längsgestellten Wandelementen einen umschlossenen Raum bildet, finden Diskussionen, Konzerte und Filmvorführungen statt. Das Tageslicht fällt durch ein hochgelegenes Fensterband ein. An eine Seite des Vortragssaales grenzt ein kleines Restaurant, das an einem Innenhof liegt.

7. Ein Teil der Ausstellung ist der Struktur und dem Wuchs des Baumes gewidmet. Die vierzig Jahre alte Kiefernwurzel, die an der Decke hängt, wurde aus dem Boden gelöst, indem die Feuerwehr das Erdreich fortschwemmte. Nur auf diese Weise konnten auch die feinen Wurzelfasern erhalten werden.

8. Der Innenhof von der Eingangshalle her gesehen. Über die Treppe gelangt der Besucher ins Freie und in das Arboretum, den Lehrgarten mit vielen Baumarten.

8

9

10

9. Die aufgehängte Baumwurzel von unten gesehen.
10. Eine Auswahl von Holzstühlen zeigt, wie verschiedene Techniken (und Stile) zu verschiedenen Formen führen.
11, 12. Die Besucher sollen nicht nur den optischen Sinn gebrauchen und werden beispielsweise dazu angeleitet, Holz an seinem Geruch zu erkennen oder die Oberflächen zu betasten.
13. Eine Schautafel, die die Wirkung des Werkzeugs auf die Struktur der Schnittfläche deutlich macht. Durch die bildliche Darstellung des Werkzeugs werden Erläuterungen überflüssig.
14. Spielerische Formen und Fotografien demonstrieren die vielseitige Verwendbarkeit des Holzes; die oberen Ausstellungsgegenstände kommentieren die unten gezeigten.

11

12

13

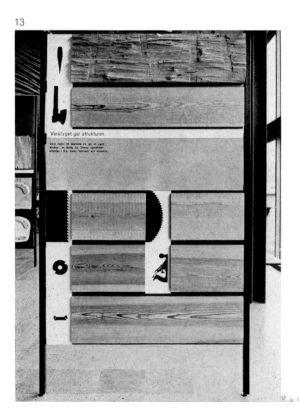

14

Provincial Museum, Falun, Sweden (1960–62)

Architect: Hakon Ahlberg

Provinzmuseum, Falun, Schweden (1960–62)

Architekt: Hakon Ahlberg

The new museum building had to adjoin an existing art gallery but had to have its main entrance some distance from the gallery on the traffic route from the town centre. Yet the point of entry itself ought, it was thought, be central to the whole group of buildings. The problem was solved by entering the site through a gateway under part of the building and approaching the main entrance hall, which now has direct access to the various sections of the museum, by walking along one side of a triangular courtyard.

Bei der Planung des neuen Museumsgebäudes war zu berücksichtigen, daß es an eine bereits bestehende Kunstgalerie anschließen sollte. Außerdem mußte der Haupteingang in einiger Entfernung von der Galerie an der Hauptverkehrsstraße vom Stadtzentrum her liegen. Der Eingangsbereich seinerseits sollte jedoch den Mittelpunkt des gesamten Gebäudekomplexes bilden. Das Problem wurde auf folgende Weise gelöst: Der Besucher geht durch einen Torweg unter einem Gebäudeteil hindurch und gelangt über den dreieckigen Hof in die Haupteingangshalle, von der aus die verschiedenen Abteilungen des Museums zu erreichen sind.

Site plan / Lageplan.
1 Entrance from street / Eingang von der Straße her
2 Main entrance / Haupteingang
3 Entrance to cafeteria / Eingang zur Cafeteria
4 Cafeteria terrace / Terrassenrestaurant
5 Existing Art Gallery / Ältere Kunstgalerie
6 River Faluån / Fluß Faluån

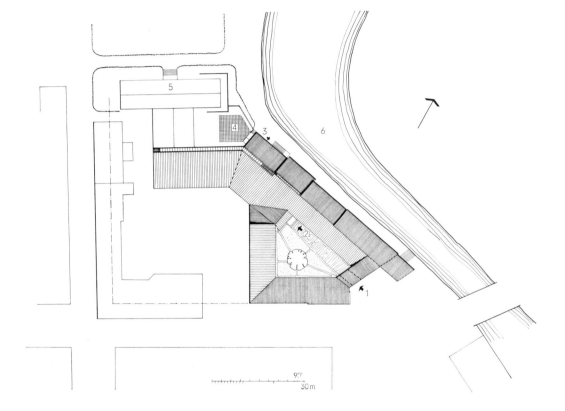

1. The new building faces the river; the steps to the bar and cafeteria are in the foreground. A terrace between the new building and the old art gallery to the right of this view looks out on the river and is used for outdoor eating. The main entrance to the museum is to the right of the bridge in the distance.
2. The entrance gateway and the court separating it from the entrance hall. A form of shop window display gives a clue to the function of the building.

1. Das neue Gebäude liegt am Fluß; im Vordergrund der Treppenaufgang zu Bar und Cafeteria. Die Stufen rechts im Bild führen zu einem Terrassenrestaurant mit Blick auf den Fluß, das zwischen dem neuen Gebäude und der alten Kunstgalerie liegt. Rechts neben der Brücke im Hintergrund ist der Haupteingang des Museums.
2. Torweg und Hof vor der Eingangshalle. Das »Schaufenster« links weist auf die Funktion des Gebäudes hin.

1   2

3. Copper household utensils are displayed on glass shelves in a room on the first floor overlooking the bridge over the river Faluån and shops in which not too dissimilar copper ware might be bought.

4. The main part of the museum is devoted to peasant art and industry from the province of Dalarna. This room on the first floor shows paintings and the costume hall can be seen through the doorway. The simplest possible means – whitewashed brickwork, boarded panels – are used to create a setting. A muslin canopy diffuses the light getting in through the high side windows. Additional lighting is provided by spotlights, which are mounted on the screens.

3. Haushaltsgegenstände aus Kupfer sind in einem Raum des ersten Geschosses auf Glasplatten angeordnet. Von dem Fenster im Hintergrund blickt der Besucher auf die Brücke über den Fluß Faluån und auf kleine Läden, in denen er recht ähnliche Kupferwaren erwerben kann.

4. In dem Museum sind hauptsächlich Volkskunst und Kunsthandwerk aus der Provinz Dalarna vertreten. Dieser Raum im ersten Geschoß zeigt Malerei, der Trachtenraum ist im Hintergrund zu erkennen. Für die Innengestaltung wurden äußerst einfache Mittel verwendet: weiß geschlämmte Ziegel, Stellwände aus Holz. Eine Deckenbespannung aus Musselin verteilt das aus den hochliegenden Seitenfenstern einfallende Tageslicht. Zusätzliche Beleuchtung erfolgt durch Spotlights, die an den Stellwänden angebracht sind.

3

4

Wasa Dockyard Museum, Stockholm (1961)

Architects: Hans Åkerblad and Björn Howander

The hull of a Swedish warship, the Wasa, was raised from the bed of Stockholm harbour in 1961 and is now being reconditioned. The enclosed pontoon which forms the major part of this museum allows this work to be carried out and at the same time provides walkways and viewing platforms for visitors. Preservation and display occur thus in this instance in the same place.

The timber of the hull which has been submerged for so long must dry out very gradually and is therefore being sprayed with a wood preservative solution and the interior of the building maintained at present at a relative humidity of 95 %. This will be progressively reduced over a number of years. The dockyard museum is a temporary arrangement likely to last seven years. The eventual position of the ship has not yet been decided.

Wasa-Schiffswerft-Museum, Stockholm (1961)

Architekten: Hans Åkerblad und Björn Howander

Das Wrack des alten schwedischen Kriegsschiffes *Wasa* wurde 1961 vom Grund des Stockholmer Hafens gehoben und wird zur Zeit renoviert und rekonstruiert. Diese Arbeit geht in dem umschlossenen Ponton vor sich, der den größten Teil des Museums bildet. Umgänge und Plattformen erlauben es dem Besucher, den Werftarbeitern bei ihrer Tätigkeit zuzusehen. Bei diesem Museum sind also Ausstellung und Restaurationsarbeiten an einem Platz vereinigt. Das Holz des Schiffsrumpfes, der lange Zeit unter Wasser gelegen hatte, darf nur allmählich trocknen. Es wird deshalb mit einem Konservierungsmittel besprüht; im Inneren des Pontons herrscht eine relative Luftfeuchtigkeit von 95%, die im Laufe der Jahre nach und nach verringert wird. Das Schiffswerft-Museum ist eine befristete Einrichtung, die etwa sieben Jahre lang bestehen wird. Wohin die *Wasa* dann kommt, ist noch nicht entschieden.

1

2

3

4

5

1. The main building has at its landward side a courtyard with an exhibition hall and restaurant on the south side and a group of offices and workshops on the north side. The yard, which is divided by a covered walkway, will eventually display some of the larger objects as they are raised from the sea.
2. Perspective showing the entrance.
3. Section through the pontoon and its superstructure which consists of pre-stressed concrete portals covered in corrugated aluminium.
4. The main building seen from the southwest is at the seaward end of a group of new structures and is very much part of Stockholm harbour.
5. A corner of the restaurant which has an oblique view of the harbour; the cafeteria and its balcony also act as assembly points for conducted tours.
6. The exhibition hall has the whole of one side open onto the courtyard and is meant to be used for a number of exhibitions which will be organised as the work on the Wasa proceeds.
7, 8. The lower and upper viewing galleries within the main building allow the hull of the *Wasa* to be seen from all sides. The work of reconditioning the ship is done from the scaffolding. The lower gallery is glazed on one side and the harbour and skyline of Stockholm are continually visible.

6

7

8

1. An der Landseite des Pontons liegt ein Hof, der südlich von einer Ausstellungshalle und einem Restaurant, nördlich von Büros und Werkstätten begrenzt wird. Der Hof, der durch eine überdachte Passage unterteilt ist, soll später Ausstellungsgegenstände aufnehmen, die vom Meeresgrund geborgen werden.
2. Perspektive mit Blick auf den Haupteingang.
3. Schnitt durch den Pontonaufbau; die vorgespannten Betonrahmen sind mit Wellblech aus Aluminium verkleidet.
4. Ansicht von Südwesten. Der schwimmende Pontonbau des Museums ist zu einem Bestandteil des Stockholmer Hafens geworden; die weiteren Museumsgebäude befinden sich auf dem Land hinter dem Ponton.
5. Von einer Ecke des Restaurants kann der Besucher auf den Hafen blicken. Die Teilnehmer an Gruppenführungen treffen sich im Restaurant und auf dem davorliegenden Balkon.
6. Die Ausstellungshalle öffnet sich auf ihrer nördlichen Seite zum Hof hin. In dem Maße, wie die Arbeit an der *Wasa* fortschreitet, sollen hier wechselnde Ausstellungen des Schiffszubehörs gezeigt werden.
7, 8. Von der oberen und unteren Zuschauergalerie im Pontongehäuse kann man die *Wasa* von allen Seiten betrachten. Die Restaurationsarbeiten werden auf Gerüsten durchgeführt. Die untere Galerie wurde auf einer Seite verglast, so daß Hafen und Stadtsilhouette von Stockholm sichtbar sind.

Bird Migration Museum, Öland, Sweden (1960)

Architect: Jan Gezelius

Zugvogel-Museum, Öland, Schweden (1960)

Architekt: Jan Gezelius

This museum is no more than a small barn. What makes it remarkable is that it was able to remain a barn and yet combine structure, lighting and exhibition space into coherent architecture. It does this moreover in the face of extraordinarily dramatic competition from great flocks of migratory birds (see Fig. 1). The exhibition is devoted to showing the annual rhythm of the many species which pass this point.

Das Zugvogel-Museum auf Öland ist im Grunde nicht mehr als eine kleine Scheune, errichtet in unmittelbarer Nachbarschaft eines Leuchtturms. Bemerkenswert wird es dadurch, daß es trotzdem durch Konstruktion, Beleuchtung und Gestaltung des Ausstellungsbereichs ein einheitliches architektonisches Bild bietet und sich in seiner äußeren Erscheinung sogar gegenüber der außerordentlich dramatischen Konkurrenz der großen Zugvogelscharen (Abb. 1) behauptet. Die Ausstellung des Museums demonstriert den Jahresrhythmus der vielen Vogelarten, die über die Insel ziehen.

2. The south point of Öland, an island in the Baltic off the coast of Sweden, seen here from the East, ends in a peninsula about 200 yards wide. The museum is the first building to be met as one approaches from the land side. It is placed there so that it may attract visitors and keep them away from the research area near the light house.
3. The museum seen from the approach road.

2. Blick von Osten auf die etwa 180 m breite Südspitze von Öland, einer Insel in der Ostsee vor der schwedischen Küste. Den Besuchern vom Festland stellt sich als erstes Gebäude das Museum entgegen. Es wurde an dieser Stelle errichtet, weil es die Besucher anziehen und informieren, gleichzeitig aber von dem Forschungsbereich um den Leuchtturm herum fernhalten soll.
3. Blick von Norden auf das Museum, im Hintergrund der Leuchtturm.

1

2

3

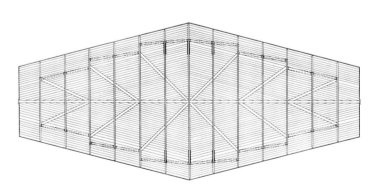

Ceiling plan / Deckenuntersicht.

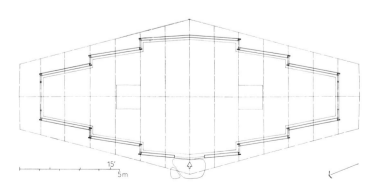

15'
5m

Plan, ground floor / Grundriß Erdgeschoß.

4. The entrance; the boarding is painted blue, the remainder white.

5. The staggered walls act as display panels and are side-lit by narrow windows screened by white cotton curtains. There is no artificial lighting.

6. The black and white photographs describing the nesting and breeding in the north are on moss green, blue and indigo panels; those showing life in the south are on a sand or light ochre coloured background. The mural facing the entrance combines these two colour groups.

4. Der Eingang des Museums; die Holzverkleidung ist blaugestrichen, die übrigen Flächen sind weiß.

5. Die stufenförmig angeordneten Wände nehmen die Ausstellungstafeln auf. Das Licht fällt seitlich durch schmale Fenster sowie durch Oberlichter ein und wird von weißen Baumwollgardinen gefiltert. Künstliche Beleuchtung ist nicht vorgesehen.

6. Die Schwarz-Weiß-Fotografien, die den Nestbau und das Brüten der Vögel im Norden darstellen, sind an moosgrünen, blauen und indigofarbenen Platten befestigt; die Abbildungen, die das Leben im Süden zeigen, hängen vor einem sandfarbenen oder hell ocker getönten Hintergrund. Die Wandbespannung gegenüber dem Eingang vereint diese beiden Farbengruppen.

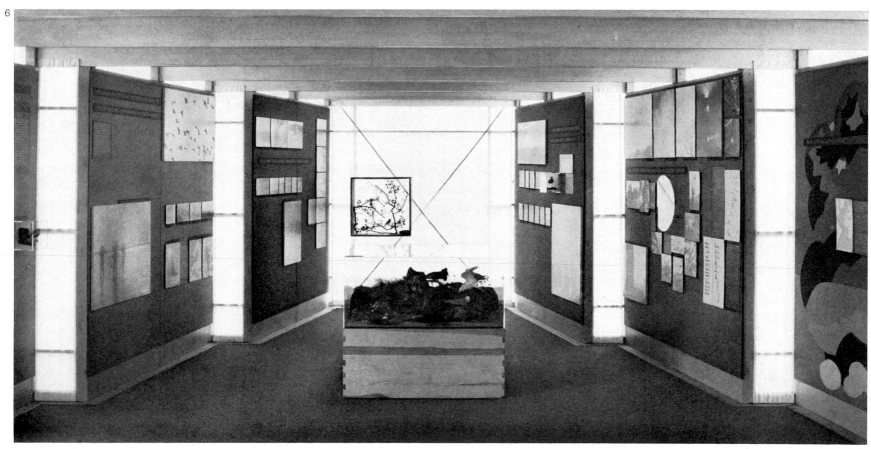

The tradition, except perhaps in Switzerland, is that of great national collections: the Louvre, the museums in Berlin, Munich, or Dresden, the Kunsthistorisches Museum in Vienna. Certain of these have recently been remodelled, have had the amount on display reduced and their lighting improved. At the Alte Pinakothek in Munich, for instance, the change is considerable. This activity has been paralleled by the building of relatively small institutions devoted to showing work unconnected with the historical collections – modern art, technology, ethnography.

The museum on the sea front of Le Havre, the Fernand Léger Museum at Biot, the Maeght Foundation at St. Paul-de-Vence, the small Kunsthalle at Darmstadt, the Folkwang Museum at Essen, the Reuchlinhaus at Pforzheim and the Austrian Pavilion of the Brussels Exposition which has now been rebuilt in Vienna are all devoted to showing modern art; the new arrangements within the Deutsches Museum in Munich and the Swiss Transport Museum at Lucerne deal with technology; the addition at Neuchâtel with ethnography. The design of most of these buildings – Sert's Maeght Foundation perhaps excepted – has been based on the desire to achieve rather anonymous, neutral spaces which would be highly flexible in use. In practice this has generally meant large spaces and controlled top-lighting. The emphasis thus differs considerably from the Italian and the Scandinavian attitudes except where old buildings were used as at the Grimaldi Museum at Antibes or the Schnütgen Museum at Cologne.

Frankreich, Deutschland und Österreich verfügen über traditionsreiche Nationalsammlungen wie etwa den Louvre, die Sammlungen in Berlin, München oder Dresden und das Kunsthistorische Museum in Wien. Einige dieser großen Museen sind in der letzten Zeit neu organisiert worden, die Zahl der Ausstellungsgegenstände wurde eingeschränkt und die Beleuchtung verbessert. In der Alten Pinakothek in München wurden beispielsweise bedeutende Umbauten vorgenommen. Außerdem entstanden in allen diesen Ländern relativ kleine Museumsneubauten, die sich nicht mit historischen Sammlungen, sondern mit moderner Kunst, Technik und Völkerkunde befassen. Moderne Kunst zeigen das Museum in Le Havre, das Léger Museum in Biot, die Fondation Maeght in St. Paul-de-Vence, die kleine Kunsthalle in Darmstadt, das Museum Folkwang in Essen, das Reuchlinhaus in Pforzheim und der Österreichische Pavillon der Brüsseler Weltausstellung, der in Wien wieder aufgebaut wurde. Die neuen Ausstellungen des Deutschen Museums in München und das Verkehrshaus der Schweiz in Luzern beschäftigen sich mit der Technik, der Anbau in Neuchâtel mit Völkerkunde. Bei allen diesen Bauten – vielleicht mit Ausnahme von Serts Fondation Maeght – war der Grundsatz vorherrschend, anonyme, neutrale und vielseitig verwendbare Räumlichkeiten zu schaffen. In der Praxis führte dieses Prinzip zu großen Ausstellungsflächen mit regulierbarem Oberlicht. Die Entwicklungstendenzen unterscheiden sich also beträchtlich von der italienischen und skandinavischen Einstellung zur Museumsarchitektur, mit Ausnahme der Museen, die in alten Bauwerken untergebracht wurden, wie das Musée Grimaldi in Antibes oder das Schnütgen-Museum in Köln.

1

2

1, 2. The Swiss Transport Museum at Lucerne was opened in 1959 and consists of a number of pavilions around a large court in which the oldest Swiss steamship dating from 1847 has been placed. This has now been fitted out as the museum restaurant. The group is on the edge of the lake just outside the town and was designed by Dreyer, Käppeli and Huber.

1, 2. Das Verkehrshaus der Schweiz in Luzern von Dreyer, Käppeli und Huber wurde 1959 eröffnet und liegt nahe bei der Stadt am Vierwaldstätter See. Mehrere Pavillons sind um einen Hof angeordnet, in dem das älteste Schweizer Dampfschiff aus dem Jahre 1847 – heute das Museumsrestaurant – einen Platz fand.

Musée Maison de la Culture, Le Havre (1961)

Architects: Guy Lagneau, Michel Weill, J. Dimitrijevic, and R. Audigier

This is the first art gallery the French State has built since 1937; the other two new museums in France – the Musée Fernand Léger at Biot which opened in 1960 and the Maeght Foundation at Vence – are private institutions. The building at Le Havre, apart from being a museum, also acts as a cultural centre to the rebuilt town. It thus includes a film projection room, photographic studios, a library, a conference room and a club. The exhibition space is a single illuminated volume standing on a podium of subsidiary rooms. Side lighting is controlled by venetian blinds, top lighting by a canopy of aluminium louvres – a horizontal brise-soleil – placed clear above the glass roof. Within this totally lit space there are several levels of exhibition space which can be sub-divided by suspended planes and screens held between a regular grid of floor and ceiling fittings.

Transverse section / Querschnitt.
A Lower ground floor / Untergeschoß
B Ground floor / Erdgeschoß
C First floor / Erstes Geschoß

Musée Maison de la Culture, Le Havre (1961)

Architekten: Guy Lagneau, Michel Weill, J. Dimitrijevic und R. Audigier

Das Maison de la Culture ist das erste Museum, das der französische Staat seit 1937 errichtete. Die beiden anderen neuen Museen in Frankreich – das Musée Fernand Léger in Biot (eröffnet 1960) und die Fondation Maeght in Vence – entstanden auf private Initiative. Das Maison de la Culture in Le Havre ist nicht nur ein Museum, sondern auch ein Kulturzentrum für die neuerstandene Stadt. Es enthält unter anderem einen Filmvorführraum, Fotoateliers, eine Bibliothek, einen Vortragssaal und einen Clubraum. Der Bau besteht aus einem einzigen Volumen, das sich über einem Sockel von Nebenräumen erhebt. Das Seitenlicht wird durch Lamellenstores reguliert, das Oberlicht durch einen Filter aus Aluminium-Blenden (eine Art horizontale brise-soleil), der frei über dem Glasdach angebracht ist. Innerhalb dieses voll ausgeleuchteten Bereichs liegen die Ausstellungsflächen auf verschiedenen Niveaus. Aufgehängte Platten und Trennwände, die in ein regelmäßiges Raster an Boden und Decke eingepaßt sind, unterteilen den Raum.

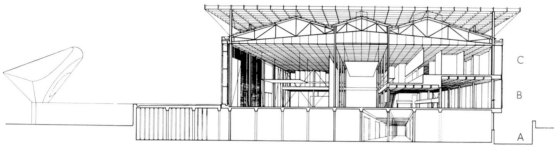

C
B
A

1. The museum from the sea front with Georges Henri Adam's sculpture thrust forward on a prow. It is seen from both the outside and the inside and acts as a sort of visual pivot.

1. Eine Skulptur von Georges Henri Adam kragt über einer bugförmigen Mauer aus. Sie ist von innen und außen sichtbar und bildet eine Art visuellen Orientierungspunkt.

1

5

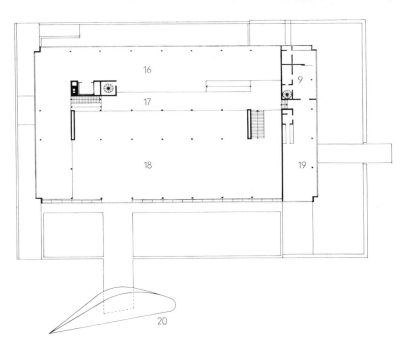

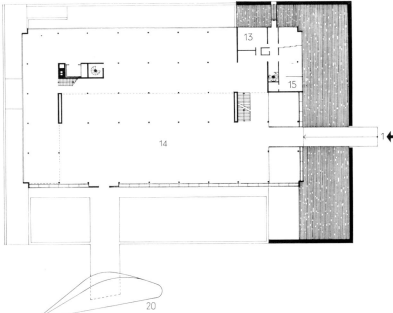

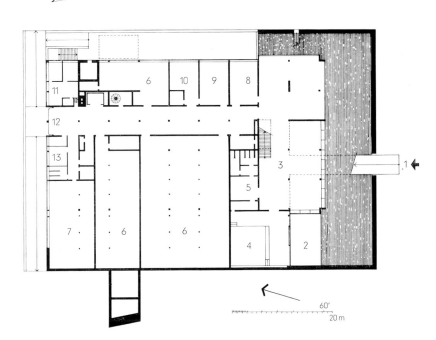

60'
20 m

Plan, first floor / Grundriß erstes Geschoß.
Plan, ground floor / Grundriß Erdgeschoß.
Plan, lower ground floor / Grundriß Untergeschoß.
 1 Entrance ramp / Eingangsrampe
 2 Terrace / Terrasse
 3 Lower exhibition gallery / Unterer Ausstellungsraum
 4 Lecture room / Vortragssaal
 5 Cloak room / Garderobe
 6 Store / Magazin
 7 Art school / Kunstschule
 8 Study collection / Studiensammlung
 9 Workshop / Werkstatt
10 Photography / Fotoatelier
11 Porter / Pförtner
12 Reception and dispatch / Anlieferung und Versand
13 Office / Büro
14 Main gallery / Hauptausstellungssaal
15 Library / Bibliothek
16 Exhibition gallery / Ausstellungsraum
17 Balcony / Balkon
18 Upper part of main gallery / Luftraum Hauptausstellungssaal
19 Club / Clubraum
20 Sculpture / Skulptur

2. The building is surrounded by a pool on three sides and the entrance is reached by crossing a bridge.

2. Das Museum ist auf drei Seiten von einem Teich umgeben. Um zum Eingang zu gelangen, muß der Besucher eine Rampe überqueren.

3. Part of the roof canopy of aluminium louvres.

3. Die Aluminium-Blenden des oberen Daches.

3

4

4. Museums are, or at least should be, used a great deal at night and their illuminated appearance is thus of considerable importance.

4. Museen sollten auch abends zugänglich sein; deshalb ist auch die Wirkung des erleuchteten Gebäudes außerordentlich wichtig.

5. The main exhibition hall looking west out over the outer harbour.
6. The stairs going up from the entrance to the first floor; the door to the club room is at the top on the right.

5. Der große Ausstellungssaal mit Blick auf den Hafen.
6. Treppe vom Eingang zum ersten Geschoß; rechts oben die Tür zum Clubraum.

5

6

7. The main hall seen from above with the three levels again visible. The continuous and uncontrolled striving for transparency makes the actual viewing of objects difficult; the belief that given an almost non-existent or at least invisible enclosure, the display will become more prominent, has in fact turned out to be mistaken.

8. The lower part of the entrance space.

9. The three levels of the exhibition area: the upper part of the first floor on the left, the balcony level in the centre and the void of the main hall on the right.

7. Der große Saal von oben gesehen; die drei Niveaus sind auch hier zu erkennen. Die Neigung zu weitgehender Transparenz macht es schwierig, die Kunstwerke einzeln zu betrachten. Die Annahme, daß die Objekte bei kaum vorhandener oder zumindest unsichtbarer Umschließung betont werden, hat sich als falsch herausgestellt.

8. Der untere Teil des Eingangsbereiches.

9. Die drei Niveaus des Ausstellungsbereichs: links der obere Teil des ersten Geschosses, in der Mitte das Balkon-Niveau, rechts der leere Raum über dem großen Saal.

Museum of the Maeght Foundation, St. Paul-de-Vence, France (1961–64)

Architects: Sert, Jackson and Gourley

The museum was founded by Aimé Maeght whose art gallery in Paris has exhibited many of the artists represented in the museum and whose publishing house has issued a considerable number of books on modern art. He commissioned the architects after seeing the studio Sert designed for Miró in Mallorca.

The buildings form a kind of village on a hillside opposite Saint Paul-de-Vence and overlook the Bay of Antibes. They are grouped as if about a "Village Square" and "Town Hall"; behind them are the Maritime Alps. The buildings and their connecting stonewalls form a continuity of internal and external spaces, each space usually used for the display of the work of a particular painter or sculptor. The rooms, buildings and spaces between buildings thus tend to be in scale with the display as well as the existing vernacular buildings in the area.

The basement of the museum is used for deliveries, storage, workshops, offices and mechanical equipment providing heating, ventilation and humidity control. There is also a cinema seating a hundred

Although the buildings form a highly irregular group on the pine covered slope, the museum is intended to be seen in a particular sequence. The path from the car park curves around the porter's lodge and ticket booth and crosses an entrance court at an angle. From the entrance hall, reached across a bridge between two pools, the visitor is meant to turn left and go through a series of galleries and ante-rooms around a central grassed court. After returning to the entrance hall he goes into the two-storey high "Town Hall" part, ascends to the roof garden to see the curved roofs and terraces from above, and the sea beyond, then returns to the ground and a terraced garden with labyrinthine stone walls enclosing sculpture by Miró and Artigas. From the lowest terrace some steps lead to a door-like opening which gives on to the paved main court with the entrance hall at the far end. After passing through this and crossing the bridge again, the visitor can turn left and go to a small chapel which is built with old stone walls but roofed with the same concrete shells as the museum. Its stained glass windows are by Braque and Ubac.

1. Model of site / Modellaufnahme.

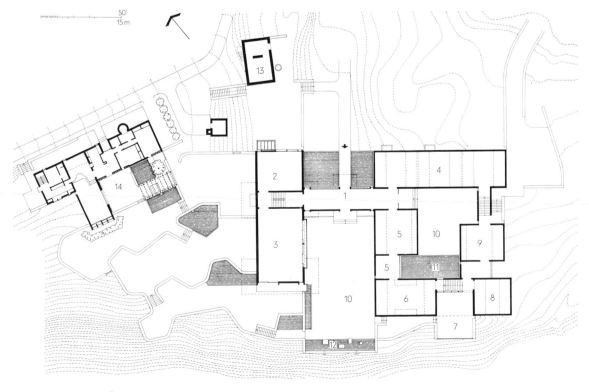

Site plan / Lageplan.
1 Entrance hall / Eingangshalle
2 Exhibition gallery (books and prints) / Ausstellungsraum für Bücher und Druckgraphik
3 Conference hall / Versammlungsraum
4 Exhibition gallery / Ausstellungsraum
5 Exhibition gallery (Braque) / Ausstellungsraum (Braque)
6 Exhibition gallery (Miró) / Ausstellungsraum (Miró)
7 Courtyard (Miró) / Hof (Miró)
8 Exhibition gallery (Chagall) / Ausstellungsraum (Chagall)
9 Exhibition gallery (Giacometti) / Ausstellungsraum (Giacometti)
10 Courtyard / Hof
11 Pool / Wasserbecken
12 Pool with Giacometti sculptures / Wasserbecken mit Skulpturen von Giacometti
13 Chapel / Kapelle
14 Director's house / Haus des Direktors

Museum Fondation Maeght, St. Paul-de-Vence, Frankreich (1961–64)

Architekten: Sert, Jackson & Gourley

Das Museum wurde von Aimé Maeght gegründet, der in seiner Pariser Kunstgalerie viele der im Museum vertretenen Künstler ausgestellt und in seinem Verlag zahlreiche Bücher über moderne Kunst veröffentlicht hat. Maeght beauftragte die Architekten mit dem Bau des Museums, nachdem er ihr Ateliergebäude für Miró auf Mallorca gesehen hatte.

Die Gebäude bilden eine Art Dorf auf einem Berg gegenüber St. Paul-de-Vence und haben Ausblick auf die Bucht von Antibes; dahinter erheben sich die französischen Seealpen. Die Bauten, die um einen »Dorfplatz« und ein »Rathaus« angeordnet sind, und die verbindenden Steinmauern schaffen eine kontinuierliche Folge von Innen- und Außenräumen. Jeder Bezirk ist als Ausstellungsfläche für einen einzelnen Maler oder Bildhauer vorgesehen. Die Innenräume, die Bauvolumen und die Bereiche zwischen den Gebäuden entsprechen im Maßstab den ausgestellten Kunstwerken wie auch der ortsüblichen Architektur der Gegend.

Das Untergeschoß des Museums enthält Anlieferung, Lagerräume, Werkstätten, Büros und technische Anlagen für Heizung, Ventilation und Feuchtigkeitskontrolle. Auch ein Filmvorführraum ist vorhanden, der hundert Personen Platz bietet.

Obwohl die Gebäude auf dem mit Pinien bewachsenen Berghang eine völlig unregelmäßige Gruppe bilden, ist das Museum auf eine bestimmte Abfolge hin angelegt. Der Weg vom Parkplatz her führt um die Pförtnerloge und Kartenverkaufsstelle herum durch einen Vorhof. Von der Eingangshalle, die der Besucher über eine Brücke zwischen zwei Wasserbecken erreicht, wendet er sich nach links und geht durch Ausstellungsräume und Vorräume, die um einen mit Gras bewachsenen Innenhof liegen. Wenn er zur Eingangshalle zurückgekehrt ist, gelangt er in das zwei Geschosse hohe »Rathaus«, steigt auf die Dachterrasse, die ihm einen Blick auf die geschwungenen Dächer und das Meer im Hintergrund bietet, und steigt dann wieder herunter in einen terrassenartig angelegten Garten mit labyrinthischen Steinmauern, in dem Skulpturen von Miró und Artigas aufgestellt sind. Von der untersten Terrasse führen einige Stufen zu einer türähnlichen Öffnung, hinter der der gepflasterte Haupthof mit der Eingangshalle liegt. Wenn der Besucher durch diese Eingangshalle zurückgegangen ist und wiederum die Brücke überquert, kann er sich nach links wenden und gelangt dann zu einer kleinen Kapelle, bei der alte Mauerreste verwandt wurden, die aber mit den gleichen Betonschalen gedeckt ist wie das Museum. Die Glasfenster stammen von Braque und Ubac.

2

3

Section through exhibition gallery / Schnitt durch den großen Ausstellungsraum.

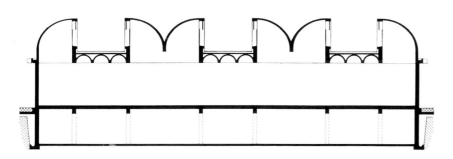

Section through "Town Hall" / Schnitt durch das »Rathaus«.
1 Conference room / Versammlungsraum
2 Exhibition gallery / Ausstellungsraum

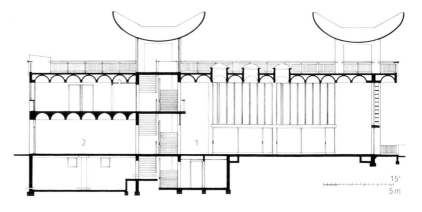

4

2. The main entrance to the museum; the path from the car park becomes a bridge between two pools.
3. The galleries of this part of the museum are entirely lit from above but the small ante-rooms between them look out onto this grassed court with pine trees and the sculpture by Miró seen at left.
4, 5. The largest of the rooms in the section to the left of the entrance hall (5). This is used to show the work of young painters and sculptors. Like all other galleries in this section it is lit from above by daylight reflected off the curved shells. The smaller barrel vaults between the larger shells carry channels for artificial lighting tracks (4).
6. Two of the concrete shells which reflect light from the monitor windows glazed with translucent diffusing glass.

2. Der Haupteingang des Museums; der Weg vom Parkplatz her wird zur Brücke zwischen zwei Wasserbecken.
3. Die Ausstellungsräume in diesem Teil des Museums werden ausschließlich durch Oberlichter beleuchtet; die dazwischen liegenden kleinen Vorräume haben jedoch Öffnungen auf den Hof mit den Pinien und der Plastik von Miró (links).

4, 5. Der größte Ausstellungsraum links von der Eingangshalle, der für junge Maler und Bildhauer bestimmt ist (5). Wie alle anderen Ausstellungsräume der Abteilung ist auch dieser Raum durch Tageslicht beleuchtet, das oben einfällt und von den gekrümmten Schalen reflektiert wird. Die kleineren Tonnengewölbe zwischen den Schalen, wie sie Abb. 4 im Miró-Raum zeigt, enthalten die Installationen für künstliche Beleuchtung.
6. Zwei der Betonschalen, die das Licht der Oberlichter reflektieren. Die Oberlichter sind mit milchigen, lichtstreuenden Scheiben verglast.

5

6

7

7. The main court with the "Town Hall" on the left. This two storey building has a large exhibition and meeting room 18′ 6″ high on the ground floor at its southern end. This is lit by roof lights and side windows screened by grilles of white glazed volcanic stone.

8, 9. The main court paved with terracotta tiles seen during the day and at night. Giacometti's *Personnages* occupy this regular almost village like square. On the south side, opposite the entrance hall, there is a view to the sea across a rectangular pool which terminates the square.

7. Der Haupthof, links das »Rathaus«. Das zwei Geschosse hohe Gebäude enthält im Erdgeschoß nach Süden einen großen Ausstellungs- und Versammlungsraum, der 5,65 m hoch ist. Dieser Raum wird durch Oberlichter und durch seitliche Fenster erhellt, die durch Gitter aus weißem Vulkanstein abgeschirmt sind.

8, 9. Tages- und Nachtaufnahme des Haupthofes, der mit Terrakottaplatten gepflastert ist. Giacomettis *Personnages* sind in diesem Hof aufgestellt, der beinahe den Charakter eines Dorfplatzes hat. Auf der Südseite gegenüber der Eingangshalle kann man über ein rechteckiges Wasserbecken, das den Platz begrenzt, bis zum Meer blicken.

8

9

Kunsthalle, Darmstadt, Germany (1956)

Architect: Theo Pabst

Kunsthalle Darmstadt (1956)

Architekt: Theo Pabst

The photographs show the first stage of the gallery designed to replace the building of the Art Club destroyed during the war. The budget for the building was limited and the design is thus extremely simple, using all the available space for display. Exhibitions are not only staged in the top-lit main room which will eventually be the central space of the building but also in the narrow side-lit entrance hall. The art gallery as a whole gains from this change in character between the two areas.

Das Museum, dessen erster Teil fertiggestellt ist, soll das kriegszerstörte Gebäude des Kunstvereins ersetzen. Für den Bau standen nur begrenzte Mittel zur Verfügung; das Bauwerk wurde deshalb außerordentlich einfach konzipiert, die gesamte Fläche ist für Ausstellungszwecke genutzt. Die Ausstellungen finden nicht nur in dem von oben beleuchteten Hauptraum statt, der später den Mittelpunkt des Gebäudes bilden wird, sondern erstrecken sich auch auf die schmale, mit Seitenlicht versehene Eingangshalle. Der Gesamteindruck der Kunsthalle gewinnt durch den verschiedenartigen Charakter dieser beiden Bereiche.

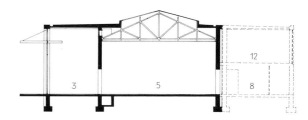

Section / Schnitt.

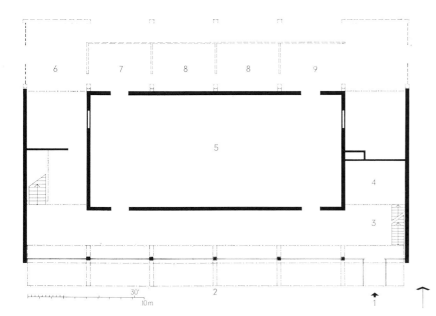

Plan, ground floor / Grundriß Erdgeschoß.

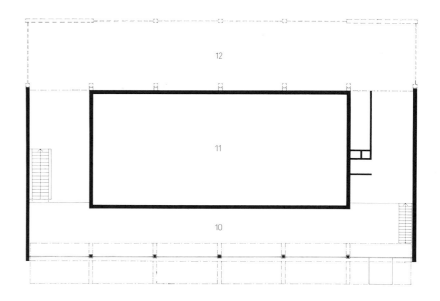

Plan, first floor / Grundriß erstes Geschoß.

The dotted lines on the north side show the future extension of the building.
Die gestrichelten Linien an der Nordseite bezeichnen die geplante Erweiterung des Gebäudes.

1 Entrance / Eingang
2 Horizontal sun-breaker at clerestory level / Lamellen-Vordach, das die gegenüberliegende Wand vor Sonnenlicht schützt
3 Entrance hall (side lit) / Eingangshalle (Seitenlicht)
4 Coats / Garderobe
5 Main picture gallery (top lit) / Hauptausstellungsraum (Oberlicht)
6 Lecture room / Vortragssaal
7 Ante-room / Vorraum
8 Office / Büro
9 Workspace / Arbeitsbereich
10 Void over entrance hall / Luftraum Eingangshalle
11 Void over picture gallery / Luftraum Hauptausstellungssaal
12 Exhibition area (side lit) / Ausstellungsbereich (Seitenlicht)

1. The south side faces a small square. The entrance to the gallery is on the right.

1. Die Südseite der Kunsthalle liegt an einem kleinen Platz; rechts der Eingang zu den Ausstellungsräumen.

2

3

2, 3. A slatted canopy which continues into the inside shields the south facing glass wall of the entrance space.

2, 3. Ein Lamellen-Vordach, das sich im Inneren fortsetzt, schützt die verglaste Südfassade der Eingangshalle gegen Sonneneinfall.

4, 5. The proportions of this space are sometimes altered for temporary exhibits. In this display of Yoruba art a sloping ceiling has been suspended on wires.

4, 5. Die Dimensionen des Eingangsbereichs können bei Wechselausstellungen verändert werden. Für diese Ausstellung von Yoruba-Kunst wurden eine schräggeneigte Decke an Drähten aufgehängt und Stellwände eingezogen.

4

5

6–9. The top-lit hall is also used for temporary exhibitions and its volume is usually subdivided by high screens.
6, 7. Mexican folk art.
8. Work by Wilhelm Grimm.
9. Yoruba sculpture.

6–9. Der Oberlichtraum nimmt ebenfalls Wechselausstellungen auf; er wird gewöhnlich durch hohe Stellwände unterteilt.
6, 7. Mexikanische Volkskunst.
8. Arbeiten von Wilhelm Grimm.
9. Yoruba-Plastik.

7

6

8

5

9

Badisches Landesmuseum, Karlsruhe, Germany (1959)

Architect: State Building Department, Karlsruhe; Interior Dieter Quast

Badisches Landesmuseum, Karlsruhe (1959)

Architekt: Staatliches Hochbauamt Karlsruhe; Innenausstattung Dieter Quast

Like so many Italian museums the castle at Karlsruhe was damaged during the war. It was gutted by a fire in an air-raid in 1944 and the rebuilding of its interior was not started until 1956. The surviving 18th-century facade has been restored but the interior spaces are completely new and were designed to house what remained of the several collections which originally formed the Landesmuseum. These were the Hall of Antiquities of the Grand Dukes of Baden which included trophies captured from the Turks; a museum of arts and crafts founded in 1890 with various collections of pottery, furnishings and tiled stoves; Greek, Etruscan and Roman antiquities and a collection of weapons and finally, a very large collection of coins. The number of exhibits in the newly arranged rooms has been deliberately kept small in the belief that a few selected objects which can really be seen and understood will convey more than a vast number indiscriminately crowded together.

Wie so viele italienische Museen wurde auch das Schloß in Karlsruhe während des Krieges beschädigt. Es brannte 1944 nach einem Luftangriff aus, und die Wiederherstellung des Inneren konnte erst 1956 begonnen werden. Die erhaltene Fassade aus dem 18. Jahrhundert wurde restauriert; die Innenräume wurden dagegen völlig neu gestaltet und nehmen die Sammlungen des Landesmuseums auf. Zu diesen gehören: vor- und frühgeschichtliche Bestände; eine umfangreiche Antiken-Abteilung mit griechischen und etruskischen Vasen, Terrakotten, Bronzen und Schmuck sowie ägyptische und römische Altertümer; die türkische Trophäensammlung des Markgrafen Ludwig Wilhelm von Baden; Skulpturen und Kunsthandwerk vom frühen Mittelalter bis zur Gegenwart; badische Volkskunst und ein Münzkabinett. Die Zahl der ausgestellten Gegenstände ist in den neuorganisierten Räumen absichtlich klein gehalten worden. Man ging von der Voraussetzung aus, daß wenige ausgewählte Objekte einen stärkeren Eindruck vermitteln als zahllose unübersichtlich angeordnete Ausstellungsstücke.

1

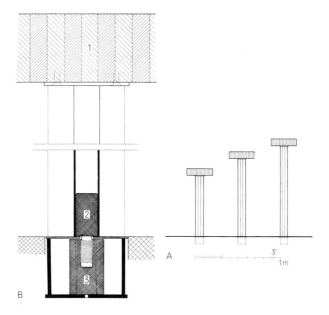

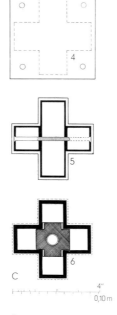

A

3′
1m

Removable pedestals, Mediaeval section / Ständerkreuze Abteilung Mittelalter.
A Elevation (three standard heights) / Ansicht (drei Standardhöhen)
B Section / Schnitt
C Plans / Grundrisse
1 Teak top / Teakholzplatte
2 Steel socket / Stahlsockel
3 Steel base in floor / In den Boden eingelassene Stahlbasis
4 Top plate / Kopfplatte
5 Cruciform pedestal composed of three hollow rectangular sections screwed together / Ständerkreuz, aus drei hohlen rechteckigen Profilen zusammengeschraubt
6 Cruciform base set in floor / In den Boden eingelassene kreuzförmige Basis

B

C

4″
0,10 m

2

3

10

1. The restored 18th-century castle is surrounded by a park at the apex of the fan-shaped layout of the city. The town centre is only a few minutes away.

2–4. Views in the two large rooms to the right and left of the main entrance are carefully controlled and show the application of some of the lessons of recent Italian design. Floor sockets have been let into the corners between the limestone paving slabs and pedestals can be fixed to these. Screens are often placed diagonally to the windows so that the light should show up the relief of the sculptures. Stained glass is placed either in front of windows or in cases artificially lit from behind.

5. The upper garden room, white with a blue carpet and its light diffused by muslin curtains, houses porcelain and wood carvings of the Rococo and has something of the character of that period. The angel by J. A. Feuchtmayer carved in 1750 hangs in front of a white screen held between floor and ceiling; behind it there is a group of furniture.

1. Das restaurierte Schloß aus dem 18. Jahrhundert, das im Scheitelpunkt der fächerförmigen Stadtanlage liegt, ist von einem Park umgeben. Das Museum ist nur wenige Minuten vom Stadtzentrum entfernt.

2–4. Die Blickwinkel sind in den beiden großen Räumen rechts und links vom Haupteingang sorgfältig berechnet, und die Aufstellung erinnert an italienische Beispiele. An den Ecken der Sandsteinplatten wurden in den Boden Buchsen eingelassen, in denen Ständerkreuze befestigt werden können. Die Stellwände stehen häufig diagonal zum Fenster, damit das Licht die Reliefs der Skulpturen zur Geltung bringt. Glasmalereien sind entweder vor den Fenstern angebracht oder in Kästen, wo sie künstliche Beleuchtung von hinten erhalten.

5. Der obere Gartensaal mit seinem blauen Teppich, den weißen Wänden, den Musselinvorhängen und dem diffusen Licht hat etwas von dem Charakter der Epoche, die hier vertreten ist: Porzellan und Holzschnitzereien aus dem Rokoko. Der Engel von J. A. Feuchtmayer (1750) hängt vor einer weißen Schirmwand, die an Fußboden und Decke befestigt ist; dahinter eine Möbelgruppe.

5

4

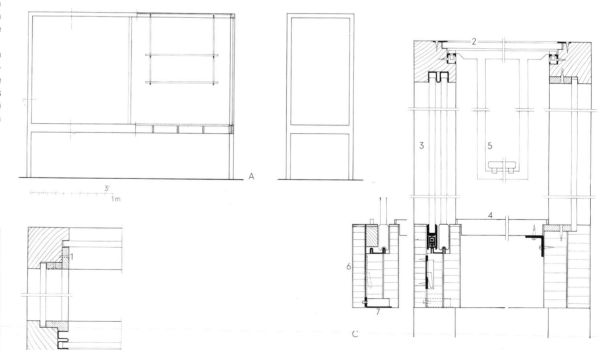

A

B

C

Wooden showcase, Rococo section / Vitrine, ahornfurniert, Abteilung Rokoko.
A Elevation and section of maple case / Ansicht und Schnitt
B Detail of corner, plan / Eckendetail, Grundriß
C Detail sections / Detailschnitte

1 Plate glass held by maple beads / Glasplatte, in das Holz eingelassen und mit Schrauben befestigt
2 Glass top / Glasscheibe
3 Glass sliding doors / Glasschiebetüren
4 Maple veneered plywood / Ahornfurnierte Tischlerplatte
5 Suspended frames for glass shelves / Eingehängte Rahmen für Glasplatten
6 Removable cover / Abnehmbare Abdeckleiste
7 Lock / Schloß

6

7

8

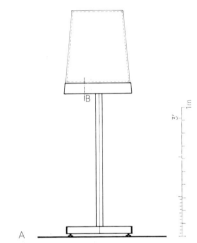

A

B

9

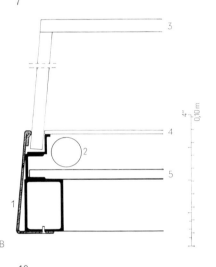

10

Pedestal showcase, Marble room / Vitrine mit Ständer, Marmorsaal.
A Elevation / Ansicht
B Section through case / Schnitt durch die Vitrine
1 Anodized aluminium edge / Eloxiertes Aluminium-profil
2 Light fitting / Beleuchtung
3 Glass / Glas
4 Etched glass / Geätztes Glas
5 Perforated plywood base / Perforierte Tischlerplatte

6–8. Many of the smaller cases not individually lit have sloping sides to prevent the disturbing effect of reflection.
9. Exhibits are often related to maps or, as here, to an enlarged etching of a battle scene.
10. The armour of a knight and horse are mounted on supports at a natural height and thus make the relation obvious.

6–8. Viele kleinere Vitrinen, die zum Teil nicht einzeln beleuchtet werden, haben abgeschrägte Seiten, um störende Lichtreflexe auszuschalten.
9. Die Ausstellungsgegenstände sind häufig zu Landkarten oder – wie hier – zu dem vergrößerten Stich einer Schlachtszene in Beziehung gesetzt.
10. Harnisch und Roßstirn, deren Aufstellung in natürlicher Höhe den Zusammenhang unmittelbar augenfällig macht.

11

12

11–14. On part of the third floor there is an exceptionally simple and effective display of folk art.
The design of the fitments shown in connection with this museum is protected by registration; designs can not be reproduced without prior permission.

11–14. In einem Teil des dritten Geschosses sind Gegenstände der Volkskunst mit einfachen Mitteln hervorragend zur Geltung gebracht.
Die Ausstellungsinstallationen des Museums (Vitrinen, Stellwände, Sockel usw.) stehen unter Gebrauchsmusterschutz.

13

14

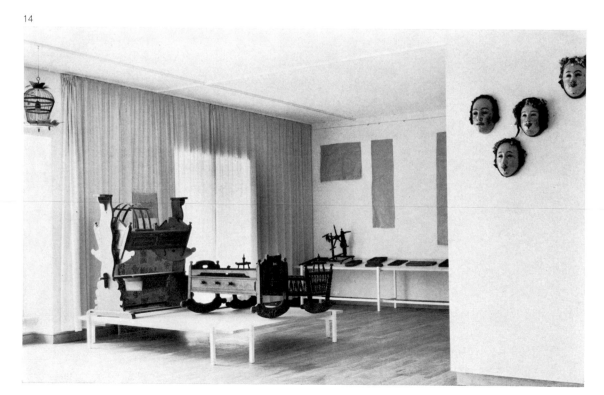

Reuchlinhaus, Pforzheim, Germany (1957–61)

Architect: Manfred Lehmbruck

Reuchlinhaus, Pforzheim (1957–61)

Architekt: Manfred Lehmbruck

Pforzheim, a town of about 80,000 between Karlsruhe and Stuttgart, is well known for the manufacture of jewellery and clocks. The Reuchlinhaus is a group of linked pavilions in the town park which the municipality erected after the war to rehouse in one place the destroyed buildings which had previously displayed the various collections and which had been used by the public library and for the town archives. The new complex now includes a jewellery museum, a folk museum, the town historical collection, the public library, the town archives, the rooms of the local Arts and Crafts Society and the workshops of two guilds. It is named after Johannes Reuchlin, a 15th century humanist born in Pforzheim.

The four pavilions of the group spiral around the entrance hall and only the library has a separate entrance. Between these there are planted terraces and a sunk courtyard used for exhibition purposes. Each pavilion has very much its own character, both internally and externally.

Das Reuchlinhaus, benannt nach dem 1455 in Pforzheim geborenen Humanisten Johannes Reuchlin, wurde in Pforzheim als kulturelles Zentrum der rund 80 000 Einwohner zählenden Goldschmiede- und Uhrmacherstadt errichtet. Der Komplex liegt inmitten des Stadtgartens und besteht aus einer Gruppe miteinander verbundener Pavillons. Das Reuchlinhaus übernimmt die Aufgaben verschiedener im Kriege zerstörter Bauten, in denen früher die Sammlungen, die öffentliche Bibliothek und das Stadtarchiv untergebracht waren. Der neue Bau umschließt daher Schmuckmuseum, Heimatmuseum, stadtgeschichtliche Sammlung, Stadtbücherei, Stadtarchiv, Räumlichkeiten für den Kunst- und Kunstgewerbeverein und Werkstätten für die Zünfte.

Die vier pavillonähnlichen Baukörper gruppieren sich um die Eingangshalle, und nur die Bibliothek hat einen getrennten Eingang. Dazwischen sind bepflanzte Terrassen und ein tiefer gelegter Hof. Jeder Baukörper behauptet sowohl in der Innengestaltung wie in der Außenansicht einen eigenen Charakter.

1. The library is seen from the main approach to the group of buildings. Both the library and the exhibition areas are open in the evenings – the latter on one day a week until 10 p.m. – so that the appearance after dark is extremely important.
2. Looking across the courtyard to the entrance hall which links the jewellery museum on the right with the temporary exhibitions gallery on the left.
3. The sunk courtyard between two of the pavilions; the lecture room is on the lower floor of the building on the far side, the gallery for temporary exhibitions on the upper floor.
4. The upper floor of the entrance hall, a glazed space from which the separate pavilions are clearly visible; the entrance to the jewellery museum is on the left.

Key to plans / Legende zu den Plänen:
1 Entrance hall / Eingangshalle
2 Courtyard / Skulpturenhof
3 Pool / Wasserbecken
4 Lecture room / Vortragssaal
5 Town historical collection / Stadtgeschichtliche Sammlung
6 Modern jewellery exhibition / Ausstellung von modernem Schmuck
7 Coats / Garderobe
8 Lavatories / Toiletten
9 Kitchen / Teeküche
10 Boiler room, mechanical equipment / Heizung und technische Anlagen
11 Workshop / Werkstatt
12 Restaurant / Kellerschenke
13 Guild room / Zunftraum
14 Storage / Magazin
15 Jewellery museum / Schmuckmuseum
16 Folk museum / Heimatmuseum
17 Library and reading rooms / Bibliothek und Leseräume
18 Main exhibition gallery / Großer Ausstellungssaal
19 Void over main exhibition gallery / Luftraum Ausstellungssaal
20 Caretaker's apartment / Hausmeisterwohnung
21 Discussion room / Diskussionsraum
22 Offices / Büros
23 Void over library / Luftraum Bibliothek
24 Town archives / Stadtarchiv

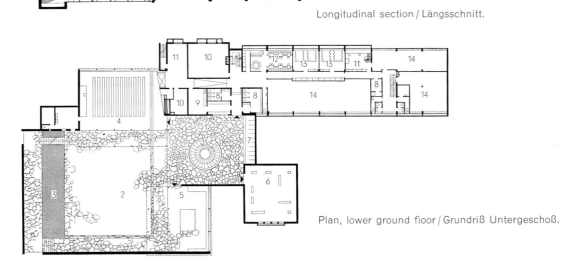

Longitudinal section / Längsschnitt.

Plan, lower ground floor / Grundriß Untergeschoß.

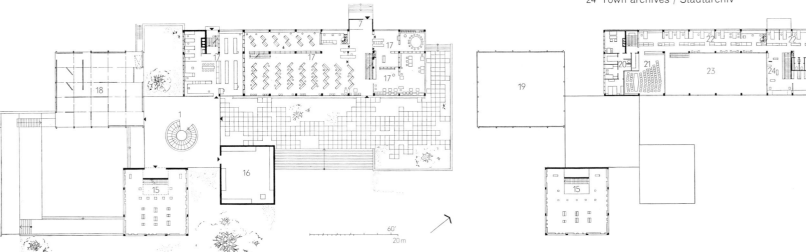

60′
20 m

Plan, ground floor / Grundriß Erdgeschoß.

Plan, first floor / Grundriß Obergeschoß.

1. Blick auf die Bibliothek von der Eingangsterrasse. Bibliothek und Ausstellungsräume sind auch abends geöffnet – die Ausstellungen an einem Wochentag bis 22 Uhr –, so daß die Nachtansicht besondere Bedeutung gewinnt.

2. Blick über den Hof zur Eingangshalle, die das Schmuckmuseum rechts mit dem Saal für Wechselausstellungen links verbindet.

3. Der Skulpturenhof wird an zwei Seiten von Pavillons begrenzt. Das Ausstellungsgebäude, das für Wechselausstellungen gedacht ist, enthält im Untergeschoß einen Vortragssaal.

4. Das obere Geschoß der verglasten Eingangshalle, von der aus die einzelnen Pavillons sichtbar sind; links der Eingang zum Schmuckmuseum.

5. The entrance hall, a pivotal point and a transitional zone between the outside and the various displays.
6. The main exhibition gallery is a two-storey flexible space used principally for temporary exhibitions. A system of movable screens based on a light metal structure makes various groupings possible; the screens may for instance be placed at an angle outside the grid. The amount of daylight is regulated by aluminium venetian blinds. Sidelight can be excluded by placing the screens in front of the windows.

5. Die Eingangshalle wirkt als eine Art »Drehscheibe« zwischen den einzelnen Pavillons und vermittelt zwischen Freiraum und Ausstellungsräumen.
6. Der große Ausstellungssaal hat eine Höhe von zwei Geschossen und wird vor allem für Wechselausstellungen benutzt. Ein System von Montagewänden mit Zusammensetzprofilen aus Leichtmetall ermöglicht die verschiedenartigsten Raumgruppierungen; unter anderem lassen sich die Wandelemente auch außerhalb des Rasters schräg aufstellen. Der Helligkeitsgrad des Tageslichts wird durch Lamellenstores aus Aluminium geregelt. Das Seitenlicht kann durch geschlossene Wandelemente ganz ausgeschaltet werden.

5

6

7, 8. The upper floor of the smallest of the pavilions contains the folk museum within four unpierced walls. – Clear panels can be introduced into the ceiling so as to allow daylight from the skylights above to enter. The large wall showcases have splayed glass fronts and receive direct daylight from above. The exhibits are supported by cantilevered glass shelves.

9, 10. The lower of the two floors of the jewellery museum; brilliantly glowing exhibits, lit by special 24 volt bulbs having a point source, are suspended or stand within a dark space. A similar but more flexible arrangement of hanging showcases is used in the room for modern jewellery under the folk museum and is shown on page 191. The wall showcases are lit by daylight reflected by mirrors and by artificial light.

8

7

7, 8. Das Obergeschoß des kleinsten Pavillons, dessen Wände fensterlos sind, enthält das Heimatmuseum. Die Oberlichtfelder der Decke sind auswechselbar. Die wandhohen Schaukästen mit schräggestellten Scheiben erhalten von oben direkte Tageslichtbeleuchtung; die gezeigten Gegenstände werden von auskragenden Glasplatten getragen.

9, 10. Das Erdgeschoß des Schmuckmuseums zeigt glitzernde Juwelen in Hänge- oder Pultvitrinen. Die Vitrinen in dem sonst relativ dunklen Raum besitzen 24-Volt-Speziallampen, die eine punktförmige Lichtquelle haben. Die Wandvitrinen werden mit Tageslicht durch Spiegelreflexion und mit gleichgerichtetem Kunstlicht belichtet. Ein ähnliches, aber flexibleres System von Hängevitrinen wird in dem Raum für modernen Schmuck unter dem Heimatmuseum verwendet (vgl. Seite 191).

10

9

3

Ernst Barlach House, Hamburg (1962)

Architect: Werner Kallmorgen

The museum displays the work of Ernst Barlach (1870 to 1938) collected over a number of years by its founder, Hermann F. Reemtsma. It is thus intended for a static collection of known objects. These include sculpture, drawings, prints, manuscripts and books. The bulk of the area is designed to exhibit fifty pieces of relatively small sculpture and the sequence and nature of the spaces could be arranged at the time of design to take account of these.

These exhibition spaces are on four sides of a courtyard with one of the rooms considerably larger and higher than the remainder. To one side of these galleries and adjacent to the entrance there is a separate group of rooms consisting of a library, an office and a lecture theatre which can be enlarged so that part of the first gallery becomes the lecture platform of the hall.

Ernst-Barlach-Haus, Hamburg (1962)

Architekt: Werner Kallmorgen

Das Museum zeigt die Werke Ernst Barlachs, die der Stifter, Hermann F. Reemtsma, im Laufe der Jahre erworben hat. Es ist also für eine permanente Ausstellung bestimmter Objekte gedacht, zu denen Plastik, Zeichnungen, Drucke, Manuskripte und Bücher gehören. Der größte Teil des Gebäudes ist für die fünfzig relativ kleinen Skulpturen konzipiert worden, die bereits beim Entwurf die Abfolge und Gestaltung der Räume bestimmten.
Die Ausstellungsräume sind um einen Innenhof angeordnet. Einer der Räume ist sehr viel höher und größer als die anderen. Neben dem Eingang an einer Seite der Ausstellungsräume liegen Bibliothek, Büro sowie ein Vortrags- und Theatersaal, der so vergrößert werden kann, daß ein Ausstellungsraum zum Podium des Saales wird.

1

Plan, ground floor / Grundriß Erdgeschoß.
1 Entrance / Eingang
2 Library / Bibliothek
3 Office / Büro
4 Coats / Garderobe
5 Store / Magazin
6 Ante-room / Vorraum
7 Lecture theatre / Vortrags- und Theatersaal
8 Room 1 / Raum 1
9 Room 2 / Raum 2
10 Lowering wall / Versenkbare Wand
11 Room 3 / Raum 3
12 Room 4 / Raum 4
13 Room 5 / Raum 5
14 Room 6 / Raum 6
15 Room 7 / Raum 7
16 Courtyard / Innenhof
17 Loggia
18 Caretaker's flat / Hausmeisterwohnung

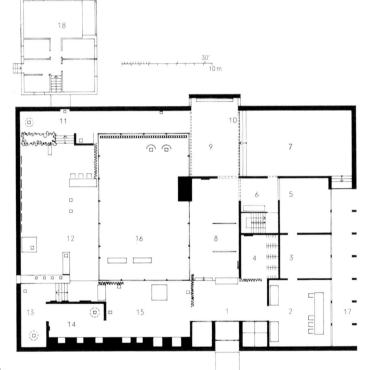

1. The museum is a precise white horizontal brick mass among the tall trees of the park. The entrance is on the left, the loggia in front of the library and the office is on the right.
2. Room 4, the largest of the exhibition spaces, with the statue of Moses to the left of the steps.
3. The same room looking in the opposite direction. Steps lead up to Room 5 behind the low wall.
4. The courtyard seen from Room 7; the entrance hall is immediately to the right. This enclosed paved space, showing the organisation of the museum, can be seen immediately on entering.
5. The platform of the lecture theatre is created by lowering into the floor the wall dividing it from Room 2. The glass wall to the courtyard is behind the curtains at the back of the platform.
6. Room 3, the narrowest of the four exhibition spaces around the courtyard, terminating in the top-lit figure of *Moses*.
7. A low relief in Room 6 is side-lit and emphasised by a continuous recessed fitting in the flanking wall.
8. Several of the more important exhibits are naturally top-lit, in this case a teak carving of *Mother and Child* in Room 6. At night an electric fitting within the recess maintains the directional nature of the lighting.
9. The last gallery, Room 7. The steps leading up from Room 4 are behind the glass case on the right. Small exhibits are in illuminated recesses of a hollow wall on the left. An even distribution of electric bulbs recessed into the ceiling provides the remainder of the artificial lighting.

2

3

4

5

1. Das Museumsgebäude liegt als klarer, weißverputzter horizontaler Ziegelsteinblock zwischen den hohen Bäumen des Parks. Links der Eingang, rechts die Loggia vor der Bibliothek und dem Büro.

2. Der größte Ausstellungsbereich, Raum 4; links von der Treppe die Plastik *Moses*.

3. Der gleiche Raum in der Gegenrichtung gesehen. Hinter der niedrigen Zwischenwand führen Stufen hinauf zu Raum 5.

4. Der Innenhof, von Raum 7 gesehen. Rechts liegt die Eingangshalle. Der Besucher erblickt also, sobald er das Museum betritt, den umschlossenen, gepflasterten Hof, der die räumliche Organisation deutlich macht.

5. Die Wand zwischen dem Vortragssaal und Raum 2 kann in den Boden versenkt werden, so daß Raum 2 das Podium des Saales bildet. Hinter den Vorhängen am Ende des Podiums die Glaswand zum Hof.

6. Raum 3, der schmalste der vier Ausstellungsflügel um den Innenhof. Am Ende die von oben beleuchtete Plastik *Moses*.

7. Das Flachrelief in Raum 6 wird von einer durchgehenden Leuchtröhre, die in die angrenzende Wand eingelassen ist, seitlich beleuchtet und dadurch in seiner Linienführung hervorgehoben.

8. Einige der bedeutenderen Skulpturen erhalten Tageslicht von oben; hier die Holzplastik *Mutter mit Kind* in Raum 6. Abends fällt Kunstlicht aus einer in der Deckenöffnung angebrachten Lichtquelle in der gleichen Richtung wie bei Tage ein.

9. Raum 7, der letzte Ausstellungsraum. Hinter der Glasvitrine rechts führt die Treppe von Raum 4 herauf. Die

Hohlwand links nimmt kleinere Gegenstände in beleuchteten Nischen auf. In die Decke sind in gleichmäßigen Abständen Leuchten eingelassen, die für die künstliche Allgemeinbeleuchtung des Raumes sorgen.

6

7

8

9

Wilhelm Morgner House, Soest, Germany (1962–63)

Architect: Rainer Schell

The two storey Wilhelm Morgner House consists of three separate but linkable elements: an exhibition gallery, a group of teaching and club rooms and a large lecture hall. The first two occupy the northern half of the building, the third the southern part. They can be joined at both floor levels. The building was thus thought of as a small cultural group in the centre of the town and it is in fact part of a sequence of buildings and open spaces which includes the town hall, the square and the cathedral.

The entrances to both halves of the building occur from a diagonal pedestrian route on the south side of the cathedral which widens under the northern part of the building into a covered courtyard with a small pool. This creates an urban resting space and opens the lower part of the exhibition area to view.

Both in scale and placing the building is a careful insertion within an existing urban group which has evolved slowly over several centuries. It faithfully continues the pattern of making small pedestrian spaces between the important town buildings. Both the museum and the town undoubtedly benefit from this close juxtaposition.

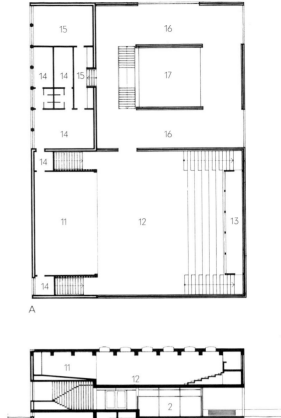

A

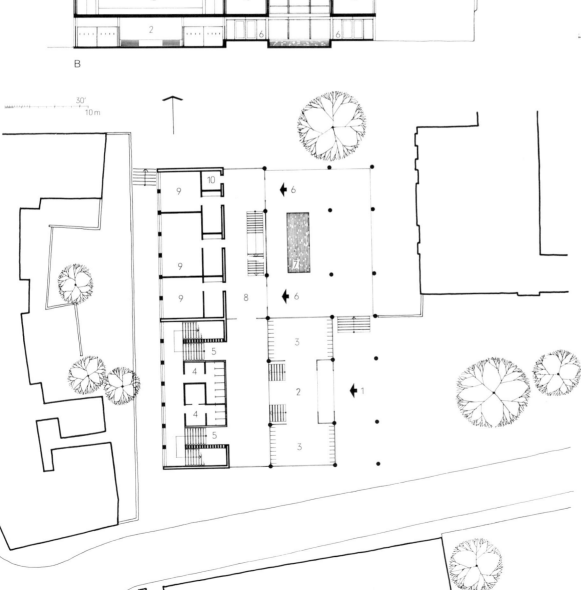

B

C

D

A Plan, first floor / Grundriß erstes Geschoß.
B North-south section / Schnitt in Nord-Süd-Richtung.
C East-west section / Schnitt in Ost-West-Richtung.
D Plan, ground floor / Grundriß Erdgeschoß.
1 Entrance to lecture theatre / Eingang zum Vortrags- und Theatersaal
2 Foyer
3 Coats / Garderoben
4 Lavatories / Toiletten
5 Stairs to lecture theatre / Treppen zum Vortrags- und Theatersaal
6 Entrance to museum and classrooms / Eingang zum Museum und zu den Arbeitsräumen der Volkshochschule
7 Pool / Wasserbecken
8 Lower exhibition gallery / Unterer Ausstellungsbereich
9 Classrooms with ante rooms / Arbeitszimmer der Volkshochschule mit Vorräumen
10 Porter / Pförtner
11 Stage / Bühne
12 Lecture theatre / Vortrags- und Theatersaal
13 Projection room and lighting gallery / Projektionsraum und Beleuchtungsanlage
14 Green rooms and adjoining rooms to stage / Künstlergarderoben und Nebenräume zur Bühne
15 Prints and drawings gallery / Graphisches Kabinett
16 Main exhibition gallery / Hauptausstellungsbereich
17 Void / Luftraum
18 Youth club / Clubraum

1

Wilhelm-Morgner-Haus, Soest (1962–63)

Architekt: Rainer Schell

Das zwei Geschosse hohe Bauwerk besteht aus drei getrennten Elementen, die jedoch auf beiden Geschoßebenen miteinander verbunden werden können: ein Ausstellungsbereich und eine Gruppe von Arbeits- und Clubräumen im Nordteil des Gebäudes sowie ein großer Vortragssaal im südlichen Teil. Das Wilhelm-Morgner-Haus ist als kleine Kulturstätte im Zentrum der Stadt konzipiert und gehört zu einem Komplex von Bauwerken und offenen Plätzen wie Rathaus, St. Patroklus und Marktplatz.
Die Eingänge zu den beiden Gebäudeteilen sind von einer diagonal verlaufenden Fußgängerpassage an der Südseite von St. Patroklus zu erreichen, die sich unter dem nördlichen Teil des Gebäudes zu einem gedeckten Innenhof mit einem kleinen Wasserbassin erweitert. Dadurch entsteht ein Ruheplatz mitten in der Stadt, und der untere Ausstellungsbereich kann vom Hof aus eingesehen werden.
Mit seinen Proportionen und seiner Lage ist das Bauwerk sorgfältig in die bestehende Gruppe von Bauten eingeordnet, die sich im Laufe der Jahrhunderte langsam entwickelt hat. Es führt die Tradition kleiner Fußgängerbereiche zwischen den wichtigen Gebäuden der Stadt getreulich fort. Sowohl das Museum als auch die Stadt profitieren zweifellos von diesem engen Nebeneinander.

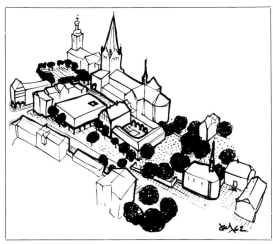

1

3

2

1. The Wilhelm Morgner House is placed on the south side of the cathedral and is part of a pedestrian area lying between the west doors of the cathedral and the church of St. Nicholas in the foreground.
2. The entrance side of the building; the doors to the lecture hall on the left, those to the gallery on the far side of the covered area on the right. The cathedral and the baroque spire of St. Peter's form the backdrop.
3. The ground floor entrance hall to the lecture theatre which is on the first floor. The intermediate level runs through on the right to become the entrance hall to the gallery and club rooms.

1. Das Wilhelm-Morgner-Haus liegt an der Südseite von St. Patroklus und gehört zu einem Fußgängerbereich, der sich von der Westfassade des Münsters bis zur Nikolaikapelle im Vordergrund erstreckt.
2. Die Eingangsseite; links die Türen zum Vortrags- und Theatersaal, am Ende des überdeckten Innenhofs rechts der Eingang zum Ausstellungsbereich. St. Patroklus und der barocke Turm der Petrikirche bilden den Hintergrund.
3. Die im Erdgeschoß liegende Eingangshalle zum Vortragssaal, der sich im Obergeschoß befindet. Das Zwischengeschoß setzt sich nach rechts fort und wird zur Eingangshalle für Ausstellungsbereich und Clubräume.

4

5

6

4. The northern part of the entrance hall; the doors lead to the teaching and club rooms, the stair up to the main exhibition space.
5. The upper exhibition gallery receives natural side-light through plate-glass windows and glass blocks, and artificial light from screened fluorescent tubes as well as spotlights in the boarded ceiling. It has views of the cathedral and also down into the entrance courtyard. Most of this gallery is given over to showing the work of the Expressionist painter Wilhelm Morgner who was born in Soest in 1891.
6. The lecture theatre on the first floor; the doors on the right wall lead into the exhibition gallery.

4. Der nördliche Teil der Eingangshalle; die Türen führen zu den Arbeits- und Clubräumen, die Treppe nach oben zum Hauptausstellungsbereich.
5. Die Ausstellungsfläche im Obergeschoß erhält seitliches Tageslicht durch Spiegelglasscheiben und Glasbausteine und Kunstlicht von Leuchtstoffröhren hinter Blenden sowie Scheinwerfern an der holzriemenverkleideten Decke. Der Besucher hat einen Ausblick auf St. Patroklus und den Eingangshof. Der größte Teil des Ausstellungsbereichs ist dem Schaffen des expressionistischen Malers Wilhelm Morgner gewidmet, der 1891 in Soest geboren wurde.
6. Der Vortragssaal im Obergeschoß; die Türen in der rechten Wand führen in den Ausstellungsbereich.

Page / Seite 119:

2. The lower floor contains an area for the permanent collection opening on to a museum garden on the west. The large central cores are for mechanical services and lavatories. The goods entrance is on the south side with receiving and dispatch to the east and administration on the west. The peripheral service area along the east side contains stores.
2. Das Untergeschoß nimmt Räume für die ständige Ausstellung auf, die sich im Westen zum Museumsgarten hin öffnen. In den großen Festpunkten sind Maschinenräume und Toiletten untergebracht. An der Südseite liegt ein Liefereingang, der rechts von An- und Auslieferung und links von den Räumen der Verwaltung begrenzt wird. Die Nebenräume entlang der Ostseite dienen als Lager.
1 Hall / Treppenhalle
2 Permanent collection / Ständige Ausstellung
3 Museum garden / Museumsgarten
4 Mechanical services / Maschinenräume
5 Lavatories / Toiletten
6 Goods entrance / Liefereingang
7 Receiving and dispatch / An- und Auslieferung
8 Administration / Verwaltung
9 Store rooms / Lagerräume

3. The upper floor, a 27′ 6″ high glazed room, contains a foyer and an exhibition hall. The two areas are screened from each other by low wood panelled cores accommodating cloakrooms and the ticket desk.
3. Das obere Geschoß, ein 8,40 m hoher verglaster Raum, enthält ein Foyer und eine Ausstellungshalle. Niedrige holzverkleidete Kuben, die Garderobe und Kartenschalter aufnehmen, trennen die beiden Bereiche voneinander.
1 Foyer
2 Exhibition hall / Ausstellungshalle
3 Cloakrooms / Garderoben

Gallery of the 20th Century, Berlin (Project)

Architect: Ludwig Mies van der Rohe

Galerie des 20. Jahrhunderts, Berlin (Projekt)

Architekt: Ludwig Mies van der Rohe

Mies van der Rohe's design for a museum and exhibition hall follows the ideas first suggested in his project for a Museum for a Small City in 1942 (see Figs. pages 26/27) and later developed at Cullinan Hall (see pages 135–137). It was based on the belief that a single great room, a universal space, provides the greatest degree of flexibility and is thus the most desirable solution. Mies has said in relation to this particular project that "it is my belief that this kind of exhibition hall provides rich and varied possibilities not normal in the usual museum".

The Gallery of the 20th century is part of a new cultural centre being erected in Berlin. Scharoun's angular Philharmonic Hall is 330 yards to the north. Mies returned to an older tradition however and one which has been among his principal formal influences. "After considering several possibilities I finally decided," he has explained, "upon a solution which located the exhibition hall on a terrace over the museum. This solution permitted a clear and strong building which, in my opinion, is in harmony with the Schinkel tradition in Berlin."

The building is organised on two levels, the upper being an open space divided by low enclosures and two service shafts, the lower sub-divided into rooms for the permanent collection, offices, workshops, storage and mechanical services. The upper part is a welded structure of steel plates at about 11' 9" centres spanning between four edge beams. These make up a 196 ft. square roof supported through pin jointed connections on eight cruciform peripheral columns. The lower part is a reinforced concrete structure with columns on a square grid of approximately 23' 6".

Mies van der Rohes Entwurf für Museum und Ausstellungshalle beruht auf den Gedankengängen, die er zum erstenmal 1942 bei seinem Projekt eines Museums für eine kleine Stadt (Abb. S. 26/27) entwickelte und später mit der Cullinan Hall (S. 135–137) weiterführte. Der Architekt ging von der Überzeugung aus, daß ein einziger großer Einheitsraum ein Höchstmaß an Flexibilität erlaube und deshalb die günstigste Lösung darstelle. Mies sagte über seinen Entwurf: »Ich bin der Ansicht, daß eine solche Ausstellungshalle reiche und vielfältige Möglichkeiten birgt, die das herkömmliche Museum nicht bietet.« Die Galerie des 20. Jahrhunderts gehört zu einem neuen Kulturzentrum, das in Berlin errichtet wird. Die winklig gebrochene Baumasse von Scharouns Philharmonie liegt 300 Meter weiter nördlich. Mies schöpfte freilich aus einer älteren Tradition, einer Tradition, die seine Formvorstellungen weitgehend beeinflußt hat. »Nachdem ich verschiedene Möglichkeiten in Betracht gezogen hatte«, erklärte er, »entschloß ich mich schließlich für eine Lösung, bei der die Ausstellungshalle auf einer Terrasse über dem Museum liegt. Diese Lösung führte zu einem klaren, kraftvollen Bauwerk, das meiner Meinung nach in Einklang mit der Schinkelschen Tradition Berlins steht.«

Das Gebäude besitzt zwei Bereiche auf verschiedenen Niveaus; der obere Bereich ist ein offener Raum, der durch niedrige Trennwände und zwei Festpunkte unterteilt wird, der untere enthält neben den Räumen für die ständige Ausstellung Büros, Werkstätten, Lager und Maschinenräume. Den oberen Teil des Bauwerks bildet eine Konstruktion von verschweißten Stahlplatten mit Achsabständen von 3,60 m, die sich zwischen vier Randträgern spannen. Das quadratische Dach hat 64,80 m Seitenlänge und wird auf Bolzengelenken von acht Außenstützen mit kreuzförmigem Querschnitt getragen. Der untere Gebäudeteil ist eine Stahlbetonkonstruktion mit Stützen, die auf einem quadratischen Raster von 7,20 m angeordnet sind.

1. East-west section. The suspended ceiling visible under the grid of steel plates in the upper exhibition hall and foyer will be the main source of general and uniform artificial lighting. Further localised lighting on particular paintings or sculpture will be possible from floor outlets. The upper and lower exhibition areas will be air-conditioned with humidity control at all times from two plant rooms in the centre of the lower floor.

1. Schnitt in Ost-West-Richtung. Die eingehängte Zwischendecke unter der Stahlplattenkonstruktion sorgt in der oberen Ausstellungshalle und im Foyer für eine gleichmäßige künstliche Allgemeinbeleuchtung. Darüber hinaus ermöglichen Bodenanschlüsse Punktbeleuchtung für bestimmte Bilder oder Skulpturen. Oberer wie unterer Ausstellungsbereich erhalten Klimaanlagen mit Feuchtigkeitskontrolle, die ständig von zwei Maschinenräumen in der Mitte des Untergeschosses aus reguliert werden.

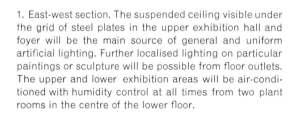

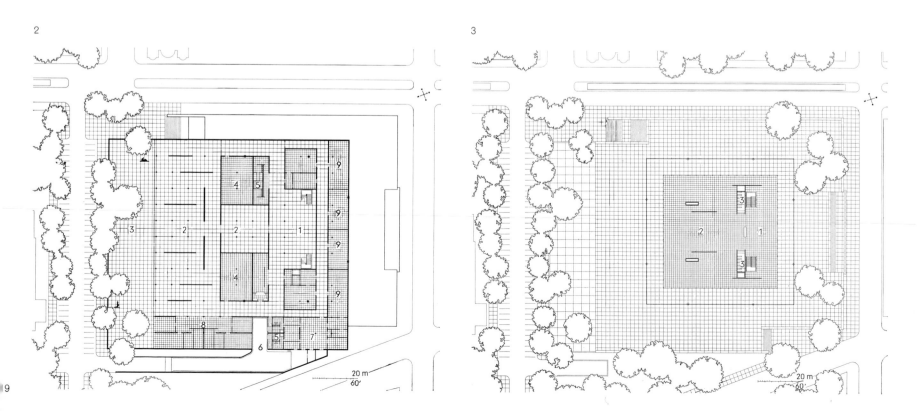

4

4. Ansicht von Südosten. Die Galerie des 20. Jahrhunderts, die südlich der neuen Philharmonie liegt, ist ein von Grünanlagen umgebener, großer verglaster Pavillon auf einer erhöhten Terrasse.

5. Eingangsseite an der Potsdamer Straße. Treppenstufen führen auf die Terrasse und zu einer Reihe von Türen. Die räumliche Kontinuität des Obergeschosses wird nur durch die niedrigen Kuben und die beiden Festpunkte unterbrochen.

6. Auch von Nordwesten her führen Treppen auf die Terrasse; der Museumsgarten liegt hinter der Mauer rechts. Die Glaswand der oberen Ausstellungshalle ist um zwei Trägereinheiten (7,20 m) vom Dachrand zurückgesetzt.

7. Ein Teil der ständigen Ausstellung im Untergeschoß mit Blick in den Museumsgarten. Der Raum ist 4 m hoch. Obwohl die unteren Räume sehr viel kleiner und niedriger sind als die obere Ausstellungshalle, stellen sie – was Dimensionen und Anordnung der Ausstellungsobjekte angeht – ähnliche Probleme wie die Cullinan Hall, Probleme, die sich bei Einheitsräumen immer zu ergeben scheinen.

4. The Gallery, south of the new Philharmonic Hall, is a great glazed pavilion on a terraced podium among parkland. The building seen from the south-east.

5. The entrance side facing the Potsdamer Straße. A flight of steps leads up to the terrace and a range of doors. The low cores and the two service shafts are the only interruption of the interior volume.

6. A flight of steps leads up from the north-west corner on to the terrace; the museum garden is behind the wall on the right. The glass wall of the upper hall is set back two girder modules (23′ 6″) from the roof edge.

7. Part of the permanent collection overlooking the museum garden on the ground floor. This space is 13 ft. high. Although these spaces are much smaller and lower than the upper gallery they already pose some of the problems of scale and display obvious at Cullinan Hall and, it would seem, inherent in the notion of universal space.

5

6

7

Museum of the 20th Century, Vienna (1958 and 1962)

Architect: Karl Schwanzer

Museum des 20. Jahrhunderts, Wien (1958 und 1962)

Architekt: Karl Schwanzer

Although Vienna played an important role in the history of contemporary art and the possibility of a museum of modern art was discussed even before the beginning of this century, it was not until the pavilion which the Austrian Government had erected at the Brussels Exposition in 1958 was dismantled and re-erected in Vienna that such a museum became a reality.

The structural tour-de-force – the four central columns support the whole building – which had something to do with the interest the pavilion aroused at an international exhibition, adds nothing to its quality as a museum. The two-storey volume with its open central well is treated as one great loft space, the lower floor enclosed with clear glass and opening onto terraces, the upper floor translucent and oriented towards the central void. Within this space all pictures are hung on movable partitions and all sculpture placed on free-standing pedestals.

Wien hat eine bedeutende Rolle in der Geschichte der modernen Kunst gespielt, und die Errichtung eines Museums für moderne Kunstwerke wurde schon vor der Jahrhundertwende geplant. Dieses Projekt nahm aber erst Gestalt an, als der Österreichische Pavillon der Brüsseler Weltausstellung 1958 abmontiert und in Wien neu errichtet wurde.

Der konstruktive Gewaltakt – vier innere Stützen tragen das gesamte Bauwerk –, der auf der Weltausstellung Auf-

sehen erregt hatte (und erregen sollte), erweist sich als nicht sonderlich ergiebig für die Zwecke eines Museums. Das zwei Geschosse hohe Bauwerk mit dem offenen Zentralbereich ist als ein großer Raum konzipiert, wobei das untere Geschoß verglast wurde und sich zu Terrassen hin öffnet, während das obere Geschoß mit Mattglas verkleidet wurde und sich zu dem offenen Zentralbereich hin orientiert. Die Bilder hängen an beweglichen Trennwänden, die Plastik ist auf frei stehenden Sockeln ausgestellt.

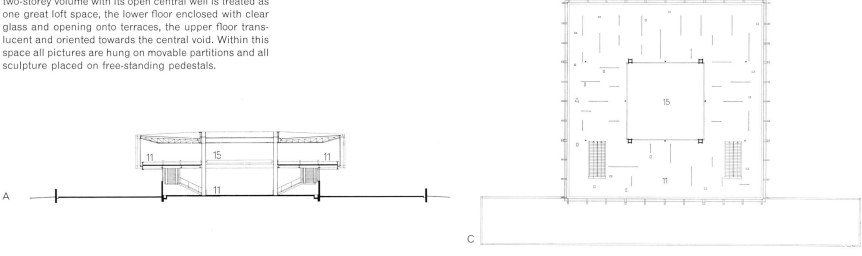

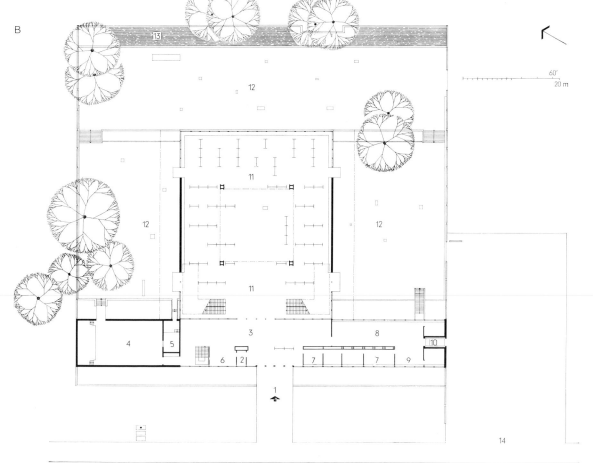

A Section / Schnitt.
B Plan, ground floor / Grundriß Erdgeschoß.
C Plan, first floor / Grundriß erstes Geschoß.
1 Entrance / Eingang
2 Porter / Pförtner
3 Hall / Vorhalle
4 Cinema and lecture theatre / Filmvorführraum, Vortrags- und Theatersaal
5 Projection room / Projektionsraum
6 Coats / Garderobe
7 Offices / Büros
8 Reading room / Lesesaal
9 Library / Bibliothek
10 Goods hoist / Lastenaufzug
11 Exhibition galleries / Ausstellungsräume
12 Terrace / Terrasse
13 Water / Wasserbecken
14 Parking / Parkplatz
15 Central void / Luftraum des Zentralbereichs

1. The low building in the foreground was added to the original square pavilion when it was re-erected in Vienna and contains the entrance hall, a lecture theatre and other ancillary rooms.
2. The two-storey volume with its central well created by the space left between the four steel columns which are the only supports for the upper floor and roof. In its original form at Brussels the lower floor remained unglazed.

1. Ansicht von Westen. Das niedrige Gebäude im Vordergrund wurde neu errichtet, als der quadratische Pavillon in Wien wieder aufgebaut wurde. Es enthält die Eingangshalle, einen Vortrags- und Theatersaal sowie weitere Nebenräume.
2. Der zwei Geschosse hohe Raum mit dem Zentralbereich zwischen den vier Stahlstützen, die allein das obere Geschoß und das Dach tragen. Auf der Brüsseler Weltausstellung war das untere Geschoß des Pavillons nicht verglast.

1

2

3

4

5

3. Trennwände unterteilen den Ausstellungsbereich. Die Lichtbänder an der Decke (mit Leuchtröhren) schaffen für das ganze Geschoß und sämtliche Ausstellungsgegenstände gleichförmige Lichtverhältnisse. Wie ungünstig sich ein solches System auswirken kann, läßt sich an der Büste rechts erkennen.

4. Die Stellwände stehen frei und sind am Boden mit Metallfüßen befestigt, die gefährlich weit in den Raum vorstehen.

5. Von jeder Seite des Haupteingangs führt eine Doppeltreppe in das obere Geschoß, in dem die Wände mit Mattglas verkleidet sind. Die Bilder sind an Tafeln angebracht, die an Stäben von der Decke hängen. Diese Stäbe laufen auf Schienen, die in die Decke eingelassen sind.

6. Die größte der drei gepflasterten Terrassen, die sich auf den Gartenseiten an das Gebäude anschließen und für Plastikausstellungen benutzt werden.

6

3. Screens subdivide the available open space. The lines of fluorescent lighting in the ceiling provide the same lighting conditions for the entire floor area and for all exhibits and the weakness of such a system can be seen from the lighting of the bust on the right.

4. The screens are free standing and are stabilised by feet projecting rather far into the normal walking space.

5. Two double staircases, one on each side of the main entrance, lead to the upper floor. Here the walls are translucent and the screens are hung on rods sliding in tracks recessed within the ceiling.

6. The largest of the three paved terraces which extend the building on its garden sides and which are used for the display of sculpture.

Kunsthaus, Zürich (1955–58)

Architects: Hans and Kurt Pfister

The Kunsthaus has undergone the transformations usual in such a building: the first part was designed by Karl Moser in 1910 and he was also responsible for its first addition in 1925. In 1944 when there was a need for expansion and a greater variety of spaces a competition was held. This was won by the Pfisters who were able to build the present wing, a reinforced concrete structure, between 1955 and 1958. There is now a sculpture court between the new wing and the old building and this space flows into a foyer leading to a lecture room holding 750 seats on one side and a restaurant on the other. Below this floor there are store rooms, above it, the main exhibition space. The rooms are mostly top-lit with some sidelight through windows on the east and west sides.
The new wing is interesting for its technical adjuncts which have been given a good deal of space. This makes maintenance easy and ensures that there is room to spare for changes which may have to be made. The void above the ceiling of the gallery contains the installations for air-conditioning and lighting (see page 178).

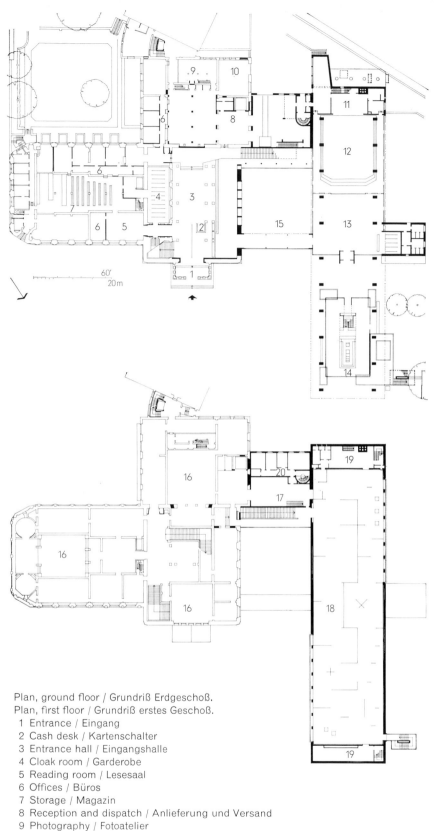

1. The windows have movable metal louvres to control the light. The lecture room on the floor below opens out onto a garden to the west.

1. Bewegliche Metall-Lamellen vor den Fenstern regulieren das Licht. Der Vortragssaal im Erdgeschoß öffnet sich auf einen Garten an der Westseite des Flügels.

Plan, ground floor / Grundriß Erdgeschoß.
Plan, first floor / Grundriß erstes Geschoß.
 1 Entrance / Eingang
 2 Cash desk / Kartenschalter
 3 Entrance hall / Eingangshalle
 4 Cloak room / Garderobe
 5 Reading room / Lesesaal
 6 Offices / Büros
 7 Storage / Magazin
 8 Reception and dispatch / Anlieferung und Versand
 9 Photography / Fotoatelier
10 Garage
11 Chair store / Stuhllager
12 Lecture hall / Vortragssaal
13 Foyer
14 Festaurant
15 Sculpture court / Skulpturenhof
16 Existing exhibition galleries / Ältere Ausstellungsräume
17 Exhibition assembly / Vorbereitung der Ausstellungen
18 New exhibition gallery / Neuer Ausstellungsbereich
19 Exhibition material storage / Lager für Ausstellungsmaterial
20 Flat / Wohnung

Kunsthaus Zürich (1955–58)

Architekten: Hans und Kurt Pfister

Das Kunsthaus hat alle die Veränderungen mitgemacht, die für ein solches Gebäude typisch sind: Der erste Teil wurde 1910 von Karl Moser entworfen, der auch für die erste Erweiterung (1925) verantwortlich zeichnet. Als 1944 mehr Raum und variablere Ausstellungsflächen benötigt wurden, wurde ein Wettbewerb veranstaltet. Die Brüder Pfister gewannen den ersten Preis und errichteten zwischen 1955 und 1958 den neuen Flügel als Stahlbetonkonstruktion. Zwischen dem alten Gebäudeteil und diesem Flügel erstreckt sich ein Skulpturenhof, der in ein Foyer übergeht. Vom Foyer aus gelangt man auf der einen Seite in einen Vortragssaal mit 750 Plätzen und auf der anderen in das Restaurant. Unter diesem Geschoß liegen die Lagerräume, über ihm die Ausstellungsräume. Die Beleuchtung erfolgt im wesentlichen durch Oberlicht; außerdem erhält der Bau durch Fenster im Osten und Westen Seitenlicht. Im neuen Flügel nehmen die technischen Nebenräume relativ viel Platz ein. Dadurch wird die Instandhaltung erleichtert, und es bleibt für künftige Veränderungen genügend Raum verfügbar. In der Dachzone über der Decke der Galerie befinden sich die Installationen für Klimaanlage und Beleuchtung (vgl. Seite 178).

2. The space under the suspended ceiling is subdivided by partitions which have four standard heights ranging from 7′ 9″ to 16′ 6″. The lighting levels on the exhibits are high and may reach 700 lux when the spotlights are in use.
3–5. Three views of the temporary exhibition of Mexican Art; coloured walls, stands, and the omission of top lighting in certain zones, can help to modify the single space and thus to subdivide it into comprehensible units.

2. Die Ausstellungsfläche unter der eingehängten Zwischendecke ist durch bewegliche Stellwände in vier verschiedene Höhen von 2,40 m bis 5 m unterteilt. Die Lichtstärke ist verhältnismäßig hoch und kann bei Benutzung der Scheinwerfer 700 lx erreichen.
3–5. Drei Ansichten der Ausstellung über Mexikanische Kunst. Farbig getönte Flächen und Abschirmung des Oberlichts in bestimmten Zonen wirken als räumliche Trennung und teilen den Ausstellungssaal in leicht überschaubare Einheiten.

As in France and Germany, it is the great collections – the British Museum, the Victoria and Albert and the National Gallery – which are the important institutions. Little has however happened to them in the post-war period. Nor has any important new museum been completed. While there is considerable interest in conservation, so much so that the cleaning of pictures at the National Gallery caused something of a public controversy, there is no comparable awareness of the importance of display.

A small museum has been built in Durham to house an oriental collection and at Leicester the ground floor of a college building now being finished will house certain antiquities and relate these to an adjacent Roman site. The first new gallery of any size will not be seen until the complex of buildings being built by the Greater London Council on the South Bank of the Thames is ready. This is likely to be followed by the art gallery which will stand next to the new University Library in Glasgow.

The Commonwealth Institute serves a rather specialized function in that it is a display gallery of ethnography, geography, commerce and art devoted to showing these aspects for each Commonwealth country as an educational venture in London.

Wie in Frankreich und Deutschland sind auch in Großbritannien die großen Museen vorherrschend: das British Museum, das Victoria and Albert Museum und die National Gallery. In der Nachkriegszeit sind diese Institutionen jedoch kaum verändert worden; ebenso wenig wurden Museumsneubauten fertiggestellt. An Konservierungsproblemen besteht lebhaftes Interesse, so daß die Reinigung von Bildern der National Gallery öffentliche Debatten hervorruft; ausstellungstechnische Fragen dagegen stoßen viel eher auf Gleichgültigkeit.

In Durham wurde ein kleines Museum gebaut, das für eine Sammlung orientalischer Gegenstände gedacht ist, und in Leicester nimmt das Erdgeschoß eines jetzt vollendeten Collegegebäudes Altertümer auf und bezieht sie auf ein benachbartes Grundstück mit römischen Ausgrabungen. Die erste neue Gemäldegalerie überhaupt soll mit dem Baukomplex entstehen, den der Greater London Council am Südufer der Themse errichtet. Eine weitere Galerie wird wahrscheinlich in der unmittelbaren Nachbarschaft der neuen Universitätsbibliothek in Glasgow gebaut.

Eine recht spezielle Aufgabe erfüllt das Commonwealth Institute in London, das in einem pädagogischen Experiment die völkerkundlichen, geographischen, wirtschaftlichen und kunstgeschichtlichen Aspekte der einzelnen Commonwealth-Staaten veranschaulicht.

1, 2. A new complex of buildings adjacent to the existing Royal Festival Hall on the South Bank of the river Thames was designed by the Architect's Department of the Greater London Council (Hubert Bennett, Architect to the Council). It will include a small concert hall, a recital room, an entrance to the existing National Film Theatre and 20,000 square feet of exhibition space. This space occurs on two floors, the upper gallery being toplit and connected to three large terraces for the display of sculpture.

3. Glasgow University is to have a new building by William Whitfield which will combine a library and art gallery. The tall building with the shaft-like staircases is the library; this is surrounded by an art gallery of low enclosed volumes which will be entirely top-lit. These galleries will be used to exhibit pictures but one is being planned to contain the rebuilt interior of Charles Rennie MacIntosh's own house.

1, 2. Die Architekturabteilung des Greater London Council (Hubert Bennett) hat einen Baukomplex entworfen, der sich an die bereits bestehende Royal Festival Hall am Südufer der Themse anschließen soll. Das Programm umfaßt einen kleinen Konzertsaal, einen Vortragssaal, einen Eingang zu dem schon existierenden National Film Theatre und etwa 1860 qm Ausstellungsfläche, die sich auf zwei Geschosse verteilt. Der obere Saal hat Deckenlicht und ist mit drei großen Terrassen für die Aufstellung von Skulpturen verbunden.

3. Für die Universität in Glasgow hat William Whitfield ein neues Gebäude entworfen, das in sich eine Bibliothek und Gemäldegalerie vereinigen wird. Der hohe Bau mit dem Treppenturm enthält die Bibliothek, er ist von niedrigeren kompakten Volumen umgeben, die für Ausstellungsräume vorgesehen sind und durchweg Oberlicht haben. Diese Räume werden eine Gemäldegalerie enthalten. Weiterhin ist geplant, in einem Raum das Innere des Hauses von Charles Rennie MacIntosh zu rekonstruieren.

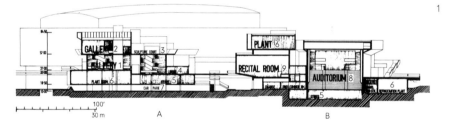

1

Section / Schnitt.
A Art Gallery / Gemäldegalerie
B Concert Hall / Konzertsaal
1 Gallery 1 / Ausstellungsraum 1
2 Gallery 2 / Ausstellungsraum 2
3 Sculpture court / Skulpturenhof

4 Lobby / Halle
5 Store / Magazin
6 Plant room / Technische Anlagen
7 Car park / Parkgarage
8 Auditorium
9 Recital room / Vortragssaal

2

3

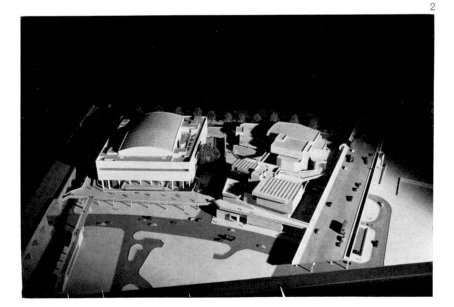

Commonwealth Institute, London (1960–62)

Architects: A. R. Matthew and Stirrat Johnson-Marshall

Commonwealth Institute, London (1960–62)

Architekten: A. R. Matthew und Stirrat Johnson-Marshall

This building houses a semi-permanent exhibition which puts on display in London certain aspects of the life and resources of the countries forming the Commonwealth. It does so in a single square space with two balcony floors going around the perimeter. The approach from the pavement leads across a bridge over moving water into an entrance hall and up a shallow ramp to a circular platform in the middle of this square. This becomes the pivotal point from which one can move up or down to any particular section of the hall. Beyond this main hall there is a cinema and above it an art gallery for temporary exhibitions. Particular attention was given to the design of the gallery lighting, and models were tested by the Building Research Station before a solution was accepted.

Das Gebäude beherbergt eine – zum Teil wechselnde – Ausstellung, die das Leben und die wirtschaftlichen Grundlagen der Commonwealth-Länder zeigt. Der Hauptbau besteht aus einem einheitlichen quadratischen Raum mit zwei Galerien um einen offenen Kern. Der Zugang führt vom Bürgersteig über eine Brücke, unter der Wasser fließt, in die Eingangshalle und von dort über eine kurze Rampe zu einer kreisförmigen Plattform in der Mitte des Quadrats. Diese Plattform bildet den Mittelpunkt, von dem aus sämtliche höher oder tiefer liegenden Teile der Halle erreichbar sind. Neben dem Hauptbau liegt ein Lichtspieltheater und darüber der Saal für wechselnde Kunstausstellungen. Die sehr sorgfältig gelöste Beleuchtung des Saales wurde durch Modellversuche der Building Research Station ermittelt.

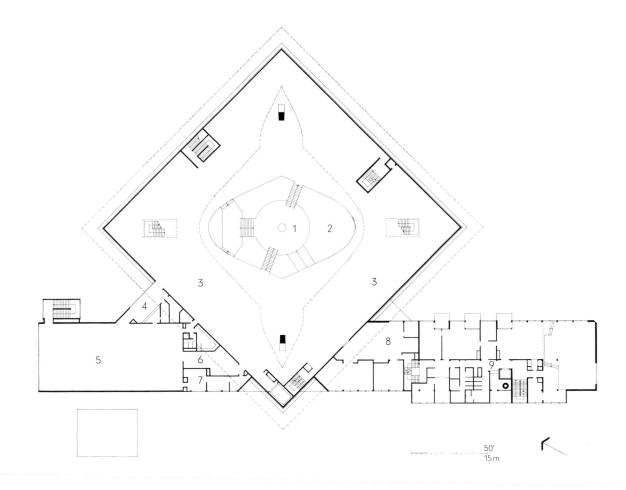

50'
15 m

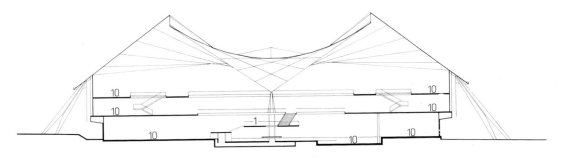

Plan, first floor / Grundriß erstes Geschoß.
Transverse section / Querschnitt.
1 Central platform / Zentrale Plattform
2 Void / Luftraum
3 Main exhibition galleries / Hauptausstellungsbereich
4 Foyer
5 Art gallery / Saal für Wechselausstellungen
6 Store / Magazin
7 Offices / Büros
8 Studio
9 Administration wing / Verwaltungsflügel
10 Exhibition areas / Ausstellungsbereich

1

2

3

1. The new building is at the southern end of Holland Park and is approached by a long covered way which crosses a pool. This canopy excludes a good deal of the sky from view and thus helps to adapt the eye to the very much lower levels of illumination to be found inside.

2. From the central platform it is possible to move down to the main floor of the exhibition area or up to the lower of the two balconies. The whole of the exhibition space can be understood from this vantage point.

3. The main area is covered by five hyperbolic paraboloid roofs. The display below these consists chiefly of rather brightly individually lit exhibits in a relatively dark space.

4. The art gallery is a single room 95 ft. × 45 ft. × 13 ft. high and is top-lit from 144 deep coffers. A detail of the ceiling is shown on page 129. At the north end there is a window with a low head to cut out the sky. The screens are supported by aluminium posts which are sprung between the floor and recesses in the underside of the ceiling. Although the aim of this and similar designs is to provide a high degree of flexibility, the uniformity of space which tends to result from this approach is in many ways an unexpectedly limiting factor.

1. Der Neubau liegt am Südende des Holland Park. Ein langer überdachter Gang, der über einen Teich führt, schließt den Blick auf den Himmel zum guten Teil aus und hilft daher dem Auge, sich auf die sehr viel geringeren Lichtwerte der Innenräume einzustellen.

2. Von der zentralen Plattform aus ist sowohl die Ausstellungsfläche des Hauptgeschosses erreichbar wie auch die untere der beiden Galerien. Der gesamte Ausstellungsraum wird von diesem Angelpunkt aus verständlich.

3. Der Hauptbau ist mit fünf hyperbolischen Paraboloiden eingedeckt. Die einzelnen Ausstellungsgegenstände sind im Vergleich zu dem verhältnismäßig dunklen Haus jeweils hell ausgeleuchtet.

4. Der Saal für Wechselausstellungen ist ein einheitlicher Raum von 29 × 13,70 m Grundfläche und 3,96 m Höhe. Er erhält Oberlicht durch ein Deckenraster mit 144 Feldern (vgl. Detail Seite 129). Die Stellwände sind an Aluminiumprofilen befestigt, die mit Hilfe von Federn zwischen Fußboden und Deckenkanten eingespannt sind. Lösungen dieser Art sollen weitgehende Flexibilität ermöglichen, aber die Monotonie des Raumeindrucks, der dabei entsteht, erweist sich als hinderlicher Faktor.

Detail of roof light in art gallery / Detail des Oberlichts im Saal für Wechselausstellungen.

1 Softwood strip, with a recess along the centre of each length to take top of screen post / Weichholzverblendung. In der Mitte jeder Rastereinheit sind Vertiefungen, in die die Aluminiumprofile eingespannt werden
2 Plasterboard / Gipsplatte
3 Blackout roller blind / Verdunkelungsjalousie
4 Fluorescent fittings / Leuchtstoffröhren
5 Glass in aluminium frame / Glas in Aluminiumrahmen

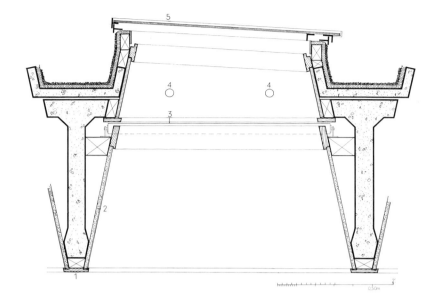

Picture Gallery for Christ Church, Oxford
(Project, 1964)

Architects: Powell and Moya

This small gallery is to be built in the grounds of the College so that its collection of paintings and drawings may be properly displayed. The paintings are mostly Italian and date from between the 14th and 17th centuries; the 2000 drawings are from the 15th–17th centuries. In view of the small site which was available, not all the exhibits could be shown at the same time so that adequate storage had to be devised.

The design of the gallery accepts the principles which Gardella pursued in his Milan pavilion where a clear relationship was established between the character, lighting and size of space and the character, lighting needs and size of exhibit. Within the L-shaped plan of the Christ Church gallery there are four distinct categories of space and each of these is related to a common reference line, the cloister circulation space, which has a view of the garden.

The largest and boldest paintings are in a big top lit room; Italian primitives and other small scale paintings are in smaller galleries, also top lit but with a less dominant section; modern exhibits are in a separate alcove and prints are in a totally artificially lit room with baffled entrances to exclude daylight.

The picture galleries provide both artificial and natural light from the same overhead zone. The fluorescent lighting tubes are held within the metal baffles which control the daylight coming through the diffusing glass. These baffles also act as burglar protection. To bring out the texture of the paintings in the large gallery there are also incandescent spotlights.

The print room will have a low level of lighting, preferably tungsten, which, it is hoped, will be switched on automatically when a visitor enters the room. This should reduce the hours of exposure of the vulnerable prints.

All the exhibition spaces will be air-conditioned, using wherever possible the hollow walls to contain the ducts.

A. Detail of junction between large gallery and gallery I / Anschlußdetail zwischen großem Ausstellungsraum und Raum I.
1 Large gallery / Großer Ausstellungsraum
2 Timber louvred ceiling with fluorescent background lighting / Holzriemendecke mit künstlicher Beleuchtung durch Leuchtstoffröhren
3 Precast paving slabs on asphalt / Vorgegossener Plattenbelag auf Asphalt
4 "Plyglass" – a double glazed insulating and diffusing glass in aluminium frames / Doppelschichtiges, isolierendes und lichtstreuendes Verbundglas in Aluminiumrahmen
5 Stone roof finish on asphalt / Steinplattenbelag des Daches auf Asphalt
6 Pressed metal louvres with fluorescent lighting tubes / Metallamellen mit Leuchtstoffröhren
7 Picture hanging rail with nylon suspension cords / Schiene mit Nylonschnüren für die Befestigung der Bilder
8 Tungsten spotlights / Punktleuchten mit Glühbirnen
9 Gallery I / Raum I
10 Suspended plaster ceiling / Abgehängte Gipsdecke
11 Timber louvres / Holzlamellen
12 Fluorescent tubes / Leuchtstoffröhren

B. Section through print room display wall / Schnitt durch die Wand des Graphikkabinetts.
1 Air-conditioning duct and grills / Leitung und Filter der Klimaanlage
2 Leather covered rail / Lederbezogene Schiene
3 Print frame / Einrahmung eines Graphikblatts
4 Tungsten spotlight / Punktleuchte

1. A view of the model from the south-west showing the relation of the gallery to one of the existing college buildings and to the Dean's garden which continues as a ramp over the cloister so as to be able to include a large part of the roof within its area.

1. Ansicht des Modells von Südwesten. Das Galeriegebäude mit einem der vorhandenen Collegebauten und dem Garten des Dekans, der mit einer Rampe über dem Kreuzgang weitergeführt ist und daher einen großen Teil der Dachfläche mit einbegreift.

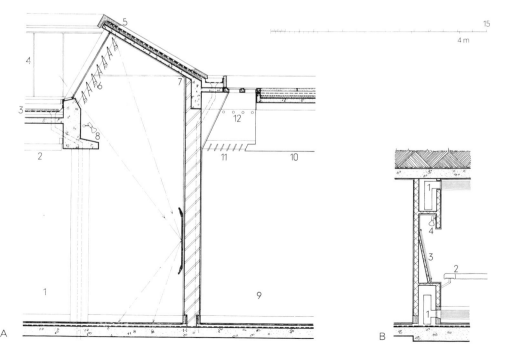

A   B

13

Kunstgalerie der Christ Church, Oxford
(Projekt, 1964)

Architekten: Powell und Moya

Die kleine Kunstgalerie soll auf dem Gelände des College errichtet werden, um der Sammlung von Gemälden und Zeichnungen zu einem angemessenen Gehäuse zu verhelfen. Die – hauptsächlich italienischen – Bilder stammen aus dem 14. bis 17. Jahrhundert, die 2000 Zeichnungen aus dem 15. bis 17. Jahrhundert. Da nur ein kleines Grundstück verfügbar ist, kann nicht der ganze Bestand gezeigt werden; ausreichender Magazinraum mußte daher vorgesehen werden.

Der Entwurf des Ausstellungsgebäudes beruht auf den Prinzipien, die Gardella bei seiner Galerie in Mailand anwandte: Gardella stellte eine klare Beziehung zwischen dem Charakter, den Lichtverhältnissen und der Größe des Raumes einerseits und dem Charakter, der erforderlichen Beleuchtung und der Größe der Ausstellungsgegenstände andererseits her. Der L-förmige Grundriß der Kunstgalerie in Oxford weist vier verschiedene Raumkategorien auf; jeder dieser Räume ist auf den gemeinsamen Orientierungspunkt bezogen, auf den Kreuzgang, der einen Ausblick auf den Garten bietet.

Die größten und anspruchsvollsten Bilder sind in einem großen Saal mit Oberlicht untergebracht; frühe italienische Malerei und andere kleinformatige Bilder sollen in Räumen von weniger beherrschenden Dimensionen gezeigt werden, die ebenfalls Oberlicht erhalten; moderne Ausstellungsgegenstände finden in einem besonderen Raum Platz, und die Graphik nimmt ein Raum mit künstlicher Beleuchtung auf, dessen Eingänge versetzt und so gegen das Eindringen von Tageslicht geschützt sind.

Künstliches Licht wie auch Tageslicht kommen von der Deckenzone der Ausstellungsräume. Die Leuchtstoffröhren sind in den Metalllamellen angebracht, die das durch Verbundglas einfallende Tageslicht dämpfen. Die Lamellen dienen gleichzeitig als Schutz gegen Einbrüche. Im großen Ausstellungsraum sollen außerdem Punktleuchten die Oberflächenstruktur der Bilder betonen.

Für das Graphikkabinett ist niedrigere Beleuchtungsstärke vorgesehen – nach Möglichkeit Glühbirnen, die automatisch eingeschaltet werden, sobald ein Besucher den Raum betritt. Auf diese Weise soll die Zeitdauer verkürzt werden, in der die empfindlichen Blätter der Einwirkung des Lichts ausgesetzt sind.

Sämtliche Ausstellungsräume werden mit Klimaanlagen versehen, deren Installationen so weit wie möglich von den hohlen Wänden aufgenommen werden.

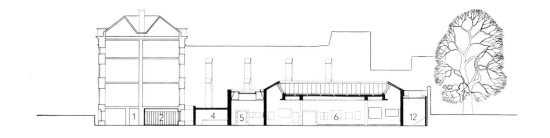

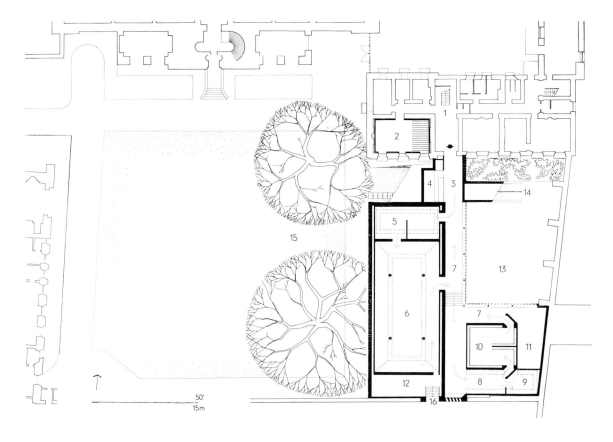

North-south section / Schnitt in Nord-Süd-Richtung.
Plan, ground floor / Grundriß Erdgeschoß.
 1 Existing building / Bestehendes Gebäude
 2 Picture storage / Bildermagazin
 3 Entrance / Eingang
 4 Custodian / Wärter
 5 Gallery I – Italian Primitives / Raum I – Frühe italienische Malerei
 6 Large gallery / Großer Ausstellungsraum
 7 Cloister / Kreuzgang
 8 Smaller pictures / Kleinformatige Bilder
 9 Modern exhibits / Moderne Ausstellungsgegenstände
10 Print room / Graphikkabinett
11 Study and picture store / Studienraum und Magazin
12 Air-conditioning plant room / Klimaanlage
13 Garden / Garten
14 Grass ramp up / Grasrampe aufwärts
15 Dean's garden / Garten des Dekans
16 Exit for tall pictures / Ausgang für große Bilder

2. Sectionalised perspective through the gallery for smaller pictures, the print room and the cloister.
2. Perspektivischer Schnitt durch den Raum für kleinformatige Bilder, Graphikkabinett und Kreuzgang.

There has been a very great increase in museum going in the States during the last fifteen years which has brought with it a considerable programme of museum building. In 1931 New York State had 200 museums, it now has twice that number. The new construction has generally been of medium sized institutions which have taken up the example set by the Museum of Modern Art in New York and built both galleries and generous ancillary spaces.

The enthusiasm which has taken large numbers to see the permanent collections and the many temporary exhibitions has also affected the commercial galleries. These have increased greatly in number and several of them have experimented with methods of display. Kiesler's World Art Gallery in New York is undoubtedly the most far reaching of these. Walls, floor and ceiling have been merged into a continuous curving surface so that the whole of the enclosure is unified.

The interest in pictures and sculpture has not been confined to viewing only. There is an interest in lectures and the explanations given through high-frequency receivers which can be hired as one enters. There is a desire to participate in painting and drawing classes. All this has architectural repercussions on museum planning, greatly increasing in size and variety the spaces which must adjoin the actual exhibition areas. The danger is always that these secondary activities will become so absorbing that they will not aid but hinder the prime objective; the communication of art to an observer. To some extent both planning and display technique can guard against this. They must always emphasise the primary aim by the manner in which spaces are related and by the visual importance given to the objects on display. I.M.Pei's proposal for a museum in Syracuse does something to restore the proper balance.

In den letzten fünfzehn Jahren hat die Zahl der Museumsbesucher in den Vereinigten Staaten ständig zugenommen, was zu einer beträchtlichen Erweiterung des Museumsbauprogramms führte. 1931 hatte der Staat New York 200 Museen – heute sind es doppelt so viele. Die neuen Bauten wurden im allgemeinen von mittelgroßen Institutionen errichtet, die dem Beispiel des Museum of Modern Art in New York folgten und außer den Kunstgalerien auch großzügige Nebeneinrichtungen einplanten.

Das Interesse an ständigen Ausstellungen und Wechselausstellungen zeitgenössischer Kunst wirkte sich auch auf die privaten Galerien aus. Viele neue Galerien sind entstanden, von denen einige mit verschiedenen Ausstellungstechniken experimentieren. Zu den extremsten Beispielen zählt zweifellos die World Art Gallery in New York von Kiesler. Wände, Boden und Decke bilden eine einzige fließende, geschwungene Fläche, so daß die Raumbegrenzungen völlig einheitlich wirken.

Die Begeisterung für Malerei und Plastik beschränkt sich nicht nur auf die optischen Eindrücke. Auch Mal- und Zeichenkurse, Vorträge und Erklärungen über Hochfrequenz-Empfänger, die man am Eingang mancher Museen ausleihen kann, werden immer beliebter. Alles das hat sich natürlich auf die architektonische Gestaltung der Museen ausgewirkt: Die Nebenräume, die sich an die eigentlichen Ausstellungsflächen anschließen, sind heute größer und vielseitiger verwendbar. Allerdings besteht bei dieser Entwicklung die Gefahr, daß die sekundären Einrichtungen allmählich zuviel Raum einnehmen und das ursprüngliche Ziel – Vermittlung der Kunst an den Museumsbesucher – nicht fördern, sondern eher behindern. In gewissem Maße können aber sowohl die Planung wie auch die Ausstellungstechnik einer solchen Tendenz entgegenwirken, indem sie die wichtigste Aufgabe des Museums durch architektonische und visuelle Mittel unterstreichen. I. M. Peis Projekt für ein Museum in Syracuse, New York, ist ein Beitrag in dieser Richtung.

1. The Corning Glass Center includes a museum (1951), attached to part of the glass works at Corning, N.Y. and contains a great historical collection of glass as well as displays demonstrating various current uses of the material. It is possible to go from the Hall of Science and Industry on the right through a link covered with glass tubing into the small Steuben factory on the left and follow the process of glass blowing, finishing and engraving. The Center also serves as the cultural centre for the area and musical and theatrical performances take place within it. The Glass Center and the administration building in the background were both designed by Harrison, Abramovitz and Abbe.

2. The Museum of Art, Science and Industry in Fairfield County, Conn. by John M. Johansen, which includes a planetarium on the middle floor, was built in 1962 and belongs to what might be called the second generation of museum building: flexibility is achieved within a variety of volumes and its range thus considerably increased.

1. Zum Corning Glass Center gehört ein Museum (1951), das sich an einen Teil der Glasfabrik in Corning, New York, anschließt. Das Museum enthält eine große historische Glassammlung und zeigt außerdem die verschiedenen Anwendungsmöglichkeiten des Materials in unserer Zeit. Von der Halle der Wissenschaft und Industrie (im Bilde rechts) gelangt man durch einen mit Glasröhren verkleideten Verbindungsgang in die kleine Steuben-Fabrik links, wo man die Vorgänge des Glasblasens und der weiteren Bearbeitung beobachten kann. Das Corning Glass Center dient gleichzeitig als Kulturzentrum für die Umgebung und veranstaltet Konzerte und Theateraufführungen. Das Glass Center und das Verwaltungsgebäude im Hintergrund wurden von Harrison, Abramovitz & Abbe entworfen.

2. Das Museum of Art, Science and Industry in Fairfield County, Connecticut (1962), von John M. Johansen gehört der »zweiten Generation« der Museumsbauten an. Durch eine Vielfalt von Raumvolumen wird große Flexibilität erreicht, und die Möglichkeiten des Museums werden dadurch beträchtlich erweitert. Im mittleren Geschoß ist ein Planetarium untergebracht.

1

2

Yale University Art Gallery, New Haven, Connecticut (1953)

Architect: Louis I. Kahn

Yale University Art Gallery, New Haven, Connecticut (1953)

Architekt: Louis I. Kahn

The Yale Art Gallery is probably one of the very few examples in which the idea of flexibility did not at once lead to an architecture of anonymous voids. Though Kahn now regrets not having subdivided the space by columns related to the triangular ceiling grid and the museum has seriously suffered through the clothing of some of its brick walls – as if their nudity were offensive – and the abandonment of the original panel system, it is still potentially a museum environment which bears comparison with the best Italian reconstructions. The space is organised by two dominant elements, a staircase drum which is the circulation node and a deep tetrahedral ceiling. Both are in shuttered concrete. Ducts, sound absorbent material and electric conduit and fittings are carried within the hollow spaces of this ceiling structure. Ceiling and drum provide the order and control which in fact brings out the individuality of the objects on display. They are, as Vincent Scully Jr. – Kahn's biographer and Professor of the History of Art at Yale – has remarked, a kind of landscape to which the works of art are related. In the original design all panels were free of the floor and ceiling so that the continuity of these major surfaces should remain uninterrupted. The panels were kept in place by rubber tipped spring-mounted feet and by a similar projection pressing against the ceiling. They were thus wedged between two rigid planes. This made it possible to arrange the screens in any position.

Die Yale Art Gallery gehört zu den wenigen Beispielen, bei denen der Wunsch nach Flexibilität nicht zu einer Architektur der anonymen Leere führte. Zwar bedauert es Kahn heute, daß er den Raum nicht durch Stützen unterteilte, die dem dreieckigen Raster der Decke entsprochen hätten. Außerdem ist die Wirkung des Museums durch die Verkleidung einiger Backsteinwände, deren Kahlheit offenbar anstößig wirkte, und den Wegfall des ursprünglichen Stellwand-Systems stark beeinträchtigt. Aber die Yale Art Gallery hält trotzdem noch jedem Vergleich mit den besten italienischen Museums-Neueinrichtungen stand. Das Innere des Museums wird beherrscht durch die plastisch wirkende Decke aus Tetraedern und den Treppenhaus-Zylinder, der den Mittelpunkt der Zirkulation bildet. Decke und Treppe sind aus Schalbeton. In den Hohlräumen der Decke liegen Kanäle, schalldämpfende Platten, elektrische Leitungen und Leuchtkörper. Decke und Treppenhaus vermitteln einen Eindruck der Einheitlichkeit und Ordnung, so daß die ausgestellten Gegenstände um so stärker ihre individuelle Wirkung entfalten können. Wie Vincent Scully jr. – der Biograph Kahns, Professor für Kunstgeschichte in Yale – sagte, sind diese beiden architektonischen Elemente eine Art Landschaft, zu der die Kunstwerke in Beziehung gesetzt werden. In Kahns ursprünglichem Entwurf reichten die Stellwände nicht vom Boden bis zur Decke, denn Kahn wollte die Kontinuität dieser Hauptflächen nicht unterbrechen. Die Wände wurden durch federnde Fußstücke mit Gummipuffern und durch eine ähnliche Vorrichtung an der Decke eingespannt. Sie waren also zwischen zwei festen Ebenen eingekeilt und konnten deshalb überall aufgestellt werden.

2. The gallery from Weir Hall courtyard; two sides of the building are almost wholly glazed and there are thus frequent views of trees and other university buildings from the inside. Part of the building has for many years also housed the School of Architecture.

2. Die Galerie vom Hof der Weir Hall gesehen. Zwei Seiten des Gebäudes sind fast vollständig verglast, so daß innen von vielen Stellen aus ein Blick auf die Bäume und die anderen Universitätsgebäude möglich ist. Ein Teil des Bauwerks hat einige Jahre lang die Architektur-Fakultät aufgenommen.

1. Ceiling plan / Plan der Decke.

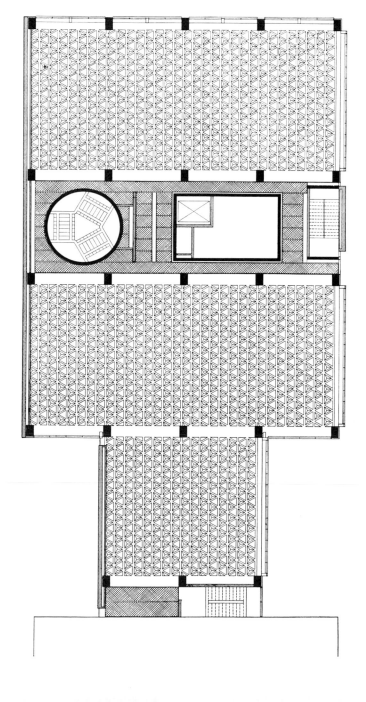

3

4

3. The circular drum containing the main stair; this like the ceiling is in shuttered concrete. Stair enclosure and ceiling provide the visual continuity between the museum spaces.

4, 5. Two views of the galleries in their altered and, unfortunately, weakened form. Lighting is provided by two types of fixtures, a low brightness fitting to illuminate general areas and a swiveling shielded fitting for specific objects in the display areas.

6. An exhibition of musical instruments held in the spring of 1960 which uses the original display panel in the foreground but not in the rear behind the harpsichord.

3. Das zylindrische Treppenhaus mit der Haupttreppe, die wie die Decken aus Schalbeton besteht.

4, 5. Zwei Innenansichten der Galerie in der geänderten und dadurch weniger eindrucksvollen Form. Für die Beleuchtung sorgen zwei verschiedene Systeme: Leuchtkörper mit niedrigen Helligkeitswerten für die Allgemeinbeleuchtung und drehbare, abgeschirmte Scheinwerfer für die Ausleuchtung einzelner Objekte.

6. Eine Ausstellung von Musikinstrumenten, die im Frühjahr 1960 gezeigt wurde. Im Vordergrund das ursprüngliche Stellwandsystem, hinter dem Cembalo die neue Lösung.

5

6

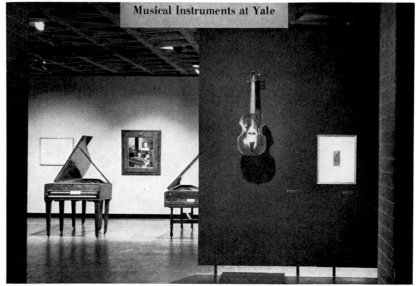

Cullinan Hall, Museum of Fine Arts, Houston, Texas (1958)

Architect: Ludwig Mies van der Rohe

Despite Mies van der Rohe's important design for a "Museum for a Small Town" (see p. 26/27), this is his only executed museum and is in fact only an addition to an existing building. The Houston Museum of Fine Arts was a symmetrical building with two projecting wings and Cullinan Hall fills the space between these. The hall is for temporary exhibitions. The basement of Cullinan Hall contains storage, studios for the Museum school and further exhibition rooms. Foundations and the floor slab of the ground floor are of reinforced concrete, the superstructure is a steel frame. The roof slab is hung from four steel plate girders which pass above the roof. This construction made it possible to span the main space without any supports. Cullinan Hall is only the first stage of the museum's reconstruction. The glass side of the hall is eventually to open into a two-storey building containing 30 galleries running parallel with the street. The hall will then become an enclosed sculpture court; whether even then its volume will be in scale with the exhibits remains to be seen.

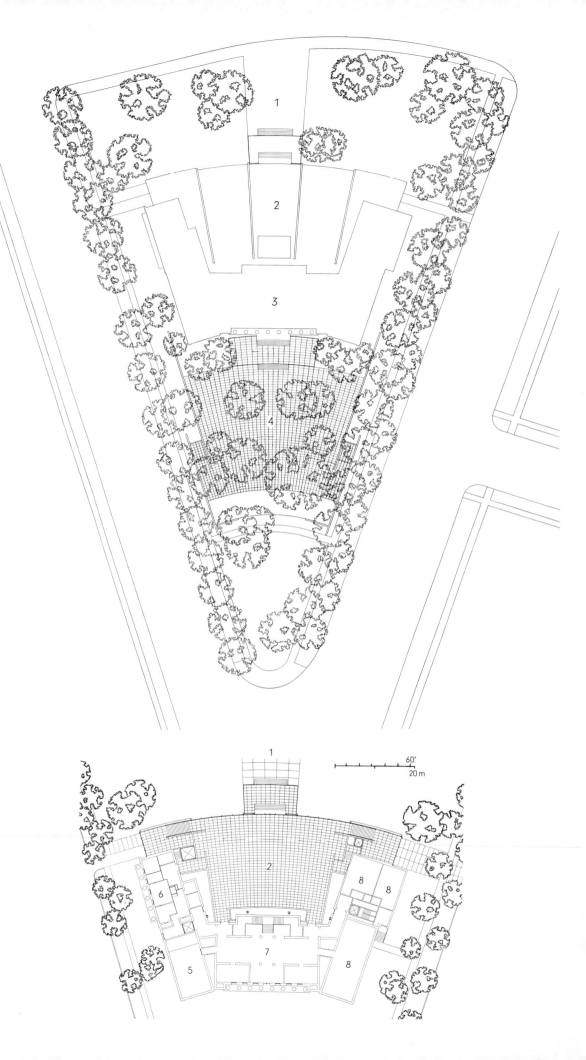

Site plan / Lageplan.
Plan, ground floor / Grundriß Erdgeschoß.
1 Main entrance / Haupteingang
2 Cullinan Hall
3 Existing building / Bereits bestehendes Gebäude
4 Proposed sculpture court / Geplanter Plastikhof
5 Lecture hall / Vortragssaal
6 Offices / Büros
7 Previous main foyer / Altes Foyer
8 Class rooms / Museumsschule

Cullinan Hall, Museum of Fine Arts, Houston, Texas (1958)

Architekt: Ludwig Mies van der Rohe

Mies van der Rohe, von dem der bedeutende Entwurf eines »Museums für eine kleine Stadt« stammt (vgl. Seite 26/27), hat nur einen einzigen Museumsbau ausgeführt. Seine Cullinan Hall liegt zwischen den beiden Flügeln des symmetrisch gegliederten Museum of Fine Arts in Houston, das bereits 1924 eröffnet wurde. Die Cullinan Hall, die Wechselausstellungen aufnimmt, bildet die erste Phase in einem Erweiterungsprogramm des Museum of Fine Arts. Im Untergeschoß sind Magazine, Studios der Museumsschule und weitere Ausstellungsräume untergebracht. Fundamente und Bodenplatte des Erdgeschosses wurden in Stahlbeton ausgeführt, der Oberbau als Stahlskelettkonstruktion. Die Dachplatte ist an vier über dem Dach verlaufenden Stahlplattenträgern aufgehängt. Diese Konstruktion ermöglichte eine stützenfreie Überspannung des Hauptraums. Die verglaste Seite der Halle soll sich später auf ein zweigeschossiges Gebäude hin öffnen, dessen dreißig Ausstellungsräume parallel zur Straße laufen werden. Aus der Halle wird dann ein umschlossener Plastikhof; ob das Raumvolumen dann im richtigen Verhältnis zu den Ausstellungsgegenständen steht, bleibt abzuwarten.

1

1, 2. The grey glass wall of the hall seen from the street during the day and at night. The sides have a brick infill. The stairs and platform lead up to the entrance, which is now the new main entry to the entire museum.
3, 4. Shown here is the first exhibition to be staged in the new addition. It was called "The Human Image" and was "to reflect man's changing image of himself through the ages". Though the great room which held it, 10,000 sq. ft. in area and 30 ft. high, may be in scale with the space which existed between the two wings of the earlier museum, it is barely so with the objects now within it. The situation may change when the second building is added. The room is lit by ceiling lights and by sidelight from the north; additional electrical connections are provided in the ceiling and in the green terrazzo floor. The stairs at the side lead to the basement and to the mezzanine which connects Cullinan Hall with the upper floors of the old wing and will eventually lead to the upper floor of the planned new building.
5. A photomontage showing the garden which is to be built at the rear opposite the previous entrance to the museum.

2

1, 2. Tag- und Nachtansicht der Wand aus grauem Tafelglas, von der Straße her gesehen. Die Seitenteile sind mit Ziegelstein ausgefacht. Stufen und Plattform führen zum Eingang, der zugleich der neue Haupteingang des gesamten Museums ist.
3, 4. Die erste Ausstellung, die in der neuen Cullinan Hall gezeigt wurde, hatte den Titel »The Human Image« (Das Bild des Menschen) und sollte demonstrieren, wie sich die menschliche Selbstdarstellung im Laufe der Jahrhunderte gewandelt hat. Die Maße des großen Ausstellungsraumes (Höhe 9,15 m, Fläche etwa 930 qm) entsprechen zwar seiner Lage zwischen den beiden Flügeln des älteren Gebäudes. Zu den gezeigten Kunstwerken stimmen seine Proportionen jedoch kaum. Das kann sich freilich ändern, wenn das neue Gebäude errichtet wird. Die Beleuchtung des Saales erfolgt durch das von Norden einfallende Seitenlicht und Deckenlichter; zusätzliche Anschlüsse sind in dem grünen Terrazzoboden und der Decke vorgesehen. Die seitlichen Treppen führen ins Untergeschoß und zu Mezzaningeschossen, die die Cullinan Hall mit den Obergeschossen des älteren Flügels verbinden und zu dem Obergeschoß des geplanten Neubaus führen sollen.
5. Die Fotomontage zeigt den Skulpturengarten, der auf der Rückseite gegenüber dem früheren Haupteingang des Museum of Fine Arts angelegt werden soll.

3

4

5

Museum of Art, Munson-Williams-Proctor Institute, Utica, N.Y. (1960)

Architect: Philip Johnson

The new building, facing the main street of the town, is part of a community centre for the arts which also includes a restored 19th century house and two large stables now used by the art school. In its design Philip Johnson, who had for 22 years been director of the Department of Architecture and Design at the Museum of Modern Art in New York, applied a good many of the beliefs he had formed during that period, in particular the notion that art is not necessarily best displayed in undifferentiated rooms purged of all architectural distinction and that there is a great need in all museums for a focal space. The latter especially is a recurring theme in Philip Johnson's thinking.

"Whether it is Le Corbusier or Mies or Wright or even myself, we all feel that the public, upon entering a museum and choosing one of six or seven things to do, require space, like a dog who, upon entering a room, will sniff in one or two circumambulations of the room and will at last coil himself in one particular spot. I assure you, orientation space is not waste.

"In the same sense, space for visual escape or space for orientation reference points in the galleries are not waste. The human eye, even the human spirit, droops from uniformity of lighting and space. A view back to the entrance, an opening into a court or garden, can be of greater functional use to the museum director than another two galleries. Space that helps us look at paintings is not waste space."

Museum of Art, Munson-Williams-Proctor Institute, Utica, N.Y. (1960)

Architekt: Philip Johnson

Das neue Museum an der Hauptstraße von Utica ist Teil eines Kunstzentrums, zu dem auch ein restauriertes Gebäude aus dem 19. Jahrhundert und zwei große Stallbauten gehören, die heute von der Kunstschule benutzt werden. Der Architekt des Neubaus, Philip Johnson, hat 22 Jahre lang die Architekturabteilung des Museum of Modern Art in New York geleitet. Beim Entwurf des Museums wandte er manche Einsicht an, die er während dieser Zeit gewonnen hatte. Johnson ist keineswegs der Meinung, daß Kunst in undifferenzierten Räumen bar jeder architektonischen Individualität am besten zur Geltung gelangt. Das Museum braucht einen Mittelpunkt – eine Forderung, die Johnson immer wieder stellt.

»Seien es Le Corbusier, Mies van der Rohe, Wright oder auch ich selbst, wir alle glauben, daß das Publikum Raum braucht, wenn es ein Museum betritt und zwischen sechs oder sieben Möglichkeiten wählt – genau wie ein Hund, der im Zimmer erst einmal umherschnüffelt, ehe er sich auf einem bestimmten Fleck zusammenrollt. Ich versichere Ihnen: Raum, der zur Orientierung dient, ist nicht vergeudet. Und auch in den Ausstellungssälen ist Raum für die visuelle Ablenkung oder für Orientierungspunkte nicht vergeudet. Das menschliche Auge, ja der menschliche Geist werden durch Gleichförmigkeit von Licht und Raum ermüdet. Ein Blick zurück auf den Eingang, eine Öffnung zu einem Hof oder Garten können für den Museumsdirektor mehr funktionellen Wert haben als zwei weitere Säle. Raum, der uns hilft, Bilder zu betrachten, ist kein vergeudeter Raum.«

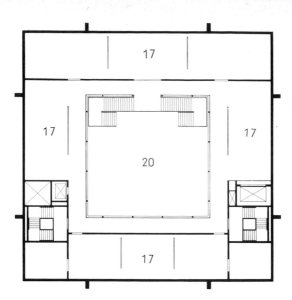

Plan, upper floor / Grundriß Obergeschoß.

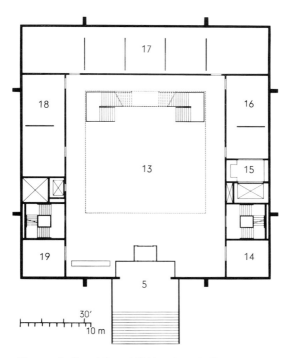

Plan, main floor / Grundriß Hauptgeschoß.

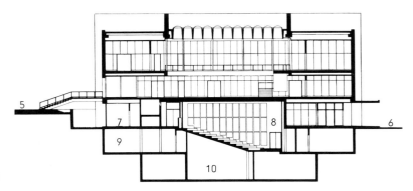

Section / Schnitt

Site plan / Lageplan.

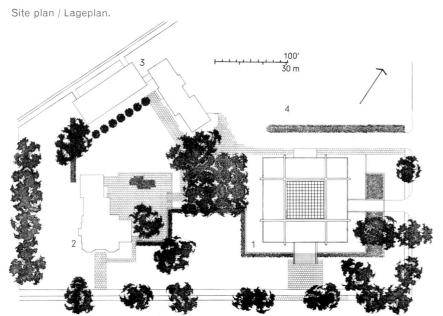

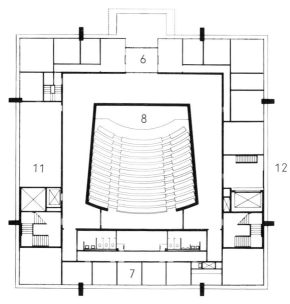

Plan, lower ground floor / Grundriß unteres Erdgeschoß. 13

1

1. The entrance steps face the main street. The square building is supported by eight bronze-clad columns of reinforced concrete holding four intersecting exterior beams. The two upper floors of the museum are enclosed by unpierced walls sheathed in grey Canadian granite.
2. The building has a dry moat on three sides onto which ancillary rooms face. A bridge across this moat leads to the main entrance.

1. Die Eingangstreppe liegt an der Hauptstraße. Das quadratische Gebäude hat acht bronzeverkleidete Stahlbetonstützen, auf denen zwei sich kreuzende Paare von Außenträgern aufliegen. Die beiden oberen Geschosse des Museums zeigen geschlossene Wände, die mit grauem kanadischem Granit verkleidet sind.
2. Das Gebäude ist auf drei Seiten von einem trockenen Graben umgeben, auf den sich die Nebenräume im Untergeschoß öffnen. Der Haupteingang führt über eine Brücke, die den Graben überquert.

2

Key to plans / Legende zu den Plänen:
 1 Museum of Art / Kunstmuseum
 2 Fountain Elms (existing house) / Fountain Elms (älteres Gebäude)
 3 Art School (existing stables) / Kunstschule (ältere Stallbauten)
 4 Car parking / Parkplatz
 5 Front entrance / Eingang von der Hauptstraße
 6 Rear entrance / Haupteingang
 7 Offices / Büros
 8 Auditorium
 9 Storage / Magazin
10 Mechanical equipment / Technische Anlagen
11 Library and music room / Bibliothek und Musikzimmer
12 Loading dock / Laderampe
13 Central hall / Zentrale Halle
14 Coats / Garderobe
15 Kitchen / Küche
16 Member's room / Raum für Mitglieder des Instituts
17 Exhibition gallery / Ausstellungsraum
18 Children's room / Kinderspielzimmer
19 Shop / Verkaufsraum
20 Void of central hall / Luftraum zentrale Halle

3

4

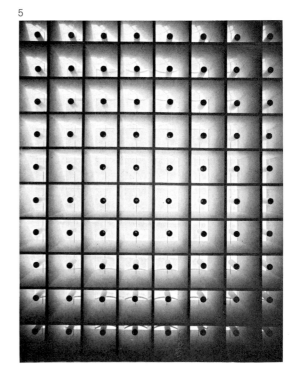

5

3, 4. The central hall completely fulfills its intended role. It acts as a continuous reference point to the galleries opening off it and its top-lit volume provides a different sort of spatial experience to the surrounding enclosed and artificially lit rooms. The lower walls panelled in teak are deliberately recessive, the upper ones covered with woven Philippine palm fibre intentionally dominant.

5. The hall is top-lit from skylights shielded by very deep coffers. Inset into the centre of each is a drum-like lighting fixture. These produce in the evening an effect similar to daylight.

6. The children's room on the main floor is equipped with games and special light racks on which patterns can be created.

7. The steeply sloping auditorium is entered at lower ground floor level and is used for films, talks, music and plays. The auditorium, like the whole of the remainder of the building, is wired for television to be used either on a closed circuit or to originate programmes which can be beamed from the roof direct to a near by television tower. The auditorium seats 300 and the sound reflection from the side walls is controlled by panels covered in gold leaf mosaic.

8. At the back of the central hall on the main level there is a long room entered on either side of the double stair. Screens are held in grooves in the ceiling; these can also take additional light fittings. Permanent walls are lit by fittings recessed into the ceiling. The ceiling also contains outlets for air conditioning. The floor material is travertine.

3, 4. Die zentrale Halle erfüllt die Funktion, die Johnson ihr zuwies. Sie bildet den Mittelpunkt für die Ausstellungsräume, die von hier aus erschlossen werden. Ihr durch Oberlicht beleuchtetes Raumvolumen bildet außerdem einen starken Kontrast zu den geschlossenen und ausschließlich künstlich beleuchteten Nachbarräumen. Die unteren, mit Teakholz verkleideten Wände treten bewußt zurück; die Wände oberhalb der Galerien sind mit einem philippinischen Palmfasergewebe bespannt und wirken absichtlich beherrschend.

6

7

8

5. Das Licht fällt in der Halle durch tiefe Deckenkassetten ein. In der Mitte jeder Kassette sind zylindrische Leuchtkörper installiert, die abends eine ähnliche Wirkung wie das Tageslicht hervorrufen.

6. Der Spielraum im Hauptgeschoß ist mit Spielzeug und Leuchtkästen ausgestattet, auf denen die Kinder bunte Muster bilden können.

7. In das steil abfallende Auditorium, das für Filme, Diskussionen, Musik- und Theatervorführungen benutzt wird, gelangt man vom Untergeschoß. Wie die übrigen Teile des Gebäudes ist das Auditorium mit Installationen für das Fernsehen ausgerüstet. Die Fernseheinrichtung ermöglicht eine Richtübertragung über Kabel; sie kann auch über Richtfunk zu einem in der Nähe befindlichen Sendeturm an das allgemeine Programmnetz angeschlossen werden. Das Auditorium hat 300 Plätze. Die Schallreflexion von den Seitenwänden wird durch Platten mit Goldblatt-Mosaik reguliert.

8. An der Rückseite der Haupthalle befindet sich auf dem Hauptniveau ein langgestreckter Raum, der von beiden Seiten der Doppeltreppe zugänglich ist. Die Stellwände werden in Deckenschienen befestigt, an denen auch zusätzliche Leuchtkörper angebracht werden können. Die feststehenden Wände werden durch Lampen beleuchtet, die in die Decke eingelassen sind. Die Klimaanlage ist ebenfalls in der Decke installiert. Das Material des Fußbodens ist Travertin.

The Solomon R. Guggenheim Museum, New York (1956–59)

Architect: Frank Lloyd Wright

Frank Lloyd Wright has described the design of the building in a number of letters to its founder, Solomon R. Guggenheim, and in several statements made during the time of its design and construction. Both Wright and Guggenheim died before the museum was completed.

"To understand the situation as it exists in the scheme for the Guggenheim Memorial all you have to do is imagine clean beautiful surfaces throughout the building, all beautifully proportioned to human scale. These surfaces are all lighted from above with any degree of daylight (or artificial light from the same source) that the curator or the artist himself may happen to desire. The atmosphere of great harmonious simplicity wherein human proportions are maintained in relation to the picture is characteristic of your building. . . .

"This advanced painting has seldom been presented in other than the incongruous rooms of the old static architecture. Here in harmonious fluid quiet created by this building-interior the new painting will be seen for itself under favourable conditions. . . .

"The paintings themselves are in perfectly air-conditioned chambers, chambers something like those of 'the chambered nautilus'. . . .

"The Solomon R. Guggenheim Museum's walls and spaces, inside and outside, are one in substance and effect. Walls slant gently outward forming a giant spiral for a well defined purpose: a new unity between beholder, painting and architecture. As planned, in the easy downward drift of the viewer on the giant spiral, pictures are not to be seen bolt-upright as though painted on the wall behind them. Gently inclined, faced slightly upward to the viewer and to the light in accord with the upward sweep of the spiral, the paintings themselves are emphasized as features in themselves and are not hung 'square' but gracefully yield to movement as set up by these slightly curving massive walls. In a great upward sweep of movement the picture is seen framed as a feature of architecture. The character of the building itself as architecture amounts to 'framing'. The flat-plane of the picture thus detached by the curve of the wall is presented to view much as a jewel set as a signet ring. Precious – as itself.

"Slightly tilted curving away of the walls against which the pictures are thus placed not only presents no difficulty but facilitates viewing; the wide curvature of the main walls is, to the painting, a positive asset. Occasional sculpture may arise from oval or circular masonry pedestal of the same colour and material as the floor and walls of the Museum. Comfortable low seats of the same character are placed conveniently at the base of the structural webs forming the sides of the alcoves. The gentle upward, or downward, sweep of the main spiral-ramp itself serves to make visitors more comfortable by their very descent along the spiral, viewing the various exhibits: the elevator is doing the lifting, the visitor the drifting from alcove to alcove."

Key to plans / Legende zu den Plänen:
 1 Entrance / Eingang
 2 Vestibule / Vestibül
 3 Main gallery / Hauptausstellungsraum
 4 Reception / Rezeption
 5 Loggia
 6 Pool / Wasserbecken
 7 Elevators / Aufzüge
 8 Beginning of ramp / Beginn der Rampe
 9 Coats / Garderobe
10 Kitchen / Küche
11 Café
12 Storage / Magazin
13 Sales desk / Verkaufsstand
14 Information booth / Informationsschalter
15 Loading platform / Laderampe
16 Ramp to auditorium / Rampe zum Auditorium
17 Auditorium
18 Machine room / Maschinenraum
19 Void / Luftraum
20 Grand gallery / Großer Ausstellungssaal
21 Print room / Graphikkabinett
22 Offices / Büros
23 Library / Bibliothek
24 Workroom / Werkstatt
25 Visitor's lounge / Aufenthaltsraum für Besucher
26 Guard room / Wärter
27 Caretaker's apartment / Pförtnerwohnung

1

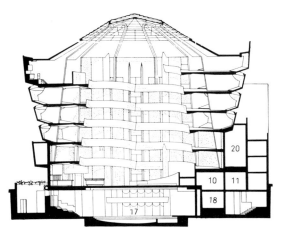

Section through the main exhibition space. The diameter of the spiral increases as it ascends so that the depth of the chambers is as a result greater at the upper levels. The partitions between the chambers act as bearing walls.

Schnitt durch den Hauptausstellungsbereich. Der Durchmesser der Spirale nimmt nach oben zu; der Durchmesser der kreisförmigen offenen Mitte bleibt in allen Geschossen gleich. Die einzelnen Kojen nehmen daher auf den oberen Niveaus an Tiefe zu. Die Trennwände zwischen den Kojen sind zugleich tragende Wandscheiben.

Plan, ground floor / Grundriß Erdgeschoß.

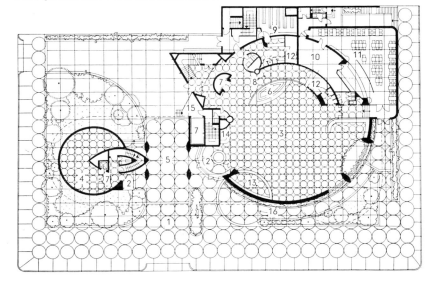

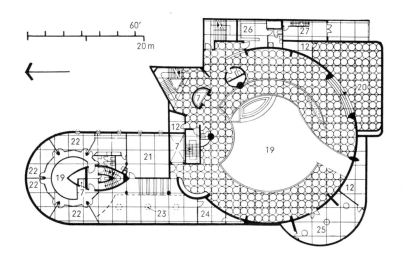

Plan, first floor / Grundriß erstes Geschoß.

The Solomon R. Guggenheim Museum, New York (1956–59)

Architekt: Frank Lloyd Wright

Frank Lloyd Wright hat seinen Entwurf in mehreren Briefen an Solomon R. Guggenheim, den Begründer des Museums, und in Erklärungen während der Planungs- und Bauzeit immer wieder analysiert. Sowohl Wright als auch Guggenheim starben, bevor das Bauwerk vollendet wurde.

»Um den Entwurf für das Guggenheim Memorial zu verstehen, müssen Sie sich nur klare, schöne Flächen vorstellen, die alle harmonisch auf den menschlichen Maßstab zugeschnitten sind. Diese Flächen werden von oben mit dem Helligkeitsgrad von Tageslicht (oder künstlichem Licht ebenfalls von oben) beleuchtet, den der Kurator oder der Künstler selbst jeweils für richtig halten. Die Atmosphäre großer harmonischer Einfachheit, in der die menschlichen Proportionen im Verhältnis zum Kunstwerk erhalten bleiben, ist charakteristisch für Ihren Bau...

Die moderne Malerei ist selten anders ausgestellt worden als in den unangemessenen Räumen der alten statischen Architektur. Hier, in harmonischer, fließender, ruhiger

Hauptwand wirkt sich auf die Kunstwerke positiv aus. An einigen Stellen können Skulpturen auf ovalen oder runden Mauersockeln aufgestellt werden, die in Farbe und Material mit dem Boden und den Wänden des Museums übereinstimmen. Bequeme niedrige Sitzplätze, die ebenfalls im Charakter passen, stehen an den Trennwänden der Kojen. Die sanfte Aufwärts- oder Abwärtsbewegung der Spiralrampe macht es ihrerseits den Besuchern bequem, wenn sie an der Spirale entlang nach unten gehen und dabei die ausgestellten Werke betrachten: Der Aufzug übernimmt den Transport nach oben, der Museumsbesucher läßt sich von einer Koje zur anderen treiben.«

1. The museum is on Fifth Avenue and faces Central Park. It is entered under the overhang between the four-storey administration building on the left and the museum on the right. A semi-circular vestibule leads straight into the main gallery.
2, 3. The ramp rises as an unbroken line to the dome 92 ft. above which is gradually revealed as one moves forward.

1. Das Museum liegt an der Fifth Avenue gegenüber dem Central Park. Der Eingang befindet sich unter der Auskragung zwischen dem viergeschossigen Verwaltungsgebäude links und dem Museum rechts. Ein halbkreisförmiges Vestibül führt geradenwegs in den Hauptausstellungsraum.
2, 3. Die Rampe führt als ununterbrochene Kurve mit einer Steigung von 3% bis zu der etwa 28 m hohen Kuppel empor. Ihre räumliche Wirkung enthüllt sich, je weiter man zur Raummitte vorschreitet.

2

3

Umgebung, wird das neue Kunstwerk unter günstigen Bedingungen individuell zur Geltung kommen...

Die Bilder selbst sind in Kojen mit Klimaanlagen untergebracht, Abteilungen, die an die Kämmerchen im Kalkgehäuse der Perlbootschnecke erinnern...

Die Wände und Räume des Solomon R. Guggenheim Museums sind innen und außen in Substanz und Wirkung eins. Die Wände neigen sich sanft nach außen; sie bilden eine Riesenspirale zu einem wohldefinierten Zweck: eine neue Einheit zwischen Betrachter, Kunstwerk und Architektur. Da der Betrachter in der Riesenspirale fast unmerklich nach unten gezogen wird, sieht er die Bilder nicht starr und aufrecht, als seien sie auf die Wand dahinter gemalt. Sie sind dem Besucher und dem Licht leicht entgegengeneigt, entsprechend der Aufwärtsbewegung der Spirale. So werden die Bilder als individuelle Kunstwerke betont; sie hängen nicht ›viereckig‹, sondern geben anmutig der Bewegung nach, die die leicht geschwungenen massiven Wände hervorrufen. In dem starken Bewegungsfluß nach oben wirkt das Bild wie ein gerahmtes Element der Architektur. Der architektonische Charakter des Gebäudes selbst kommt einem ›Rahmen‹ gleich. Die Ebene des Bildes, die sich von der ausschwingenden Wand löst, präsentiert sich dem Betrachter wie ein Juwel, das in einen Siegelring gefaßt ist. Kostbar – ein individuelles Objekt.

Die leichte Kurvung der Wände, vor denen die Bilder hängen, bietet deshalb keine Schwierigkeiten, sondern erleichtert die Betrachtung. Der weite Schwung der

4. The view across the museum from the second level; the steps into the two-storey grand gallery are in the distance on the level below.
5. Looking down from the top onto a pool shaped like a seed-pod which marks the beginning of the ramp. Brancusi's white figure is in the centre of the floor.

4. Blick quer durch das Museum vom zweiten Niveau; die Treppe zu dem zwei Geschosse hohen großen Ausstellungssaal (im Hintergrund) liegt auf dem ersten Niveau.
5. Blick von oben auf das Wasserbecken am Ausgangspunkt der Rampe, das wie eine Samenschote aussieht. Die weiße Plastik in der Mitte stammt von Brancusi.

9. The ramp galleries are now lit by a combination of fluorescent fittings between the skylight and a lower sheet of frosted glass, and front light fixtures hung on the ceiling and following the U-shaped form of each compartment. The pictures are attached to square rods which project about four feet from the walls. The wall and the sloping portion of the floor are matt white and the paintings appear to float against this background. The skylights illuminate the walls, the ceiling fittings the paintings and the balance between them is so controlled that the rods should not cast a shadow. The light intensity on the face of most paintings reaches the extraordinary value of 170 foot candles (1800 lux).

9. Die Galerien auf den Rampen werden durch Leuchtstoffröhren erhellt, die zwischen dem Oberlicht und einer darunter angebrachten Mattglasscheibe installiert sind. Für zusätzliche Beleuchtung sorgen bandförmige Deckenlampen, die der U-Form der Kojen entsprechend angeordnet sind. Die Bilder sind an rechteckigen Stangen befestigt, die etwa 1,20 m von den Wänden abstehen. Wände und Rampen sind in Mattweiß gehalten, so daß die Bilder vor dem Hintergrund zu schweben scheinen. Die Oberlichter leuchten die Wände aus, die Deckenlampen die Bilder. Die Helligkeitsgrade sind so gut ausgewogen, daß die Stangen keinen Schatten werfen. Die Lichtintensität auf der Fläche der meisten Bilder erreicht die außergewöhnliche Stärke von 1800 lx.

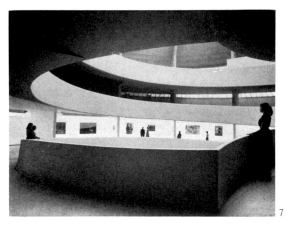

6. On one side of the circular space on the ground floor, there is a view out to Fifth Avenue and a sunken garden with a ramp which forms a direct entrance to the auditorium in the basement.
7. The topmost part of the ramp is used for storage and some of the racks can be seen on the left on the level above.
8. The main gallery as seen on entering.

6. An einer Seite der kreisförmigen Fläche im Erdgeschoß blickt man auf die Fifth Avenue und auf einen tieferliegenden Garten mit einer Rampe. Von dort aus gelangt man direkt in das Auditorium im Untergeschoß.
7. Der höchste Teil der Rampe wird als Lagerraum benutzt; auf dem oberen Niveau links sind einige Gestelle der Bilder zu erkennen.
8. Der Hauptausstellungsraum vom Eingang aus.

10. The museum is capable of holding large crowds – 750,000 came during the first nine months – and to make the great open space a social gathering place. This spiral-enclosed room is, as Peter Blake has remarked, "undoubtedly the most valuable piece in the Guggenhelm Collection." The cylindrical shaft contains the service core; the lifts are installed in another shaft semicircular in shape.

10. Das Museum kann eine große Zahl von Besuchern aufnehmen (in den ersten neun Monaten nach der Eröffnung kamen 750 000 Menschen), und aus dem großen offenen Raum wird bisweilen ein gesellschaftlicher Treffpunkt. Dieser von der Spirale umschlossene Raum ist, wie Peter Blake bemerkte, »zweifellos das wertvollste Stück in der Sammlung Guggenheim«. Der zylindrische Schaft enthält den Installationskern. Die Aufzüge sind in einem weiteren Schaft von halbkreisförmigem Grundriß untergebracht.

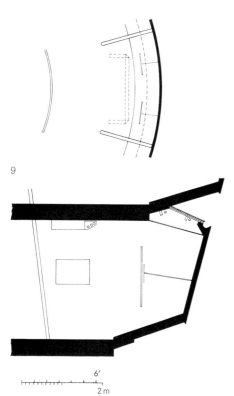

9

6'

2 m

10

11. Although pictures are neither lit nor hung as intended by Wright, their arrangement preserves his original intention that they should appear free in space. Looking across the open well more than one level is always visible and the juxtaposition of paintings seen at a distance becomes significant; many compartments of "the chambered nautilus" are revealed as soon as one looks inwards.

11. Obwohl die Bilder weder so beleuchtet noch so gehängt wurden, wie Wright es plante, ist doch seine ursprüngliche Vorstellung verwirklicht, daß sie frei im Raum zu hängen scheinen. Der Blick über die offene Mitte hinweg zeigt stets mehr als nur ein Niveau; von der Ferne her wird die Zusammenstellung der Bilder in den zahlreichen gleichzeitig sichtbaren Kammern der »Schnecke« bedeutungsvoll.

11

Albright-Knox Art Gallery, Buffalo, N.Y. (1962)

Architects: Skidmore, Owings & Merrill

Albright-Knox Art Gallery, Buffalo, N.Y. (1962)

Architekten: Skidmore, Owings & Merrill

The design of the addition to the Albright-Knox Art Gallery faced the problem of adding a wing equal in site area to the existing precise Neo-classical building of 1905. It does so without in any way belittling the original temple forms or compromising the present solution. The white marble walls of the new wing extend the podium of the old buildings and the auditorium rises from these as a complimentary precise form of dark grey glass.

Beim Entwurf des Anbaus war zu berücksichtigen, daß der neue Flügel eine annähernd gleiche Fläche des Grundstücks einnehmen sollte wie das bestehende neoklassizistische Gebäude von 1905. Der Neubau respektiert die älteren Tempelformen, ohne daß ein Kompromiß entstanden wäre. Die weißen Marmorwände des neuen Flügels führen den Sockel des alten Gebäudes weiter; darüber erhebt sich das Auditorium als klares Volumen aus dunkelgrauem Glas.

1, 2. Day and at night views of the museum; only the auditorium and the new entrance lobby protrude beyond the unpierced marble walls of the new wing.

1, 2. Tag- und Nachtansicht des Museums. Nur das Auditorium und der neue Eingang heben sich von den geschlossenen Marmorwänden des neuen Flügels ab.

1

Key to plans / Legende zu den Plänen:
1 Existing building / Altes Gebäude
2 New wing / Neuer Anbau
3 New entrance / Neuer Eingang
4 Entrance corridor / Eingangskorridor
5 Stair to galleries in existing building / Treppe zu den Ausstellungsräumen im alten Gebäude
6 Coat room / Garderobe
7 Lavatories / Toiletten
8 Offices / Büros
9 Courtyard / Innenhof
10 Dining room / Speiseraum
11 Kitchen / Küche
12 Exhibition gallery / Ausstellungsraum
13 Stairs to auditorium / Treppen zum Auditorium
14 Main gallery / Hauptausstellungsraum
15 Auditorium seating 348 / Auditorium mit 348 Sitzplätzen

2

3. The rooms of the new wing are grouped around a courtyard. Picture galleries occur on two sides, ancillary rooms on the other two.
4, 5. The boardroom and sitting area face the courtyard with Henry Moore's *Reclining Figure Number One* on the left and Reg Butler's *Manipulator* on the right. The rooms on the far side of the court are museum offices. The two higher elements of the building group, the old museum and the new auditorium, provide added enclosure to the large court.

3. Die Räume des Anbaus sind um einen Hof gruppiert. An zwei Seiten liegen Bildergalerien, an den beiden anderen Nebenräume.
4, 5. Von der Sitzgruppe und dem Konferenzraum aus erblickt man im Hof links die *Reclining Figure Number One* von Henry Moore und rechts Reg Butlers *Manipulator*. Auf der anderen Seite des Hofes liegen Büroräume. Durch die beiden höheren Bauten des Komplexes, das alte Museum und das neue Auditorium, wirkt der Hof noch stärker umschlossen.

1

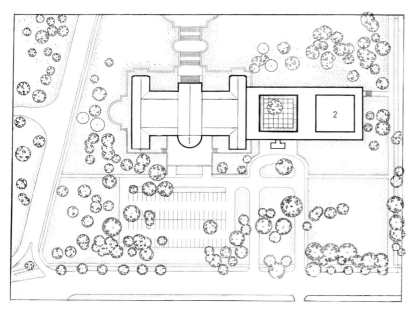

Site plan / Lageplan.

3

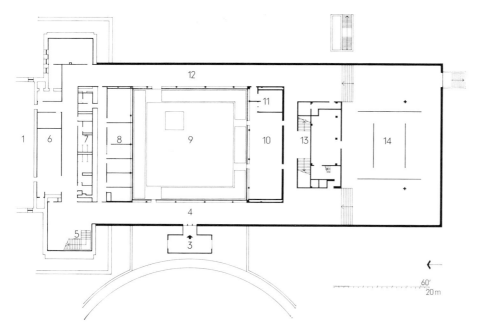

Plan, ground floor / Grundriß Erdgeschoß.

60'
20 m

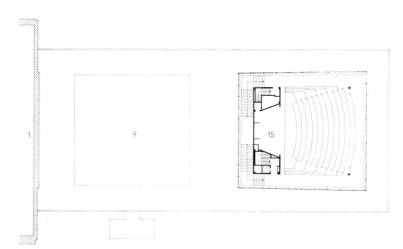

Plan, first floor / Grundriß erstes Geschoß.

4

5

6

6, 7. The space under the auditorium has a higher ceiling and is subdivided by movable screens into a number of galleries. The fixed outer walls are lit by fittings recessed into circular openings in the suspended ceiling; the partitions by drum-like fittings attached to lighting bridges which fasten to the tracks recessed in the ceiling on a regular grid. The tracks also stabilize the vertical supports of these partitions. The floor is covered with 18″ × 36″ rubber tiles.

8. The new staircase connects the new wing to the existing building. The picture galleries of the old museum were renovated and had new lighting installed. One of these rooms is illustrated on page 175.

9. The 350 seat auditorium is fitted with rear projection and the dark grey glass makes possible its use during the day without necessarily drawing the curtains. The seats are upholstered in red cloth.

6, 7. Der Saal unterhalb des Auditoriums hat eine höhere Decke und wird durch bewegliche Stellwände in verschiedene Räume aufgeteilt. Die feststehenden Außenwände werden durch Leuchtkörper erhellt, die in kreisrunde Löcher in der eingehängten Decke eingelassen sind. Die Beleuchtung der Trennwände übernehmen zylindrische Spotlights. Sie sind an Lichtbrücken be-

festigt, die in einem regelmäßigen Raster von Deckenschienen angebracht wurden. Die Schienen nehmen auch die vertikalen Stützen der Stellwände auf. Der Fußboden ist mit 45×90 cm großen Gummiplatten belegt.

8. Eine neue Treppe verbindet den Anbau mit dem älteren Gebäude. Die Ausstellungsräume des alten Museums wurden renoviert und mit neuen Beleuchtungsanlagen versehen (vgl. Seite 175).

9. Das Auditorium faßt 350 Personen. Die dunkelgraue Farbe des Glases ermöglicht es, die Projektionsanlage an der Rückseite des Auditoriums auch bei Tage zu benutzen, ohne daß die Vorhänge zugezogen werden müssen. Die gepolsterten Sitze sind mit rotem Stoff bespannt.

7

8

9

14

Rose Art Center, Brandeis University, Waltham, Massachusetts (1962)

Architects: Harrison & Abramovitz

Rose Art Center, Brandeis University, Waltham, Massachusetts (1962)

Architekten: Harrison & Abramovitz

The small Greek temple plan has been adapted for a small museum pavilion on the campus of Brandeis University outside Boston. The belief that art requires to be enshrined – even for undergraduate visitors – persists with remarkable tenacity.
The two storey volume of the museum is entered at the upper level. A staircase cantilevered over a pool leads to the lower floor. Future development will be linked to this lower level.

Der kleine Museumspavillon der Brandeis University bei Boston wurde über einem Grundriß errichtet, der an griechische Tempel erinnert. Die These, daß Kunstwerke als Heiligtum verwahrt werden müssen – selbst wenn die Besucher jüngere Studenten sind –, hält sich mit bemerkenswerter Hartnäckigkeit.
Der Eingang zu dem zwei Geschosse hohen Volumen liegt im oberen Geschoß. Eine Treppe, die über ein Wasserbassin auskragt, führt zum Untergeschoß. Spätere Erweiterungsbauten werden mit dem unteren Geschoß verbunden.

1, 2. The recessed entrance of the museum, a limestone clad pavilion on the undulating ground of the university campus, is reached by a flight of steps from a raised terrace.

1, 2. Ansicht von Südosten. Der zurückgesetzte Eingang des Museums. Das Gebäude ist mit Kalksteinplatten verkleidet. Es liegt auf dem welligen Gelände der Brandeis University und ist über Treppen von einer erhöhten Terrasse aus zugänglich.

1

2

3. The entrance doors are behind the translucent screen in the distance. The two levels of the museum are connected by a dominant central staircase. This central well is lit by deep roof lights.
4. Pictures on white plaster walls are artificially lit by lights concealed in troughs behind the edge of the suspended ceiling. Further general lighting is given by circular recessed downlights in the sound absorbent ceiling. The floor is Italian travertine.
5. The lower level is a four-sided gallery around a central pool with natural clerestory lighting on three sides.

3. Die Eingangstüren liegen hinter der Mattglasscheibe im Hintergrund. Eine Treppe in der Mitte verbindet die beiden Geschosse des Museums. Der Treppenbereich wird durch schachtartige Oberlichter beleuchtet.
4. Für die künstliche Beleuchtung der Bilder auf der weißen Wand im Obergeschoß sorgen Lichtquellen, die in den kastenförmigen Vertiefungen seitlich der Zwischendecke angebracht sind. Die Allgemeinbeleuchtung übernehmen Scheinwerfer, die in die schallschluckende Decke eingelassen wurden. Der Fußboden besteht aus italienischem Travertin.
5. Im unteren Geschoß ist der Ausstellungsbereich um ein zentrales Wasserbecken angeordnet; auf drei Seiten fällt durch Oberlichtstreifen Tageslicht ein.

Longitudinal section / Längsschnitt.
Plan, lower floor / Grundriß Untergeschoß.
Plan, main floor / Grundriß Hauptgeschoß.
1 Entrance / Eingang
2 Upper exhibition gallery / Oberer Ausstellungsbereich
3 Stairs to lower level / Treppe zum Untergeschoß
4 Lower exhibition gallery / Unterer Ausstellungsbereich
5 Pool / Wasserbecken
6 Office / Büro
7 Mechanical plant / Technische Anlagen

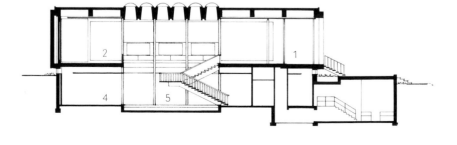

5

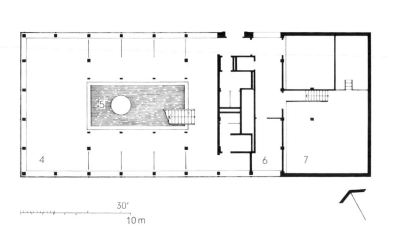

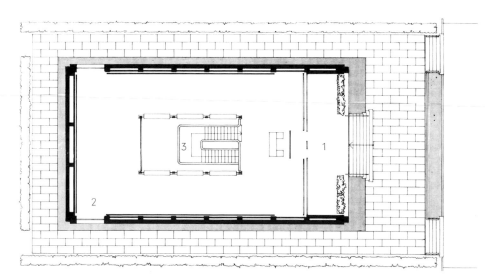

30'
10 m

Sheldon Memorial Art Gallery, University of Nebraska, Lincoln, Nebraska (1963)

Architect: Philip Johnson

This gallery, like the Rose Art Center at Brandeis, is part of a university campus and is thus both exhibition space and teaching area. The basement, for example, contains a group of storage and viewing rooms for students and visiting specialists. The building owes a great deal to Johnson's earlier designs; the central space to that at the Munson-Williams-Proctor Institute, the outside to the tapered columns of the Amon Carter Museum as also, of course, to early 19th century neo-classical precedent which it closely follows in its organisation and room planning. It is not surprising, therefore, that, as at Brandeis, art appears to be enshrined somewhat remotely.

1

Plan, ground floor. To the left of the central entrance hall and sculpture gallery there is a 300 seat theatre with projection room; to the right, picture galleries and offices.
Plan, first floor. The two groups of picture galleries are linked by a bridge in the double height entrance hall.

Grundriß Erdgeschoß. Links neben Eingangshalle und Plastikgalerie liegt ein Vortragssaal mit 300 Plätzen, zu dem ein Projektionsraum gehört; rechts Gemäldegalerie und Büros.
Grundriß Obergeschoß. Die Ausstellungsräume links und rechts sind durch eine Brücke im zwei Geschosse hohen Mittelraum verbunden.

1. The main entrance side of the gallery.
2. The opposite side of the building with a single flight of steps leading to the central hall. Both the tapered and curving concrete pilasters, 16ft. apart, and the infilling walls are sheathed in travertine. The black discs at the foot of the columns hold fittings for lighting the building at night.
3. The rhythm of columns, arches and infilling walls continues into the 30 ft. high entrance hall and thus divides the gallery into two separate but linked pavilions. The link is made by a bronze covered bridge and stair. The ceiling of the hall is made up of shallow saucer domes holding gold leaf covered discs with recessed light fittings.

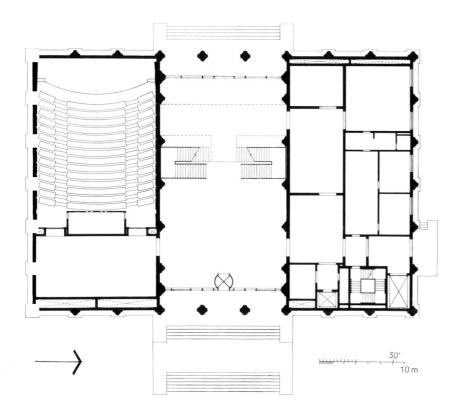

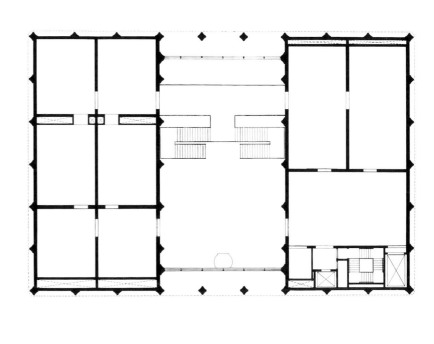

30'
10 m

Sheldon Memorial Art Gallery, University of Nebraska, Lincoln, Nebraska (1963)

Architekt: Philip Johnson

Die Sheldon Art Gallery ist, wie das Rose Art Center an der Brandeis University, einer Universität angegliedert und dient deshalb gleichzeitig als Ausstellungsgebäude und als Lehrstätte. Das Untergeschoß enthält zum Beispiel eine Reihe von Magazinen und Studienräumen für Studenten und interessierte Besucher. Das Gebäude ist offensichtlich von Johnsons früheren Arbeiten hergeleitet. So erinnert der große Mittelraum an den des Munson-Williams-Proctor Institute und das Äußere an die ausgebuchteten Profile des Amon Carter Museum wie auch an neoklassizistische Bauten des frühen 19. Jahrhunderts, denen die Sheldon Art Gallery in Organisation und Raumaufteilung eng verwandt ist. Wie beim Rose Art Center wirken deshalb die Kunstwerke distanziert, als seien sie von einer Art Schrein umschlossen.

1. Die Haupteingangsseite des Museums.
2. Die entgegengesetzte Seite des Gebäudes; durchgehende Treppenstufen führen zur zentralen Halle. Die Arkaden aus Stahlbeton mit ihren ausgebuchteten Pfeilerprofilen im Achsabstand von 4,8 m und die Füllwände sind mit Travertin verkleidet. Die schwarzen Scheiben am Fuße der Stützen enthalten die elektrischen Installationen für die nächtliche Beleuchtung.
3. Der Rhythmus von Stützen, Bögen und Füllwänden setzt sich in der 9 m hohen Eingangshalle fort, die das Museum in zwei miteinander verbundene Flügel unterteilt. Für die Verbindung sorgen bronzeverkleidete Treppen und Rampen. Die Decke der Halle besteht aus flachen Kuppeln. In die mit Goldblatt belegten Scheiben in den Kuppeln sind elektrische Installationen eingelassen.

2

4. One of the group of enfiladed rooms on the upper floor The walls are covered in biscuit coloured cotton pile carpet which provides a slightly textured surface and does not show the marks of nails used for hanging pictures or fixing labels. All the lighting is by incandescent fittings in the ceiling; there is no natural light and the building is fully air conditioned.

4. Eine der axial angeordneten Raumfolgen im Obergeschoß. Die Wände sind mit genopptem beige Wollstoff bespannt, auf dessen leicht strukturierter Oberfläche die Nagelspuren der Bilder oder der Schilder nicht zu sehen sind. Für die Beleuchtung sorgen Leuchtstoffröhren an der Decke; Tageslichtbeleuchtung ist nicht vorgesehen. Das Gebäude ist vollklimatisiert.

3

4

Museum, Oakland, California (Project)

Architect: Eero Saarinen & Associates

This new building is planned to house the three existing museums of the town so that they should form a unified group yet keep some of their identity. The site overlooks Lake Merrit and is to be the beginning of a great terraced slope connecting a number of public buildings.

The entire site becomes in this solution a sequence of planted terraces formed by the roofs of the three museums stepping back behind each other. Both the inside and the outside spaces of the building become thus areas of public enjoyment and even when the museum is closed its site is an asset to the city. Seldom before has museum design been considered in such close relation to the urban plan; perhaps not since the Athenian stoa have the two been so integrated.

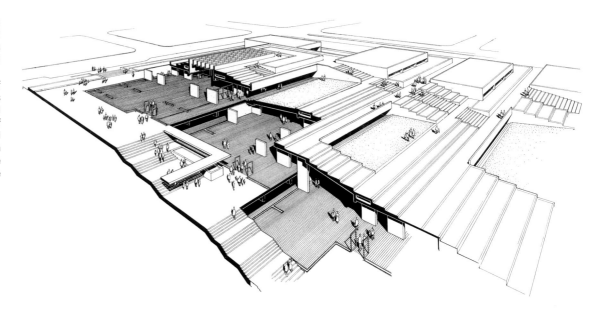

1. Sectionalised perspective. The ruled lines delineate the interior spaces of the three museums which will combine to make a single building on the hillside. Each museum is accessible separately from the main flight of external stairs seen in the foreground.

1. Perspektivischer Schnitt. Die schraffierten Flächen stellen das Innere der drei Museen dar, die sich auf dem Hügel nach außen hin zu einem einzigen Bauwerk verbinden. Jedes Museum hat von dem im Vordergrund sichtbaren, im Freien befindlichen Treppenaufgang aus einen gesonderten Eingang.

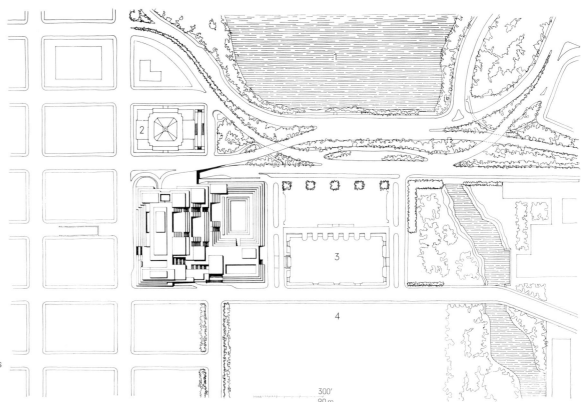

Site plan / Lageplan.
1 Lake Merrit
2 Existing County Building / Bestehendes öffentliches Gebäude
3 Existing Auditorium / Bestehendes Auditorium
4 Peralta Park

300'
90 m

Museum, Oakland, Kalifornien (Projekt)

Architekt: Eero Saarinen & Associates

Der geplante Gebäudekomplex wird die drei Museen der Stadt Oakland aufnehmen, die eine geschlossene Gruppe bilden und bis zu gewissem Grade doch ihren individuellen Charakter beibehalten sollen. Das Gelände liegt über dem Lake Merrit an einem in Terrassen gegliederten Hügel; diese Plattformen sollen verschiedene öffentliche Bauten locker miteinander verbinden.
Die gesamte Museumsanlage präsentiert sich nach außen hin als eine Folge bepflanzter Terrassen, die dadurch entstehen, daß die Dächer der drei Museen hintereinander gestaffelt sind. Selbst wenn das Museum nicht geöffnet ist, stellt die Anlage einen Gewinn für die Stadt dar. Seit der Stoa in Athen dürfte nur selten ein Museum so weitgehend in die Stadtplanung einbezogen worden sein.

2

2, 3. The steps and terraces which form the pedestrian space are landscaped and used for the display of sculpture. Below these are the three main exhibition areas.

2, 3. Auf den Treppen und den gärtnerisch gestalteten Terrassen und Plattformen werden Skulpturen ausgestellt. Darunter liegen die drei Hauptausstellungsräume.

3

Everson Museum of Art, Syracuse, New York (Project)

Architects: I. M. Pei & Associates

The design of this museum is, particularly in terms of ideas current in the U.S.A., a further step from the belief that only the most anonymous and variable spaces can provide a satisfactory museum. As at Philip Johnson's building in Utica and Le Corbusier's in Tokyo, the galleries are here related to a central two storey focal space which is seen as one crosses from gallery to gallery. The four linked galleries on the top floor are however only the uppermost portion of a considerable building which contains studios, an auditorium, club facilities, offices and other ancilliary rooms.

A system of recessed incandescent down lights illuminates the sculpture court in which the more permanent works of art are displayed. This reduces somewhat the extreme contrast created by the natural light entering from above and the side. The four major galleries on the second floor require, on the other hand, a fairly flexible lighting system to deal with the demands imposed by the changing circulating type of exhibition. Parallel to each wall, therefore, there will be a recessed lighting track along the entire length of which incandescent directional fixtures can be installed. These provide an ven ewash of light throughout the complete height of the wall. Additional accent lights can also be installed.

The building faces the street on one side, a new pedestrian square with a rectangular pool on the other. Adjacent to this community Plaza are various existing county and city buildings and a proposed Music Hall. The building of the museum is to be part of the revival of the town centre.

Everson Museum of Art, Syracuse, New York (Projekt)

Architekten: I. M. Pei & Associates

Das Museum von Syracuse entfernt sich um einen weiteren Schritt von der besonders in Amerika vorherrschenden Auffassung, daß nur die anonymsten und variabelsten Räumlichkeiten sich für ein Museum eignen. Wie bei Philip Johnsons Museum in Utica oder bei Le Corbusiers Museum in Tokio sind auch hier die einzelnen Ausstellungsräume auf einen zwei Geschosse hohen zentralen Raum bezogen, den der Besucher überblickt, wenn er von einem Saal zum nächsten geht. Die vier miteinander verbundenen Ausstellungsbereiche des Obergeschosses bilden allerdings nur den obersten Teil des großen Gebäudes, das Studios, ein Auditorium, Klubeinrichtungen, Büros und weitere Nebenräume enthält. Für die Beleuchtung des Plastikhofes mit seinen größtenteils permanenten Ausstellungsobjekten sorgt ein System von Lichtquellen, die in die Decke eingelassen sind und tagsüber den Kontrast zwischen Oberlicht und Seitenlicht mildern. Die vier Hauptausstellungsräume im Obergeschoß erforderten ein möglichst flexibles Beleuchtungssystem, da in diesen Räumen Wechselausstellungen untergebracht werden sollen. Deshalb sind Schienen vorgesehen, die parallel zu den Wänden verlaufen und an denen Leuchtkörper angebracht werden, die für eine gleichmäßige Allgemeinbeleuchtung sorgen. Außerdem können zusätzliche Punktscheinwerfer montiert werden. Eine Seite des Museums liegt an der Straße, die andere an einem neuen Platz für Fußgänger mit einem rechtwinkligen Wasserbecken. An diesen Platz grenzen verschiedene bereits bestehende städtische Gebäude, und auch die geplante Konzerthalle soll hier errichtet werden. Das Museum ist so in die Neugestaltung des Stadtzentrums einbezogen.

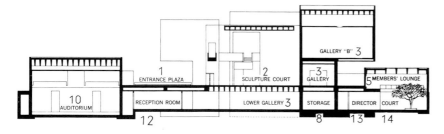

Longitudinal section / Längsschnitt.

Plaza level floor plan / Grundriß auf dem Niveau des Eingangshofs.

1 Entrance Plaza / Eingangshof
2 Sculpture court / Plastikhof
3 Exhibition galleries / Ausstellungsräume
4 Bridge / Verbindungsbrücke
5 Member's lounge / Aufenthaltsraum für Mitglieder
6 Library / Bibliothek
7 Gifts and information / Verkauf und Auskunft
8 Storage / Magazin
9 Coats / Garderobe
10 Auditorium
11 Space above auditorium / Luftraum über Auditorium
12 Reception room / Empfangsraum
13 Director / Direktion
14 Court / Hof

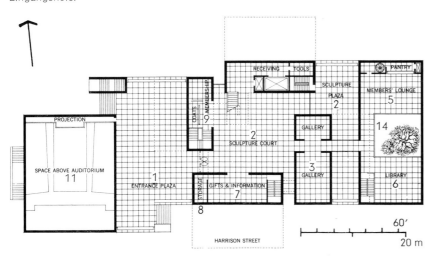

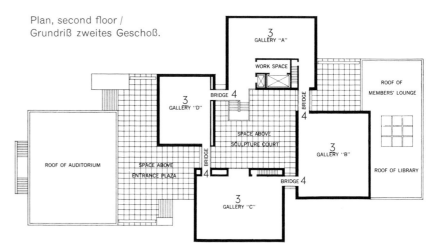

Plan, second floor / Grundriß zweites Geschoß.

1

2

1. The north side of the museum seen from the new precinct formed by the museum and its surrounding civic buildings. Both the podium and the four cantilevered galleries are to be granite aggregate concrete with a rough bush hammered finish. They are to be treated as if they were the "product of a sculptor's tool".
2. The two storey central sculpture court through which the bridges linking the four main galleries pass at first floor level. Internally some walls are also to be bush hammered concrete, others carrying pictures will be surfaced with cloth.

1. Die Nordseite des Museums, von der neuen Platzanlage her gesehen. Der Sockel und die vier auskragenden Säle sind aus Beton mit Granitbeimischung und erhalten eine gestockte Oberfläche. Sie sollen wirken, als seien sie das Werk eines Bildhauers.
2. Der zwei Geschosse hohe zentrale Plastikhof, den in der Höhe des ersten Geschosses die Verbindungsbrükken der vier Hauptsäle überqueren. Auch innen sind einige Wände in gestocktem Beton vorgesehen; andere Wände, an denen Bilder hängen, sollen mit Stoff bespannt werden.

The Sao Paulo Museum of Art, established in 1947, has exerted considerable influence on museum thinking through the reputation it acquired from its Biennales and International Exhibitions of Architecture as well as its policy of making drawing classes for adults and children and the teaching of dancing, music and industrial design part of its functions. It was among the first to break the narrow conception of the museum as an area of display adjacent to a depository.

The Museum of Modern Art in Rio de Janeiro has also followed this policy and part of its ground floor is used by the School of Design and a whole wing is devoted to a theatre seating a thousand.

The less wealthy areas of South and Central America have not been able to match the building activity of Brazil and Mexico but have concentrated on small regional museums, frequently in converted old buildings, which are safeguarding the remains of local cultures often under pressure in a period of transition.

Das Kunstmuseum in São Paulo, das 1947 eingerichtet wurde, hat einen großen Einfluß auf das Museumswesen ausgeübt. Es erwarb seinen guten Ruf vor allem durch seine Biennale-Ausstellungen und durch die Internationalen Architekturausstellungen, aber auch durch Zeichenkurse für Erwachsene und Kinder und durch Kurse für Tanz, Musik und industrielle Formgebung. Das Museum übernahm als eines der ersten solche Funktionen und schlug damit eine Bresche in die herkömmliche Auffassung, daß Museen nur Kunstwerke einlagern und zur Schau stellen sollten.

Das Museum moderner Kunst in Rio hat diese Entwicklung weitergeführt; einen Teil des Erdgeschosses nimmt die Kunstschule ein, und ein ganzer Flügel ist für ein Theater mit 1000 Plätzen bestimmt.

Die weniger wohlhabenden Länder Süd- und Zentralamerikas waren nicht in der Lage, eine ähnliche Bautätigkeit wie Brasilien und Mexiko zu entfalten. Sie haben sich dafür auf kleine Regionalmuseen konzentriert, die häufig in neugestalteten alten Gebäuden untergebracht sind und die Überreste der heimischen Kultur pflegen.

1

2

1, 2. Sao Paulo's Museum of Art by Lina Bo Bardi occupies two floors of an office building in the centre of town. It interprets its functions as a museum freely and has become known for the wide range of both its exhibitions and educational activities.

1, 2. Das Kunstmuseum in São Paulo von Lina Bo Bardi nimmt zwei Geschosse eines Bürohauses im Zentrum der Stadt ein. Es legt die Aufgaben eines Museums großzügig aus und ist durch die Vielfalt seiner Ausstellungen und seiner pädagogischen Tätigkeit bekannt geworden.

Museum of Modern Art, Rio de Janeiro
(Started in 1954)

Architect: Affonso Eduardo Reidy

This complex of buildings on the shore of the bay of Rio includes a theatre seating 1000 persons, the actual exhibition building with its reinforced concrete frames sloping outwards and a low wing containing administrative offices, a restaurant and a school of design. The success of this building as a museum can not yet be judged as the main exhibition area is still incomplete. This will consist of two levels of display space over a mainly open ground floor. The ceiling of the second floor will consist of suspended translucent plastic distributing the light of the fluorescent tubes above. Spotlights for local lighting will also be provided. Apart from this, there will be sidelighting which will be regulated by aluminium venetian blinds on the north side. The landscape of the bay will thus again be introduced into the viewing areas through the north and south windows. Judging by the temporary exhibitions so far held on the first floor of the south wing, the reconciliation between bright dramatic landscape and small scale exhibition is not always easy in this particular situation.

1–3. The still unfinished main part of the building; when complete this will have a floor 426 ft. long and 85 ft. wide free of columns.

1–3. Der noch nicht fertiggestellte Haupttrakt des Gebäudes. Die stützenfreie Geschoßfläche ist 130 m lang und 26 m breit.

Museu de Arte Moderna, Rio de Janeiro
(begonnen 1954)

Architekt: Affonso Eduardo Reidy

Der Baukomplex, unmittelbar am Ufer der Bucht von Rio gelegen, umfaßt außer einem Theater für 1000 Zuschauer das eigentliche Ausstellungsgebäude mit seinen schräg nach außen geneigten Stahlbetonrahmen und einen teils ein-, teils zweigeschossigen flachen Baukubus, der Verwaltung, Restaurant und Kunstschule aufnimmt. Wie das Gebäude seine Funktionen erfüllen wird, bleibt abzuwarten, da der Ausstellungsbereich im Hauptgebäude noch nicht fertiggestellt ist. Er wird zwei stützenfreie Niveaus umfassen, die über dem weitgehend offenen Erdgeschoß liegen. Die Decke des zweiten Geschosses besteht aus transparenten Plastikplatten, die das Licht der darüber befindlichen Leuchtstoffröhren gleichmäßig streuen; auch Scheinwerfer für punktförmige Lichtführung sind vorgesehen. Der Raum soll neben dem Decken- auch Seitenlicht erhalten, das durch Aluminiumjalousien an der Nordseite reguliert werden kann. Die Bucht von Rio wird durch die Nord- und Südfenster in das Blickfeld des Betrachters einbezogen. Wenn man nach den Wechselausstellungen urteilt, die bisher im Obergeschoß des Südflügels, dem späteren Restaurant, veranstaltet wurden, erscheint die Verbindung von dramatischer Landschaft und kleinformatigen Ausstellungsgegenständen nicht ganz unproblematisch.

Page / Seite 161:

4, 5. The ramp from the court leads to a terrace overlooking the bay and the city. Temporary exhibitions are now staged in the room facing this terrace.

4, 5. Die Rampe führt vom Hof auf die Terrasse, die einen Blick über Bucht und Stadt bietet. Wechselausstellungen werden zur Zeit provisorisch in dem Raum untergebracht, der an die Terrasse grenzt.

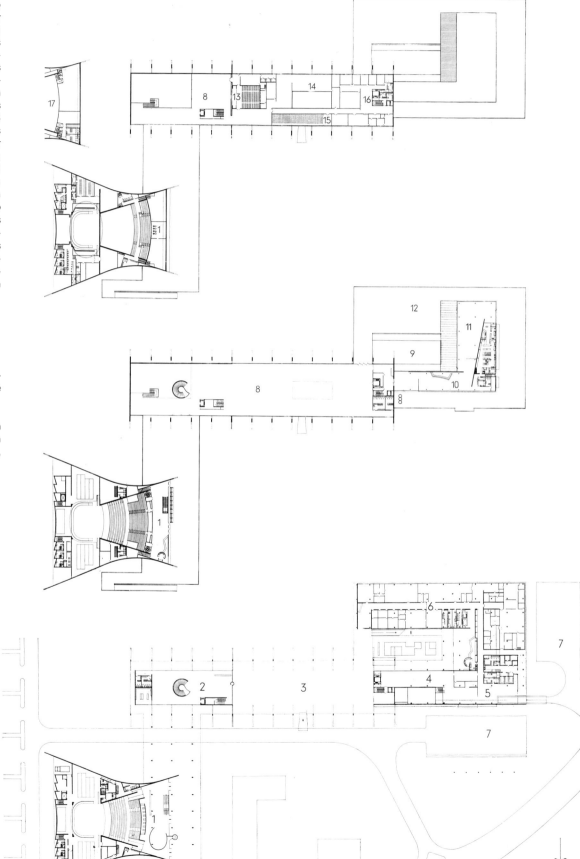

Plan, second floor / Grundriß zweites Geschoß.
Plan, first floor / Grundriß erstes Geschoß.
Plan, ground floor / Grundriß Erdgeschoß.
 1 Theatre wing / Theatergebäude
 2 Entrance hall / Eingangshalle
 3 Open area / Offene Fläche
 4 Exhibition preparation / Ausstellungsvorbereitung
 5 Loading and unloading / Anlieferung und Versand
 6 School of Design / Kunstschule
 7 Car parking / Parkplatz
 8 Exhibition galleries / Ausstellungsräume
 9 Courtyard / Innenhof
10 Bar
11 Restaurant
12 Roof terrace / Dachterrasse
13 Auditorium
14 Library / Bibliothek
15 Storage / Magazin
16 Offices / Büros
17 Mezzanine of theatre wing / Zwischengeschoß des
   Theatergebäudes

60'
20m

4

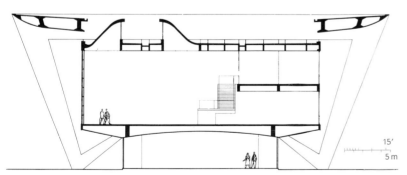

Sections through main exhibition gallery / Schnitte durch
den Hauptausstellungsraum.

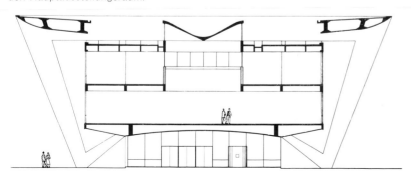

5

6

7

6. Roberto Burle-Marx has landscaped the three-sided court between the main building and the School of Design. It is overlooked by what will become the restaurant terrace.
7. Sculpture by Alexander Calder is shown on the terrace and in the courtyard.

6. Roberto Burle-Marx gestaltete den an drei Seiten umbauten Innenhof zwischen dem Hauptgebäude und der Kunstschule. Darüber die spätere Restaurantterrasse.
7. Skulpturen von Alexander Calder werden wie im Hof auch auf der Terrasse gezeigt.

8–11. Two visiting exhibitions in the long room now being used for display: an exhibition of Ben Nicholson and Ten British Sculptors and one of Finnish Glass and Rugs. The considerable impact which the landscape makes within the building may be appropriate in a room which is to become a restaurant but is likely to be excessive if equally uncontrolled in the main exhibition gallery. The deep fin-like columns will, of course, do something to modify the impact, particularly in the oblique view.

8

9

8–11. Zwei Ausstellungen mit Leihgaben in dem langgestreckten Raum, der vorläufig zu Ausstellungszwecken verwendet wird: Werke von Ben Nicholson und zehn britischen Bildhauern sowie finnische Gläser und Läufer. Daß die Landschaft den Gesamteindruck so stark beherrscht, mag angemessen sein für einen Raum, der später zum Restaurant umgewandelt werden soll. Wenn sie aber im großen Ausstellungssaal nicht abgeschirmt wird, könnte sie eine zu große Konkurrenz zu den Kunstwerken darstellen. Die breiten, flossenähnlichen Stützen werden freilich – besonders in der Schrägsicht – die Wirkung der Landschaft um einiges abschwächen.

10

11

As in South America, new museum building has occurred in the wealthiest areas. It is thus not accidental that most new museums are in Japan or that Le Corbusier's museum in India was built at Ahmedabad which is the centre of the cotton industry. Elsewhere collections in old colonial buildings have been re-organised – frequently, as at Saigon, for instance, with considerable success – or regional and site museums have been created. These will probably do more to preserve a large variety of relatively undocumented cultures than any ambitious programme of building national museums.

What has not however been attempted in either Asia or Africa is the design of museums specifically intended to become institutions of visual communication for a continually increasing urban population. These may well require methods which have no European precedent.

Wie in Südamerika hat sich auch in Asien die Errichtung neuer Museen auf die wohlhabendsten Gebiete beschränkt. Es ist deshalb kein Zufall, daß die meisten neuen Museen in Japan entstanden oder daß Le Corbusiers indisches Museum in Ahmedabad, dem Zentrum der Baumwollindustrie, gebaut wurde. In anderen Städten wurden die Sammlungen in alten Kolonialbauten neu arrangiert – häufig sogar mit beträchtlichem Erfolg, wie beispielsweise in Saigon –, oder es wurden regionale und lokale Museen geschaffen. Diese kleinen Museen tragen vielleicht mehr dazu bei, eine große Vielfalt relativ unbekannten Kulturgutes zu bewahren als irgendein ehrgeiziges Programm für den Bau von Nationalmuseen.

Was bisher in Asien wie in Afrika fehlt, ist die Planung von Museen, die als spezifische Instrumente visueller Kommunikation der ständig zunehmenden Stadtbevölkerung dienen. Für solche Projekte werden Methoden nötig sein, die in Europa keine Vorgänger haben.

1

1, 2. Kiyonori Kikutake's Shimane Prefectural Museum at Matsue was completed in 1959 and is one of several distinguished museum buildings recently designed in Japan. The main exhibition area is on the second floor. Its end walls consist of three-pronged pivotting vertical louvres made up of two solid and one glass blade.

1, 2. Das Shimane-Präfekturmuseum in Matsue von Kiyonori Kikutake wurde 1959 fertiggestellt und zählt zu den bemerkenswertesten Museumsbauten, die in der letzten Zeit in Japan entstanden. Der Hauptausstellungsbereich liegt im zweiten Obergeschoß. An den Seitenwänden sind schwenkbare vertikale Lamellen von dreiarmigem Querschnitt angebracht; sie bestehen jeweils aus zwei massiven und einem verglasten Element.

2

The National Museum of Western Art, Tokyo (1959)

Architect: Le Corbusier

Le Corbusier's earlier ideas of a growing square spiral museum where "the illumination has become an integral part of the museum's impression on the visitor", and where "it is raised to the level of emotive power; it has become a determining element of the architecture", have not been fulfilled in this building nor, for that matter, in his museum at Ahmedabad. The Tokyo museum, although following the plan laid down by Le Corbusier, is in its detail and use of materials in any case quite uncharacteristic of his later work. It bears the stamp of his collaborators.

The museum, a reinforced concrete structure clad with precast concrete elements, is situated in the Ueno Park which overlooks the city and which also contains other cultural buildings. The new museum displays a collection of Impressionist painting and sculpture acquired by Kojiro Matsukata while resident in Paris. The collection was held as a war prize by the French Government until restored to the Japanese on condition that it would be publicly displayed.

Nationalmuseum für abendländische Kunst, Tokio (1959)

Architekt: Le Corbusier

Weder bei diesem Museum noch in Ahmedabad ist Le Corbusiers alte Idee eines quadratischen, wachsenden Spiralmuseums verwirklicht, in dem »die Beleuchtung wesentlich zum Eindruck des Museums auf den Besucher beiträgt«, in dem »sie auf das Niveau einer emotionellen Kraft erhoben wird« und »einen entscheidenden Bestandteil der Architektur« bildet. Obwohl das Museum in Tokio durchaus in der allgemeinen Konzeption dem Entwurf Le Corbusiers entspricht, sind Details und verwendete Materialien nicht charakteristisch für sein Spätwerk. Der Bau trägt den Stempel seiner Mitarbeiter.

Das Museum, eine Stahlbetonkonstruktion, die mit präfabrizierten Betonelementen verkleidet ist, liegt über der Stadt im Ueno-Park, wo sich noch andere kulturelle Bauten befinden. Ausgestellt wird eine Sammlung impressionistischer Malerei und Plastik, die Kojiro Matsukata während eines Aufenthaltes in Paris erworben hatte. Die französische Regierung konfiszierte die Sammlung während des Krieges und gab sie später unter der Bedingung an Japan zurück, daß sie öffentlich ausgestellt werden sollte.

1 Open area / Offene Fläche
2 Entrance hall / Eingangshalle
3 Central gallery / Zentraler Ausstellungsraum
4 Ramp to upper floor / Rampe zum nächsten Geschoß
5 Storage / Magazin
6 Workshop / Werkstatt
7 Goods lift / Warenaufzug
8 Offices / Büros
9 Cloakroom / Garderobe
10 Kitchen / Küche
11 Stairs down to basement / Treppe zum Untergeschoß
12 Future extension – library / Zukünftige Erweiterung – Bibliothek
13 Exhibition galleries / Ausstellungsräume
14 Terrace / Terrasse
15 Future extension – lecture hall / Zukünftige Erweiterung – Vortragssaal

16 Upper part of exhibition galleries / Oberer Teil der Ausstellungsräume
17 Upper part of central gallery / Luftraum zentrale Ausstellungshalle
18 Lighting gallery / Lichtgalerie
19 Balcony / Balkon
20 Air conditioning plant / Klimaanlage

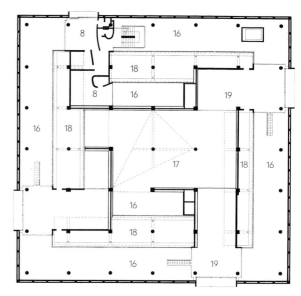

Plan, second floor / Grundriß zweites Geschoß.

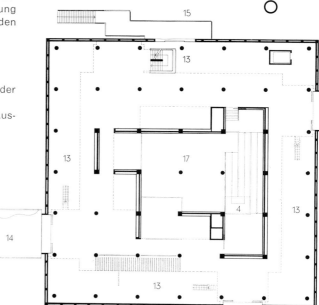

Plan, first floor / Grundriß erstes Geschoß.

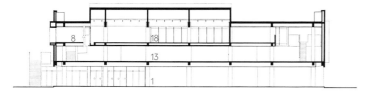

Section through side gallery / Schnitt durch eine Seitengalerie.

Section through central gallery / Schnitt durch den zentralen Ausstellungsraum.

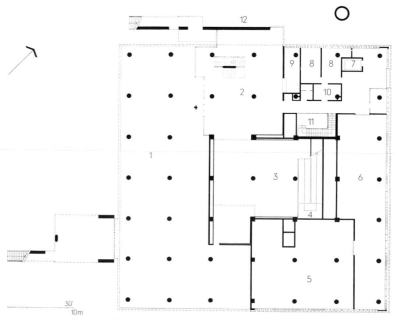

Plan, ground floor / Grundriß Erdgeschoß.

1

1. View from the west. The museum was to form part of a cultural centre clustered around a paved square. The group was to include a pavilion for temporary exhibitions, a "Box of Miracles" (a pavilion for theatrical experiments, particularly with lighting), a library, an amphitheatre and a restaurant. Rodin's *The Thinker* and *The Burghers of Calais* stand in the square and act as an introduction to the works inside.
2. Detail of the southwest side.
3. The roof clearly shows the organisation of the building: four galleries turbining about a central space top-lit by a large pyramidal skylight.
4. The central nodal space of the museum seen from the first turning of the ramp leading to the upper level. It is possible to look into this space as one goes around the galleries.

5. The lighting galleries protrude through the roof. Daylight gets in through the heat absorbing wire glass of the upper sidelights and is directed through the diffusing glass below onto the walls of the galleries. These are half a floor lower down and run along both sides of the lighting galleries. Fluorescent lighting and reflectors are also within this enclosure. The idea derives from stage lighting but seems to have adopted neither its versatility nor its ability to throw light for some distance.
6, 7. Two of the four galleries which surround the circulation space; that on the east side (see Fig. 6) has sliding panels on which pictures are hung and these can be pulled out by visitors themselves. The rooms are lit by a combination of natural and artificial light directed through the glass screens at mezzanine level.

1. Ansicht von Westen. Das Museum war als Teil eines Kulturzentrums geplant, das sich um den gepflasterten Hof gruppieren sollte. Der Komplex sollte einen Pavillon für Wechselausstellungen, einen »Wunderkasten« (einen Pavillon für Theater- und Lichtexperimente), eine Bibliothek, ein Amphitheater und ein Restaurant umfassen. Rodins Skulpturen *Der Denker* und *Die Bürger von Calais*, die auf dem Hof aufgestellt sind, stimmen auf die im Inneren des Museums gezeigten Werke ein.
2. Detail der Südwestseite.
3. Das Dach demonstriert deutlich die Einteilung des Gebäudes: vier Galerien umgeben einen zentralen Raum, der durch das große, pyramidenförmige Oberlicht erhellt wird.
4. Der Zentralraum des Museums, von der ersten Kehre der Rampe her gesehen, die zum oberen Niveau führt. Von den Galerien aus ist ein Blick nach unten in diesen Raum möglich.
5. Die Lichtgalerien reichen über das Dach hinaus. Das Tageslicht fällt durch die hitzeabsorbierenden Drahtglasscheiben der oberen Seitenlichter ein und wird durch die unteren, lichtstreuenden Glasflächen auf die Wände der Bildersäle gelenkt, die ein halbes Geschoß tiefer zu beiden Seiten der Lichtgalerie liegen. Leuchtstoffröhren und bewegliche Punktscheinwerfer sind ebenfalls in dem Zwischengeschoß untergebracht. Das System ist von der Bühnenbeleuchtung hergeleitet, doch fehlt ihm deren Beweglichkeit und die Fähigkeit, das Licht über eine größere Entfernung hinweg zu lenken.
6, 7. Zwei der vier Galerien, die den Zirkulationskern umgeben; in der Galerie an der Ostseite (vgl. Abb. 6) sind links Platten mit aufgehängten Bildern angebracht, die auf Schienen laufen und von den Besuchern an einem Griff herausgezogen werden können. Die Galerien werden durch eine Kombination von natürlichem und künstlichem Licht erleuchtet, das durch die Glasscheiben in halber Höhe fällt.

2

3

4

5

6

7

Gandhi Memorial Museum, Ahmedabad, India (1963)

Architect: C. M. Correa

Gandhi-Museum, Ahmedabad, Indien (1963)

Architekt: C. M. Correa

This building, which is to be a museum, a memorial and a centre for the study of Gandhi's thought and philosophy, was built less than a 100 yards from the Sabarmati Ashram where Gandhi lived from 1917 until he left to start on the Dandi March in 1930 vowing not to return until India achieved independence.

The museum will exhibit letters, photographs and other documents related to Gandhi's activities. There are, for instance, 400 manuscripts of his newspaper articles and a considerable collection of photographs depicting him from childhood to death. There is also a library housing 4000 books from the Sabarmati Ashram and a further 3000 volumes from the collection of Gandhi's secretary and associate, Shri. Mahader Desai.

These and other collections, such as the index of letters written to and by Gandhi, will be continually augmented as further material becomes available. The museum plan had to recognise this fact and have an organisation which allowed for growth for many years to come. The plan is thus of an additive kind; the museum at any one time is the sum of a number of simple 20 ft. × 20 ft. squares each covered with a pyramidal roof. Courtyards are formed by omitting these squares and such openings act as visual reference points and rest areas.

The materials of the building are simple and used with great discretion: tile roofs, timber lined ceilings, concrete beams and floors, brick piers, stone paving, timber louvres. There is no glass in any of the wall openings.

Both in its design assumptions and in its architectural execution the museum seems wholly appropriate to its setting, to the nature of its display and to the elemental directness of Gandhi's teaching. Nehru opening the museum on May 10th 1963 remarked "this building – so simple, so beautiful – is the proper Sanghralaya for this holy ground".

1. Part of the library and its display with a reading desk and a cushion for squatting on the left.
2. Photographs are mounted and grouped on a sloping display stand very similar to the reading desk in the library. The slotted display stands have the same simplicity as the building and allow only parts of the exhibition to be seen at any one time.

Das Gebäude ist als Museum, Gedächtnisstätte und Studienzentrum für die Philosophie Gandhis konzipiert. Es wurde weniger als 100 Meter von Sabarmati Ashram entfernt errichtet, wo Gandhi von 1917 an lebte, bis er 1930 den Dandi-Marsch unternahm und gelobte, erst dann zurückzukehren, wenn Indien die Unabhängigkeit erlangt hätte. Das Museum wird Briefe, Fotografien und andere Dokumente ausstellen, die mit Gandhis Tätigkeit verbunden sind. Es existieren zum Beispiel 400 Manuskripte seiner Zeitschriftenartikel und eine umfangreiche Fotosammlung, die Bilder von seiner Kindheit bis zu seinem Tode enthält. Außerdem sind eine Bibliothek mit 4000 Büchern aus Sabarmati Ashram sowie weitere 3000 Bände von Gandhis Sekretär und Partner Mahader Desai vorhanden. Diese und andere Sammlungen wie zum Beispiel ein Verzeichnis der Briefe an und von Gandhi werden ständig erweitert. Der Entwurf mußte daher so organisiert werden, daß zukünftige Vergrößerungen leicht möglich sind. Der Grundriß ist additiv: Das Gebäude besteht jeweils aus Quadraten von 6×6 Metern, die mit pyramidenförmigen Dächern überdeckt sind. Wo diese Quadrate nicht überbaut wurden, entstanden Höfe, die zur visuellen Orientierung und als Ruheplätze dienen.

Das Material des Bauwerks ist einfach und mit größter Zurückhaltung verwandt: Ziegeldächer, mit Holzriemen verkleidete Decken, Stahlbetonträger und -böden, Backsteinstützen, Steinplatten und hölzerne Blenden. Keine der Öffnungen ist verglast.

In Entwurf und Ausführung ist das Museum seiner Umgebung, dem Charakter seiner Ausstellungsobjekte und der spontanen Unmittelbarkeit von Gandhis Lehre voll und ganz adäquat. Als Nehru das Museum am 10. Mai 1963 eröffnete, erklärte er, daß »dieses schlichte und schöne Haus das wahre Sanghralaya für diesen heiligen Boden darstellt«.

1. Ansicht der Bibliothek; links Lesepult und Sitzkissen.
2. Auf einem Exponatträger mit schräger Fläche, der dem Lesepult in der Bibliothek ähnelt, sind Fotografien angeordnet. Die ineinander verzapften Exponatträger sind ebenso einfach konstruiert wie das Gebäude selbst. Sie sorgen dafür, daß nur begrenzte Teile der Ausstellung gleichzeitig gesehen werden können.

3. There is a viewing platform between the end of the car park and the head of the steps going down to the entrance.
4. The entrance to the building is on the left and leads past two courtyards, one pebble filled, the other grassed, to the central square pool. The central pool is surrounded by long galleries terminating in other courtyards or views of the outside.
5. The floor of the building is raised off the ground and carried by plinth beams spanning between the brick piers. This was necessary in view of the poor soil conditions but also enables the area of the building to be clearly delineated yet open to the outside. All the electric wiring is concealed in the floor; there is none in the walls or roof.
6. A view across the square pool and through a further courtyard to the steps leading down to the Sabarmati River. The rainwater from the tiled roofs is carried by deep gutters which are also beams.

3. Blick von Südwesten. Zwischen dem Parkplatz und den Stufen, die hinunter zum Eingang führen, liegt eine Aussichtsterrasse.
4. Der Eingang zu dem Gebäude befindet sich links (außerhalb des Bildes). Der Besucher gelangt vorbei an den zwei Höfen, von denen der eine mit Kieseln belegt und der andere mit Gras bewachsen ist, zu dem quadratischen Becken in der Mitte der Anlage. Das zentrale Wasserbecken ist von langgestreckten überdachten Gängen umgeben, die entweder in andere Höfe münden oder Ausblicke nach draußen gewähren.
5. Die Bodenfläche des Gebäudes ist angehoben und wird von Balken getragen, die sich zwischen den Backsteinpfeilern spannen. Eine solche Konstruktion war wegen der ungünstigen Bodenverhältnisse notwendig; außerdem ist das Bauwerk dadurch klar hervorgehoben und öffnet sich trotzdem nach außen hin. Die elektrischen Leitungen sind im Boden verlegt, Wände und Dach sind frei von Leitungen.
6. Blick über das quadratische Becken durch einen weiteren Innenhof auf die Treppen, die hinunter zum Sabarmati-Fluß führen. Das Regenwasser von den Ziegeldächern wird über tiefe Rinnen abgeleitet, die gleichzeitig als Träger dienen.

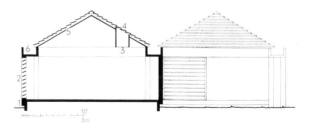

Section / Schnitt.
1 Plinth beam / Sockelträger
2 Openable wooden louvres / Verstellbare Holzblenden
3 Frosted glass / Milchglas
4 Glass tiles / Glasziegel
5 Wooden boarding / Holzverkleidung
6 Concrete gutter and beam / Abflußrinne und Träger aus Beton

3

4

5

6

Plan, ground floor / Grundriß Erdgeschoß.
1 Entrance / Eingang
2 Car parking / Parkplatz
3 Viewing platform / Aussichtsterrasse
4 Entrance to building / Eingang zum Gebäude
5 Collection of Gandhi's letters / Sammlung von Gandhis Briefen
6 Office / Büro
7 Pool / Wasserbecken
8 Gandhi photographs / Fotografien von Gandhi
9 Library / Bibliothek
10 Meeting room / Versammlungsraum
11 Rock courtyard / Steingarten
12 Pebble filled courtyard / Mit Kieseln belegter Hof
13 Lawn courtyard / Grasbewachsener Hof
14 Lavatories / Toiletten
15 Steps to Sabarmati River / Treppen zum Sabarmati-Fluß
16 Place of Gandhi's prayer platform / Platz der Gebetsstätte Gandhis

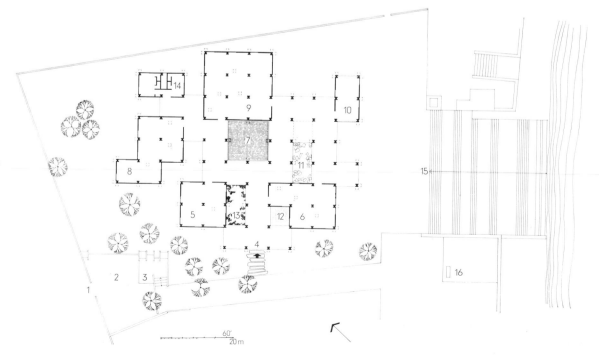

To be seen, objects require light. The amount of light which is needed is however not a quantity which can be specified easily but is dependent on the situation and the context of that situation within the sequence of museum viewing. What matters enormously in museum viewing, that is to say in a situation in which work is not being performed, is the relative brightness of objects, i. e. the quality of light.

As all light and ultra-violet light in particular will deteriorate most items on display in a museum with the exception of metal, stone and glass it would seem important to work with the lowest possible illumination levels and to make certain that these are maintained for the shortest possible time. This means that measures should be devised to adapt the eye to progressively lower levels of light in the transition from outdoors to indoors and to use, wherever suitable, lighting which in view of its lower colour temperature – its apparent warmth of tone – appears relatively bright. It also suggests that all natural light sources should be capable of being obscured so that light can be modulated when it becomes excessive and totally excluded during the hours of daylight when the museum is closed to the public. There may for instance be as many as five hours of daylight before a museum opens.

Table 1 gives maximum recommended levels related to certain groups of exhibits where these maxima are derived from a need for conservation. These levels will in practice give perfectly adequate viewing.

Table 2 by way of comparison lists levels recommended by the Illuminating Engineering Society. That for pictures is higher than the advisable limit given in Table 1. Levels for other rooms are also included and it will be seen that where a task has to be performed these are considerably higher.

Table 3 gives the equivalent colour temperature of a number of light sources. The colour temperature is measured in degrees absolute ($^\circ$C + 273) and is the temperature a perfect black body radiator would have to reach in order to emit light of that spectral value.

The very close relation between the levels of brightness which we find agreeable and the prevailing colour temperature can be seen from Figure A, which is a chart adapted from certain work done on an admittedly limited number of subjects by A. A. Kruithof but nevertheless generally valid.

Fluorescent tubes are available in three ranges of colour temperature; the upper range equivalent to north light at over 6000°K, a middle range equivalent to afternoon sunlight at about 4200°K and a lower range around 3000°K which is meant to equal tungsten. If fluorescent lighting is used, the middle range is generally considered the most suitable for museum illumination since it will seem agreeable in view of its warmer tone at lower intensities. If a still warmer tone is wanted, tungsten lamps should be used as they are safer from a conservation point of view.

The considerations just set out apply equally to daylight and artificial lighting. Greater intensities will be found necessary under north light roof glazing (in the north temperate zone) than east or west facing sidelighting. While it is usually necessary to exclude direct sunlight in order to prevent glare and the damaging effect of its ultra-violet component, it is not essential to rely on north lighting or on daylight of a high colour temperature even where this comes from north lighting. The colour of the incoming light can be modified, for example by reflection from wood louvres, as at the Castello Sforzesco in Milan.

From whatever direction daylight is used, the opening admitting it should be designed so that the light is graded and glare avoided by excessive contrast of dark objects with light. Openings should also be placed in such a position or screened in such a manner so that the eye will not see the sky or other bright areas, such as white paving or buildings in sunlight, once it has adjusted itself to the lower levels of illumination found inside.

The brightness of the object will of course not only depend on the intensity of light but on the reflectivity of the surface illuminated. It is the reflected light which we see and judge. As the surface of the exhibit cannot be changed – we must inevitably accept this as found – the lighting has to vary with the reflecting characteristics of the display.

As ultra-violet radiation has been shown to be harmful it would appear to be advisable to filter all daylight and light from fluorescent tubes. Filters which may be either a transparent sheet or a varnish applied to glass must be placed between the light source and the object to be protected. In practice this means the filter is over the light source, or behind the glass of a showcase, or the glass over a picture. The first is greatly to be preferred since the yellow tint of the filter may be visible and be objectionable in a case or over a picture. An ultra-violet filter can be placed between two sheets of glass, like the film in safety glass, and this form of glazing is made in some countries, though it must be remembered that the filter has a limited life, perhaps about five years outside the tropics and very much less under tropical light.

It should be remembered that in all museum lighting the object to be seen can not be changed and must be protected; the eye on the other hand, given the opportunity, is a highly flexible instrument able to perform effectively through a great range of conditions.

Table 1

Recommended Maximum Illumination and Types of Illuminant

Objects insensitive to light (e. g. metal and stone)	Daylight, Fluorescent light at about 6,500°K or about 4,200°K	Rarely necessary to exceed 300 lux (30 lm/sq.ft.) except for special emphasis
Most museum objects, including oil and tempera paintings	Daylight, Tungsten light, Fluorescent light at about 4,200°K	Not more than 150 lux (15 lm/sq.ft.)
Specially sensitive objects (watercolours, textiles, tapestries, etc.)	Preferably tungsten filament lamps	Not more than 50 lux (5 lm/sq.ft.) and less if possible

Notes:

1. The illumination values are the highest that need be used under good conditions of adaptation. In many cases the curator may be able to use lower values, and to use other devices for keeping sensitive exhibits out of the light for as long as possible.
2. in order that daylight does not exceed the maximum, there is often no practical alternative to the installation of automatic shutters. Ultra-violet filters should also be used.
3. At present the only lamps known to the author in the 4,200°K category with a reasonable colour rendering are the Philips 34 and the A.E.I. (Mazda) Kolor-rite. It is hoped that others will soon be available.
4. Mixtures of fluorescent and tungsten fittings can be used where the technical knowledge is available.
5. Since the illumination values of fluorescent lamps fall after a short initial period, the fixtures may be so arranged as to give up to a third more light when the tubes are new. Evidence suggests that there is no detectable change in colour rendering of fluorescent lamps as they age.
(Table and Notes from "A New Look at Colour Rendering. Level of Illumination, and Protection from Ultraviolet Radiation in Museum Lighting" by Garry Thomson, in: Studies in Conservation, Vol. 6, No. 2 and 3, 1961. See also "Control of deteriorating effects of light upon museum objects" by Robert L. Feller in Museum, Vol. XVII, No. 2, 1964.)

Tabelle 1

Empfohlene Maximalbeleuchtung und Beleuchtungsart

Lichtunempfindliche Gegenstände (zum Beispiel Metall und Stein)	Tageslicht, Leuchtstoffröhren mit etwa 6500°K oder 4200°K	Muß selten mehr als 300 lx betragen, wenn nicht besondere Hervorhebung gewünscht wird
Die meisten Museumsgegenstände einschließlich Öl- und Temperabildern	Tageslicht, Glühlampen, Leuchtstoffröhren mit etwa 4200°K	Nicht mehr als 150 lx
Besonders lichtempfindliche Gegenstände (Aquarelle, Textilien, Tapisserien usw.)	Möglichst Glühlampen	Nicht mehr als 50 lx, wenn möglich weniger

Anmerkungen:

1. Die Beleuchtungswerte sind die höchsten, die unter guten Anpassungsverhältnissen in Frage kommen. In vielen Fällen kann die Museumsleitung niedrigere Werte anwenden oder Möglichkeiten finden, um empfindliche Objekte so lange wie möglich vom Licht fernzuhalten.
2. Wenn das Tageslicht die äußerste Grenze nicht überschreiten soll, gibt es in der Praxis oft keine andere Möglichkeit als automatisch gesteuerte Fensterblenden. Darüber hinaus sollten ultraviolette Filter benutzt werden.
3. In der Kategorie um 4200°K mit guter Farbwirkung gibt es zur Zeit nur die Philips 34 und die A.E.I. (Mazda) Kolor-rite. Es ist zu hoffen, daß auch noch weitere Leuchtkörper dieses Bereichs in den Handel kommen.
4. Wo die technischen Vorrichtungen vorhanden sind, läßt sich Leuchtstoff- und Wolframlicht mischen.
5. Da die Helligkeitswerte von Leuchtstoffröhren nach kurzer Zeit stark abfallen, ist bei der Installation der Leuchtkörper zu berücksichtigen, daß neue Röhren bis zu einem Drittel mehr Licht abgeben. Im übrigen ist erwiesen, daß sich die Farbwirkung von Leuchtstoffröhren auch nach längerem Gebrauch nicht merklich ändert.
(Tabelle und Anmerkungen stammen aus dem Artikel »A New Look at Colour Rendering, Level of Illumination, and Protection from Ultraviolet Radiation in Museum Lighting« von Garry Thomson, in: Studies in Conservation, Band 6, Nr. 2–3, 1961. Siehe auch »Control of deteriorating effects of light upon museum objects« von Robert L. Feller in Museum, Vol. XVII, Nr. 2, 1964.)

Table 2

Levels of lighting in public and some ancillary rooms, extracted from: *The I.E.S. Code: Recommendations for Good Interior Lighting,* 1961, by the Illuminating Engineering Society, London

	lm/sq.ft.	limiting glare index
Museums:		
General	15	16
Displays	special	16
Art Galleries:		
General, with separate picture lighting	10	10
without separate picture lighting	20	10
Paintings, on vertical surface	20	10
Libraries:		
Reading Rooms	20	19
Reading tables	30	19
Offices:		
General offices	30	19
Drawing offices – General	30	16
Boards and Tracing	45	16
Workshops:		
Laboratories, general	30	19
Leather working, grading and matching	100	19
Paint works, colour matching	70	19
Pottery, enamelling, colouring, decorating	45	19
Textile weaving, fine cloth	70	19

The amount of light shown to be required in the Code is dependent on the reflection factor of the object and the distance at which detail of a given size has to be viewed and distinguished. It must also be borne in mind that the colour quality of the light is obviously very important in many of these instances. The glare index must, like all lighting design, be worked out by a qualified illuminating engineer.
Conversion to metric values: 1 lm/sq.ft. = 10.76 lux;
$1 \text{ lm/m}^2 = 1 \text{ Lx.}$

Tabelle 2

Helligkeitswerte in öffentlichen Räumen und Nebenräumen, aus: *The I.E.S. Code: Recommendations for Good Interior Lighting,* 1961, herausgegeben von der Illuminating Engineering Society, London.

	lx (lm/m²)	Maximaler Blendwert
Museen:		
Allgemeinbeleuchtung	162,4	172,16
Ausstellungsgegenstände	variiert	172,16
Kunstmuseen:		
Allgemeinbeleuchtung bei besonderer Beleuchtung der Bilder	107,6	107,6
ohne besondere Beleuchtung der Bilder	215,2	107,6
Beleuchtung von Bildern auf vertikaler Fläche	215,2	107,6
Bibliotheken:		
Leseräume	215,2	204,44
Lesetische	322,8	204,44
Büroräume:		
Allgemeinbeleuchtung von Büroräumen	322,8	204,44
Allgemeinbeleuchtung von Zeichensälen	322,8	172,16
Beleuchtung von Zeichentischen	485	172,16
Werkstätten:		
Allgemeinbeleuchtung von Laboratorien	322,8	204,44
Lederzurichtung, Sortieren und Einfärben	1076	204,44
Malerarbeiten, Farbvergleiche	753,2	204,44
Töpfer-, Emaillier-, Färbe- und Dekorationsarbeiten	485	204,44
Textilweberei, feine Tuche	753,2	204,44

Die Helligkeitswerte der Tabelle hängen im übrigen von dem Reflexionsfaktor des Objekts ab sowie von der Entfernung, aus der ein Detail gegebener Größe erkannt und unterschieden werden muß. Darüber hinaus ist in vielen Fällen die Farbqualität des Lichtes von Bedeutung. Die Blendungsziffern müssen wie alle Beleuchtungsfragen von einem qualifizierten Fachmann für Beleuchtung ausgearbeitet werden.

Ausstellungsgegenstände brauchen Licht, damit sie gesehen werden können. Wieviel Licht sie benötigen, kann allerdings nicht ohne weiteres angegeben werden, sondern hängt von der Placierung der Objekte und von ihrer Position innerhalb der Raumfolge des Museums ab. Wesentlich für die Sichtverhältnisse im Museum – das heißt also für Sichtverhältnisse, bei denen keine Arbeit ausgeführt werden muß – ist die relative Helligkeit der Objekte und die Vermeidung von Blendwirkungen.
Da Licht und vor allem ultraviolettes Licht die meisten Ausstellungsgegenstände mit Ausnahme von Metall, Stein und Glas schädigen, muß mit den niedrigstmöglichen Helligkeitsgraden gearbeitet werden, die ihrerseits nur für eine möglichst kurze Zeitdauer einwirken dürfen. Das Auge sollte deshalb beim Übergang von außen nach innen an immer geringere Helligkeitswerte gewöhnt werden. Außerdem sollte, wo immer dies möglich ist, eine Beleuchtung mit niedriger Farbtemperatur installiert werden, die auf Grund ihres warmen Tonwerts relativ hell wirkt. Natürliche Lichtquellen müssen sich verdunkeln lassen, damit das Licht gedämpft oder auch ganz ausgeschlossen werden kann, wenn das Museum an einigen

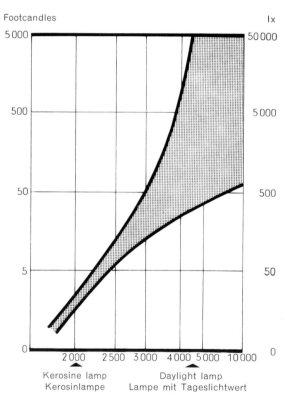

A. "Amenity Curve" showing relationship between intensity and colour of light, the shaded area representing the generally acceptable zone; in the area above this zone colours appear unnatural, in the area below, dim or cold. (From A. A. Kruithof, *Philips Technische Rundschau,* 1941, No. 6.)

A. Diagramm, das die Verbindung zwischen Helligkeitsgrad und Farbtemperatur deutlich macht. Das dunkle Feld stellt den Bereich dar, der als angenehm empfunden wird. Bei höheren Werten wirken die Farben unnatürlich, bei niedrigeren matt oder kalt. (Aus: A. A. Kruithof, *Philips Technische Rundschau,* Nr. 6, 1941.)

Table 3

Equivalent Colour Temperature of various Light Sources measured in degrees absolute

Light Source	Equivalent Colour Temperature (°K)
Blue Sky	10,000–20,000
Overcast Sky	5,000– 7,000
Direct Sunlight	ca. 5,000
Low Sunlight	ca. 4,000
Carbon Arc	3,750
Photographic lamp	3,200
Tungsten incadescent lamp for general lighting	2,400– 3,000
Candle	1,900

Tabelle 3

Farbtemperaturen verschiedener Lichtquellen, in absoluten Graden gemessen:

Lichtquelle	Farbtemperatur (°K)
Blauer Himmel	10 000–20 000
Bedeckter Himmel	5 000– 7 000
Direktes Sonnenlicht	ca. 5 000
Niedrig stehende Sonne	ca. 4 000
Bogenlampe	3 750
Fotografenlampe	3 200
Glühlampe für die Allgemeinbeleuchtung	2 400– 3 000
Kerze	1 900

Stunden des Tages dem Publikum nicht zugänglich ist (ein Museum erhält manchmal bis zu fünf Stunden Tageslicht, bevor es geöffnet wird).

Tabelle 1 gibt die maximalen Helligkeitsgrade für bestimmte Gruppen von Ausstellungsgegenständen an, wobei die Werte von dem Gesichtspunkt der Konservierung bestimmt sind. Für den Betrachter reichen sie vollständig aus.

Tabelle 2 nennt zum Vergleich die von der Illuminating Engineering Society empfohlenen Lichtwerte. Die Maximalgrenze für Bilder liegt hier höher als bei Tabelle 1. Auch für andere Räumlichkeiten sind Werte angegeben, und es läßt sich deutlich ablesen, daß die Maximalwerte in den Räumen größer sind, in denen Arbeiten ausgeführt werden.

Tabelle 3 enthält die Farbtemperatur einer Reihe von Lichtquellen. Die Farbtemperatur wird in absoluten Graden gemessen ($°C + 273$) und entspricht der Temperatur, die ein schwarzer Strahlungskörper erreichen müßte, um Licht dieses bestimmten Spektralwertes auszustrahlen. Die enge Verbindung zwischen dem als angenehm empfundenen Helligkeitsgrad und der Farbtemperatur ist aus der Abbildung A ersichtlich. Das Diagramm basiert auf Versuchen, die A. A. Kruithof mit einer begrenzten Zahl von Objekten anstellte, besitzt aber trotzdem allgemeine Gültigkeit.

Leuchtstoffröhren sind in drei verschiedenen Farbtemperaturen erhältlich; der obere Bereich mit über 6000° K entspricht dem Nordlicht, der mittlere mit etwa 4200° K dem Sonnenlicht am Nachmittag und der niedrigste mit ungefähr 3000° K den Glühlampen. Für ein Museum kommt hauptsächlich der mittlere Bereich in Frage, da er durch seine warme Tönung bei geringerer Intensität angenehm wirkt. Wenn eine noch wärmere Tönung erwünscht ist, empfehlen sich Glühlampen, die vom Standpunkt der Konservierung günstiger sind.

Diese Überlegungen beziehen sich sowohl auf Tageslicht als auch auf künstliche Beleuchtung. Bei einem Oberlicht von Norden sind größere Intensitäten erforderlich als bei Seitenlicht von Osten oder Westen. Direktes Sonnenlicht muß im allgemeinen ausgeschlossen werden, damit keine Blendung entsteht und damit sich die ultravioletten Strahlen nicht schädlich auswirken. Es ist jedoch nicht notwendig, nur mit Nordlicht oder mit Tageslicht hoher Temperatur zu arbeiten, auch wenn es von Norden einfällt. Die Farbe des einfallenden Lichts kann zum Beispiel durch Reflexion an Holzblenden gemildert werden, wie es beim Castello Sforzesco in Mailand geschieht.

Von welcher Richtung auch immer das Tageslicht kommt, die Einlaßöffnung sollte so beschaffen sein, daß das Licht abgestuft und Blendung durch zu starke Leuchtdichtekontraste vermieden wird. Darüber hinaus sollten die Öffnungen so angeordnet oder abgeschirmt werden, daß das Auge nicht den Himmel oder andere helle Zonen wie etwa weißes Pflaster oder Gebäude im Sonnenlicht sieht, nachdem es sich an die niedrigeren Helligkeitsgrade des Innenraums gewöhnt hat.

Die Helligkeit des Objekts hängt natürlich nicht nur von der Intensität des Lichtes ab, sondern auch von der Reflexion der beleuchteten Oberfläche: Was wir sehen, ist das reflektierte Licht. Da die Oberfläche eines Ausstellungsgegenstandes nun einmal nicht geändert werden kann, muß sich die Beleuchtung nach den Reflexionseigenschaften des Objekts richten.

Da ultraviolette Strahlung sich als schädlich erwiesen hat, ist es angebracht, Tageslicht und Licht von Leuchtstoffröhren zu filtern. Die Filter, die aus transparentem Material oder getöntem Glas bestehen können, müssen zwischen der Lichtquelle und dem Objekt angeordnet wer-

1

den. In der Praxis bedeutet dies, daß sich der Filter direkt vor der Lichtquelle, an einer Vitrinen- oder Bilderverglasung befindet. Dabei wird die erstere Anbringungsmöglichkeit bevorzugt, da die gelbliche Färbung des Filters sonst sichtbar werden und bei einer Vitrine oder vor einem Bild stören könnte. Ein ultravioletter Filter kann wie ein verglastes Dia zwischen zwei Glasschichten geschoben werden. Eine solche Art der Verglasung ist in einigen Ländern üblich, wobei allerdings zu beachten ist, daß ein Filter nur eine begrenzte Lebensdauer von etwa fünf Jahren in Gebieten außerhalb der Tropen und sehr viel weniger unter tropischem Licht besitzt.

Entscheidend ist bei allen Fragen der Museumsbeleuchtung, daß der ausgestellte Gegenstand nicht verändert werden kann und geschützt werden muß; das Auge ist hingegen außerordentlich flexibel und kann sich wechselnden Bedingungen anpassen.

2

3

4

1. White venetian blinds. Palazzo Bianco Museum, Genoa. Architect: Franco Albini.

2. Curtains and baffle incorporating light fittings Orrefors Exhibition Building, Orrefors, Sweden. Architect: Bengt Gate.

3. Rendered wall and reveal. Castello Sforzesco Museum, Milan. Architects: Studio Architetti BBPR.

4. Kenneth Armitage Exhibition, Museum Boymans-van Beuningen, Rotterdam. Architect: A.J.v.d. Grinten.

5, 6. Apart from using built form or accessories as light control, dense planting close to the building can to a considerable extent perform this function. Robert Woods Bliss Collection of Pre-Columbian Art, Dumbarton Oaks, Washington, D. C. Architect: Philip Johnson.

1. Weiße Lamellenstores. Museo di Palazzo Bianco, Genua. Architekt: Franco Albini.

2. Vorhänge und Blende, die die Beleuchtungsinstallation aufnimmt. Orrefors-Ausstellungsgebäude, Orrefors, Schweden. Architekt: Bengt Gate.

3. Verputzte Mauer. Museo del Castello Sforzesco, Mailand. Architekten: Studio Architetti BBPR.

4. Ausstellung Kenneth Armitage, Museum Boymans-van Beuningen, Rotterdam. Architekt: A.J. v. d. Grinten.

5, 6. Außer Bauelementen oder speziellen Schutzvorrichtungen kann auch dichte Bepflanzung nahe am Gebäude das Licht weitgehend abhalten. Robert Woods Bliss Collection, Präkolumbianische Kunst, Dumbarton Oaks, Washington, D.C. Architekt: Philip Johnson.

Light coming through windows can and ought to be graded by reveals and can be controlled by curtains, venetian blinds and horizontal or vertical baffles. In top-lit rooms further screening by muslin panels, for instance, will not only subdivide the space but also cut out oblique views of the bright ceiling.

Licht, das durch Fenster einfällt, sollte durch Laibungen abgestuft und durch Vorhänge, Jalousien und horizontale oder vertikale Blenden gemildert werden. In Räumen mit Oberlicht dient zum Beispiel ein Musselinschirm nicht nur dazu, den Raum zu unterteilen, sondern er lenkt auch den Blick von der hellen Decke ab.

5

6

7

Overhead lighting, whether natural or artificial, can be modified or totally excluded by movable louvres. The total exclusion of daylight while the gallery is not open to the public may be important in terms of conservation. The space between the control elements and the sky-lights ought to be accessible. Artificial light sources are usually placed below the roof glazing so that they may on occasion reinforce daylight, but can also be positioned outside the building.

7. Double layer of movable shaped American larch louvres. Castello Sforzesco Museum, Milan. Architects: Studio Architetti BBPR.
8. Movable gantry for maintenance. Castello Sforzesco Museum, Milan. Architects: Studio Architetti BBPR.
9. Gallery lit by skylight above deep vertical baffles. Kasmin Gallery, London. Architects: Ahrends, Burton and Koralek.
10. Movable white fabric louvres controlling natural and artificial lighting. Kasmin Gallery, London. Architects: Ahrends, Burton and Koralek.
11. Exterior flood lights. Art Gallery, Lund, Sweden. Architect: Klas Anshelm.

Natürliche oder künstliche Deckenbeleuchtung kann durch bewegliche Lamellen gemildert oder ganz ausge-schaltet werden. Für die Konservierung der Ausstellungs-gegenstände ist es günstig, das Tageslicht völlig auszu-schließen, wenn das Museum nicht geöffnet ist. Der Raum zwischen den Kontrollelementen und den Ober-lichtern sollte zugänglich sein. Künstliche Lichtquellen werden gewöhnlich unter der Dachverglasung installiert, damit sie, wenn nötig, das Tageslicht ergänzen. Sie kön-nen natürlich auch außen angebracht werden.

7. Doppelte Lage von Holzblenden aus amerikanischer Lärche. Museo del Castello Sforzesco, Mailand. Architek-ten: Studio Architetti BBPR.
8. Bewegliches Gerüst für Instandhaltungsarbeiten. Museo del Castello Sforzesco, Mailand. Architekten: Studio Architetti BBPR.
9. Der Ausstellungsraum wird durch Oberlichter über tiefen Lichtschächten beleuchtet. Kasmin Gallery, Lon-don. Architekten: Ahrends, Burton und Koralek.
10. Verstellbare weiße Kunststofflamellen regulieren Ta-ges- und Kunstlicht. Kasmin Gallery, London. Architek-ten: Ahrends, Burton und Koralek.
11. Außen angebrachte Scheinwerfer. Kunstgalerie, Lund, Schweden. Architekt: Klas Anshelm.

8

9

11

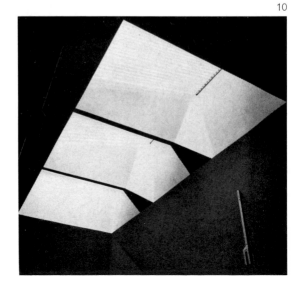

10

Kasmin Gallery, London. Transverse section / Querschnitt.
1 Existing skylight / Vorhandenes Oberlicht
2 Fluorescent tubes / Leuchtstoffröhren
3 Pivotting fabric louvres / Verstellbare Kunststofflamellen
4 Plaster baffles / Lichtschächte
5 New plaster lining on timber framework set within
   existing building / Neue Gipswand auf Holzrahmen,
   die in das alte Gebäude eingesetzt wurde
6 Aluminium supports for booms to carry pictures or
   lighting / Aluminiumhalterungen für Ausleger, die
   Bilder oder Leuchtkörper tragen

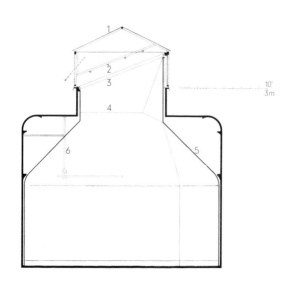

174

12

13

14

The simplest and most effective wall lighting consists of placing sources parallel with the wall and directed at the paintings at an angle of about 30°. These sources can be either continuous or movable.

Für die einfachste und wirksamste Wandbeleuchtung werden die Lichtquellen parallel zur Wand angebracht und mit einem Winkel von etwa 30° auf die Gemälde gerichtet. Die Lichtquellen können entweder aus durchlaufenden Röhren bestehen oder beweglich installiert sein.

12. Movable tungsten fittings. Albright-Knox Art Gallery, Buffalo, New York. Architects: Skidmore, Owings & Merrill.
13. Cold cathode tubes. Palazzo Bianco Museum, Genoa. Architect: Franco Albini.
14. Movable spot lights. Art Gallery, Lund, Sweden. Architect: Klas Anshelm.

12. Bewegliche Glühlampen. Albright-Knox Art Gallery, Buffalo, New York. Architekten: Skidmore, Owings & Merrill.
13. Kalte Leuchtstoffröhren. Museo di Palazzo Bianco, Genua. Architekt: Franco Albini.
14. Bewegliche Scheinwerfer. Kunstgalerie, Lund, Schweden. Architekt: Klas Anshelm.

The three diagrams show certain accepted positions for light sources; they by no means preclude other methods and should merely be taken as guides to general practice.
A. Picture lighting angle and room dimensions related to the size of the painting; it is suggested that the horizontal dimensions be increased by 35 cm for every 30 cm increase in the height of the painting.
B. Sculpture lighting angles.
C. Light sources should be placed in the upper or lower concealment zone; the surface being looked at acts like a mirror and any object within the reflected field will be visible as a reflected image. It is important therefore to reduce the mirror-like quality of the display, by the removal of glass for example, and by reducing the brightness of objects within the reflected field.
(Diagrams A and B are based on those by Lawrence Harrison, Diagram C is taken from *Architectural Lighting Graphics* by John E. Flynn and Samuel M. Mill, Reinhold Publishing Corporation, New York, 1962.)

Die drei Diagramme zeigen verschiedene Möglichkeiten für die Placierung der Lichtquellen; sie sollen nur als Empfehlungen für die Praxis gelten und schließen andere Methoden selbstverständlich nicht aus.
A. Lichteinfallswinkel für die Beleuchtung von Bildern und Raumdimensionen bezogen auf die Höhe der Bilder. Es wird vorgeschlagen, die horizontalen Raumabmessungen jeweils um 35 cm zu vergrößern, wenn die Höhe des Bildes um 30 cm zunimmt.
B. Lichteinfallswinkel für die Beleuchtung von Plastiken.
C. Lichtquellen sollten oberhalb oder unterhalb der reflektierten Zone angebracht werden. Die Bildebene wirkt wie ein Spiegel und macht jeden Gegenstand innerhalb des Reflexionsbereichs als reflektiertes Bild sichtbar. Es ist

deshalb wichtig, die spiegelnden Eigenschaften des Ausstellungsgegenstandes etwa durch Entfernen von Verglasungen möglichst auszuschalten und die Helligkeit von Objekten innerhalb des reflektierten Bereichs zu verringern. (Die Diagramme A und B nach Lawrence Harrison, Diagramm C ist entnommen aus *Architectural Lighting Graphics* von John E. Flynn und Samuel M. Mill, Reinhold Publishing Corporation, New York, 1962.)

1 Central axis of gallery / Mittelachse des Ausstellungsraumes
2 Visitors' circulation / Zirkulation der Besucher
3 Upper concealment zone / Zone oberhalb des reflektierten Bereichs
4 Limit of reflected field / Reflektierter Bereich
5 Lower concealment zone / Zone unterhalb des reflektierten Bereichs
6 Approximate minimum / Mindestabstand

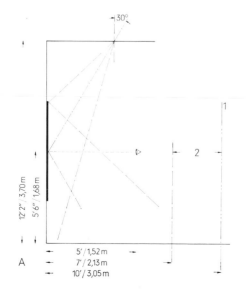

12'2" / 3,70 m
5'6" / 1,68 m
5' / 1,52 m
7' / 2,13 m
10' / 3,05 m
A

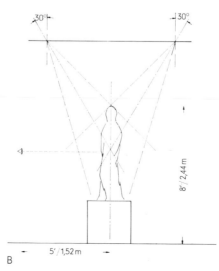

8' / 2,44 m
5' / 1,52 m
B

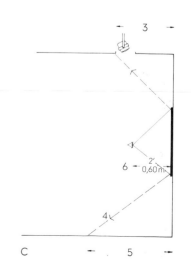

6 — 2' / 0,60 m
C

Small objects and objects whose surface requires emphasis will need more localized lighting. This can be directed by a spotlight or provided by lights related to showcases.

15. Exhibition of Museology, XI Triennale, Milan. Architects: Cesari, Amicis, Pallavicini, Raboni and Rezzonico.
16. Exhibition of Glass. Architect: Carlo Scarpa.
17. Jewellery. Badisches Landesmuseum, Karlsruhe. Interior: Dieter Quast.
18. Musée de Bretagne, Rennes, France. Many exhibits are affected by ultraviolet light and need yellow filters over the light source to protect them. The corner of this case contains fluorescent fittings and swivelling tungsten sources behind a sheet of coated glass. The lights are accessible through a hinged cover from above and this is perforated to ensure ventilation.

15

16

Kleinere Ausstellungsgegenstände und Objekte, deren Oberfläche betont werden muß, brauchen gezieltes Licht. Für punktuelle Beleuchtung sorgen Scheinwerfer oder Punktleuchten, die an den Vitrinen installiert sind.

15. Ausstellung für Museumswesen, XI. Triennale, Mailand. Architekten: Cesari, Amicis, Pallavicini, Raboni und Rezzonico.
16. Glasausstellung. Architekt: Carlo Scarpa.
17. Schmuckvitrine. Badisches Landesmuseum, Karlsruhe. Innengestaltung: Dieter Quast.
18. Musée de Bretagne, Rennes, Frankreich. Viele Ausstellungsobjekte werden durch ultraviolettes Licht beschädigt, so daß zu ihrem Schutz Gelbfilter vor der Lichtquelle angebracht werden müssen. Die Ecke dieser Vitrine enthält hinter einer getönten Glasscheibe Leuchtstoffröhren und bewegliche Glühlampen. Die Lichtquellen sind von oben durch die mit Scharnieren versehene Abdeckung zugänglich; die Abdeckung ist perforiert, um Ventilation zu ermöglichen.

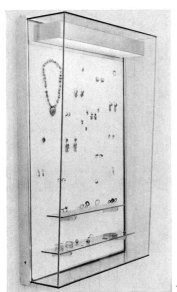

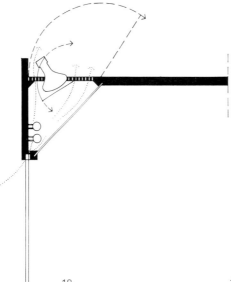

17

18

19

Confined localized lighting within relatively dark spaces will tend to focus attention on the illuminated areas; the display becomes a series of television screens. This method may be particularly useful if very small or delicately moulded items are shown.
Örtlich begrenzte Beleuchtung in relativ dunklen Räumen lenkt die Aufmerksamkeit auf die erhellten Zonen; die Ausstellung wirkt wie eine Folge von Fernsehschirmen. Diese Methode ist besonders dort günstig, wo sehr kleine oder fein geformte Gegenstände gezeigt werden.

19. Exhibition "5000 Years of Persian Art", Gewerbemuseum der Bayerischen Landesgewerbeanstalt, Nuremberg, Germany. Interior: C. Heigl.
20. Oceanic and African Art Gallery, Brooklyn Museum, Brooklyn, New York. Architects: Edward Bryant and Frieda Tenenbaum.
21. Exhibition "Rumanian Folk Art", Gewerbemuseum der Bayerischen Landesgewerbeanstalt, Nuremberg, Germany. Interior: C. Heigl.

19. Ausstellung »5000 Jahre persische Kunst«, Gewerbemuseum der Bayerischen Landesgewerbeanstalt, Nürnberg. Innengestaltung: C. Heigl.
20. Ausstellung ozeanischer und afrikanischer Kunst, Brooklyn Museum, Brooklyn, New York. Architekten: Edward Bryant und Frieda Tenenbaum.
21. Ausstellung »Rumänische Volkskunst«, Gewerbemuseum der Bayerischen Landesgewerbeanstalt, Nürnberg. Innengestaltung: C. Heigl.

20

21

17

22

23

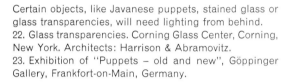

24

Certain objects, like Javanese puppets, stained glass or glass transparencies, will need lighting from behind.
22. Glass transparencies. Corning Glass Center, Corning, New York. Architects: Harrison & Abramovitz.
23. Exhibition of "Puppets – old and new", Göppinger Gallery, Frankfort-on-Main, Germany.

Paintings can also be lit from below and the source screened by a seat or similar baffle.
24. Jackson Pollock Exhibition, Whitechapel Art Gallery, London. Architect: Trevor Dannatt.

Gewisse Objekte wie zum Beispiel avanische Schattenpuppen oder Glasmalereien müssen von hinten beleuchtet werden.
22. Glastransparente. Corning Glass Center, Corning, New York. Architekten: Harrison & Abramovitz.
23. Ausstellung »Puppenspiele – alt und neu«, Göppinger Galerie, Frankfurt am Main.

Bilder können auch von unten beleuchtet werden, wobei die Lichtquelle durch eine Sitzbank oder eine Blende abgeschirmt wird.
24. Jackson-Pollock-Ausstellung, Whitechapel Art Gallery, London. Architekt: Trevor Dannatt.

Illumination of the exterior of the building and its approaches should also be considered since museums are likely to be used late in the evening.
25. Entrance to the new wing, Albright-Knox Art Gallery, Buffalo, New York. Architects: Skidmore, Owings & Merrill.
26. Entrance to exhibition building of the Art Club at Hameln, Germany. Architect: Dieter Oesterlen.

Auch die Beleuchtung des Äußeren ist von Bedeutung, da Museen oft auch abends geöffnet sind.
25. Eingang zum neuen Flügel der Albright-Knox Art Gallery, Buffalo, New York. Architekten: Skidmore, Owings & Merrill.
26. Eingang zum Studio des Kunstkreises Hameln. Architekt: Dieter Oesterlen.

25

26

Every museum has an obvious responsibility to make certain that the objects in its care will survive and will remain intact to communicate in the future. The mere fact that they are in a museum does not necessarily insure this. On the contrary, the switch from an environment to which the object has adapted – a wood panel to a certain humidity for example – to the new surroundings of the museum may in itself cause considerable damage. Nor are conditions within a museum, with its emphasis on lighting and the need for public access, always ideal for the preservation of certain exhibits.

Deterioration is caused mainly by two factors: the action of the atmosphere and the effect of light. The first is dealt with in this section, the second in the section on lighting, see page 170. Most of the atmospheric action is dependent on the effects of humidity and the lack of stable conditions. Clean air and a uniform environment at a relative humidity of about 55 % appear to give the best conditions for the largest variety of items likely to be found in museums.

Metals are, for instance, attacked by oxygen in the presence of moisture and this is hastened if hygroscopic particles of dust, fabric or salt adhere to the metal absorbing the water vapour in the air. Stone is attacked by acids and salts in the presence of moisture; these move inwards and outwards as the humidity changes and this movement produces stresses which cause a break-up. Organic materials vary in their resistance; they may either become brittle from excessive dryness or, when the humidity is high, become rotten and deteriorate from biological effects. The growth of fungi and moulds usually occurs if the relative humidity is 70 % or over and the temperature at least 68°F. This is the point at which spores start to germinate.

The deteriorating effect of humidity is increased in urban situations where acids are present and where dust and other forms of industrial pollution will settle on objects and absorb moisture. The extent of this can perhaps be gauged by the fact that a fan delivering 5,000 cubic feet of air an hour working for 10 hours in an only moderately dirty metropolitan area will bring into the museum 17 cubic inches of loosely packed dirt. In an industrial area the amount would be twice this, in a rural area, a third.

It becomes important therefore to create a building which either by natural or mechanical means will preserve stable climatic conditions and exclude as much pollution as possible. This will be affected by orientation, the relation of glass to solid in the outer walls, the thermal capacity of the building, the method of natural ventilation and a number of factors which can be gauged for each particular site. It will also be influenced by the actual placing of objects so that these do not touch cold walls, for instance, or become damp from open windows.

Mechanical means also exist to produce a partially or fully controlled environment. Relatively simple devices will change the humidity only. Humidifiers produce a fine spray of water particles, dehumidifiers absorb moisture either by refrigerating the air and disposing of the condensed water or by using a dehydrating chemical such as silica gel. There are also simple means of partially cleaning air by using a fan and a filter of fibres coated with a tacky fluid.

More complex systems will provide complete air conditioning i.e. control temperature, humidity, ventilation and air pollution. The most suitable form for museums washes the air by direct contact between the air and sprays of chilled slightly alkaline water. Electrostatic filters in which particles are charged and then deposited on plates of an opposite charge may, if the field is too strong, produce ozone which is a highly destructive agent.

The cost of installing and running a complete system of air conditioning may well be offset against a very much lower cost of conservation. Pictures from the National Gallery, London which were painted on wood and which needed constant attention while in the gallery, needed none after being stored for some time in controlled conditions of 58 % Relative Humidity at 63°F during the war. This experience was sufficient to persuade the gallery to install an air conditioning system in its building.

1. Air-conditioning ducts and lighting in the void between the rooflights and the suspended ceiling. Kunsthaus, Zürich. Architects: Hans and Kurt Pfister.

1. Leitungen der Klimaanlage und Beleuchtung in dem leeren Raum zwischen den Oberlichtern und der eingehängten Decke. Kunsthaus Zürich. Architekten: Hans und Kurt Pfister.

Jedes Museum ist dafür verantwortlich, daß die Kunstwerke, die es bewahrt, der Nachwelt unversehrt überliefert werden. Die bloße Tatsache, daß die Werke in einem Museum untergebracht sind, genügt nicht unbedingt. Wenn man zum Beispiel ein auf Holz gemaltes Bild, das ständig einem bestimmten Feuchtigkeitsgrad ausgesetzt ist, aus seiner Umgebung entfernt und in ein Museum bringt, können beträchtliche Schäden entstehen. Auch innerhalb des Museums, in dem ja Beleuchtung und Publikumsverkehr eine große Rolle spielen, sind die Voraussetzungen für die Erhaltung mancher Ausstellungsgegenstände nicht immer ideal.

Die Hauptursachen für Schäden sind atmosphärische Einflüsse und Einwirkungen des Lichts (vgl. Seite 170). Die atmosphärischen Einflüsse hängen weitgehend von der Luftfeuchtigkeit und von den Bedingungen der Umgebung ab. Reine Luft und eine relative Luftfeuchtigkeit von etwa 55% sind günstig für die meisten Kunstwerke, die gewöhnlich in Museen zu finden sind.

Metalle oxydieren bei Feuchtigkeit; dieser Vorgang wird noch beschleunigt, wenn hygroskopische Staub-, Gewebe- oder Salzpartikel an dem Metall haften und den in der Luft enthaltenen Wasserdampf absorbieren. Stein wird bei Feuchtigkeit von Säuren und Salzen angegriffen, die sich bei wechselnden Feuchtigkeitsgraden nach innen oder außen bewegen. Die Spannungen, die dadurch entstehen, können zu Rissen führen. Organische Materialien sind von unterschiedlicher Widerstandsfähigkeit; bei zu großer Trockenheit werden sie spröde, bei zu starker Feuchtigkeit faulen sie und verderben durch biologische Einwirkungen. Pilze und Schimmel treten im allgemeinen dann auf, wenn die relative Luftfeuchtigkeit 70% oder mehr und die Temperatur 20°C oder mehr beträgt, denn unter solchen Voraussetzungen beginnen die Sporen zu keimen.

Die schädigenden Einflüsse der Feuchtigkeit wirken sich besonders in den Städten aus, wo Säuren vorhanden sind und wo sich Staub sowie andere Ausscheidungen der Industrie auf den Gegenständen festsetzen und die Feuchtigkeit anziehen. Das Ausmaß der Verunreinigung läßt sich daran erkennen, daß ein Ventilator, der in einer Stunde ca. 140 m³ Luft zuführt und zehn Stunden in einer Stadtzone mittleren Verschmutzungsgrades tätig ist, etwa 280 cm³ Staub in ein Museum bringt. In einem Industriegebiet wäre diese Zahl doppelt so groß, auf dem Lande beträgt sie nur ein Drittel.

Es ist deshalb bei Museumsbauten wichtig, daß durch natürliche oder mechanische Mittel gleichmäßige klimatische Verhältnisse geschaffen werden und daß eine Luftverschmutzung so weit wie möglich ausgeschlossen wird. Von Einfluß sind die Orientierung des Gebäudes, das Verhältnis von Glasflächen zu massiven Außenwänden, die Heizfähigkeit, die natürliche Ventilation und eine Reihe weiterer Faktoren, die bei den verschiedenen Museumsbauten variieren. Wichtig ist auch der genaue Aufstellungsort der Gegenstände, die zum Beispiel nicht an kalten Wänden oder in der Nähe von bisweilen geöffneten Fenstern stehen sollten.

Für eine partielle oder völlige Klimakontrolle des Museums gibt es auch mechanische Einrichtungen. Relativ einfache Geräte übernehmen nur die Feuchtigkeitsregulierung. Luftbefeuchter sorgen für einen feinen Sprühschleier von Wasserpartikeln, Entfeuchter absorbieren die Feuchtigkeit, indem sie entweder die Luft abkühlen und das kondensierte Wasser auffangen oder eine absorbierende Chemikalie wie Silikagel verwenden. Für die teilweise Reinigung der Luft gibt es ebenfalls einfache Vorrichtungen wie zum Beispiel einen Ventilator mit Stoffilter, der mit einer klebrigen Flüssigkeit bestrichen ist.

Für eine vollständige Klimakontrolle sorgen kompliziertere Geräte, die Regulierung von Temperatur und Feuchtigkeit, Ventilation und Reinigung der Luft übernehmen. Bei dem für Museen tauglichsten System dieser Art wird die Luft durch direkten Kontakt mit Sprühschleiern aus abgekühltem Alkaliwasser gereinigt. Bei elektrostatischen Filtern werden Partikel geladen und auf Platten mit entgegengesetzter Ladung abgelagert; wenn das Kraftfeld zu stark wird, kann dabei allerdings Ozon entstehen, der äußerst schädliche Wirkungen ausübt.

Die Installations- und Bedienungskosten einer vollständigen Klimaanlage können in vielen Fällen durch niedrigere Erhaltungskosten kompensiert werden. Auf Holz gemalte Bilder der Londoner National Gallery erforderten zum Beispiel im Museum ständige Konservierungsarbeiten; als sie während des Krieges bei ca. 17°C und einer relativen Luftfeuchtigkeit von 58% eingelagert wurden, waren keine solchen Arbeiten mehr notwendig. Diese Erfahrung brachte die National Gallery dazu, in ihrem Gebäude eine Klimaanlage zu installieren.

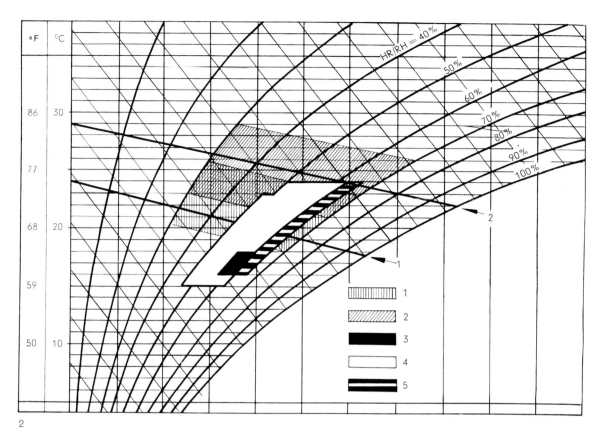

2

1 Winter comfort zone / Behaglichkeitszone im Winter
2 Summer comfort zone / Behaglichkeitszone im Sommer
3 Safety zone of paintings / Sicherheitszone für Gemälde
4 Safety zone of archives / Sicherheitszone für Archive
5 Safety zone of diverse collections / Sicherheitszone für verschiedenartige Sammlungen

2. The hygrometric diagram relates the limits of comfort to those of safety recommended for different types of collections. In the diagram defining atmospheric conditions, an attempt has been made to correlate the limits which are acceptable as zones of comfort with those recognised as satisfactory for museums. There are numerous points in common, but it should be noted in the first place (left part of the diagram), that the limits of comfort extend to hygrometric regions that are much too dry for many kinds of objects, the relative humidity being less than 40%. As a result museums ought to be air-conditioned with regard to the collections rather than the staff. In the second place, archives etc. can be stored in conditions far removed from the limits of comfort (see bottom of diagram). Since it is well known that human beings cannot comfortably perform sedentary work at temperatures lower than 20°C, it would in this case be necessary to provide sedentary staff with suitable local heating. (Originally published in *Museum*.)

2. Hygrometrisches Diagramm, das die Behaglichkeitszonen sowie die Sicherheitszonen für verschiedene Arten von Sammlungen angibt. In dieser graphischen Darstellung der atmosphärischen Verhältnisse stellen die Behaglichkeitszonen die Bereiche dar, die vom Menschen als angenehm empfunden werden; sie sind in Beziehung gesetzt zu den Zonen, die für ein Museum als geeignet gelten. Die Bereiche überschneiden sich zum Teil; links im Diagramm ist jedoch zu erkennen, daß die Behaglichkeitszone sich auf Regionen erstreckt, die für zahlreiche Ausstellungsgegenstände zu trocken sind, da ihre relative Luftfeuchtigkeit unter 40% liegt. Das Museum muß also mehr im Hinblick auf die Sammlungen als auf das Personal klimatisiert werden. Wie sich unten im Diagramm feststellen läßt, können zum Beispiel die Archive in Bereichen untergebracht werden, die weit von der Behaglichkeitszone entfernt sind. Bei sitzender Tätigkeit wird die Arbeitskraft bekanntlich durch Temperaturen unter 20°C beeinträchtigt; es wäre deshalb in einem solchen Fall notwendig, für das Personal eine örtlich begrenzte Heizanlage vorzusehen. (Aus: *Museum*.)

Museum collections should, like every other valuable – or even irreplaceable – set of objects be protected from loss or accidental destruction. This means devising security arrangements in terms of theft, disfigurement and fire. Those against theft fall into two categories; those in operation while the building is open to the public and those while it is closed. Guards on duty in the galleries are the traditional method of dealing with the first problem. They can be greatly helped by being able to set off an alarm system which shows on a central switchboard and which can cause all doors to close so as to trap the thief. The actual removal of objects can also be made much more difficult by their mounting or hanging. Pictures suspended on metal rods, for instance, can be padlocked to them. It is also possible to connect objects to electric systems which set off an alarm as soon as there is a disturbance of the exhibit.

Night time security depends, in addition to patrols, on preventing entry, or if this has been achieved, its immediate detection. Openings can be protected by grilles or shutters and they can also be wired to a central system so that if they should be opened an alarm is set off. There are further methods in which an infra-red light is directed from a projector at a receiving unit, which may be up to 2,500 feet away, and an alarm is given off if the ray is broken. The units can be camouflaged by exhibits or furniture. Another method, particularly useful for storage rooms, works by having a fan blow air into or out of the area to be protected at a predetermined pressure. A diaphragm elsewhere monitors the difference between the inside and the outside pressures. As soon as an entry is made the pressure alters, the diaphragm reacts and the alarm is set off.

There are many forms of fire and smoke detection available. These can be linked directly to alarm switchboards at the nearest Fire Brigade Station. It is important that they are sensitive to both temperature rise and smoke. Museums should in addition have their own fire extinguishing apparatus readily available and distributed throughout the building.

Museumssammlungen sollten, wie alle wertvollen oder gar unersetzlichen Gegenstände, gegen Diebstahl, Beschädigung und Feuer geschützt werden. Die Maßnahmen gegen Diebstahl fallen unter zwei Kategorien: solche, die tagsüber wirksam sind, wenn das Museum dem Publikum zugänglich ist, und solche, die nachts angewandt werden. Die Beschäftigung von Museumswärtern stellt die traditionelle Lösung des ersten Problems dar. Die Wärter können durch Alarmsysteme unterstützt werden, die zu einer Zentrale führen und alle Türen automatisch schließen. Der Diebstahl von Gegenständen kann auch durch ihre Aufstellung oder Hängung erschwert werden. Bilder, die an Metallstäben hängen, können zum Beispiel mit einem Vorhängeschloß daran befestigt werden. Darüber hinaus ist es möglich, Gegenstände an ein elektrisches System anzuschließen, das Alarm auslöst, sobald das Objekt berührt wird.

Die Sicherung beruht – außer auf Kontrollgängen der Wärter – auf dem wirksamen Schutz der Eingänge und auf der Möglichkeit, Eindringlinge sofort zu entdecken. Öffnungen und Zugänge zum Museum können durch Gitter oder Rolläden geschützt und an ein Alarmsystem angeschlossen werden. In manchen Museen wird infrarotes Licht von einem Projektor zu einem Empfänger geleitet, der bis zu 760 m entfernt liegen kann; wenn der Lichtstrahl durchbrochen wird, wird Alarm ausgelöst. Die Empfangszellen können durch Ausstellungsgegenstände oder Möbel verborgen werden. Eine andere Methode, die besonders für Lagerräume Verwendung findet, funktioniert folgendermaßen: Ein Ventilator bläst Luft in den zu schützenden Bereich oder führt sie ab, wobei ein festgesetzter Druck eingehalten wird. Eine Membrane reagiert auf Unterschiede zwischen den Innen- und Außendrücken; sobald sich der Luftdruck verändert, löst die Membrane Alarm aus.

Gegen Feuer gibt es eine Vielfalt von Schutzvorrichtungen. Sie können direkt mit den Alarmanlagen der nächsten Feuerwehrstation verbunden werden und sollten erhöhte Temperaturen genauso registrieren wie Rauchentwicklung. Die Museen müssen im übrigen über eigene Feuerlöschapparate verfügen, die im ganzen Gebäude verteilt sein sollten.

These four elements of museum display put the object to be seen within the field of vision of a standing observer who may be either an adult or a child. They may also serve to protect the exhibits, to carry lighting and to subdivide spaces.

The field of vision of an observer occupies a cone which is roughly defined by an angle of 40°. The total field of vision is greater than this and is greater horizontally than vertically but normally it is easier to move one's head than to turn both eyes beyond the limits shown in Figure B. As a result the amount of surface which can be comfortably seen at certain distance can be found and is shown in Figure C.

Since only a limited area is seen at any one time it becomes possible to position the exhibits so that only a single object or a related group of objects is seen within the field of vision. Head movement or movement of the observer to a new position will bring further objects into view. As Herbert Bayer has shown, Figure A, all surfaces of a display space can be organised in these terms. Museum viewing consists of looking at a succession of such fields. There is an advantage in terms of visual comfort if succeeding fields are not always at the same distance but, that within each field, the distance between objects in depth is not too great; there is a limit to the eye's depth of focus particularly at close range.

Diese vier Elemente der Ausstellungsgestaltung bringen das Objekt in das Blickfeld eines stehenden Betrachters, sei es eines Erwachsenen oder eines Kindes. Darüber hinaus schützen sie die Gegenstände, tragen die Leuchtkörper und unterteilen die Räume.

Das Blickfeld des Betrachters umfaßt einen Kegel, der etwa einem Winkel von 40° entspricht. Das gesamte Blickfeld ist zwar größer und in horizontaler Richtung weiter als in vertikaler; im allgemeinen ist es aber einfacher, den Kopf zu wenden als beide Augen über die in Abbildung B angegebenen Grenzen hinaus zu bewegen.

Die Flächen, die sich von einer bestimmten Entfernung aus bequem überblicken lassen, sind in Abbildung C gezeigt.

Da der Sehbereich in einem bestimmten Augenblick begrenzt ist, können die Ausstellungsgegenstände so aufgestellt werden, daß jeweils nur ein einziges Objekt oder eine Gruppe zusammengehöriger Objekte in das Blickfeld treten. Wenn der Betrachter den Kopf wendet oder eine neue Position einnimmt, erblickt er weitere Ausstellungsstücke. Herbert Bayer hat gezeigt (Abbildung A), daß alle Flächen eines Ausstellungsraumes sich nach diesen Gesichtspunkten organisieren lassen. Der Museumsbesucher betrachtet also eine Folge solcher Einzelbereiche. Für den optischen Eindruck ist es günstig, wenn aufeinanderfolgende Zonen nicht in gleichem Abstand vom Betrachter liegen; innerhalb eines jeden Bereichs sollten die Distanzen jedoch nicht allzusehr variieren, da die Akkomodation des Auges bei geringen Entfernungen begrenzt ist.

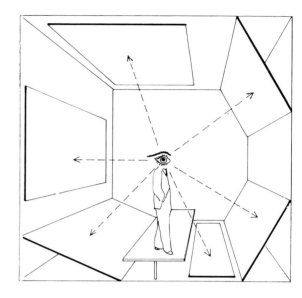

A. Diagram for an exhibition. Herbert Bayer, 1939.

A. Diagramm für eine Ausstellung. Herbert Bayer, 1939.

B. Diagram showing the normal limits of the horizontal angular sweep of the eyes without turning the head; the total field of binocular vision is 120° but it is usually not used since it is more comfortable to turn the head. (From *Sight, Light & Work* by H. C. Weston, H. K. Lewis, London 1962, Second Edition.)

B. Diagramm der normalen Begrenzung des horizontalen Sehbereichs, den das Auge ohne Wendung des Kopfes überblicken kann; der gesamte Blickwinkel hat 120°, wird aber im allgemeinen nicht ausgenutzt, da es bequemer ist, den Kopf zu drehen. (Aus: *Sight, Light and Work* von H. C. Weston und H. K. Lewis, London 1962, 2. Auflage.)

LE = Left eye / Linkes Auge
RE = Right eye / Rechtes Auge

C. The three diagrams show the size of the square which can be inscribed within the base of a 40° cone dependent on the distance between the eye and the picture plane.

C. Die drei Diagramme zeigen die Größe des Quadrats, das entsprechend der Entfernung zwischen Auge und Bildebene in die Grundfläche eines Kegels von 40° eingeschrieben werden kann.

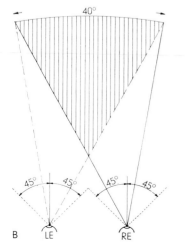

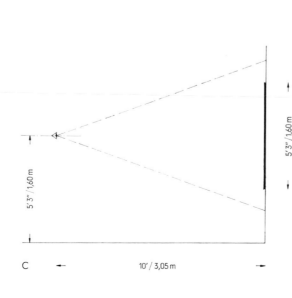

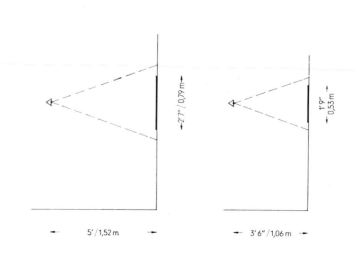

Walls / Wände

The wall has been the most readily available support surface in traditionally constructed buildings.

It is possible, and occasionally desirable, to modify the wall surface by colour or by the addition of a further surface. This may be particularly appropriate where a reduction in the scale of the setting seems necessary.

Die Wand stellt bei traditionellen Gebäudekonstruktionen die einfachste Stell- und Hängefläche dar.

Es ist möglich und häufig wünschenswert, die Wände durch farbigen Anstrich oder durch Hinzufügen einer weiteren Fläche zu variieren. Das ist besonders dort angebracht, wo die Ausmaße der Wandflächen in keinem günstigen maßstäblichen Verhältnis zum ausgestellten Gegenstand stehen.

1. Farbig gestrichene Putzfläche. Uffizien, Florenz. Architekten: Ignazio Gardella, Giovanni Michelucci, Carlo Scarpa, Guido Morozzi.
2. Holztafeln, die mit Scharnieren an der Wand befestigt sind. Uffizien, Florenz.
3. Aufgehängte Ausstellungstafeln aus Holz. Gewerbemuseum der Bayerischen Landesgewerbeanstalt, Nürnberg. Innengestaltung: C. Heigl.

1. Farbig gestrichene Putzfläche. Uffizien, Architekten: Ignazio Gardella, Giovanni Michelucci, Carlo Scarpa, Guido Morozzi.
2. Holztafeln, die mit Scharnieren an der Wand befestigt sind. Uffizien, Florenz.
3. Aufgehängte Ausstellungstafeln aus Holz. Gewerbemuseum der Bayerischen Landesgewerbeanstalt, Nürnberg. Innengestaltung: C. Heigl.

Panels / Tafeln

These are in effect additional wall, floor, or ceiling planes, and fulfil the same functions: support, background and space separation. They have the obvious advantage that they are movable and thus changeable. The kind of space they define can be altered and their position related to light, other exhibits and the movement of the observer for each particular occasion.

Tafeln sind zusätzliche Wand-, Boden- oder Deckenflächen und erfüllen entsprechende Funktionen: Sie dienen als Träger, als Hintergrund und als Raumteiler und haben den Vorteil, daß sie beweglich und deshalb variabel sind. Die Größe des Raumes, den sie begrenzen, kann verändert werden; ihre Anordnung kann sich beliebig nach der Lichtquelle, nach ihrem Verhältnis zu anderen Ausstellungsgegenständen und nach der Zirkulation der Besucher richten.

8

Panels, adding to the area of available display surface, need not invariably be movable elements nor always vertical.
4. Blockwork wall panels. Jackson Pollock Exhibition, Whitechapel Art Gallery, London. Architect: Trevor Dannatt.
5. Movable screens. Frank Lloyd Wright Exhibition, XI Triennale, Milan. Architect: Carlo Scarpa.
6. Timber screens. L. Baskin Exhibition, Boymans-van Beuningen Museum, Rotterdam. Architect: A. J. v. d. Grinten.
7. Exhibition of Experimental Painters, Stedelijk Museum, Amsterdam. Interior: F. A. Eschauzier.

Wandtafeln erweitern die verfügbare Ausstellungsfläche. Sie sind nicht in allen Fällen beweglich und nicht immer vertikal angeordnet.
4. Wände aus Hohlblocksteinen. Jackson-Pollock-Ausstellung, Whitechapel Art Gallery, London. Architekt: Trevor Dannall.
5. Bewegliche Stellwände. Frank-Lloyd-Wright-Ausstellung, XI. Triennale, Mailand. Architekt: Carlo Scarpa.
6. Holzwände. L.-Baskin-Ausstellung, Museum Boymans-van Beuningen, Rotterdam. Architekt: A. J. v. d. Grinten.
7. Ausstellung experimenteller Malerei. Stedelijk Museum, Amsterdam. Innengestaltung: F. A. Eschauzier.

9

Panels, particularly movable panels, are not stable unless held at the top, or side, or support each other by their geometric arrangement.
8. Side supported panels incorporating glass covered recesses. Bellini Room, Galleria dell' Accademia, Venice. Architect: Carlo Scarpa.
9. Cloth covered panels on metal uprights. Castello Sforzesco Museum, Milan. Architects: Studio Architetti BBPR.

Stellwände und vor allem bewegliche Stellwände sind nicht standfest, wenn sie nicht oben oder an der Seite gehalten werden oder sich gegenseitig durch eine geometrische Anordnung stützen.
8. Stellwände, die seitlich von der Wand aus gestützt werden; die Bilder sind in Vertiefungen angebracht, die mit Glas abgedeckt wurden. Bellini-Raum, Galleria dell' Accademia, Venedig. Architekt: Carlo Scarpa.
9. Mit Stoff bespannte Stellwände zwischen Metallträgern. Museo del Castello Sforzesco, Mailand. Architekten: Studio Architetti BBPR.

10

11

The object on display can itself be a panel within a supporting framework or be suspended on wires.
10. Uprights held between floor and ceiling grid of wires. Room for temporary exhibition, Palazzo Bianco Museum, Genoa. Architect: Franco Albini.
11. Pictures are suspended on wires. "Family of Man" photographic exhibition, Museum of Modern Art, New York. Architect: Paul Rudolph.

Panels can also provide enclosure and emphasis, carry lighting and control circulation.
12. Demountable panels. "Forms from Israel" travelling exhibition, Baltimore Museum of Art, Baltimore, Maryland. Architect: Nathan Shapiro.
13. Plywood screen incorporating top and side lighting. Carlo Crivelli Exhibition, Palazzo Ducale, Venice. Architect: Egle Trincanato.

Der ausgestellte Gegenstand kann selbst eine Art Wand bilden, wenn er in einer Rahmenkonstruktion angebracht oder an Drähten aufgehängt wird.
10. Die Metallträger sind zwischen dem Boden und einem System von Drähten an der Decke eingespannt. Raum für Wechselausstellungen, Palazzo Bianco, Genua. Architekt: Franco Albini.
11. Die Bildtafeln sind an Drähten aufgehängt. Fotoausstellung »Family of Man«, Museum of Modern Art, New York. Architekt: Paul Rudolph.

Stellwände können die Ausstellungsgegenstände umschließen und betonen, sie können die Leuchtkörper aufnehmen und die Zirkulation lenken.
12. Flexible Stellwände. Wanderausstellung »Forms of Israel«, Baltimore Museum of Art, Baltimore. Architekt: Nathan Shapiro.
13. Stellwand aus Sperrholz, die Decken- und Seitenbeleuchtung trägt. Carlo-Crivelli-Ausstellung, Palazzo Ducale, Venedig. Architekt: Egle Trincanato.

Page / Seite 185:

The glass surfaces of showcases will act as light reflectors and should be positioned, or have their sides sloped, in such a way that they do not reflect light sources to an onlooker.
G. Opposite a window.
H. In front of a window.
I. Lighted cases facing each other.
K. Under overhead lighting.

Die Glasflächen von Vitrinen reflektieren das Licht und sollten deshalb so angeordnet oder an den Seiten so abgeschrägt werden, daß sie den Besucher nicht blenden.
G. Aufstellung gegenüber dem Fenster.
H. Aufstellung vor dem Fenster.
I. Beleuchtete Vitrinen, die einander gegenüberstehen.
K. Vitrinen unter Deckenbeleuchtung.

12

13

Cases / Vitrinen

These enclose and protect objects and normally also bring them to a reasonable viewing height. The protection they offer is threefold: theft is much more difficult, dust and insects are excluded, and climatic conditions within are much more constant and can additionally be altered by inserting, for instance, hygroscopic material. The diagrams show various methods of opening cases.

Vitrinen umschließen die Ausstellungsgegenstände und präsentieren sie in angemessener Sichthöhe. Sie bilden einen Schutz gegen Diebstahl und gegen das Eindringen von Staub oder Insekten, und sie schaffen konstante klimatische Verhältnisse, die zusätzlich noch durch hygroskopische Materialien verbessert werden können. Die Zeichnungen zeigen verschiedene Methoden, die Vitrinen zu öffnen.

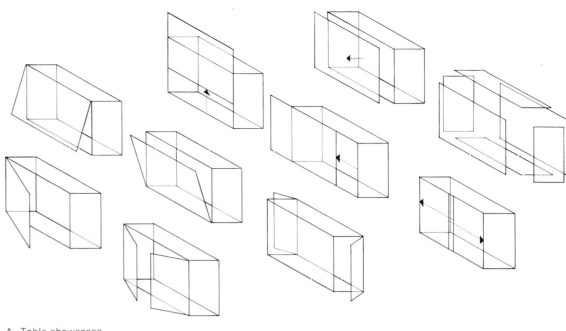

A. Table showcases.
A. Tischvitrinen

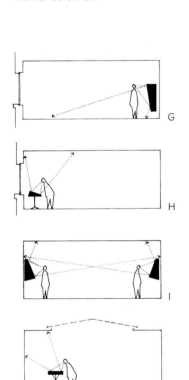

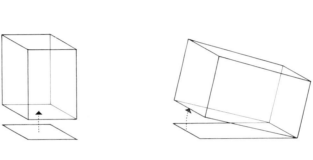

B. Free standing vertical showcases with hoods.
B. Frei stehende vertikale Vitrinen mit Abdeckung.

C. Other free standing vertical showcases; several of these methods are equally applicable to wall cases.
C. Weitere frei stehende vertikale Vitrinen; einige dieser Systeme sind auch auf Wandvitrinen anwendbar.

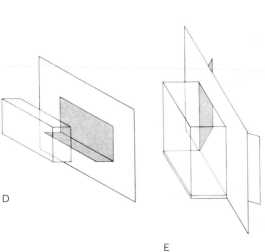

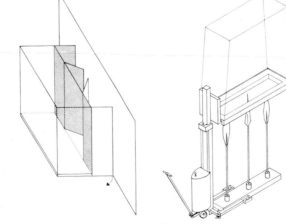

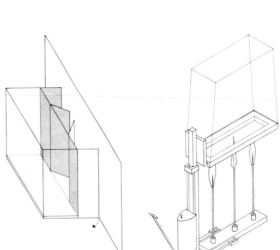

D. Wall cases where the display, support, and the enclosure can be separated.
E. Upright wall cases where access from the rear is possible.
F. In some instances large enclosures can be moved mechanically by a fork lift or jacked-up onto a trolley.

D. Wandvitrinen, bei denen Exponatträger und Umschließung voneinander getrennt werden können.
E. Wandvitrinen, die von hinten zugänglich sind.
F. In einigen Fällen können große Rahmenkonstruktionen mechanisch durch Gabelstapler bewegt oder mit Winden auf einen Karren gehoben werden.

(The drawings on this page are taken from Museum, Vol. XIII, No. 1, 1960, a special number devoted to an article on "Museum Showcases" by G. H. Rivière and Herman F. E. Visser.)
(Die Zeichnungen auf dieser Seite stammen aus Museum, XIII, Nr. 1, 1960, einer Sondernummer mit einem Artikel über Museumsvitrinen von Georges H. Rivière und Herman F. E. Visser.)

D

E

F

14. Islamic glass. Corning Glass Center, Corning, New York. Architects: Harrison & Abramovitz.
14. Islamisches Glas. Corning Glass Center, Corning, New York. Architekten: Harrison & Abramovitz.

Open cases, shelves and tables put small objects at their proper viewing level and can give them some visual emphasis by related screening or localized lighting.
Offene Vitrinen, Regale und Tische präsentieren die Ausstellungsobjekte in Sichthöhe. Kleinere Gegenstände können durch Unterteilungen oder durch Punktleuchten visuell hervorgehoben werden.

15, 16. Demountable display. Exhibition "5000 Years of Persian Art", Gewerbemuseum der Bayerischen Landesgewerbeanstalt, Nuremberg, Germany. Interior: C. Heigl.
17. Related objects grouped together on screens and tables without, however, recreating period rooms. Danish Handicrafts Exhibition, Copenhagen (1962). Design: Hans Lassen.

15, 16. Ausstellung »5000 Jahre persische Kunst«, Gewerbemuseum der Bayerischen Landesgewerbeanstalt, Nürnberg. Innengestaltung: C. Heigl.
17. Verwandte Objekte sind auf Stellwänden und Tischen angeordnet, ohne daß dadurch »Stil«-Räume entstehen. Dänische Kunstgewerbeausstellung, Kopenhagen (1962). Gestaltung: Hans Lassen.

19

20

21

Cases can create a setting which is in scale with the size of the object being shown.

18. Wall case subdivided by shelves and a coloured background. National Archeological Museum, Gela, Sicily. Architect: Franco Minissi.

22. Tetrahedral cases subdivided by cloth-covered tetrahedra. International Exhibition of Modern Jewellery 1890–1961, Goldsmith Hall, London. Architect: Alan Irvine.

Vitrinen können eine Umgebung schaffen, die den Proportionen der gezeigten Objekte gerecht wird.

18. Wandvitrine, die durch Fachböden und einen farbigen Hintergrund unterteilt ist. Museo Archeologico Nazionale, Gela, Sizilien. Architekt: Franco Minissi.

22. Die Vitrinen in Tetraeder-Form enthalten stoffbespannte Tetraeder. Die Beleuchtung erfolgt durch Pendelleuchten. Internationale Ausstellung modernen Schmucks von 1890 bis 1961, Goldsmith Hall, London. Architekt: Alan Irvine.

Glass cabinets provide protection through enclosure.

19. Metal and glass case incorporating lighting. Villa Aurea, Agrigento, Sicily. Architect: Franco Minissi.

20. Metal and glass case. Badisches Landesmuseum, Karlsruhe. Architects: State Building Department and Dieter Quast.

21. Similar glass enclosed panels used on the wall and on freestanding supports. Print Room, Uffizi Gallery, Florence. Architects: Edoardo Detti and Carlo Scarpa.

A. Layout of Room 1, 1890–1914 (see Fig. 22) / Grundriß von Raum 1, 1890–1914 (vgl. Abb. 22).

B. Plan of ¾″ blockboard supports, painted black / Plan der 19 mm dicken Stützen aus Schichtholz, die schwarz gestrichen wurden.

C. Detail of junction between base and glass / Plan der Verbindung zwischen Basis und Glas.

1 ¼″ plate glass, cemented corner joints / 6,3 mm dickes Tafelglas, verkittete Eckverbindung

2 Brass angle, lacquered black / Schwarzlackierte Kupferwinkel

3 Fabric covered ¾″ blockboard / 19 mm dickes, mit Tuch bespanntes Holz

Glasvitrinen umschließen und schützen die Ausstellungsgegenstände.

19. Beleuchtete Glasvitrine auf Stahlstützen. Villa Aurea, Agrigent, Sizilien. Architekt: Franco Minissi.

20. Glasvitrine auf Stahlträgern. Badisches Landesmuseum, Karlsruhe. Architekten: Staatliches Hochbauamt Karlsruhe und Dieter Quast.

21. Mit Glas bedeckte Tafeln an der Wand und auf frei stehenden Trägern. Graphikraum, Uffizien, Florenz. Architekten: Edoardo Detti und Carlo Scarpa.

B

22

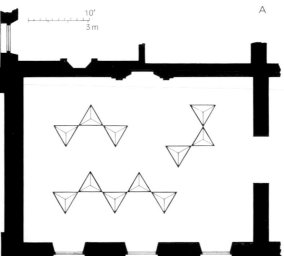

A

C

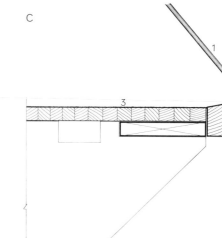

87

23

Supports / Exponatträger

These serve a variety of functions especially as the category really includes all methods of holding up an object which cannot be described as wall, panel or case. Normally these supports provide stability at a desirable level, some fixing to prevent removal and often differentiate the display from its surroundings.

Zu den Exponatträgern zählen alle Vorrichtungen, die Ausstellungsgegenstände stützen oder halten und nicht als Wände, Tafeln oder Vitrinen bezeichnet werden können. Die Träger sorgen für Stabilität sowie für eine günstige Sichthöhe und sind in manchen Fällen direkt mit dem Ausstellungsgegenstand verbunden, damit dieser nicht entfernt werden kann.

The whole room, or part of the room, can itself become a display case. This has been a long accepted solution where period rooms are being shown.
23. Folk Art, Badisches Landesmuseum, Karlsruhe. Architects: State Building Department and Dieter Quast.
24. Shop. American Museum in Britain, Claverton Manor, Bath. Interior: Ian McCallum.
25. Bedroom. American Museum in Britain, Claverton Manor, Bath. Interior: Ian McCallum.

Der ganze Raum oder ein Teil des Raumes kann selbst zum »Schaukästen« werden, vor allem dann, wenn es sich um Zimmereinrichtungen einer bestimmten stilistischen Epoche handelt.
23. Volkskunstabteilung, Badisches Landesmuseum, Karlsruhe. Architekten: Staatliches Hochbauamt Karlsruhe und Dieter Quast.
24. Ladeneinrichtung. American Museum in Britain, Claverton Manor, Bath. Inneneinrichtung: Ian McCallum.
25. Schlafzimmer. American Museum in Britain, Claverton Manor, Bath. Inneneinrichtung: Ian McCallum.

24

25

Supports provide not only stability but are able to emphasize an object by setting it apart from its immediate surroundings.
26, 27. Crucifix by Cimabue. Metal floor support into separate stone base, metal ties to wall. Uffizi Gallery, Florence. Architects: Ignazio Gardella, Giovanni Michelucci, Carlo Scarpa, Guido Morozzi.
28. Metal and stone sculpture stands (in the background). Exhibition of Museology, XI Triennale, Milan. Design: Cesari, De Amicis, Pallavicini, Raboni and Rezzonico.

Exponatträger sorgen nicht nur für Stabilität, sondern können auch ein Objekt betonen, indem sie es aus seiner unmittelbaren Umgebung herausheben.
26, 27. Kruzifix von Cimabue. Die untere Stütze aus Metall ist in einen Steinsockel eingelassen; der obere Teil des Kruzifixes ist mit Metallstangen an der Wand befestigt. Uffizien, Florenz. Architekten: Ignazio Gardella, Giovanni Michelucci, Carlo Scarpa, Guido Morozzi.
28. Exponatträger aus Stein und Metall (im Hintergrund der Abbildung). Ausstellung Museumswesen, XI. Triennale, Mailand. Gestaltung: Cesari, De Amicis, Pallavicini, Raboni und Rezzonico.

The easel is a traditional picture support and is as useful in the museum as in the studio.
29. Metal easels. Museo Correr, Venice. Architect: Carlo Scarpa.

Die Staffelei, ein traditioneller Bilderträger, ist im Museum genauso nützlich wie im Atelier.
29. Metallstaffelei. Museo Correr, Venedig. Architekt: Carlo Scarpa.

26

27

28

29

Walls, floors and ceilings can be designed to have prepared positions for the location of supports. These can be combined with electric points.

30. Walnut top on bronze cruciform legs fitting into floor bases. Castello Sforzesco Museum, Milan. Architects: Studio Architetti BBPR.

31. Textiles hung from curtain tracks set 16 inches apart between every other ceiling board. Scandinavian Textile Hall, Lund, Sweden. Architect: Klas Anshelm.

32. Sculpture on wooden bases screwed to supports held on bronze wall pegs. Castello Sforzesco Museum, Milan. Architects: Studio Architetti BBPR.

33. Vertical supports can be fitted into floor sockets spaced at regular intervals; these include an electric point and can be capped when not in use. Forestry Museum, Gävle, Sweden. Architects: Erik Herløw and Tormod Olesen with Sven H. Wranér and Gunar Aagaard Andersen.

34. Movable illuminated cases for jewellery suspended from a ceiling grid. Reuchlinhaus, Pforzheim, Germany. Architect: Manfred Lehmbruck.

30

31

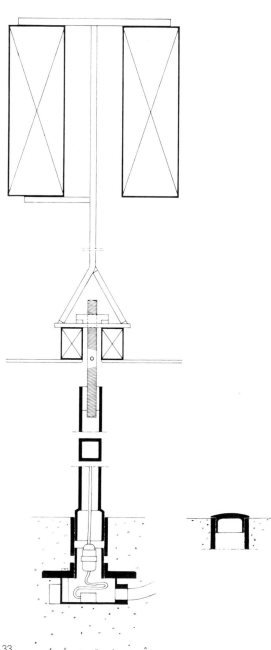

32

33

In manchen Museen sind in den Decken, im Fußboden oder in den Wänden Halterungen vorgesehen, an denen die Exponatträger in variabler Anordnung befestigt werden können. Diese Vorrichtungen lassen sich auch mit elektrischen Anschlüssen kombinieren.

30. Die Platte aus Walnußholz liegt auf bronzenen Stützen mit kreuzförmigem Durchschnitt, die am Boden in entsprechende Öffnungen eingesetzt sind. Museo del Castello Sforzesco, Mailand. Architekten: Studio Architetti BBPR.

31. Die Textilien hängen von Vorhangschienen herunter, die 40 cm voneinander entfernt zwischen jedem zweiten Holzbrett der Decke angebracht sind. Skandinavische Textilausstellung, Lund. Architekt: Klas Anshelm.

32. An der Wand Plastiken auf Holzkonsolen; die Platten sind an Bronzehalterungen geschraubt, die in Wanddübeln befestigt wurden. Museo del Castello Sforzesco, Mailand. Architekten: Studio Architetti BBPR.

33. Vertikale Stützen können in Bodenöffnungen eingelassen werden, die in regelmäßigen Abständen angeordnet sind. Die Öffnungen enthalten auch einen elektrischen Anschluß und werden abgedeckt, wenn sie nicht benötigt werden. Museum für das Forstwesen, Cävle, Schweden. Architekten: Erik Herløw und Tormod Olesen in Zusammenarbeit mit Sven H. Wranér und Gunar Aagaard Andersen.

34. Bewegliche, beleuchtete Vitrinen für Schmuck, die an einem Deckenraster befestigt sind. Reuchlinhaus, Pforzheim. Architekt: Manfred Lehmbruck.

34

Museum storage occupies a considerable proportion of the total floor area and its design must make efficient use of the allocated space. Some of this storage ought to be in the form of study collections accessible to those interested. The ordered arrangement and proper labelling of objects is equally important in both situations.

Museumsmagazine nehmen einen beträchtlichen Teil der gesamten Geschoßfläche ein, so daß die Verwendung des verfügbaren Raumes sorgfältig geplant werden muß. Ein Teil des Magazins sollte als Studiensammlung den interessierten Besuchern zugänglich sein. Übersichtliche Anordnung und Beschriftung der Objekte ist in jedem Fall unerläßlich.

1. Wire mesh screens. National Museum of Western Art, Tokyo. Architect: Le Corbusier.

1. Tafeln aus Drahtgitter. Nationalmuseum für abendländische Kunst, Tokio. Architekt: Le Corbusier.

2. Posters on overhead supports. Stedelijk Museum, Amsterdam. Interior: F. A. Eschauzier.

2. Plakate an Hängevorrichtungen. Stedelijk Museum, Amsterdam. Inneneinrichtung: F. A. Eschauzier.

3. Aluminium ceiling grid in the attic. Palazzo Bianco, Genoa. Architect: Franco Albini.

3. An der Decke befestigtes Aluminiumgitter. Dachgeschoß des Palazzo Bianco, Genua. Architekt: Franco Albini.

4. Panels of perforated board clamped to columns. Musée Maison de la Culture, Le Havre. Architects: Lagneau, Weill, Dimitrijevic and Audigier.
5. Study collection containing 85% of the museum's total contents. Corning Glass Center, Corning, N.Y. Architects: Harrison & Abramovitz.

4. Lochplattentafeln, an Stützen schwenkbar befestigt. Musée Maison de la Culture, Le Havre. Architekten: Lagneau, Weill, Dimitrijevic und Audigier.
5. Studiensammlung, die 85% des Museumsbestandes enthält. Corning Glass Center, Corning, N.Y. Architekten: Harrison & Abramovitz.

4

5

6. Illuminated shelves and labelled drawers. National Archeological Museum, Gela, Sicily. Architect: Franco Minissi.

6. Beleuchtete Vitrinen und Schubfächer mit Beschriftung. Museo Archeologico Nazionale, Gela, Sizilien. Architekt: Franco Minissi.

6

Museum workshops, like all service areas, are often neglected zones of the building. Work of a precise and critical nature is performed in these and great care should be taken to provide an environment adequate in quality and size. This may of course be a great deal easier to do at national or regional centres specially devoted to conservation than in a museum itself. Such central institutes may also find it easier to acquire both the staff and equipment to deal with the highly specialised forms of restoration.

The following four layouts – based on plans by N. S. Brommelle, Keeper, Department of Conservation at the Victoria and Albert Museum in London – show the minimum desirable areas and equipment in studios dealing with the conservation of art objects. A specialist restorer would work in each studio. The plans illustrate principles only and are not meant to show actual room layouts.

Museumswerkstätten werden, wie alle Nebenräume, häufig vernachlässigt. Dabei wird in diesen Werkstätten schwierige Präzisionsarbeit geleistet, für die der Architekt eine angemessene Umgebung schaffen sollte. Das ist freilich in nationalen oder regionalen Zentren, die nur der Erhaltung von Kunstwerken dienen, leichter zu erreichen als in einem einzelnen Museum. Solche zentralen Institutionen gelangen auch leichter an die qualifizierten Kräfte und die technische Ausrüstung, die für die hochspezialisierten Restaurationsmethoden unerläßlich sind. Die vier abgebildeten Beispiele, die auf Plänen von N. S. Brommelle, Konservator am Victoria and Albert Museum in London, beruhen, demonstrieren die Mindestanforderungen an Größe und Ausstattung von Restaurationsateliers. Jedes Atelier ist für einen Restaurator vorgesehen. Die Pläne zeigen keine tatsächlichen Werkstattgrundrisse, sondern sollen nur als allgemeine Beispiele dienen.

A. Studio for paintings and drawings.
These must have adequate daylight – a minimum of 100 lumens/sq. ft. and a maximum of 300 lumens/sq. ft. (above this figure glare problems arise) – preferably from windows facing north rather than skylights.
B. Studio for furniture.
Ample space is needed in this room for the larger pieces of furniture since there may be several being restored at the same time. The ceiling should be strong enough to take the thrust of telescopic tubes used for holding down glued inlays etc. It is important that ordinary museum maintenance should not be done in this room.
C. Studio for textiles.
The size of this room assumes that work on large tapestries and carpets will not be performed. The left hand side of the room is given over to sewing and mending, the right hand side to laundry and cleaning.
D. Studio for metals, porcelain, stone etc.
Work on these various objects can be carried out in the room and by a single specialist. In this room, as in the furniture and textile studios, the general level of illumination should be about 50 lumen/sq. ft. and where more exacting work is done, 100 lumen/sq. ft. locally. The room really deals with the objects not specifically allocated to the previous three. It has two sections, the right hand side dealing with metal work and including a fume cupboard for cyanide treatment, the left hand side for work on porcelain, stone and marble.

1 Studio for paintings / Atelier für Gemälde
2 Studio for prints and drawings / Atelier für Druckgraphik und Zeichnungen
3 Varnishing room and stove / Firnisraum und Ofen
4 Bench / Werkbank
5 Sink / Ausguß
6 Examination and work table / Arbeitstisch
7 Lamp / Lampe
8 Easel / Staffelei
9 Hot table / Wärmetisch
10 Screen / Stellwand
11 Bench with storage below / Werkbank, darunter Lagerfläche
12 Cupboard / Schrank
13 Press / Presse
14 Washing tank / Wasserbehälter
15 Fumigation chamber / Abteil für Säurebehandlung

A. Atelier für Gemälde und Zeichnungen.
Ausreichendes Tageslicht muß vorhanden sein, mindestens jedoch 1000 lx und höchstens 3000 lx (bei höheren Werten tritt Blendung auf). Fenster nach Norden sind günstiger als Oberlichter.
B. Atelier für Möbel.
Großer Platzbedarf, da es vorkommen kann, daß mehrere große Möbelstücke gleichzeitig restauriert werden. Die Decke sollte so stark sein, daß sie die Last von Teleskoppressen aushalten kann, die beispielsweise bei geleimten Furnieren verwandt werden. Es ist wichtig, daß in diesen Werkstätten keine anderen Restaurationsarbeiten ausgeführt werden.
C. Atelier für Textilien.
Die Abmessungen dieses Raumes setzen voraus, daß keine Restaurationsarbeiten an großen Gobelins und Teppichen vorgenommen werden. Die linke Seite des Raumes ist für Näh- und Flickarbeiten bestimmt, die rechte für Waschen und Reinigen.
D. Atelier für Metalle, Porzellan, Stein usw.
Die Arbeit an Gegenständen aus diesen Materialien kann in einem Raum und von einem einzigen Spezialisten ausgeführt werden. Wie in den Ateliers für Möbel und Textilien sollte auch hier die allgemeine Beleuchtungsstärke 500 lx oder bei schwierigeren Arbeitsvorgängen punktuell bis zu 1000 lx betragen. In dem Atelier werden alle die Objekte restauriert, die nicht unter die anderen drei Gruppen fallen. Der Raum hat zwei Arbeitsbereiche, wobei der rechte der Metallbearbeitung dient und eine Anlage für Säurebehandlung enthält, während der linke für Arbeiten an Porzellan, Stein und Marmor bestimmt ist.

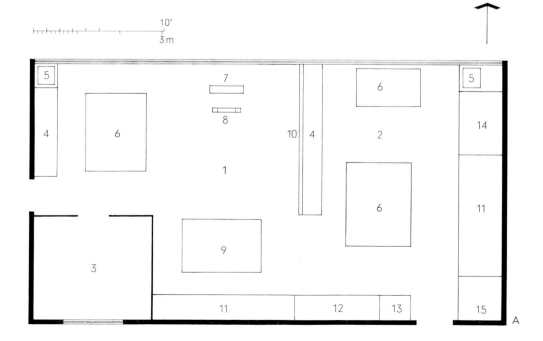

1 Safe
2 Files and workcases / Akten und Handwerkskästen
3 Inspection table / Prüftisch
4 Work table covered with linoleum / Mit Linoleum bedeckte Arbeitsplatte
5 Tool cupboard / Werkzeugschrank
6 Hot plate / Wärmeplatte
7 Sink / Ausguß
8 Layout table / Arbeitstisch
9 Storage racks for timber and veneers / Holz- und Furnierlager
10 Storage cupboards / Lagerschränke
11 Grinder / Schleifmaschine
12 Jig saw / Säge
13 Cabinet maker's bench / Werkbank des Kunsttischlers
14 Multi-purpose lathe / Drehbank

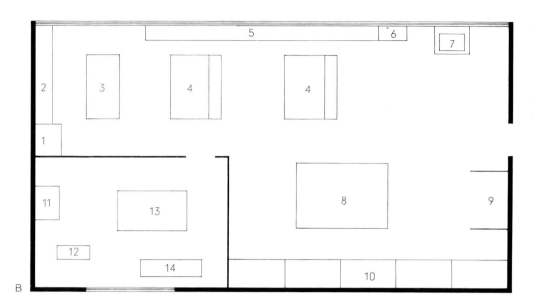

1 Enclosed dress racks / Kleiderschrank
2 Stove press / Dampfpresse
3 Materials / Arbeitsmaterial
4 Work table / Arbeitstisch
5 Sewing table / Nähtisch
6 Ironing board / Bügelbrett
7 Spotting table / Reinigungstisch
8 Hot plate / Wärmeplatte
9 Sink / Ausguß
10 Wash tank / Wasserbehälter

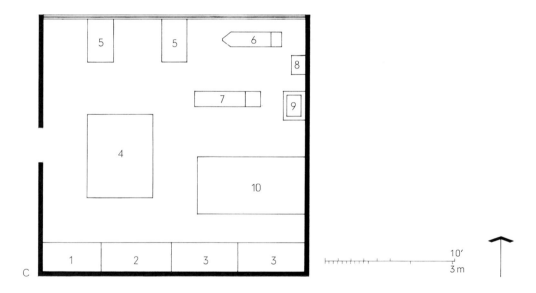

1 Studio for porcelain and stone / Atelier für Porzellan und Steine
2 Studio for metals / Atelier für Metalle
3 Records and files / Akten und Unterlagen
4 Store bins / Lager
5 Ultra-violet lamp in curtained booth / Ultraviolette Lampe in einem Abteil, das durch Vorhang abgeschirmt ist
6 Cupboard and shelves / Schrank und Regale
7 Cupboard / Schrank
8 Work trolley / Arbeitstisch auf Rollen
9 Drying oven / Trockenanlage
10 Sink and draining board / Ausguß und Abtropfbrett
11 Work table / Arbeitstisch
12 Examination table with microscope / Prüftisch mit Mikroskop
13 Balance and scales / Waage
14 Soldering and brazing / Löt- und Schweißapparate
15 Soaking and electrolytic tanks / Durchfeuchtung und elektrolytischer Trog
16 Table with drawers below / Tisch mit Schubladen
17 Sink / Ausguß
18 Fume cupboard / Schrank für Säuren
19 Lathe / Drehbank
20 Drill, vice and mandrils / Bohrer, Schraubstock und Spindeln
21 Oven / Ofen

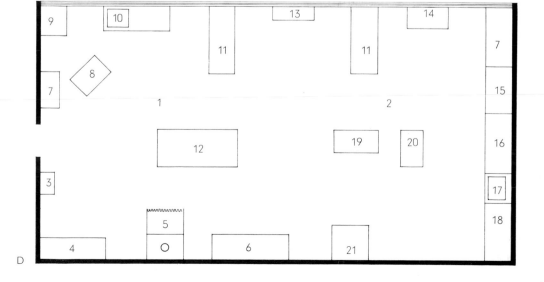

Display outdoors does not differ in its essentials from that inside a building except that there is a varying but known light source, the sky. Objects still require support, may need protection, ought to be made visible by being within a controlled field of vision and are seen in sequence. It is possible to provide such conditions as well as some control of the light source either by built form – walls, canopies, pedestals, platforms – or by the use of planting, or, of course, both. Occasionally, as in some of the pavilions at the Venice Biennale, the line of demarcation between enclosed building and the open air is deliberately left undefined.

Ausstellungen im Freien unterscheiden sich grundsätzlich nicht von solchen in Gebäuden; ihre Lichtquelle – der Himmel – ist allerdings veränderlich. Im übrigen muß den Gegenständen zur Wirkung verholfen werden, sie brauchen Schutzvorrichtungen, sind auf eine Abgrenzung des Blickfeldes angewiesen und werden in einer Abfolge betrachtet. Diese Voraussetzungen sowie in gewissem Umfang auch eine Kontrolle des Tageslichts sind entweder durch architektonische Elemente wie Wände, Überdachungen, Sockel und Plattformen oder durch Bepflanzung oder auch durch beides zu erreichen. Bisweilen (zum Beispiel bei einigen Pavillons der Biennale in Venedig) ist der Übergang zwischen umschlossenem Gebäude und Umgebung bewußt fließend gehalten.

1

2

The placing of sculpture on terraces beyond a building has strong renaissance roots; it greatly extends the range of museum display and may have repercussions on the arrangement of the interior since it may be desirable to see the outdoor exhibits from indoors.
1. Sculpture court. Museum of Modern Art, New York. Architect: Philip Johnson.
2. Sculpture terrace. Museum of the 20th Century, Vienna. Architect: Karl Schwanzer.

Die Aufstellung von Skulpturen auf Terrassen in der Nachbarschaft eines Bauwerks geht auf die Renaissance zurück; sie erweitert damit den Museumsbereich beträchtlich und kann sich auf die Anordnung im Inneren auswirken, wenn die Gegenstände im Freien auch von innen her zu sehen sein sollen.
1. Skulpturenhof. Museum of Modern Art, New York. Architekt: Philip Johnson.
2. Terrasse mit Skulpturen. Museum des 20. Jahrhunderts, Wien. Architekt: Karl Schwanzer.

3

Display cases can be made weatherproof and put out of doors to become part of the accepted surroundings of the town.
3–5. Open Air Exhibition of Industrial Art. Svenska Slöjdföreningen, Stockholm.

Wetterfeste Vitrinen können im Freien aufgestellt und somit in das Stadtbild eingefügt werden.
3–5. Freiluftausstellung von Industrial Design. Svenska Slöjdföreningen, Stockholm.

4

5

6

7

Temporary exhibitions are sometimes held in pavilions whose character is intentionally only that of an impermanent canopy.
6–9. Plastic roof draped between concrete beams. Finnish, Norwegian, and Swedish Pavilion, Biennale Park, Venice. Architect: Sverre Fehn.

Vorübergehende Ausstellungen in Pavillons, die bewußt wie ein provisorisches Schutzdach gestaltet sind.
6–9. Kunststoffdecke zwischen Betonträgern. Finnischer, norwegischer und schwedischer Pavillon, Biennale, Venedig. Architekt: Sverre Fehn.

Occasionally objects are left in their original situation and ▷ the museum created around them. Such site museums may need no more than a layout of paths. Some may, however, require enclosure and protection of the display.
10. Roman mosaic paving, Corrugated acrylic roof and wall. Piazza Armerina, Sicily. Architect: Franco Minissi.

Bisweilen werden die Ausstellungsgegenstände in ihrer ▷ ursprünglichen Position belassen, und das Museum wird um sie herum errichtet. Solche Museen brauchen unter Umständen nichts weiter als Zirkulationswege, in anderen Fällen muß das Kunstwerk umschlossen und geschützt werden.
10. Römisches Mosaikpflaster, Decke und Wände aus gewelltem Kunststoff. Piazza Armerina, Sizilien. Architekt: Franco Minissi.

8

9

Open air museums are not restricted in the size of the object they put on display and may thus show a ship or whole houses or villages specially re-erected.
11. Timber frame house, Colonial Williamsburg, Virginia.

Bei Ausstellungen im Freien unterliegt die Größe des Objekts keiner Beschränkung, so daß auch Schiffe, ganze Häuser oder rekonstruierte Dörfer gezeigt werden können.
11. Holzhaus, Colonial Williamsburg, Virginia.

10

11

Labels are rather like the title page of a book: they provide certain factual information – authorship, date, place of origin and identification – without necessarily describing the contents. This is the minimum amount to which a museum visitor is entitled. Further information can be given on the label itself, on a separate label related to a group of objects or in a catalogue. In which ever form it is conveyed some distinction ought to be made between information of general interest, such as an explanation of its historical context or method of manufacture, and items of scholarship such as attribution or a list of its previous owners.

The design of the label must carefully consider legibility at a range related to the likel positiy on of the onlooker. Occasionally it will be imposs ble for the label to be near the exhibit it refers to. In such icasesthe relation between the two must be made absolutely clear by other means such as a small reproduction of the object next to the label, arrows or other identification.

Beschriftungen sind etwa mit den Titelseiten eines Buches zu vergleichen: Sie vermitteln sachliche Information – Autor, Entstehungsdatum und -ort, Titel –, ohne dabei den Inhalt zu beschreiben. Auf diese Mindestangaben hat der Museumsbesucher ein Recht. Weitere Information kann auf dem Schild selbst, auf einem anderen Schild, das sich auf eine Gruppe von Kunstwerken bezieht, oder in einem Katalog mitgeteilt werden. In welcher Form das auch immer geschieht, es sollte zwischen Angaben von allgemeinem Interesse (Erläuterung des historischen Zusammenhangs oder der Herstellungsverfahren) und von wissenschaftlichem Interesse (Zuschreibung, frühere Eigentümer) unterschieden werden.

Bei dem Entwurf des Schildes muß beachtet werden, daß es von der wahrscheinlichen Position des Betrachters aus gut lesbar ist. Bisweilen ist es nicht möglich, die Beschriftung in der Nähe des entsprechenden Ausstellungsgegenstandes anzubringen. In solchen Fällen muß die Beziehung zwischen Schild und Objekt durch andere Mittel verdeutlicht werden, etwa durch eine kleine Reproduktion des Kunstwerkes neben dem Schild, durch Pfeile oder andere Hinweise.

1

The position of the label should be slightly peripheral in the field of vision so that it does not conflict with the object it describes.

3. Wood labels with photographic overprinting. Castello Sforzesco Museum, Milan. Architects: Studio Architetti BBPR.

Das Schild sollte am Rande des Blickfeldes angebracht werden, damit es nicht die Wirkung des Kunstwerkes stört.

3. Holztafel mit fotomechanischem Aufdruck. Museo del Castello Sforzesco, Mailand. Architekten: Studio Architetti BBPR.

2

The label can often usefully do more than provide the minimum description; it can explain the manufacture or performance of the item on view or relate it to its original situation.

1. Photographic reproduction of an engraving showing the original location of the stone fragments. Castello Sforzesco Museum, Milan. Architects: Studio Architetti BBPR.

2. Individual labels and an explanatory diagram. Museum of Technology, Deutsches Museum, Munich. Architect: Paolo Nestler.

Schilder vermitteln bisweilen mehr als nur die notwendigste Information: Sie können die Herstellung oder die Funktion des ausgestellten Gegenstandes erklären und auf seine ursprüngliche Position hinweisen.

1. Fotografische Reproduktion eines Stichs, auf dem die ursprüngliche Anordnung der Steinfragmente zu erkennen ist. Museo del Castello Sforzesco, Mailand. Architekten: Studio Architetti BBPR.

2. Einzelschilder und Erläuterungstafel. Abteilung Flugtechnik, Deutsches Museum, München. Architekt: Paolo Nestler.

3

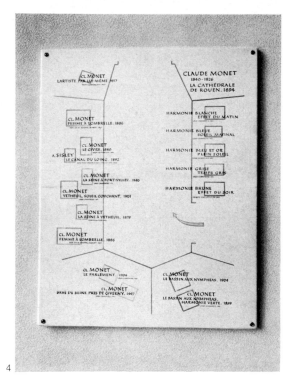

4

5

6

It may sometimes be advantageous to group labels so that display is quite unencumbered by extraneous elements.
4. Label at the entrance to the Monet Room. Jeu de Paume Museum, Paris.
5. Claude Monet's series of paintings of the Cathedral at Rouen mounted behind a slight recess in the wall. Jeu de Paume Museum, Paris.

Labels provide written information; this can also be conveyed verbally or through transistor radios carried by the museum visitor.
6. Making laboratory glassware. Corning Glass Center, Corning, New York. Architects: Harrison & Abramovitz.

In manchen Fällen ist es angebracht, die Beschriftungen zusammenzufassen, damit sie nicht die Wirkung der Kunstwerke beeinträchtigen.
4. Tafel am Eingang zum Monet-Raum. Musée Jeu de Paume, Paris.
5. Claude Monets Bilder der Kathedrale in Rouen sind in leichte Wandvertiefungen eingelassen. Musée Jeu de Paume, Paris.

Informationen können auch mündlich oder über Transistorengeräte, die der Museumsbesucher mit sich trägt, weitergegeben werden.
6. Herstellung von Glaswaren für Laboratorien. Corning Glass Center, Corning, New York. Architekten: Harrison & Abramovitz.

Individual labels or grouped labels can usefully be preceeded by further information of a more general and introductory kind applicable to a room or series of rooms.
7. Van Gogh's palette. Jeu de Paume Museum, Paris.
8. Photographs and descriptive notes on a group of painters. Jeu de Paume Museum, Paris.

Außer Einzelschildern oder Gruppentafeln können auch noch allgemeine Hinweise in die Ausstellungsgegenstände eines Raumes oder einer Folge von Räumen einführen.
7. Van Goghs Palette. Musée Jeu de Paume, Paris.
8. Fotografien und Beschreibungen einer Gruppe von Künstlern. Musée Jeu de Paume, Paris.

7

8

As museum viewing is done by a walking observer, the quality of the furniture which provides the needed rest and change is of very great importance. Furniture will be required in many parts of the museum, in its galleries as well as in restaurants, libraries, auditoria, offices and workrooms. Furniture is not a matter of afterthought but part of museum design.

Furniture, particularly in small groups, can do a great deal to affect the atmosphere of display areas.
1. Chairs by Hans J. Wegner. Louisiana Museum, Humlebæk, Copenhagen. Architects: Jørgen Bo and Vilhelm Wohlert.

Da ein Museumsbesuch bisweilen recht anstrengend ist, kommt den Möbeln, die für Entspannung sorgen, große Bedeutung zu. Möbel werden in vielen Teilen des Museums benötigt, in den Ausstellungsräumen wie auch in den Restaurants, Bibliotheken, Auditorien, Büros und Werkstätten. Die Auswahl und Anordnung der Möbelstücke ist nicht eine Frage nachträglicher Inneneinrichtung, sondern gehört zur Planung eines Museums.

Kleinere Möbelgruppen können die Atmosphäre in den Ausstellungsbereichen günstig beeinflussen.
1. Stühle von Hans J. Wegner im Louisiana Museum, Humlebæk bei Kopenhagen. Architekten: Jørgen Bo und Vilhelm Wohlert.

Furniture becomes dominant in many of the ancillary ▷ rooms and the character of these may be greatly determined by it.
4. Library, Uffizi Gallery, Florence. Architect: E. Detti.
5. Auditorium, Solomon R. Guggenheim Museum, New York. Architect: Frank Lloyd Wright.
6. Office, Albright-Knox Art Gallery, Buffalo, New York. Architects: Skidmore, Owings & Merrill.

Die Wirkung vieler Nebenräume wird weitgehend von der ▷ Möblierung beherrscht.
4. Bibliothek in den Uffizien, Florenz. Architekt: E. Detti.
5. Auditorium des Solomon R. Guggenheim Museum, New York. Architekt: Frank Lloyd Wright.
6. Büroraum in der Albright-Knox Art Gallery, Buffalo, New York. Architekten: Skidmore, Owings & Merrill.

Seats ought to be positioned in such a way that the whole room, or at least a large part of it, can be seen or, alternatively, they ought to be movable.
2. Central fixed seat. Exhibition of Carlo Crivelli, Palazzo Ducale, Venice. Architect: Egle Trincanato.
3. Stools by Charles Eames. Print Room, Uffizi Gallery, Florence. Architects: Edoardo Detti and Carlo Scarpa.

Sitzplätze sollten – sofern sie nicht beweglich sind – so aufgestellt werden, daß der Raum ganz oder teilweise zu überblicken ist.
2. Unbewegliche runde Sitzbank. Carlo-Crivelli-Ausstellung im Palazzo Ducale, Venedig. Architekt: Egle Trincanato.
3. Hocker von Charles Eames. Graphikraum in den Uffizien, Florenz. Architekten: Edoardo Detti und Carlo Scarpa.

4

5

6

Museum going is a civilised activity in which all aspects of the museum play their part.
7. Sitting area and fireplace, end room. Louisiana Museum, Humlebæk, Copenhagen. Architects: Jørgen Bo and Vilhelm Wohlert.
8. Garden restaurant and sculpture court. Museum of Modern Art, New York. Architect: Philip Johnson.

Das Museum bietet dem Besucher vielfältige Erlebnisse.
7. Sitzgruppe mit Kamin im letzten Raum des Louisiana Museums, Humlebæk bei Kopenhagen. Architekten: Jørgen Bo und Vilhelm Wohlert.
8. Gartenrestaurant und Plastikhof im Museum of Modern Art, New York. Architekt: Philip Johnson.

7

8

Entrance Halls

Eingangshallen

Entrance halls serve a double function. On the one hand they are museum service zones in which coats and packages are left; postcards, guide books and reproductions are bought; notices are displayed and directions given; friends are met and parties assembled, and where security checks can be carried out. On the other hand they exercise certain symbolic functions as the first and, usually, last museum space seen. The whole flavour of a museum can be suggested by its entrance hall. The Stedelijk, for instance, clearly establishes its character with its first space.

Eingangshallen haben eine doppelte Aufgabe. Sie dienen einmal praktischen Funktionen: Der Besucher legt Mantel und Pakete an der Garderobe ab; er kauft Postkarten, Kataloge und Reproduktionen; er liest Bekanntmachungen und Hinweise. Man verabredet sich mit Freunden, Gruppen sammeln sich, Sicherheitskontrollen können dort durchgeführt werden. Zum anderen kommt den Eingangshallen als den Räumlichkeiten des Museums, die der Besucher normalerweise als erste und als letzte sieht, ein symbolischer Wert zu. Schon die Eingangshalle kann den gesamten Charakter eines Museums andeuten, wie es zum Beispiel im ersten Raum des Stedelijk geschieht.

2

1

1. Die steigende Zahl der Museumsbesucher bedingte in der Tate Gallery, London, einen Umbau des Eingangsbereichs. Die den Verkaufsständen vorbehaltene Fläche wurde bedeutend vergrößert und umfaßt jetzt den ersten Vorraum, eine seitliche Nische sowie eine kreisrunde Halle, die den dritten Raum in der Abfolge der Eingangsräume darstellt. Ein Durchgangsraum mit einem Garderobentisch, an dem man Mäntel abgeben kann, bildet das verbindende Zwischenglied. In das Gebäude führen Drehtüren, die Luftzug ausschließen und sich im Falle eines Alarms automatisch schließen. Architekt: Colin St. John Wilson.
2. Eine der Seitennischen des Vorraums wird als kleine Galerie mit verkäuflichen Reproduktionen benutzt.
3. Die beiden Stände im Vorraum sind freistehende, bronzeverkleidete Verkaufsschalter, die mit eigenen Beleuchtungskörpern versehen sind.
4. Runder Verkaufsstand für Postkarten und Broschüren im Zentrum der kreisförmigen Halle, der eine gut sichtbare und erreichbare Ausstellungsfläche bietet.

1. The increase in the number of museum visitors made a reorganisation of the entrance area of the Tate Gallery, London, necessary. The amount of sales space has been greatly enlarged and now occurs in the first entrance lobby, in an alcove off it and in a circular hall which is third in the sequence of entrance spaces. A link with a counter at which coats are left forms an intervening space. The building is entered through revolving doors which are useful as draught excluders and which also allow simple automatic locking in case of a burglar alarm. Architect: Colin St. John Wilson.
2. One of the alcoves off the entrance is used as a small gallery showing prints which are for sale.
3. The two counters in the entrance, one on each side, are free standing pieces of furniture covered in bronze and supporting their own lighting canopy.
4. The round hall contains at its centre a circular counter which has a tiered top for face display of postcards and pamphlets. A great deal of easily reached and visible surface is thus provided.

Reports on the development of all aspects of museum activity, including new buildings and display, taking place throughout the world, are regularly given in:

Museum, published quarterly by UNESCO in Paris

In addition to this international publication there are a number of journals produced by some of the national museum organisations; these include:

Museums Journal, London
Museumskunde, Berlin
Museum News, Washington

Architectural magazines which often illustrate new museum buildings or renovations include:

Architectural Design, London
Architectural Forum, New York
Architectural Record, New York
Architectural Review, London
Arkitektur, Copenhagen
Bauwelt, Berlin
Casabella, Milan
Domus, Milan
Japan Architect, Tokyo
L'architecture d'aujourd'hui, Paris
Werk, Winterthur, Switzerland

Museum lighting is from time to time discussed in:

International Lighting Review, published by Stichting Prometheus, Amsterdam

A further selection of museum illustrations can be found in:
Musei, by Roberto Aloi, Hoepli, Milan, 1962

Museums earlier than the period covered by this volume are shown in:

Museum Buildings, by Laurence Vail Coleman, The American Association of Museums, Washington, D.C., 1950
Muséographie, Vols. I & II, Société des Nations, Office International des Musées, (based on the International Study Conference held in Madrid in 1934)

Über alle Aspekte des internationalen Museumswesens – einschließlich Neubauten und Ausstellungsgestaltung – berichtet regelmäßig:

Museum, vierteljährlich herausgegeben von der UNESCO, Paris

Außer dieser internationalen Publikation gibt es einige Zeitschriften, die von nationalen Museumsorganisationen veröffentlicht werden, darunter:

Museums Journal, London
Museumskunde, Berlin
Museum News, Washington

Zu den Architekturzeitschriften, die häufig neue oder neugestaltete Museumsgebäude publizieren, gehören:

Architectural Design, London
Architectural Forum, New York
Architectural Record, New York
Architectural Review, London
Arkitektur, Kopenhagen
Bauwelt, Berlin
Casabella, Mailand
Domus, Mailand
Japan Architect, Tokio
L'architecture d'aujourd'hui, Paris
Werk, Winterthur

Probleme der Museumsbeleuchtung werden gelegentlich erörtert in:
International Lighting Review, herausgegeben von der Stichting Prometheus, Amsterdam

Weiteres Material über Museen bietet:

Musei von Roberto Aloi, Mailand 1962

Museen, die vor den hier veröffentlichten Bauten entstanden, sind publiziert in:

Museum Buildings von Laurence Vail Coleman, The American Association of Museums, Washington, D.C., 1950
Muséographie, Band I und II, Société des Nations, Office International des Musées. (Das Werk beruht auf der International Study Conference, die 1934 in Madrid stattfand)

Index of Architects · Verzeichnis der Architekten

Photo Credits · Fotonachweis

Michel Aertsens 161 (4, 5), 162 (6, 7), 163 (8–11)
Cliché Agraci, Paris 201 (4, 5, 7, 8)
Maria Austria, Amsterdam 71 (15)
Badisches Landesmuseum (Bildarchiv), Karlsruhe 106 (1–3), 107 (5), 108 (6, 7, 9, 10), 109 (11–14), 176 (17), 187 (20) 188 (23)
Baltimore Museum of Art, Baltimore, Maryland 184 (12)
Erich Bauer, Karlsruhe 107 (4)
Gewerbemuseum der Bayerischen Landesgewerbean-stalt, Nürnberg 176 (19, 21), 182 (3, Photo G. Böhrer), 186 (15, 16)
Günther Becker, Kassel 177 (23)
Carla De Benedetti, Milano 42 (1, 2), 47 (29, 30)
Pierre Berdoy, Paris 97 (5)
Eva Besnyö, Amsterdam 67 (2), 68 (3–7), 69 (10), 70 (13), 71 (14, 16, 18, 19), 192 (2)
Lee Boltin 140 (5)
Boymans-van Beuningen Museum, Rotterdam 173 (4)
Studio Casali, Milano 37 (4, 5, 7)
Ciari, Milano 37 (3, 6)
Civici Musei (Archivio Fotografico), Venezia 7, 58 (1), 60 (10, 11), 61 (14, 16)
Comune di Genova, Direzione delle Arti 32 (1)
Comune di Venezia 19, 184 (13), 202 (2)
Connecticut Life, West Hartford 7, Connecticut 134 (3)
Corning Glass Works, Corning, New York 132 (1), 177 (22), 186 (14), 193 (5), 201 (6)
Deutsches Museum, München 200 (2)
John Donat 174 (9, 10)
Walter Dräyer, Zürich 178 (1)
Dülberg, Soest 117 (2, 3), 118 (4–6)
Friedrich Emich, Nieder-Ramstadt/Darmstadt 104 (2, 3)
Boris Engström 92 (1)
Everson Museum of Art, Syracuse, New York 157 (1, 2)
Gilbert Fernez, Le Havre 95 (1), 96 (2), 97 (3, 6), 98 (7–9), 193 (4)
Ferruzzi, Venezia 198 (6, 7), 199 (8, 9)
Fondation Maeght (Photo Claude Gaspari), St. Paul-de-Vence 99 (1), 100 (2, 3), 101 (4–6), 102 (7–9)
Jan Forsström, Stockholm 197 (3–5)
Fotogramma s. r. l., Milano 42 (3, 4), 43 (5–9), 44 (10–14), 45 (15–20), 46 (21–25), 52 (4, 5), 53 (6, 8, 9), 173 (3), 174 (7, 8), 183 (9), 190 (30, 32), 200 (1, 3)
Jørn Freddie, København 82 (12)
A. Frequin, Den Haag 66 (1, 2)
Gasparini, Genova 192 (3)
Gemeente Musea, Amsterdam 67 (1), 69 (8, 9, 11), 70 (12), 71 (17), 182 (7)
P. Grünzweig, Wien 122 (1), 196 (2)
Solomon R. Guggenheim Museum, New York, N.Y. 144 (4–6, 8), 145 (10–11)
Erik Hansen, København 186 (17)
H. Lund Hansen, København 11, 76 (1, 2), 77 (3–6), 78 (8–10)
Hedrich-Blessing, Chicago, Illinois 119 (1–3), 120 (4–7), 135, 136 (1, 2), 137 (3–5)
Heidersberger, Braunschweig 177 (26)
Ch. Hirayama, Minatoku, Tokyo 166 (1)
David Hirsch, New York, N.Y. 132 (2)
Jesper Høm, København 79 (1), 81 (3–8), 82 (9–11, 13), 83 (14–16), 202 (1), 203 (7)
Edgar Hyman, London 17, 187 (22)
Pierre Joly – Vera Cardot 97 (4)
Rollie McKenna, New York, N.Y. 196 (1), 203 (8)
H. Kessels, Bruxelles 72 (1), 73 (2–5)
Adalbert Komers-Lindenbach, Wien 122 (2), 123 (3–6)
Sam Lambert, London 177 (24), 182 (4)
Mats Lindén, Stockholm 88 (1, 2), 89 (3, 4)
London County Council, Architect's Dept., Photographic Unit, London 126 (1, 2)

Fanny Lopez 182 (6)
Louisiana Museum, Humlebæk/København 79 (2)
Arne Malm, Gävle 87 (9–14)
Hans Malmberg/Tio, Stockholm 92 (2)
Martinotti, Milano 36 (1), 37 (2)
F. Maurer, Zürich 124 (1), 125 (2–5)
Paolo Monti, Milano 22, 38 (1), 39 (3–9), 40 (10–13), 46 (26), 47 (27, 28), 49 (1–6), 50 (7–9), 52 (1–3), 53 (7), 55 (1–7), 56 (8–12), 57 (13–16), 58 (2), 59 (3–7), 60 (8, 9, 12), 61 (13, 15), 62 (1, 2), 63 (3–5), 64 (6–10), 65 (11–15), 176 (15, 16), 182 (1, 2, 5), 183 (8), 187 (21), 189 (26–29), 202 (3), 203 (4)
Museum of Modern Art, New York, N. Y. 25, 196 (1), 203 (8)
National Gallery, London 9
National Museum of Western Art, Tokyo 166 (2, 3), 167 (4–7), 192 (1)
Sigrid Neubert, München 111 (1–4), 112 (5, 6), 113 (7–10), 191 (34)
The Observer (Photo Axel Poignant), London 188 (24, 25)
Lennart Olson, Stockholm 78 (7, 11, 12), 90 (1, 4, 5), 91 (6–8), 92 (3), 93 (4–6), 174 (11), 175 (14)
AB Orrefors Glasbruk (Photo Hartmut Hipp), Orrefors 172 (2)
John Rawson, London 130
Herbert Rost, Darmstadt 103 (1), 104 (4, 5), 105 (6–9)
Oscar Savio, Roma 31 (3), 187 (19), 193 (6)
P. C. Scheier, São Paulo 158 (1, 2)
Skriver, Architektens redaktion, København 84 (1, 2), 85 (3–5), 86 (6–8)
Henk Snoek, London 128 (1–3), 129 (4)
Ezra Stoller Associates, Rye, N.Y. 139 (1, 2), 140 (3, 4), 141 (6–8), 142 (1), 143 (2, 3), 144 (7), 146 (1, 2), 147 (3–5), 148 (6–9), 149 (1, 2), 150 (3, 4), 151 (5), 152 (1), 153 (2–4), 173 (5, 6), 175 (12), 177 (25), 184 (11), 203 (5, 6)
K. Teigen 74 (1)
Eberhard Troeger, Hamburg-Großflottbek 114 (1–3), 115 (4–9)
US Information Service, American Embassy, Photograph Section, London 199 (11)
Verkehrshaus der Schweiz, Luzern 94 (1, 2)
A. Villani & Figli, Bologna 32 (2), 33 (3–6), 34 (7, 8), 35 (9–11), 172 (1), 175 (13), 184 (10)
Wasa-Foto, Stockholm 90 (2, 3)
Gerd Weiss, Karlsruhe/Baden 108 (8)
Yale University Art Gallery, New Haven, Connecticut 133 (2), 134 (5, 6)